Whose Europe?
The turn towards democracy

A selection of previous *Sociological Review* Monographs

Life and Work History Analyses[†]
ed. Shirley Dex

The Sociology of Monsters[†]
ed. John Law

Sport, Leisure and Social Relations[†]
eds John Horne, David Jary and Alan Tomlinson

Gender and Bureaucracy*
eds Mike Savage and Anne Witz

The Sociology of Death: theory, culture, practice*
ed. David Clark

The Cultures of Computing*
ed. Susan Leigh Star

Theorizing Museums*
ed. Sharon Macdonald and Gordon Fyfe

Consumption Matters*
eds Stephen Edgell, Kevin Hetherington and Alan Warde

Ideas of Difference*
eds Kevin Hetherington and Rolland Munro

The Laws of the Markets*
ed. Michel Callon

Actor Network Theory and After*
eds John Law and John Hassard

[†] Available from The Sociological Review Office, Keele University, Keele, Staffs ST5 5BG.
* Available from Marston Book Services, PO Box 270, Abingdon, Oxon OX14 4YW.

The Sociological Review Monographs

The Sociological Review has established a tradition of publishing Monographs on issues of general sociological interest. The Monograph is an edited book length collection of research papers which is published and distributed in association with Blackwell Publishers. Recent Monographs have included *Ideas of Difference* (edited by Kevin Hetherington and Rolland Munro), *Theorizing Museums* (edited by Sharon Macdonald and Gordon Fyfe). *The Sociology of Death* (edited by David Clark) and *The Sociology of Monsters* (edited by John Law). Other Monographs have been published on consumption; caste; culture and computing; gender and bureaucracy, sport-life history analyses, journalism and many other areas. We are keen to receive innovative collections of work in sociology and related disciplines with a particular emphasis on exploring empirical materials and theoretical frameworks which are currently under-developed. If you wish to discuss ideas for a Monograph then please contact the Monographs Editor, Martin Parker, at *The Sociological Review*, Keele University, Newcastle-under-Lyme, North Staffordshire, ST5 5BG. Email mnall@keele.ac.uk.

Whose Europe?
The turn towards democracy

Edited by Dennis Smith and Sue Wright

Blackwell Publishers/The Sociological Review

Copyright © The Editorial Board of the Sociological Review 1999

First published in 1999

Blackwell Publishers
108 Cowley Road, Oxford OX4 1JF, UK

and
350 Main Street
Malden, MA 02148, USA

British Library Cataloguing in Publication Data

A CIP catalogue record for this book is available from the British Library

Library of Congress Cataloging-in-Publication Data applied for

ISBN 0 631 21918 8

Printed and bound by Whitstable Litho Ltd

This book is printed on acid-free paper.

Contents

Contents

Prologue

The main themes of political sociology are nowadays being transformed by structural and political events in the real world. By and large political sociology in the 50s and 60s dealt with the structure of national societies seen as complexes of functionally related institutions or as the product of class and status conflict. Today these foci seem inadequate or misleading as we seek to come to terms with a post-national globalised world, as some nation states and empires break up giving rise to sub-national ethnic conflict, and as some of the existing nation states seek to regroup themselves in supra-national but not world wide organisations.

The essays collected here deal with all of these developments in some measure but especially the third, taking the case of western Europe which is in the process of developing into, or creating, a new political, economic, social and cultural unit. On each of these levels there are serious problems but also new possibilities leading some contributors to pessimistic, others to optimistic analyses. The contributions of the different authors are set out in the introduction by Dennis Smith and Sue Wright.

Reading these essays as a political sociologist whose roots were in the 50s, it seems to me that the major themes in the essays are those of politics and human rights and of language and culture. The basic question is how a political community comes into existence when there is cultural and linguistic diversity and what the obstacles are to this process.

One level of analysis sees the problems of the European Union as lying in the so-called democratic deficit and of course there are problems at this level. The European Parliament is much more tenuously related to its constituencies than are national parliaments and it has to share governing power with the Council of Ministers and the bureaucratic commission. This produces tensions of differing kinds for the governments and peoples of different constituent nation states. But, even if these problems were solved on the level of formal political structures it is argued here that the European Union would be unlikely to counteract this democratic deficit unless the citizens of the nation-states were able to participate in a European public sphere.

One of the editors of this book, Sue Wright, draws attention to the linguistic dimension of this issue, arguing that the deliberative demands of democracy and respect for the plurilingual nature of

Europe are difficult to reconcile, and that this tension may prove one of the stumbling blocks to European integration. She makes her case with a careful consideration of international and national languages in the past. Dennis Smith argues that relations between the warring nations of Western Europe became increasingly 'civilized' in the aftermath of American victory in 1945. He traces the social processes that led, on the one hand, to closer integration between the national polities of Europe and, on the other hand, to the disembedding of business corporations and the regions from their primary involvement in national structures. Business and the regions have increasingly operated within a European arena.

Other authors take up the themes of barriers and bridges to European integration. The role of language and communication in the creation of political entities is discussed by Simon May, Charlotte Hoffmann and co-authors Barrie Axford and Richard Huggins. Citizenship, democracy and human rights are the focus of the chapters by John Markoff, Andreas Føllesdal and David Jary. Pablo Jáuregui and Harald Wydra look at national identity and democracy in the context of long-term social processes.

For my own part I would see two interrelated problems as particularly important for Europe. One is how it deals with the problems of residents of European states who come from outside Europe and do not have citizenship in the states within whose boundaries they reside. Should they have the same right to freedom of movement as the full citizens of the different nation states? The other is that of how immigrants of all kinds are to be represented politically. So far as the first of these problems is concerned although there are repeated suggestions by policy makers that the rights of third country residents will be recognised there has as yet been no significant change in their status.

The second problem is that, so far as political representation is concerned what the European Commission has offered is a strangely conceived body called the Migrants Forum, which brings together in the same body representatives of those minorities, like the German guestworkers, who lack political citizenship, and those who are citizens but are disadvantaged through ethnic and racial discrimination like Blacks and Asians in Britain or *maghrébins* in France.

Another theme which needs to be dealt with is that of religious differences. Too often when the notion of a European identity is being discussed that identity is thought of as being White and Christian, but the residents of Europe now include millions of

Muslims of different kinds from Asia, North Africa and Turkey. If Europe's democracy is to be embedded in a culture how would it deal with this problem of multiple faiths and religions?

The problem of the recognition of third country citizens is dealt with in these essays by Andreas Føllesdal, but he does not deal with the question of how immigrants as such are to be represented politically in Europe except tangentially in a discussion of citizenship rights. (He actually takes the existence of the Migrants Forum for granted and considers its views on citizenship.) On the question of religious pluralism Føllesdal rightly points out that immigrant faiths like Islam may benefit from the religious toleration conceded for diverse Christian groups. But this has not happened automatically and in Britain until very recently, for example, the state support given to Catholic, Protestant and Jewish schools was not extended to Muslim schools. This is also true in several other European states and there are also problems which arise from the differences of rights between established churches and others.

Any search for a cultural unity is misguided and the most that can be looked for is the sharing of a public political culture, the culture of a democratic political system, perhaps based on the values of liberal or social democracy. This could lead to the development of a constitutional patriotism rather than an emotive sense of belonging to Europe as Habermas suggests (and as Jary explores further in this volume). And, once this is raised, there is the question opened up recently by writers like Yasemein Soysal of whether the important question in a post-national globalised world is not human rights rather than national or European citizenship.[1]

At the present juncture, however, while it may be important to discuss these more grandiose questions, it also has to be realised that the supra-national entity called Europe is still struggling to be born. Most of the essays contained here deal with these birthpangs. The baby may survive or die and if it survives it may grow up in good health or it may be a monster. These questions should be of concern to all of us and I am sure that the publication of this book will contribute importantly to the debate.

John Rex
University of Warwick

Note

1 See Habermas, J. (1992) *Autonomy and Solidarity*, London: Verso, Soysal, Y. (1994), *Limits of Citizenship. Migrants and Postnational Membership in Europe*, Chicago: University of Chicago Press, and the chapter by David Jary in this volume.

The turn towards democracy

Dennis Smith and Sue Wright

A spectre is haunting Europe—the spectre of democracy.

The founders of the European movement[1] back in the 1950s did not build from the bottom up, carefully consulting grassroots public opinion. Instead, they worked from the top down. The European Coal and Steel Community, the European Economic Community and, later, the European Union were fashioned by politicians, business people, diplomats, lawyers, economists and civil servants. The lynchpin of the structure was the Franco-German axis. Charles de Gaulle and Konrad Adenauer were key deal-makers in the late 1950s and early 1960s. Twenty-five years later their successors were François Mitterrand and Helmut Kohl. The close understanding between Kohl and Mitterrand and their commitment to European integration gave added authority to Jacques Delors, President of the European Commission. The outcome of their combined political will was a surge of institution-building in the late 1980s and early 1990s: for example, the Single European Act (February 1986),[2] the Social Chapter (December 1989),[3] the Schengen Convention (June 1990)[4] and the Maastricht Treaty on European Union (February 1992).[5]

The people were hardly involved in the debates surrounding this phase of the European project, which in Maastricht created a Union that went far beyond a common market. They were given what was considered good for them. However, during the 1990s democracy struck back. The makers of the Maastricht Treaty took it for granted that their national parliaments and electorates would ratify the agreement with little trouble. Not so. The Danish electorate rejected it in a 1992 referendum and only narrowly accepted it in a second referendum in 1993. In France, the Maastricht Treaty became a focus of angry public debate. President Mitterrand went to referendum and only won support by a narrow margin.[6] In

Ireland, a High Court decision forced the government to hold a referendum in 1992, which it won.

In Britain, parliament delayed ratifying the treaty until the result of the second Danish referendum was known. The whole process ruined the government's credibility. In Germany, the treaty was ratified but the government was forced to concede that any future 'European' decisions would have to be backed by two-third's majorities in the Federal Parliament and Länder governments. The German government had to delay ratification until a legal challenge was defeated. Opponents claimed that the Maastricht Treaty meant a loss of German statehood and a reduction of parliamentary competence.

In the medium term, one outcome of this widespread backlash from national parliaments and electorates was that the EU's Council of Ministers lost its sense of direction during the mid-1990s. At the European Commission, the era of Jacques Delors, the determined and shrewd French politician who had served as president since 1985, was followed by the less illustrious era of Jacques Santer, appointed president from January 1995. It is widely believed that Santer was chosen, at the insistence of the British, because he was a political nonentity incapable of exercising strong leadership.[7]

The European Commissioners, responsible for the European equivalent of national ministries, have traditionally been nominated by the EU's member governments. These governments have used their 'slots' on the Commission as a way to reward or compensate senior politicians leaving the national scene. Until 1999 governments paid very little attention to public opinion in making these appointments. This was possible because voters had little incentive to take a detailed interest in events over which they had virtually no control.

In principle, the Commission is answerable to the European Parliament.[8] In the early months of 1999, that principle acquired some reality. A 144 page report appeared entitled *Allegations regarding Fraud, Mismanagement and Nepotism in the European Commission.* The enquiry, commissioned by the European Parliament, was carried out by a Committee of Independent Experts comprising five senior lawyers and public auditors. The report focused upon seven areas: the activities of the Tourism Unit; the programmes for decentralised co-operation with the countries of the southern Mediterranean; the European Community Humanitarian Office (ECHO) whose aim was to provide aid in emergency relief situations; the Leonardo da Vinci Programme to implement a vocational training policy in support of initiatives by individual member states; the Commission's own security Service; issues relating to nuclear safety; and allegations of favouritism. The report concluded that it was difficult to find any member of the Commission who had the slightest sense of responsibility for the 'fraud, mismanagement and nepotism' uncovered.

The European Parliament cannot dismiss individual commissioners. However, it has the power to insist upon the resignation of the entire European Commission. The members of the Commission did not wait to be dismissed. Instead they resigned *en bloc*.

After these traumatic events, appointments to the Commission are bound to be a tricky business. Who will national governments be willing to send? It is unlikely they will reverse their past practices and start to send their brightest and best since that would be to strengthen the supranational body that competes with the governments of national states. Who will be willing to serve? Surely not the most ambitious since it seems likely that from now on individual commissioners will have less autonomy. There are two reasons for this. On the one hand, power on the Commission will increasingly be concentrated in the office of a reinvigorated presidency. On the other hand, the European Parliament will be eager to exercise increased control. As *The Economist* puts it, 'Commissioners will have to expect a rough and relentless ride. And they will have to explain and justify themselves as never before, because public opinion will be on the side of the parliament' (27 March 1999, 54).

These events have pushed the question of democracy in the European Union higher up the agenda. Hence the question in our title: *Whose Europe?* One way of posing this question is to ask: on whose behalf is the European Union being run? Possible candidates include: factions on the Commission, the most influential member states (Germany and France), poorer regions who receive generous funding, powerful regions (such as Baden-Württemberg and Lombardy) and re-emerging national groups (for example, the Scots and Catalans). The least plausible beneficiary at the moment is the European *demos*, an entity still taking shape.

Another way of posing the question is to ask: what identities and expectations are fuelling the politics and planning that shape the complementary processes of Europeanisation and devolution? Who are 'we' with our three-tier identities: Welsh-British-European, Catalan-Spanish-European, Flemish-Belgian-European, and so on? What do we hope to gain from the European project?

Whose Europe? is going to press in mid-1999 at a time of great

3

uncertainty in Europe. Chaos in the government of the European Union is compounded by the confusion, fear and insecurity brought by war as NATO launches attacks on the Serbian regime in Yugoslavia. This coincidence of challenges has dramatised the tensions and ambiguities surrounding the European project.

The Balkan war draws attention to two of the European Union's key external relationships: with the 'East', in other words, the ex-communist world of Eastern and South-Eastern Europe and with the United States. Eastwards, the question is how can the relationship between the European Union and the successor states of ex-Yugoslavia, the ex-Soviet Union and the ex-Soviet Bloc become stabilised? Will the intense hatreds and bitter conflicts stirred up by ethnic nationalism permit the development of 'Western' democracy in the East?[9]

In the relationship with the United States, the question is how American business and the American state will react to the possible development of the European Union as a pan-European polity which increasingly combines economic strength and military might. It would have been significant if, for example, any ground (as opposed to air-borne) operations by NATO had been carried out by European as opposed to American troops.

The end of the Cold War, defined as a global ideological conflict pitting the United States and the USSR against each other, may inaugurate an era in which the European Union has to deal with conflict on two fronts: to the east, conflict along the 'democratic' frontier with states that oppress ethnic minorities; to the west, conflict along the 'capitalist' frontier with opposing business interests. The burgeoning dispute with America over beef and bananas in the spring of 1999 may be an early indication of what is to come.

However, speculation is very dangerous. If Balkan conflicts spread with unpredictable consequences, if tensions intensify between combatant and non-combatant (or pacifist) states within the European Union, if the fragile unity of the NATO coalition crumbles, and if the Euro fails to establish itself as a strong currency—just to mention a few contingencies that might become realities—then all bets are off. The implications for democracy in Europe are difficult to foresee.

The European movement has always had this unpredictable character. Since the late 1940s, when the Americans gave Europe a hefty shove in the direction of transnational economic co-operation,[10] Europe-making has involved a relatively unco-ordinated series of advances all in the general direction of greater unity and co-operation. These advances were secured through tactical alliances between visionaries taking the long view, business people looking for economies of scale, and opportunistic politicians keen to get re-elected.

The outcome has been the growth of an increasingly large body of 'European' institutions. However, these institutions are, in many respects, opaque, inefficient and undemocratic. Europe's 'democratic deficit' is notorious. Martin Woollacott recently summed up the situation as follows:

> We have a [European] Parliament which is a monitoring body rather than a law-making assembly, an executive, in the shape of the Council [of Ministers], which acts in large matters as a legislature, and a civil service, in the shape of the [European] Commission, which is partly a law-maker and partly also an executive . . . The Council, always swayed by national interests, exercises little supervision over the commissioners, the commissioners exercise less than proper supervision of their staffs, and the Parliament, until 1999, had exercised little supervision over the Commission and none over the Council.[11]

During the 1990s, democracy, in the shape of the people's will, has been roused from slumber. The process is rather like the inhabitants of a village becoming aware that an elephant that has been tramping around the outskirts of their land is beginning to stray across their fields and gardens. The animal has grown too large and strong to be shooed away. The question is: can it be harnessed, tamed and put to work or is it going to trample down crops and houses? This awakening to Europe has arrived later and more abruptly in the case of Britain than most other member states.[12] However, all Europeans are facing the same issue. To put it more directly, it has become increasingly evident that what is decided in Brussels affects the jobs, incomes and rights of ordinary men and women. In these circumstances, how can the people's interest, the democratic interest, best be served?

It could be argued that strong government at the European level is necessary to uphold the social rights of ordinary citizens against the enormous influence of large-scale business. From this perspective, men and women in the street have a vested interest in powerful European institutions that are able to persuade business to make a sizeable contribution to the communities in which they operate. In dealing with footloose capital it is helpful to have a continent-wide polity that can ensure its rules are followed throughout its territory.

However, a triangular model that recognises just three main actors—the People, the Government and Business—is over-simple. In fact, each of these actors is an amalgam of different and often opposed interests. Business consists of ruthless competitors who are united only in resisting government regulation and taxation. Government operates at several levels, from local authorities to supra-state institutions, each level ruled by the politicians with different electorates to satisfy. Finally, there are the people, divided by language, nationality, culture and class.

Anyone trying to identify the 'democratic interest' in Europe at the turn of the millennium must be prepared to explore a complex and dynamic configuration of forces. At the centre of this configuration are the old national states that were at loggerheads during two world wars. During the last quarter of the twentieth century, Europe's national governments have had to confront two challenges to their authority. The supra-state institutions in Brussels, Strasbourg and Luxembourg that they helped to bring into existence have acquired sufficient influence to diminish the relative autonomy of national governments. European laws, regulations and judicial decisions are disciplining the national state 'from above'.

Meanwhile, the old established national states are being challenged 'from below' by assertive provincial interests whose supporters demand recognition of their nationhood and increased political autonomy through their own parliaments, legislative bodies, and so on. In Spain, Catalonia achieved such autonomy following the death of General Franco.[13] Flemish protests at Walloon dominance led to Belgium becoming a federal state in 1994 with three linguistic communities (respectively Dutch-speaking, French-speaking and German-speaking).[14] In Britain, the Scots now have their own parliament and the Welsh have an assembly. Since 1984 the Lombard League (renamed the Northern League in 1991) has campaigned for an independent state, to be called Padania, in Northern Italy.

Other regional interests, although not necessarily campaigning for political autonomy, find that the existence of the European Union gives them added leverage. The richest regions, such as the so-called 'four motors'—Baden-Württemberg, Lombardy, Rhône-Alpes and Catalonia—are able to co-operate with each other without needing to work through their respective national governments. Meanwhile, the poorest regions, especially in Greece, Portugal and parts of Spain and Italy are able to benefit from European grants.[15]

6

The significant shift in power away from the old national states as a result of Europeanisation and devolution presents a major challenge for democracy. France, Britain, Germany, Italy, Spain, Portugal and so on have each had well over a century, in some cases several centuries, of internal cultural and socio-political adjustment, often fraught and bloody. During this time, political and cultural establishments have emerged in each national state. As these societies have modernised, national education systems have developed under the control of these establishments, imposing greater uniformity, and spreading a shared culture and language.

A shared culture and language makes for easier communication between different parts of a society. In most cases, the national establishments were mainly interested in top-down communication, imposing discipline upon 'their' people, integrating them into a shared national life. However, once a shared language and culture exists, it is a resource for democracy. In other words, it allows people to articulate their wishes, debate their needs, and organise for resistance or change.

Devolution and Europeanisation both disrupt these relationships, potentially at least, especially where new language practices become prominent in the public domain. In Wales and Catalonia, for example, the successful reintroduction of Welsh and Catalan into public life may introduce new barriers to communication and participation which disadvantage those local inhabitants who only speak English or Castilian.

Language is also an issue at the level of supranational politics. Within the European Union, how can a European *demos* emerge if language differences inhibit lateral communication between populations? This issue is more than simply a matter of trouble-free tourism and smooth business dealings. European citizens are represented within a parliament whose functions and powers are increasing. This parliament acts in their name. However, what opportunities exist for citizens in different member states of the European Union to communicate with each other? How can a 'European' interest be articulated at the level of the European *demos* if Europeans are unable to debate among themselves because of language boundaries? How can they shape the agenda of the European Parliament and deliberate upon the issues that come before it? Even more than at national level, citizens tend to become passive recipients of legislation that has already been finalised without having been involved in the process.

These are urgent questions requiring research. If we wish the

European Parliament to speak for a European citizenry aware of sharing common interests and able to communicate directly across national borders, then we have to identify the socio-political and cultural factors that encourage or prevent that *demos* coming into existence in a fuller way than at present. This is a very complex problem, not least because as the European Parliament becomes more powerful the ruling parties in national governments are likely to impose greater discipline upon 'their' MEPs to ensure they speak and act in favour of the interests represented by those governments. As in the case of the European Commission, so with the European Parliament, the member states of the EU have no desire to give added muscle to institutions that put European concerns before the national interest.

In *Whose Europe?* we explore these issues. The book is organised into three sections. In the first section, entitled 'Barriers', John Markoff, Charlotte Hoffmann, Andreas Føllesdal and Sue Wright explore different aspects of the multi-level political structures that are emerging in the course of Europeanisation and devolution. Each of these contributors shows specific ways in which European polities—not only the national states but also suprastate institutions and devolved forms of government—fail to give all men and women access to the benefits and activities of citizenship on equal terms.

John Markoff argues that, although the European Union has a strong formal commitment to democratic values and despite the fact that civic freedoms are strong in member states throughout the EU, this polity nevertheless poses a challenge to democratisation. Since the eighteenth century, the development of democratic freedoms and political practices has been associated with the activities of social movements placing pressure 'from below' on government bodies, making them more accountable to the people. As more governmental power drifts upwards, above the level of the national state, the capacity of social movements to exercise influence decreases. Paradoxically, while the EU supports democracy within its member states, it remains relatively free of effective democratic control itself. During the nineteenth century, social movements reoriented themselves from local power structures to national states but they have been much less effective in making the further adjustment needed to be effective at the suprastate level.

In her chapter, Charlotte Hoffmann explores the part played by language issues in Catalonia. She traces some issues at the heart of Catalan language policy since the late 1970s and makes the case that language planning in Catalonia is no longer grounded in popu-

8

lar consensus. On the contrary, the policy is confrontational and creates conflicts of allegiance. In Hoffmann's view, political, economic, social and cultural conditions have changed so much over the last thirty years that the traditional fusion of nation-state, territory, language and identity must give way, making room for new solutions to present-day language problems.

Sue Wright points to another set of problems that derive from the way language networks and practices are developing. She argues that language is an important but often neglected aspect of political power. The language adopted by political elites acquires the role of gatekeeper. While those who possess it are not automatically included in the power nexus, those who do not are most definitely excluded. There is a certain dishonesty in maintaining the fiction that the European Union gives equal weight and respect to all official languages of the member states if, in reality, the languages which permit access to the European centres of power are one, perhaps two, dominant lingua francas: English and French.

In the next chapter, Andreas Føllesdal takes up the case of third country nationals, citizens of non-EU states who may be semi-permanent residents in member states. Føllesdal argues that, as far as such people are concerned, the present rules of European Union citizenship violate the basic democratic principle that those affected by social institutions should also enjoy political levers of influence. In his view, third country nationals (for example, Turkish residents in Germany or Algerians living in France) should enjoy full citizenship in the relevant member states as well as Union citizenship.

In the second section of this book, entitled 'Bridges', Reiner Grundmann, Steve May, joint authors Barrie Axford and Richard Huggins and, finally, David Jary analyse social tendencies that have the potential for establishing new bonds between populations within Europe. They explore the mechanisms that are creating and legitimising new identities within and beyond old national boundaries, and raise the question of how these identities may find democratic expression.

Reiner Grundmann takes a more optimistic line than John Markoff about the potential emergence of an active transnational sphere of public debate involving citizens throughout the European Union. He argues that the emergence of distinctively 'European' issues such as BSE means that a homogenisation of opinion is more likely than before to occur at the European level. This outcome is possible in spite of the fact that social movements have more leverage at the national level. In Grundmann's view, the creation of a

9

European public sphere through the synchronisation and homogenisation of cycles of media attention on contentious 'European' issues is a more realistic prospect than direct attempts to create a 'new European' identity through public education or the legal system.

When the arguments of Markoff and Grundmann are considered together, it can be seen that there is a possibility that as more European issues come to the top of the news agenda, a European public opinion may gradually take shape that can be harnessed, potentially at least, by pan-European social movements, non-governmental organisations and, perhaps, political parties. As far back as the 1960s and 1970s, student protest campaigns and peace movements in different European countries influenced each other in terms of both their tactics and their objectives. If the war in the Balkans were to be followed by a succession of similar conflicts on Europe's borders, similar processes of transnational influence might become important.

Charlotte Hoffmann's account of language policy in Catalonia is echoed by Steve May's analysis of the Welsh case. However, May is quite optimistic, arguing that Wales provides a model of ethnocultural and ethnolinguistic democracy, one that has redefined the role of language within the nation-state. Unlike Charlotte Hoffmann, who points out the sense of exclusion felt by monolingual Castilian speakers within Catalonia, May does not agonise over those who may be excluded in the new bilingual Wales. Rather, he welcomes the new opportunities for plurilingual democracy that now appear possible even in a state such as Britain where the monolingual tradition has been particularly strong.

Barrie Axford and Richard Huggins argue that the terms of the debate about democracy and identity in Europe should be fundamentally altered to take account of the prospects for a post-national network polity in Europe. Without ceasing to be a territorial entity, a united Europe is becoming a web of nodes and connections that pay little regard to spatial frontiers. They examine the developing European Information Society Project and explore the prospects for democracy in a network polity that has governance without government.

Axford and Huggins give an account of a possible future, visualized by some, in which the EU policy process is made more transparent and accessible by placing it on the Internet, where functional (as opposed to territorial) communities are given voting rights. In this future Europe, general civic rights and obligations would cease to be tied to nationality and ethnicity, and consensual problem-solving backed up by efficient regulation would replace conflictual bargaining leading to redistribution. This transformation would have to be accompanied, they assume, by changes in consciousness and culture.

They raise the question of how democratic participation by citizens could be made effective in this new world. One possibility Axford and Huggins evoke is that a networked, transnational politics would be pluralistic and involve countervailing influences. To that extent it would be democratising. However, this would not in itself overcome the practical difficulty that networks and flows are always in one particular language, a fact that excludes those who have no access to that language. As Sue Wright argues, Europe's plurilingual condition remains a major obstacle to overcoming the democratic deficit whether we are talking about a post-national network polity or a Europe rooted in peoples and territories.

It may be the case that in the very long term, if pan-European functional networks displace ethnic and national identities as the focus of identity and commitment, language may cease to be a focus of cultural and political loyalty. In such circumstances, men and women might be ready to see their local languages restricted to the local domain while a lingua franca provided for transnational communication. This would be less radical than the switch from their local currency to the Euro, since there is no suggestion that the local language should not be conserved. If the lingua franca adopted is English, it is likely to be an internationalised and pluricentric English, a language shorn of the cultural barnacles acquired in London or New York. However, it is difficult to envisage the early displacement of national and ethnic identities in a decade that has seen struggles throughout Europe for the congruence of nation, state and language. The Balkans may be the most bloody example but they are not the only one.

In his chapter, David Jary contributes to the debate about citizenship within the European Union. He takes up the challenge, implicit in Føllesdal's chapter, to identify a form of citizenship which ensures that all those affected by social institutions are able to enjoy political levers of influence. Jary sets himself against postmodern formulae that dismiss the possibility of incorporating a wide range of sub-cultures and value positions within a political framework that recognises rights and obligations common to all. He makes the argument that universal rights preserve the conditions for cultural diversification and autonomous action while also allowing social solidarity and integration to develop between different groups. Jary draws on Habermas, Held, Linklater and others to show that an inclusionary, cosmopolitan emancipatory citizenship may develop within a post-national civil state.

The chapters in the first two parts of this book all attempt realistic assessments of barriers against and bridges towards a more democratic Europe. In the third part, entitled 'Processes', we stand back a little from current political issues and prospects and return to the broader historical and comparative perspectives already present in the chapters by Markoff and Wright. Dennis Smith, Pablo Jáuregui and Harald Wydra all draw upon aspects of the work of the sociologist Norbert Elias.

Dennis Smith looks at the part played by the United States during the 1940s and 1950s in pacifying the European nations and imposing a framework of rules for the conduct of their economic and diplomatic affairs. He argues that as states in Western Europe have been increasingly locked into tight bonds of interdependence, this movement is complemented by the disembedding of regions and large businesses from their close ties to the national state. Brussels has become Europe's Versailles, a place where the courtier's skills are employed by the modern lobbyist.

For his part, Pablo Jáuregui questions the suggestion that the development of the European Union means Europe is entering a 'post-nationalist' era. Jáuregui does not believe that nationalism and Europeanism are mutually incompatible. These two phenomena may be related in a variety of ways. For example, in Britain, the idea of going into Europe was associated with a decline in national status and the 'loss of world power'. By contrast, for Spain, entering Europe meant a considerable enhancement of national prestige following the collapse of a 'backward dictatorship'.

Finally, Harald Wydra turns to Eastern Europe and challenges the vision of East and West as two isolated blocs that gradually converged. He sees the rise of democracy in Eastern Europe as a long-term social process interwoven with the fall of communism. Wydra argues that dissident movements created a 'second reality', undermining communism's official myths. Dissidents took their standards and aspirations from Western experience but found themselves largely ignored by the West. Since 1989, the influence of western models and standards has increased but, ironically, there has also been a breakdown of self-restraint and an upsurge of violence.

This last point returns us, once again, to the Balkan war. Major advances towards and away from democracy tend to be associated with the trauma of large-scale military conflict. Wars raise questions about the role of government and the rights and obligations of the people. War also dramatises identity. A war involving most of the European Union on the same side may strengthen our sense of sharing a European identity that is defined in large part by a commitment to democratic practices and the recognition of human rights. When we turn from the Balkans and look back at ourselves, do we find a European political order that lives up the values for which we went to war?

Appendix: Beginners start here

There are three big historical landmarks in the process of Europe-formation over the past four decades or so:[16] the defeat of Germany in 1945; the oil shock in 1973; and the fall of the Berlin Wall in 1989. These landmarks divide Europe-formation into three phases. In the first phase, from 1945 to 1973, West Germany was reintegrated into Western European politics and diplomacy. Between 1951 and 1965 a series of treaties[17] between 'the Six'[18] set up the European Community[19] with the object of creating a customs union and eliminating trade distortions between member states. In this period, the Six had dramatic economic growth.

In the second phase, between 1973 and 1989, the European community expanded from six to twelve member states.[20] This expansion was managed under difficult conditions. The energy crisis of 1973 ended the postwar boom in Europe. It undermined the Keynesian welfare strategies of most member states, transforming their internal power balances. Trade unions were weakened and governments cut back on spending. Business interests fought hard to protect their profits through protectionist measures, against the original spirit of the Common Market.

Broadly, the response of politicians had three elements. The first was to move towards a single internal market, harmonising regulations throughout the Community as far as possible. The second was to move in the direction of a common currency. The third was to make the European Community more like a developmental state. This last involved such measures as creating a regional development fund (1974), introducing direct elections to the European Parliament (1974), accepting qualified majority voting in the Council of Ministers (1986), and giving the European Parliament powers to delay and amend legislation (1986).[21]

The third (that is, the present) phase of Europe-making began in 1989 with the collapse of the Soviet empire in eastern and central Europe. This was soon followed by the third recession in two decades.[22] This meant that two conditions which had favoured the Common Market in the 1960s had been removed by the early 1990s. One condition was the remarkable postwar boom that had produced a climate of growth. This had ended by the early 1970s. The second conducive condition was the Cold War which had kept Germany divided and enabled West Germany to be contained with relative ease within the framework of the European Community (and NATO).

Since 1989 the Federal Republic of Germany has been released from the strait-jacket imposed by the Cold War. It has been drawn both eastwards and westwards. On the one hand, Germany has achieved reunification with the eastern Länder, the old socialist state. On the other hand, it has sought to persuade its partners in the European Union to accept a greater degree of political integration. If this comes about, it will lead towards a union in which Germany is bound to be more powerful than before. In return, Germany's partners, especially France, demanded that Germany merge the Deutschmark within a single European currency.

This agreement led to the Maastricht Treaty on European Union (drawn up in 1991, signed in 1992, implemented in 1993). This treaty makes provision for intergovernmental co-operation in foreign and security policy and also in the area of justice and home affairs. It has set up new institutions such as the Committee for the Regions and the Cohesion Fund, introduced the concept of European Union citizenship and given the European Parliament increased powers. It has also enshrined the principle of subsidiarity.[23]

Now, at the turn of the millennium, it is not clear how many more member states the European Union will acquire. Nor is it possible to say how member states (or at least eleven out the fifteen)[24] will respond to the controls imposed by the discipline of EMU (Economic and Monetary Union) which began in 1999.

Over four decades after the Treaty of Rome (1957), the European Union, with its 370 million inhabitants,[25] has some of the key characteristics of a large modern state, even if they are underdeveloped. It has an executive civil service, the European Commission, that draws up specific legislative proposals. Political direction is provided by the Council of Ministers. There is also a European Court of Justice, an elected parliament, European citizenship with the symbols of a common passport, an anthem and a flag and a common European currency.

However, there is another side to the coin. The sense of a shared European identity remains relatively weak and national feelings—the strong sense of being French, British, Spanish, German and so on—are still extremely powerful. This may explain the strong opposition within some national electorates to ratifying the Maastricht Treaty. For example, the French referendum produced a 'yes' vote by a margin of only two per cent. The British government only got the Maastricht Treaty through the House of Commons by turning the issue into a vote of confidence.[26]

Furthermore, the institutional and cultural bases for a democratic European public sphere remain relatively narrow. Language differences make it difficult to communicate across national borders, especially to older, working-class audiences. The constituencies of the European Parliament do not cross national borders either, so national issues dominate campaigns. The European Union frequently resembles a pantomime horse. In other words, beneath the stage costume you can see the individual actors struggling to go in different directions. In this respect, the politics of the European Union often seem to be primarily a struggle between different national interests.

And finally there is the issue of devolution, autonomy and independence. The current state of identities is made yet more complex because of the phenomenon whereby those territorial, cultural and ethnic identities which many had assumed to have been incorporated into the 'nation states' reemerge with ambitious cultural and political agenda. A number of groups have already had great success. We have mentioned Flanders, Scotland, Padania and Catalonia. There are many more with similar ambitions.

Notes

1 The European movement was, in part, the product of an unusual alliance between business leaders who saw the benefits of a single European market and idealists, many of them socialist, who wanted to abolish the conditions for nationalist aggression between European national states.

2 Signed in 1986, the Single European Act provided for the completion of the single internal market allowing free movement of goods, persons, services and capital. It also made economic and monetary union an objective, gave formal status to the European Monetary System, extended co-operation in monetary, social, regional, environmental, research and technology policy, increased the

scope for qualified majority voting in the Council of Ministers, gave the European Parliament more powers to delay and amend legislation, and provided for increased co-operation between governments in matters of foreign policy.

3 The Social Chapter embodied a charter of 'fundamental rights' of workers. These included rights in respect of health and safety, working conditions, equality between men and women, and protection of the unemployed. Issues relating to pay, the right to strike and the right to impose lockouts are excluded from the charter. The Social Chapter is embodied in an annexe to the Maastricht Treaty as a separate intergovernmental agreement among the member states (except the UK). A further annexe to the treaty provides for the Social Chapter to be implemented through the mechanisms of the European Union. In effect, social policy is decided within the EU's supranational framework. The UK took no part at first and negotiated an opt out to legislation relating to the Social Chapter. The Blair government reversed this decision.

4 The Schengen Convention is an agreement to remove border controls and, at the same time, develop increased co-operation between governments in respect of gathering and sharing information on wanted persons, illegal immigrants, stolen property. The convention provides also for the harmonisation of visa regulations and criteria for political asylum. It consists of two 'accords', signed in 1985 and 1990 respectively, between the Benelux countries, France and Germany. Italy, Portugal, Spain and Greece also joined the group of signatories between 1991 and 1992 although Denmark, Ireland and the UK remain outside the arrangement.

5 The Maastricht Treaty established the European Union composed of three 'pillars': (i) the European Communities (consisting of the European Community, the European Coal and Steel Community and the European Atomic Energy Community); (ii) the Common Foreign and Security Policy; and (iii) Cooperation on Justice and Home Affairs. The second and third pillars are forms of 'intergovernmental co-operation' rather than being part of the supranational framework embodied in the first pillar. The treaty expanded the European Community's responsibilities to include new policy areas in (for example) education, culture, transport, health, consumer protection and the environment. It also increased the powers of the European Parliament, set up the Committee of the Regions, established the Cohesion Fund, introduced the principle of 'subsidiarity', established the concept of EU citizenship and provided a framework for a common foreign and security policy, a common approach to judicial affairs and, eventually, a common defence policy.

6 The 'Yes' vote was 51.05%. The 'No' vote was 48.95%.

7 Santer was chosen over the much more formidable Jean-Luc Dehaene, who had become prime minister of Belgium in 1992.

8 The European Parliament's powers are restricted to the European Community, the first 'pillar' of the European Union, and do not extend to the common foreign and security policy or to intergovernmental co-operation on justice and home affairs. The parliament has the tasks of scrutinizing draft legislation and the budget, supervising the European Commission and the Council of Ministers, caring for constituents and debating current issues. It may question Commission members, including the President, amend or reject the budget, and dismiss the Commission (but not, so far at least, individual members). The 'co-operation procedure' gives the parliament limited powers to amend proposals relating to the single internal market. The 'co-decision procedure' gives the parliament powers

equal to the Council of Ministers in 14 specific policy areas, including health, education, training, science and technology, culture, health, consumer affairs, trans-European networks (energy, transport and telecommunications), environmental issues, regional policy and developmental co-operation. These are the areas in which the Council of Ministers operates under qualified majority voting. Under co-decision arrangements, introduced under the Maastricht treaty, the parliament can amend or reject legislative proposals coming from the Council. Where necessary, bipartisan conciliation committee is convened to work out compromises.

9 Membership of the EU has become a highly desired means of validating the 'democratic' and 'civilized' character of countries and regimes. Some aspects of this mechanism are explored by Pablo Jáuregui in this volume in connection with Spain. He shows that entry into the EU reinforced the collective self-image of the Spaniards as a modern democratic nation. A similar argument may be made with respect to Portugal and Greece. The potential reward of EU membership at some point in the future arguably makes certain states take action on human rights that they might not otherwise consider. This case could be made with respect to, for example, Latvia and Estonia in respect of their treatment of Russian language speakers.

10 At the time of Marshall Aid and the establishment of the Organisation for European Economic Cooperation (OEEC), which later expanded to become the Organization for Economic Cooperation and Development (OECD). See the chapter by Dennis Smith in this volume.

11 *The Guardian*, 20 March 1999, 20.

12 Awareness and acceptance of the implications of membership of the European Union have been slower to develop in Britain and Scandinavia than in countries such as Spain and Italy. In the last-named countries EU membership is widely regarded as, on the whole, enhancing rather than undermining the national interest. It is doubtful whether the Spanish and Italian governments would have been able to impose the painful economic policies required to prepare for entry into the single currency without substantial grassroots support for the European project. For a comparison of the Spanish and British cases, see the chapter by Jáuregui in this volume.

13 Following Franco's death the new Spanish constitution devolved significant power to seventeen autonomous regions. Although the Catalans, Basques and Galicians had long asserted their separate identities, many of the other regions had no special historical claims to special recognition. However, by creating so many autonomous regions the blow was softened for the military and right wing political forces. In other words, the constitutional change did not look so obviously like a victory for Catalan, Basque and Galician aspirations.

14 The federal structure is based upon three geographical regions (Flanders, Wallonia and Brussels) and, overlapping with this, three language-based cultural communities (Flemish, French and German-speaking). The central government retains control of defence, foreign policy, finance, social security and justice. The regions are responsible for all other areas with the exception of language issues, education, social policy and health which are devolved to the communities.

15 An increasingly important role is likely to be played by the Committee of the Regions, set up in 1995, which brings together representatives from regional and local authorities throughout the EU. The committee's remit includes health, education, culture, training and transport, and regional development (under the rubric of 'economic and social cohesion').

16 For further details see, for example, Middlemas 1995, Drost 1995 or Therborn 1995.

17 Most notably, the Treaty of Rome in 1957 which set up the European Coal and Steel Community and the European Economic Community.

18 France, West Germany, Italy, Belgium, Netherlands and Luxembourg.

19 More precisely, the European Communities which is the joint name of the European Coal and Steel Community (founded 1951), the European Atomic Energy Community (founded 1957) and the European Economic Community (also founded 1957) when their executives were merged in 1967.

20 Denmark, Ireland and the UK joined in 1973, Greece in 1981, Spain and Portugal in 1986.

21 The Single European Act of 1986 gave formal status to the European Monetary system, extended qualified majority voting, and set out a timetable for achieving the internal market by 1992.

22 The recession years were 1974–6, 1984–6 and 1990–93.

23 Subsidiarity is the principle that in areas that do not fall within the Community's exclusive competence it shall take action 'only if and in so far as the objectives of the proposed action cannot be sufficiently achieved by the member states and can therefore . . . be better achieved by the Community' (from article 3b quoted in Drost, 1995, 64). In the Amsterdam treaty of 1997 the powers of the European Parliament were extended still further.

24 In 1995 Austria, Finland and Sweden joined the EU.

25 Middlemas, 1995, 692.

26 The Danes initially rejected the Treaty in a referendum by 50.3% to 49.7%. After several 'opt-outs' were negotiated, they voted 'yes' in a second referendum with a majority of 56.7%. Middlemas, 1995, 197–200; Drost, 1995, 162.

Bibliography

Drost, H. (1995), *What's What and Who's Who in Europe*, London: Cassell.

Edwards, G. and Pijpers, A. (eds), *The Politics of European Treaty Reform: the 1996 intergovernmental conference and beyond*, London: Pinter.

Middlemas, K. (1995), *Orchestrating Europe. The informal politics of European union 1973–95*, London: Fontana.

Therborn, G. (1995), *European Modernity and Beyond*, London: Sage.

Barriers

Our 'common European home'—but who owns the house?

John Markoff

Abstract

In this chapter, John Markoff notes that although the European Union has a strong formal commitment to democratic values, for example in the tests it applies to new entrants, and although civic freedoms are strong throughout the EU, this body nevertheless poses a challenge to democratisation. This is because the development of democratic freedoms and political practices has, since the eighteenth century, been accompanied by the activities of social movements that have placed pressure 'from below' upon government bodies, making them accountable to the people. As more governmental power drifts upwards, above the level of the national state, the capacity of social movements to exercise influence decreases. Paradoxically, while the EU supports democracy within its member states, it remains relatively free of effective democratic control itself. During the nineteenth century, social movements reoriented themselves from local power structures to national states but they have been less effective in reorienting themselves yet again to the suprastate level.

Introduction

In the late 1960s and early 1970s many a keen observer of political life was deeply pessimistic about the world prospects of democratic advance.[1] Communist rule seemed immutable where in power and likely to advance to new locations, generals governed in most of Latin America, hopes for democratic rule in many parts of decolonized Asia and Africa had been dashed, and even in some of the most successful democratic states themselves tumultuous social movements mounted a variety of challenges to the prevailing order. In defiance of this common pessimism, the next two decades witnessed the most geographically extensive wave of democratisations in history; by the early 1990s equally keen observers were inclined to conclude that democracy was close to becoming the only legitimate political order, the 'only game in town',[2] some even held that, with the dynamic force for change of fundamental political conflict over, history itself was brought to an end.[3]

The easy optimism of the early 1990s seems no more warranted than the easy pessimism of the early 1970s. Democracy is not a fixed thing, achieved or even achievable once and for all, but an expanding, contracting, moving, continually redefined and reimagined social creation. Although the past two centuries have brought about considerable democratisation of many of the world's states, and the great wave of democratisation that began in southern Europe in the early 1970s and continued into the 1990s has been the geographically most extensive wave thus far, new challenges to a democratic future were also emerging. The challenges I will consider here are rooted in structures of power that transcend the territorial boundaries of the national states and raise questions about whether the social processes that have produced the democratisation of the states in the past will continue to be effective forces for democratisation in the future. The logic of the basic argument is simple: if we think of democratisation as a process, we may ask what have been the forces that have sustained this process; if we may expect those forces to be weaker in the future, we may wonder whether a) the future course of democratisation will run less strong or b) whether there may be other emerging forces to substitute as engines for democratisation.

The geographic focus of my observations on the challenge of transnational structures of power to the future of democratisation will be the developing institutions of the European Union (until recently the European Community). There is a sub-argument implicit in this way of framing my subject that I want to make explicit. There are many very significant democratic elements in the EU. First, its member states all govern themselves as democracies. Second, its commitment to a democratic identity shows up in, and is strengthened by, a) its unwillingness to admit Greece, Portugal and Spain until they democratised and its willingness to do so with that transformation accomplished; b) its continuing refusal to admit Turkey on the publicly stated grounds of that country's several forms of violating an implicit definition of a democratic polity (although there may be other, less openly stated, reasons as well); c) the degree to which a more or less secure democratic transformation is understood in post-Communist east-central Europe as an essential precondition for admission. Thus Slovaks may hope, after the fall of the Meciar government with its significant antidemocratic features (fall 1998), that Slovakia might join Poland, the Czech Republic and Hungary in being seriously considered for admission. This is by no means to say that a democratic polity is the only issue, but no one doubts that it is essential. Third, to the extent that one thinks of the EU as already a sort of quasi-state, it is a quasi-state many of whose powerholders are named by those democratically elected governments. By formal definitions identifying democracies as political systems in which all powerholders are directly or indirectly responsible to electorates (indirectly in the sense of being named by those so elected), the EU might be held to qualify.[4] Fourth, the civic life of the EU has much that is typical of democracies: its extensive personal freedoms include the freedom to complain, criticise and mobilise public opinion even against positions favoured by powerholders. Citizens of member countries who object to EU policies are unlikely to fear arrest (let alone worse) for attempting to persuade others.

So the larger claim made here indirectly is that if even the EU is in important ways a challenge to democratisation, how much more so will other forms of transnational power prove to be.

The intertwined histories of democratic institutions and social movements in Europe

Historians of early modern Europe (and elsewhere) have revealed the numerous ways in which the obscure people of town and country were sometimes able to resist, challenge, and alter the plans of the wealthy and powerful. Wayne te Brake has demonstrated the degree to which conflicts of local and distant élites (a town government and the centre of empire, for example) could readily furnish opportunities for 'ordinary people' to bid for the support of the one or the other.[5] It is a major challenge to historians to try to identify the points at which such interventions went beyond supporting some élite powerholder less noxious than some rival actually to formulate and advance the projects of those down below. One such moment, I would suggest, was the late eighteenth century when the word 'democrat' first began to be widely used, indicating the existence of political actors identified with—or identifying themselves with—the project of creating 'democracy'—a much older term long used in hypothetical discussions of possible political systems.[6] But what were the institutions of this democracy?

The development of the formal institutions of democracy from that eighteenth-century revolutionary moment to the present has been intertwined with the history of social movements.[7] Writing on the eve of the democratic breakthrough of the late eighteenth century, Jean-Jacques Rousseau gave vivid voice to a critique of the political institutions across the Channel that were admired by so many French reformers of the day. Commenting scornfully on British electoral practice, he observed in 1762 that:

> The people of England regards itself as free, but it is gravely mistaken. It is free only during the election of Parliament. As soon as they are elected, slavery overtakes it, and it is nothing. The use it makes of the short moments of liberty it enjoys merits losing them.[8]

Rousseau's contention about the limitations of electoral institutions was in no way superseded by the age of democratic revolution that followed. From the 1790s to the present, there have been recurrent complaints about the depth of popular involvement in political life, the reality of popular control over powerholders, and the possibility that the existence of some form of institutional channel for participation could blind publics to the inadequacy of that participation. Rousseau's critique has repeatedly appeared in one form or another and has informed movements for a more genuine democratisation.

But as a matter of simple, empirical observation, Rousseau was utterly mistaken about the British political practice he so eloquently despised. For even the occasional contests for a Parliament of uncertain authority in which only a narrowly constituted stratum had the right to vote provided occasions for the political involvement of much larger numbers, often in ways that overflowed the bounds of electoral and even legal practice. Local élites mobilised large numbers for distributing leaflets, festive parades and generally displaying enthusiasm, not to mention the occasional attempt to intimidate the partisans of rival candidates. Not only did a larger target public need to be courted than had the right to vote, but an opportunity for popular forces to bargain for their support with élites was institutionalised. Elections could easily be a time of disturbance as well as celebration, a moment for challenge as well as a ritual of orderliness.[9] And parliamentary representation created a framework for the petitioning of representatives, including the organising of petition drives by the representatives themselves.[10]

If the political institutions of early modern Europe already presented opportunities for popular action, the democratic breakthrough of the late eighteenth century linked many things together: élites claiming to rule on the basis of popular consent; the creation of new formal institutions through which the will of the people was to be shaped, made known, and asserted; the proliferation of organisational networks to influence parliaments (in the form of territorially- or issue-based associations); the explosion of journalism, as citizens sought up-to-date information on what was happening on high and those on high sought equally up-to-date information on what was happening down below; and the flowering of new forms of political struggle for those outside the centres of wealth and power.

Several distinguishable yet intertwined processes radically transformed the structures of government and the forms of popular political action. In western Europe, the increasing transfer of power from local arenas to national ones provoked (and was provoked by) a transformation of popular political action. Increasingly effective claims by distant authority were matched by a transformation of popular political action from challenges to local élites—ranging from the multiple forms of hidden resistance to open, collective and violent insurrection—to long-term campaigns to influence distant national governments.

The very broad result was the intertwined histories of new institutions of governance and the development of the modern social movement. People on high were bidding for the acquiescence or even the support of those down below; and those down below were creating new ways of threatening to disrupt the plans of those on high. The institutions of modern democracy and the modern politics of the street developed in tandem. Parliamentary and electoral processes

- provided targets for long-term mobilisation campaigns
- created channels for the exertion of influence
- displayed a model for asserting that political action was legitimate to the extent that it was carried on by the agent of 'the people', with the consent of 'the people', or on behalf of 'the people' and conflating these three claims
- increased the significance of the sheer number of people affiliated with one or another political position as the fashioning of electoral or parliamentary pluralities became an increasingly important activity for those who sought power, encouraging organisers to find the means to demonstrate that their positions had large

numbers of adherents; thus petition drives, demonstrations and electoral campaigns came to influence one another.

In these ways the development of democratic institutions encouraged popular mobilisations even against the policies and personnel of the rulers. (This is the broad picture; much detail remains to be filled in.) After North American settlers defeated the greatest maritime power of the age, French revolutionary armies dominated Europe, and Haitian ex-slaves fought off the armies of three empires, the power of democratic claims to legitimation were clear to all, and many states began to make claims that they ruled as the deputies of, with the assent of, or in the interests of 'the people' as never before. Even conservative states were coming to do so by the time the French forces went down to defeat.[11]

As states were claiming their rule reposed on popular will, challengers, at intervals, denied such claims with the counterclaim that it was they, the challengers, who spoke for the people, or for some heretofore excluded component. And as élite reformers sought to use democratic legitimations for their own agenda, élite conservatives sought to find some other principle for governance. Out of such struggles, new institutions were created. Democratisation advanced in large part in several multicontinental waves.[12] It was in no way merely the diffusion of some known, fixed model, for in the course of these struggles, new institutions were created that have redefined democracy. Innovation was a multicontinental process, with many points of innovation, although generally not in the world centres of wealth and power. Democracy has never been a finished thing, but has been continually renewed, redefined and reinvented, drawing on political struggles in many places. And in this reinvention, the interaction of social movements and élite powerholders has been crucial.

Modern democracy has never been limited to such formal practices as elections and parliamentary rule because such institutions and the democratic legitimating formula of rule by virtue of popular will encourage a whole range of additional political practices, organisations, forms of carrying on conflict. These include: political parties to contest elections; lobbying activities seeking influence with legislators and regulators; a variety of interest associations; social movement organisation and activism; and efforts of bureaucratic groups to avoid public scrutiny, resist social movement pressures, and insulate themselves from the instabilities inherent in the shifting fortunes of electoral selection of powerholders.

Key arenas of struggle among élites and between élites and social movement activists in nineteenth- and twentieth-century European states developed around the extent to which bodies accountable to electorates controlled ministerial appointments, policy and budgets and over the definition of the electorates. (Organisations battling on behalf of workers and of women were particularly important participants in democratic history.)

Before the late eighteenth century democratic breakthrough, then, the political action of ordinary people was significant, but routinised mechanisms of accountability of those on high to those down below were lacking. By the great wave of democratisation of the late twentieth century such routinised practices were the norm in a large number of states. But if the history of the intertwining of movements and democratic institutions just sketched is correct, the implications as we attempt to peer ahead into the twenty-first century are great, and troublesome, for at least two reasons. First, at the tail end of the twentieth century important decision-making power is being exercised at locations other than those democratised states. Second, the capacity of social movement action to democratise the emerging transnational structures of power as they had democratised some of the states is problematic. In what follows, I shall be examining both of these issues in the context of the developing European Union.

The challenge of transnational power

Adam Przeworski sounds an important cautionary note:

> We know very little and understand next to nothing about 'globalisation'. All we have so far is slogans and anecdotes. But we do know that the supra-national question is alarming from the point of view of democratic theory.[13]

So many of the claims made about a supposedly unprecedented and powerful increase in the role of transnational linkages are so extreme and rest on so little systematic evidence that we have some reason to approach the whole subject with a certain scepticism, as Przeworski's remarks suggest.[14]

Despite such reservations, it seems pretty clear that a wide diversity of institutions of transnational governance of various sorts, with varying relations to the states, are in process of formation.

These include:

- a quasi-state, the European Union
- multistate bodies of which the most important is the UN
- decision-making structures that are embedded in multistate economic agreements like NAFTA or the South American Mercosur
- formally constituted transnational financial institutions, in particular the World Bank and the IMF
- multinational corporations
- *ad hoc* or permanent committees making decisions for consortia of investors
- transpacific networks of finance and trade cemented by kinship ties
- multinational criminal enterprises with financial resources large enough that few states in the world have the capacity to prevent their police forces from supplementing their incomes with payments from such sources
- the governance, if that is the right word, of the Internet.

The emergence of such structures has been variously explained. They may be responses to the variety, complexity, importance and ubiquity of transnational economic linkages; they may be modes of coping with environmental or other problems now widely understood to span borders and be beyond the capacity of states to manage on their own; they may be efforts to avert interstate warfare; they may be byproducts of a cultural transformation toward transnational visions of one sort or another; they may be new modes of politically organising capitalism in the face of challenges by workers who have acquired some power at the level of the states—we shall not try to sift through the causes here (but we may note that all of the above have played some role in the history of the EU).[15]

What follows from this is that many, many important decisions affecting the lives of large numbers of people are not made by the states. While it was common in the 1990s to celebrate the sheer numbers of people who lived under governments they had the right to elect, it was by no means obvious that citizens have been acquiring more control over policies, as such nonstate or quasi-state structures—of very diverse sorts, and with very diverse relations to the states—exerted more weight. Among such structures the European Union is the one which most strongly resembles a state.[16] But it hardly follows from the democratisation of some of the states, or even many of the states at the crest of the great wave of democrati-

sations of the late twentieth century,[17] that the transnational structures in formation would be democratic ones; it does not even follow for structures co-ordinating policies for states every one of
whose individual members has a markedly democratic character.
We have now entered a historical moment in which we confront the
challenge of what creating 'postnational democracy'[18] might mean.

European union and democratic practice[19]

The EU is sufficiently different from other transnational structures
of authority and changing with sufficient rapidity that the scholarly
literature reminds one of the image of the blind men and the elephant, with each observer seizing on a different aspect of this large,
varied, unusual and complex beast, except that in this case the beast
keeps moving.[20] It has its 'intergovernmental' aspects and its 'supranational' ones. Its decision-making processes are radically different
depending on which of its three 'pillars' a particular policy arena is
in. Denmark entered on terms different than other member states
and Britain was not subject to its 'social charter' until the new
Labour government accepted it in 1997. It is publicly committed to
enlargement, but no one can be sure which new states will be admitted nor on what terms nor when. The powers of its European
Parliament vary from one issue to the next, as reflected in the varying denominations of its authority as 'consultation', 'cooperation',
and 'co-decision', but those powers have also been changing over
time. It is embarked on creating a whole new institutional structure
to control the common currency being introduced at the end of the
twentieth century. Four of its member states are not participating
(yet?) in that common currency. Its political life is shaped by a mar-
vellously diverse array of political actors, including the institutions
of the EU itself (European Commission, European Parliament,
European Court of Justice, Council of Ministers and the new
European Central Bank); the member states; the subnational
regions, buoyed up by the vision of the 'Europe of the Regions' and
embodied in various local or transnational organisations representing ethnoterritorial groups and subnational governments;[21] a
variety of lobbies; and social movement organisations. In looking
for analogous but better understood political structures, some
observers and some participants (not always a very sharp distinction) have looked to federal political systems and one finds the
expression 'The United States of Europe'[22] (although Alberta

Sbragia cogently suggests that it is German rather than US federalism that is the closer analogy).[23] As for the element of change: its membership has expanded in stages from a half-dozen to fifteen (as of the late 1990s); the policy arenas in which it makes rules have grown; its Court came to acquire a weight hardly foreseen in its initial founding; the powers of the Parliament have grown somewhat; many important decisions that once were made by a rule of unanimity can now be made by 'qualified majority'; it is now moving into the uncharted waters of currency union and accompanying central bank. Some of these changes have been tracked by the changes in self-designation of this 'emerging entity'[24] from the European Coal and Steel Community through the European Community and on to the (current) European Union (and let us not neglect the variant label much used in Britain, the Common Market).

When we ask to what degree the EU's policymakers are responsible to citizens, we can readily see how the notion of a 'democratic deficit' crops up with such frequency in these discussions. The only powerholders in the EU's key institutions directly elected by citizens are the members of the European Parliament whose competence is far less than that of the parliaments of any member state. The various rule-making bodies whose highest officials are appointed by the states work in considerable secrecy. The European Court of Justice, whose authoritative rulings have emerged as major decision points, and whose capacity to advise national courts that national laws are contrary to some EU rules has many points of resemblance to the US Supreme Court. But the European Court of Justice differs profoundly from the Supreme Court in announcing only its collective decision, rather than individual adherence to differing opinions. It may perhaps thereby cement a collective supranational identity distinct from the states that appointed its judges, but it also effaces any potential linkages of individual judges to citizens. While the European Parliament does have some significant leverage in budgetary matters, it is far from obvious that this could in time produce the parliamentary power over ministers that was characteristic of much of the history of the states, for the EU's budget is small. EU power resides in rule-making, whether by technocrats, agents of the member states, or judges, none of whom are directly elected, and none of whom are responsible to political parties (let alone broader publics) at the union level.[25] In the history of the western European states, state demands for revenue and soldiers provided important opportunities for subjects and citizens to bargain by resisting, sometimes surreptitiously, sometimes violently, the tax collector and the recruiting sergeant; and representative assemblies could, in more routine fashion, bargain with the crown as well, and ultimately gain power over ministers. An EU whose budget is low compared to the member states and with no army at all (so far)[26] may also be an EU less vulnerable to parliamentary assertiveness. If a state, for Max Weber, was virtually defined by its monopoly on legitimate force over some territory, the EU (so far) is an antistate.

Even in social welfare policy, where European states have strong histories, and the formal role of supranational institutions is very limited by virtue of the explicit decision to keep social welfare at the state level and not construct a Eurowelfare state, the capacity of electorates to influence policy is probably significantly reduced. The linkages to social policy of macroeconomic policy (in which the European Central Bank will be a powerful actor), the development of a free market in services as well as personal mobility, the erosion of the distinction between the rights of citizens and the rights of noncitizen residents all imply that national social welfare policy is going to be made under severe constraints, as Paul Pierson puts it, in which 'national governments possess diminished control over many of the policies that have traditionally supported national welfare states'.[27]

The diminution of state autonomy in this realm may be especially notable because the welfare state and political democracy have developed a profoundly symbiotic character in western Europe.[28] Many students of politics since World War Two simply assumed an inevitable connection of expanded rights of democratic participation and expanded social rights. If all adults have the vote, so the argument went, of course the large numbers of people who feel economically threatened by potential medical costs, old age, expensive education for their children, and so forth, would support programmes of social provision. Such programmes in turn would attach large numbers of people to the current constitutional order. So democratisation would promote social provision and social provision in turn would assure large majorities favouring democracy. But the first half of this relationship has suddenly and rapidly eroded—raising important questions about the second half. The strength of the movement for 'welfare reform' in the US political debate of the 1990s was not matched in European states with their much more strongly institutionalised welfare traditions,[29] but one must wonder about the more subtle challenge posed to social provision at the national level by an EU devoted in its macroeconomic policies to stressing liberalisation, with its new European Central

Bank devoted to currency stability and made quite autonomous from national political demands (or European ones, for that matter), and its judicial apparatus recognising the priority, in many matters, of Union regulations over national law.[30]

This is particularly the case with actual and potential erosion of the commitment of some publics to previous forms of social provision evident. Part of what gives antiwelfare positions their special force today is a fragmentation of political identities. To the extent that poorer people are identifiable as ethnically distinctive, including an identity as recent immigrants, some political parties are able to denounce welfare as taking from 'us' to give to 'them'. With millions of North African Moslems in France, or Turks in Germany, and Albanians and Africans moving to Italy, the mobilisation of xenophobic sentiment is readily linkable to an attack on welfare. When Surinamese or Indonesians show up on Dutch welfare rolls, the Dutch rethink their generous unemployment insurance. Moreover, the weakening of labour in the transnational marketplace reduces the likelihood of a collective identity as workers effectively overriding this fragmentation. The shift among a portion of France's workers from voting for the Communists to voting for the anti-immigrant National Front is an important sign of the power of anti-immigrant politics in an age of globalised economics.

If there should be a serious weakening in state commitments to the sorts of policies that in post-World War Two western Europe so significantly helped to cement political democracy, one wonders at the future. In the weakening of policies directed at their inclusion, in the weakening of notions of minimal acceptable standards of life guaranteed by a national community, will large numbers of poorer people feel materially or symbolically excluded from national life and simply opt out of support for a democratic practice that no longer aspires at both their inclusion and material advance? The stably high unemployment levels that economic reorganisation has produced in many western European countries may prove to be profoundly threatening to political legitimation in the absence of new social initiatives, as George Kolankiewicz suggests;[31] yet such initiatives are exactly what other scholars have persuasively argued are unlikely to characterise the EU in the near future. (28 per cent of EU citizens feel the chance of job loss in the next few years is fifty-fifty or worse; 48 per cent expect unemployment to worsen; 51 per cent want the EU to take action on unemployment.[32]) Such disaffection may be more profoundly corrosive of democracy than the direct exclusionary notions of xenophobic parties.

It is worth pausing for a moment over the currency of the expression 'democratic deficit'; after all, the Eurocrats do not occupy office by hereditary right, the judges in the European Court of Justice have not been named by generals, and the participants in the European Council are there as ministers of democratically elected regimes. To some of those in the foundational generation of late eighteenth-century democratisation the government of the European Union would not be alien. In the constitution of the new United States, balancing the interests of large and small states played a considerable role, the powers of the central government were restricted, and the state legislatures of the United States were to choose the members of the US Senate and an Electoral College the President. French Revolutionary electoral practice usually involved multistage electoral procedures. But what such eighteenth-century benchmarks leave out is the transformation of democratic conceptions and democratic practice over the past two centuries.

The EU is certainly no monolith; one scholarly monograph after another struggles to characterise the intricate relations among its varying institutions and the dizzying complexity of the interplay among union, national and subnational politics; even as the institutions change, new members join, and the interplay assumes new patterns demanding new scholarly monographs. But whether it is judges, bureaucratic regulators or national ministers meeting in secret, the relocation of decisional authority away from the national states toward this shifting intergovernmental and supranational mix, would seem to weaken, not strengthen, the democratic character of Europe. This weakening comes about in two rather different ways: first, by creating and strengthening institutions at the union level that are highly sheltered from accountability to publics; and second, by eroding the capacity of the member states to make policy autonomously thereby weakening the meaningfulness of those states' democratic processes.

The claims of democratic deficit are so frequent because the security and depth of the democracy of the member states is far stronger than in the past; and yet, at this very same moment, some significant decisional power is redeploying away from those states, sheltered by various forms of indirection, complexity and obscurity from the scrutiny of citizens. Consider that the post-war western European states were not merely reviving pre-war democracy, but deepening it. Post-war Britain ended the remnants of plural voting, France recognised the political rights of its women, Italy and Germany put democratic institutions on a relatively secure footing.

A generation later, Spain, Portugal and Greece had to democratise prior to joining the EU. So the paradox is that, on the whole, the democracy of the states ran strong as never before, and at the same time, the states were making partial cessions of sovereignty toward a structure whose democratic character was far less marked than their own. The 'pooling of sovereignty', as students of the EU put it, may well serve the interests of European peace and European prosperity, but its implications for democracy are cloudy. It may be an advance for technical rationality to have an autonomous European bank make monetary policy (or it may not—there's much to debate here),[33] but for most of the states, this means a bank far more independent of democratically accountable government than the present arrangements. Should the European Central Bank develop the habit, on the model of the Union's judicial and executive bodies, of announcing its collective decisions, but concealing the views of its individual members (who will represent the national banks), any element of accountability to citizens will vanish.

As a German jurist characterises the 'democracy gap':

> The democracy principle is valid for the member states, whose own capacities for decision are, however, dwindling; decisional powers are accruing to the European Community; but the principle of democracy is only weakly developed there. This leads to a growing need for democratic legitimation of its own for European policy, not derived from member-state governments.[34]

Let me summarise the state of EU democracy. First of all, there is a very strong democratic identification of the member states that is deeply reinforced by admissions policy.[35] In this sense, the EU has bolstered the notion of European democracy. This identification is strong enough that it has probably been casting a powerful spell over countries to the east that hope to join, where it functions as an important barrier to the potential for antidemocratic movements to form even in the face of significant economic disappointment. Indeed, on the crest of the great wave of democracy[36] that began in the 1970s, some even see a new international norm, an emerging 'right to democratic governance';[37] the EU's insistence on the democratic character of its members is an important contribution to the emergence of such talk. In this sense, we could perhaps speak of democracy as an implicit part of the Union's *acquis communautaire*, the body of secure institutional tradition and regulation. Second, and as a consequence, the freedom of citizens to express dissident views, to organise lobbies, movements, and parties to defend or advance their interests is as secure as it has ever been anywhere. If Euro-lobbies, movements, and parties are often less effective or vigorous than their member-state counterparts, it is not remotely the case that this is because they are in any sense repressed. (Indeed, the absence of a coercive apparatus is one of the more remarkable features of the EU as a quasi-state.) It is because the states remain such powerful players within the EU that in the struggle for influence resources are frequently more effectively deployed at the national than at the union level. At the same time: the only central institution whose members are elected by citizens is weaker by far than the parliamentary counterparts within any of the member states (although its authority has increased). The various decision-making bodies whose members are named by the states are prone to great secrecy and to announcing only the collective decision,[38] not the individual vote, thereby radically reducing the possibilities of indirect accountability to citizens; and the trend, from the days of the European Coal and Steel Community to the Union's European Central Bank, has been to increase the competence of such bodies.

European union and social movement practice

In assessing the state, and prospects, of democracy in our transnationalised world (including the EU), it is common to look at the vigour or lack of vigour of non-state actors (often lumped together under the NGO label), or substate actors (especially in thinking about the EU). Such discussions often take the form of assessing the prospects of a global (or European) civil society on the Tocquevillean principle that the viability of democracy depends in significant measure on the density, variety and strength of citizen associations.[39] In light of the role of social movements in the past democratisations of the states, I want quite specifically to focus here on the potential role of movements in the democratisation of transnational structures generally, and the EU in particular.

I have set forth above two principal contentions: first, that the history of modern democracy with its forms of legitimation and institutions of governance and the history of social movements as a distinctive form of contention have been profoundly intertwined; and second, that transnational structures of authority, including the EU, have an at best uneasy relationship to the democratisation of states. This has been a rather long introduction, pausing over some important issues of the eighteenth century in order to get a handle on a central issue of the twenty-first: what are the prospects of democracy in a world in which the intensity of cross-border movements of goods, people, words and images, and problems, may be generating cross-border structures of governance with complex relationships to the national states? The EU is of special interest among transnational political structures because it is the *least* threatening to the democratic character of the states and the *most* readily subject to democratisation itself—despite which it has been surrounded by controversy.

Do social movement pressures have a democratising potential analogous to the role played in the European past within the states? The question suggests looking in a rather different direction than most writing on the EU which tends to see it largely as an élite affair, both in its inception and in the major debates of the 1990s over 'widening', 'deepening', and 'variable geometry'. Yet the whole history of democratisation suggests the vital role of movements. What are the prospects for such movements in the future of the EU? The attention that scholars of social movements have been devoting to the transnational aspects of movements has been expanding so rapidly that virtually anything one says based upon current research might have to be rethought in the future (and the forms of political action may themselves be in flux). Nonetheless, I believe this recent research[40] thus far suggests the following three statements:

- Throughout the entire modern history of social movements, notions of strategy and tactics, models of organisational forms, general notions of social justice, and participants in social movement activism have frequently crossed national frontiers.
- In the past few decades, a wide variety of transnationally organised activists have made intermittently effective use of international organisations, NGO resources, and the governments of national states to address issues in particular national states. For the most part, the activities of such transnational activist networks do not include the collective, public, mass mobilisations that some see as among the defining hallmarks of social movements.
- Although the institutions of transnational power have been targets of mass mobilisations (as well as of the lobbying campaigns of transnational advocacy networks), for the most part social movement activism has continued to address national states,

although sometimes with an eye to having that state take some action on some transborder matter.

With regard to the EU's history in particular, research by Sidney Tarrow and Doug Imig on contentious events in member-states since 1984 shows a small but rising proportion of such events involving in some fashion the institutions or policies of the EU, growing from about 2 per cent in 1983 to about 7 per cent in 1995. Even those EU-oriented events for the most part involve groups targeting particular national governments who are asked to take some position within the EU. While there is some targeting of EU institutions directly, some transborder participation in collective action, some events involving cross-national organisational coalitions, for the most part even Euro-conflicts make use of familiar targets and tactics.[41]

This hardly rules out the possibility that choosing national targets and familiar tactics might have transnational and unfamiliar consequences.[42] One reason European workers, farmers and civil servants continue to engage in the tried and true forms of social movement activism that reach back into a repertoire of contention, in Charles Tilly's felicitous formulation[43], largely moulded in the nineteenth century, is precisely because such forms of contention remain effective at the level of the national states and the states are significant actors within the EU.

But what are the prospects that social movement action might exert democratising pressures upon the EU? Many observers have noted the broad sway of interest groups and networks of technical specialists that seek attention from the various agencies of policy-making in the EU, many of which are nonstate actors, either representing subnational or transnational interests (or both, as in the case of multistate associations of local, regional, or ethnoterritorial groupings). Scholarly attempts to count the existence of transnational political organisations clearly indicate their global growth, and the EU seems to be contributing its share to this broader trend,[44] but nonetheless, as indicated above, it is national rather than supranational authorities that are usually targeted. Can one anticipate something analogous to the early nineteenth-century British process documented by Tilly, in which changing forms of popular political action not only aimed at central political institutions, as consequential decision making centralised, but targeted Parliament specifically, and among parliamentary institutions shifted towards the House of Commons specifically, thereby contributing significantly to the intermixing of a centralising state, a parliamentarised élite politics, and a citizenry with rights to whom key incumbents are formally responsible?

The EU has in fact to some extent been redefining conceptions of rights. In one of the foundational texts of modern democracy, the revolutionary French *Declaration of the Rights of Man and Citizen*, there is a profound ambiguity over to what extent one has rights because one is French or because one is human. Consider its famously stirring first article: 'Men are born and remain free and equal in rights'. Is that only Frenchmen? And women? Most sociologists who have written on rights issues would probably hold that what really counted was being French: what is a right without a corresponding obligation on an Other, and often, on a state? The EU seems to be eroding this equation: noncitizens have (limited) voting rights, the European Court of Justice enforces its own sense of human rights, which are not reducible either to the lowest standard observed by any member state nor to some sort of interstate blend.[45] And in social welfare policy, member states are finding it difficult to 'limit social benefits exclusively to their citizens'.[46]

The member states that have accepted the notion that noncitizen residents can vote in nonnational-level elections (either local or supranational) have blurred the clarity of the territorial state as *the* rights-granting entity. As such, the ongoing formation of the EU is among the processes opening up new and important discussion of human rights—what such rights might be and how they are to be institutionalised if not in the states.[47]

All these things are significant and highly innovative. But they do not appear, thus far, to be pressing the EU to significantly alter its decision-making styles (a compound of the technocratic and the judicial), to significantly alter the authority of the Parliament, to bind parliamentary members into Europarties rather than national ones, or even to open up its rule-making bodies to greater public scrutiny.[48] It was not a Euromovement that generated much talk about a need for treater 'transparency' in rule-making as much as it was the rejection of participation by a Danish majority and a French near-majority in referenda in 1992.[49] Of course, movements have consequences beyond the intended ones, but the EU still seems largely shaped by élite decisions (which may take national publics into consideration, and national movements as part of their context). In short, thus far, the mix of popular and élite politics, including the invention of new forms of contention, that responded to the increasing scope of the national state by democratising it, does not seem (yet?) to be happening in the EU (nor in the emerging structures of transnational power generally).

To the extent that the citizens of member states have some sense that their rulers are accountable to them, it is not because the new, emerging Europe has pioneered new forms of democratic practice, but because the states have maintained the democracy that has come out of a past history of social struggles, including the very important ways in which democratic practice was deepened, in different ways, on different timetables, and to different degrees in different countries, in post-war Britain, Germany, France, Italy, Spain, Portugal and Greece. As the intensity of transborder connection in commerce, finance, weapons, crime, labour migration and, hardly least, ideas continues to enlarge during the twenty-first century and, alongside these flows of goods, people and symbols, the consequent incapacity of national states to manage their own affairs continues to enlarge as well, the new institutions of transnational coordination will pose many problems for the future of democracy, in the EU as elsewhere.

Further reflections

A European speculating on the future of political organisation around 1500 would have found many present models of rulership to contemplate: city-states dominated by merchant élites, claimants to universal Christian rule, federations of provinces, weak centres and powerful rural lords, complex imperial amalgams, and more or less territorially consolidated states.[50] It would not have been easy to predict that the national states of the nineteenth and twentieth centuries would not only come to dominate in Europe but provide the dominant model of governance beyond Europe; it would have been still less easy to foresee that the transfer of power from local arenas to national ones would transform patterns of conflict in ways that ultimately would democratise many of those states (including, although with some significant variation in degree, every European state).

The movements in capital, labour, and symbols; the transborder character of problems beyond the capacity of individual states, including the threat of economic processes to the human environment; the astronomical destructiveness of the twentieth century's wars even without the enormous, continuing threat of nuclear devastation—all these have given much impetus to a wide variety of mechanisms for co-ordination and control that span national frontiers. It is very far from obvious which of these existing models, if any, will in retrospect prove to have been prototypes of the governing institutions of the future,[51] but it is already clear that the emergence of any such institutions poses a deep challenge to notions of democratic rule.

Among the emerging forms of transnational governance, none is more interesting than the EU with its quasistatal character. Just as the shift in power from local to national arenas in the European past propelled a reorientation of strategies, tactics, organisation and identities on the part of the contentious, it does appear that people, as always, are adapting to new structures of authority by adopting, to some extent, new means of pressing their claims but are also continuing, to a large degree, to use familiar means of pressing their claims because those familiar means continue in effectiveness. What is a great deal less obvious is that the emerging structure of European contention is pushing the emerging institutions of Europe in democratic directions.

It is striking that issues of democratic deficit arise far more frequently in discussions of the EU than in discussions of other transnational structures. It seems rather obvious that such discussions in no way arise from some unique lack of democracy in EU governance—on the contrary, among transnational institutions, the EU is notable for the degree to which it does have democratic elements. The generality of transnational structures are to a much greater degree intergovernmental arrangements among states; those states often include some lacking a democratic identity; and few expect such intergovernmental bodies to be anything other than agencies for one or another form of interstate diplomacy. The EU, in contrast to most, has significant supranational features, has only member states with democratic identities, and is a conceivable focus for political identities itself (one might be a 'European', and maybe a 'EUropean', but is anyone a 'Naftan'?).[52] So expectations, hopes, and disappointments run stronger. Whether the emerging Europe continues to move further towards rule by a mix of unaccountable technocrats and jurists, is halted in its tracks by popular disaffections, or is challenged by new movements that reinvent democracy transnationally as they have in the past reinvented it within the states will be subjects the political scientists half a century hence will be discussing (or maybe disputing).

The combination of secrecy, unaccountability, supremacy of EU regulation over national law in many areas, eurocratic aversion to scrutiny, and expansion of competence into new domains combine to create a potential for significant narrowing of European democratic space by regulatory fiat. In 1995, to cite a rather dramatic example, the EU's Council, without public discussion, decided to place new surveillance powers over telecommunications in the hands of the police. Neither the national parliaments nor the European Parliament had any prior discussion.[53] Since major EU decision-making bodies consist, at the top, of ministers of state who meet *in camera* and act on an increasingly wide range of affairs, the national parliaments have less control over the actions of national ministers who can use the EU setting to bring about what they cannot bring about in national politics. Some hold, for example, that support by the Italian government for the creation of a common currency and a powerful European Central Bank was in order to obtain economic outcomes that they did not want to try to sell to the Italian electorate.[54] Deirdre Curtin refers to this situation as the 'multi-level deficit scenario'.[55]

Many important questions swirl around the new Europe, ranging from compound issues of identity and geography, through the possibilities of escape from a long history of warfare, to the costs and benefits of economic integration. None of these questions will be more challenging than the place of a changing Europe in the future of democracy. A managerial conception of a well-managed common European home, a nice place to live, but run by a somewhat mysterious and secretive élite, sheltered in institutional complexity and remoteness from citizens is one vision; halting the process on behalf of economic, cultural, and hardly least, political, autonomy is another. It remains to be seen what else, if anything, can be created.

Notes

1 Preparation of this essay was supported by a fellowship from the University of Pittsburgh's Center for International Studies for which I am deeply grateful.
2 For example: 'the decline of communism and of military and bureaucratic authoritarianism has left democracy almost unchallenged as the supreme principle of political legitimacy' (Yossi Shain and Juan J. Linz, *Between States: Interim Governments and Democratic Transitions*, Cambridge: Cambridge University Press, 1995, p. 8).
3 Francis Fukuyama, 'The End of History?', *National Interest*, 16, 1989, pp. 3–18.
4 See, for example, Juan Linz's definition of democracy in 'Totalitarian and Authoritarian Regimes', in Nelson Polsby and Fred Greenstein (eds), *Handbook of Political Science*, Reading, Mass: Addison Wesley, 1975, v. 3, pp. 182–183.

5 Wayne te Brake, *Shaping History: Ordinary People in European Politics, 1500–1700*, Berkeley and Los Angeles: University of California Press, 1998.

6 Robert R. Palmer, 'Notes on the Use of the Word "Democracy", 1789–1799', *Political Science Quarterly*, 68, 1953, pp. 203–226; Werner Conze and Reinhart Koselleck (eds), *Geschichtliche Grundbegriffe. Historisches Lexikon zur politisch-sozialen Sprache in Deutschland*, Stuttgart: Klett Verlag, 1972–1984, v. 1, pp. 821–899; Pierre Rosanvallon, 'The History of the Word Democracy in France', *Journal of Democracy* 6, 1995, pp. 140–154; Horst Dippel, 'Démocratie, Démocrates', in Rolf Reichardt and Eberhard Schmitt (eds), *Handbuch politisch-sozialer Grundbegriffe in Frankreich 1680–1920*, Munich: Oldenbourg, 1986, v. 6, pp. 57–97; Jens A. Christophersen, *The Meaning of 'Democracy' as Used in European Ideologies from the French to the Russian Revolutions. An Historical Study of Political Language*, Oslo: Universitetsforlaget, 1968; Robert W. Shoemaker, ' "Democracy" and "Republic" as Understood in Late Eighteenth Century America', *American Speech*, 41, 1966, pp. 83–95.

7 The very big claims made in the next few paragraphs draw on arguments developed in Charles Tilly, 'Democracy Is a Lake' and 'Parliamentarization of Popular Contention in Great Britain, 1758–1834', both in Charles Tilly, *Roads from Past to Future*, Lanham, MD: Rowman and Littlefield, 1997, pp. 193–244, and *Popular Contention in Great Britain, 1758–1834*, Cambridge, MA: Harvard University Press, 1995, pp. 193–244; Sidney Tarrow, ' "The Very Excess of Democracy": State Building and Contentious Politics in America', pp. 20–38, in Anne N. Costain and Andrew S. McFarland, *Social Movements and American Political Institutions*, Lanham, MD: Rowman and Littlefield, 1998 and *Power in Movement: Social Movements, Collective Action and Politics*, 2nd edn, New York: Cambridge University Press, 1998; Markoff, *Waves of Democracy*.

8 Jean-Jacques Rousseau, *Du Contrat social*, Book III, chapter 15, Paris: Aubier Montaigne, 1943, p. 340.

9 Frank O'Gorman, *Voters, Patrons, and Parties: The Unreformed Electoral System of Hanoverian England 1734–1832*, Oxford: The Clarendon Press, 1989 and 'Campaign Rituals and Ceremonies: The Social Meaning of Elections in England 1780–1860', *Past and Present*, no. 135, 1992, pp. 79–115.

10 Morgan, *Inventing the People*, pp. 174–233; David Zaret, 'Petitions and the "Invention" of Public Opinion in the English Revolution', *American Journal of Sociology*, 101, 1996, pp. 1497–1555.

11 Consider the constitution issued by the restored French monarchy in 1814, announced in its royal preamble as in recognition 'of the wishes of our subjects'. See 'Charte constitutionelle de 4 juin 1814', in Maurice Duverger, *Constitutions et documents politiques*, Paris: Presses Universitaires de France, 1960, p. 80.

12 Samuel P. Huntington, *The Third Wave: Democratization in the Late Twentieth Century*, Norman, OK: University of Colorado Press, 1991; *Waves of Democracy: Social Movements and Political Change*, Thousand Oaks, CA: Pine Forge Press, 1996.

13 Adam Przeworski, 'Democratization Revisited', *Items*, 51, 1997 (march), p. 11.

14 For various arguments about 'globalisation', see David Held, *Democracy and the Global Order. From the Modern State to Cosmopolitan Government*, Stanford: Stanford University Press, 1995; Martin Albrow, *The Global Age: State and Society Beyond Modernity*, Stanford: Stanford University Press, 1997; Arjun Appadurai, *Modernity at Large: Cultural Dimensions of Globalization*, Minneapolis, Minn.: University of Minnesota Press, 1996; Ulrich Beck, *The*

Reinvention of Politics: Rethinking Modernity in the Global Social Order, Cambridge, Mass.: Polity Press, 1996; Ulf Hannerz, *Transnational Connections: Culture, People, Places*, London: Routledge, 1996; A. Douglas Kincaid and Alejandro Portes, *Comparative National Development. Society and Economy in the New Global Order*, Chapel Hill, NC: University of North Carolina Press, 1994; Roland Robertson, *Globalization: Social Theory and Global Culture*, London: Sage, 1992; Saskia Sassen, *Cities in a World Economy*, Thousand Oaks, CA: Pine Forge Press, 1994; Linda Weiss, 'Globalization and the Myth of the Powerless State', *New Left Review*, no. 225, 1997, pp. 3–27; Francis Fox Piven and Richard Cloward, *The Breaking of the American Social Compact*, New York: The New Press, 1997, pp. 3–14; Immanuel Wallerstein, *Unthinking Social Science: The Limits of Nineteenth-Century Paradigms*, Cambridge: Polity Press, 1991; Charles Tilly, 'Globalization Threatens Labor's Rights', *International Labor and Working-Class History*, no. 47, 1995, pp. 1–23 (with responses by Immanuel Wallerstein, Aristide R. Zolberg, E. J. Hobsbawm, and Lourdes Beneria, pp. 24–55); Robert K. Schaeffer, *Understanding Globalization: The Social Consequences of Political, Economic, and Environmental Change*, Lanham, MD: Rowman and Littlefield, 1997; Leslie Sklair, *Sociology of the Global System*, Baltimore: The Johns Hopkins University Press, 1991; Robin Brown, 'Globalization and the End of the National Project', in John MacMillan and Andrew Linklater (eds), *Boundaries in Question. New Directions in International Relations*, London: Pinter, 1995, pp. 54–68.

15 In summarising the context of transnational connectedness, this paragraph skips over a large number of challenging questions about those connections. It ignores the variation from place to place, including very importantly variation in the degree to which existing states can manipulate the institutions of transnational power. It avoids the important question of which sorts of economic and political connection are unprecedented, which cyclically recurrent, and which long-term situations that are falsely held to be of recent vintage. It avoids the equally challenging question of which features of the current transnational order are ideological constructions, real to the degree that powerful actors act on the presumption of their reality, and which are constraints that could not be avoided even if powerful actors chose to do so. To sketch, quickly and illustratively, a few tentative assertions (some of which require a defence that I will not attempt here): postcolonial and central European states are stronger, not weaker, players in the world order as compared to, say, 1970; the powerful role of transnational finance is probably cyclically recurrent, rather than unprecedented; and sweeping claims that transnational markets require dismantling first world social safety nets are probably ideological constructions.

16 This is brought out clearly in a systematic comparison of the EU and NAFTA by Alberta Sbragia, 'The European Union and NAFTA in a Post-Cold War Global Economy: An Overview', presented at the conference on Globalization and Regionalization, Brussels, 1998.

17 John Markoff, *The Great Wave of Democracy in Historical Perspective*, Ithaca, NY: Cornell University Western Societies Occasional Papers #34, 1995.

18 Deirdre M. Curtin, *Postnational Democracy. The European Union in Search of a Political Philosophy*, The Hague:Kluwer Law International, 1997.

19 In addition to the studies cited below, this section draws on Mario Telò (ed.), *Démocratie et Construction Européenne*, Brussels: Editions de l'Université de Bruxelles, 1995; Sammy van Tuyll van Serooskerken (ed.), *Europe: Your Choice.*

Five Options for Tomorrow's Europe, London: The Harvill Press, 1995; Joseph H. Weiler, Ulrich R. Halten, and Franz C. Mayer, 'European Democracy and Its Critique', *West European Politics*, 18 (3), 1995, pp. 4–39; Renaud Dehousse, 'Constitutional Reform in the European Community: Are There Alternatives to the Majoritarian Avenue?', *West European Politics*, 18 (3), 1995, pp. 118–136; William Wallace and Julie Smith, 'Democracy or Technocracy? The Problem of Popular Consent', *West European Politics*, 18 (3), 1995, pp. 137–157; John Redmond and Glenda G. Rosenthal (eds), *The Expanding European Union. Past, Present, Future*, Boulder, CO: Lynne Rienner, 1998; Pierre-Henri Laurent and Marc Maresceau, *The State of the European Union, v. 4: Deepening and Widening*, Boulder, CO: Lynne Rienner, 1998.

20 Surveying the development and operation of the EU: Desmond Dinan, *An Ever Closer Union? An Introduction to the European Community?*, Boulder, CO: Lynne Rienner, 1994; Derek W. Unwin, *The Community of Europe. A History of European Integration Since 1945*, London: Longman, 1995; Alberta Sbragia (ed.), *Euro-Politics. Institutions and Policymaking in the 'New' European Community*, Washington, DC: Brookings Institution, 1992; Andrew Moravcsik, *The Choice for Europe. Social Purpose and State Power from Messina to Maastricht*, Ithaca, NY: Cornell University Press, 1998; Gary Marks, Liesbet Hooghe, and Kermit Blank, 'European Market Integration from the 1980s: State-Centric vs. Multi-Level Governance', *Journal of Common Market Studies*, 34, 1996, pp. 342–377.

21 Among such bodies working to influence the European Commission: the Bureau of Unrepresented Nations, the German regional governments, the Association des Régions d'Europe, the Union Nationale des Villes et Pouvoirs Locaux. See Liesbet Hooghe, 'Subnational Mobilisation in the European Union', in *West European Politics*, 18 (3), pp. 175–198.

22 Used, for example, by German Chancellor Helmut Kohl, cited in Alberta M. Sbragia, 'Thinking about the European Future', in Sbragia (ed.), p. 260n.

23 Alberta M. Sbragia, 'Thinking about the European Future', in Sbragia (ed.), *Europolitics*, pp. 283–289. Volker Bornschier suggests an even closer analogy: the Dutch Republic of early modern Europe. See Volker Bornschier, *Western Society in Transition*, New Brunswick, NJ: Transaction Books, 1996, pp. 350–351.

24 As Guy Peters at one point refers to it in 'Bureaucratic Politics and the Institutions of the European Community', in Sbragia (ed.), *Europolitics*, p. 75.

25 Important EU decision-making bodies made up of national ministers, of course, have a membership responsible to their own national parliaments and who are members of national parties.

26 The Maastricht Treaty established a Common Foreign and Security Policy with its own decision-making mechanisms (complex even by EU standards), which as of the late 1990s commands no soldiers. See Dinan, *An Ever Closer Union?*, pp. 465–497.

27 Paul Pierson, 'Social Policy and European Integration', in Andrew Moravcsik (ed.), *Centralization or Fragmentation? Europe Facing the Challenges of Deepening, Diversity, and Democracy*, New York, NY: Council on Foreign Relations, 1998, p. 143.

28 On these questions: T. H. Marshall, *Citizenship and Social Class and Other Essays*, Cambridge: Cambridge University Press, 1950; Bryan Turner (ed.), *Citizenship and Social Theory*, London: Sage, 1993; Bart van Steenbergen (ed.), *The Condition of Citizenship*, London: Sage, 1994; Charles Tilly (ed.), *Citizenship, Identity and Social History*, Cambridge: Cambridge University Press, 1996;

Michael Hanagan and Charles Tilly (eds), *Extending Citizenship, Reconfiguring States*, Lanham, MD: Rowman and Littlefield, 1999; Claus Offe, *Modernity and the State. East, West*, Cambridge, Mass: MIT Press, 1996; Frances Fox Piven and Richard Cloward, *The Breaking of the American Social Compact*, New York: The New Press, 1997.

29 Social security transfers in the 1990s continued the traditional West European pattern of much larger expenditures as a proportion of GDP than in the United States. See Göran Therborn, 'Europe in the Twenty-first Century. The World's Scandinavia?', in Peter Gowan and Perry Anderson (eds), *The Question of Europe*, London: Verso, 1997, p. 367.

30 Analyses of the complex relationships of EU institutions and national or union welfare policy, actual and potential: Peter Lange, 'The Politics of the Social Dimension', in Alberta M. Sbragia (ed.), *Europolitics: Institutions and Policymaking in the 'New' European Community*, Washington, DC: The Brookings Institution, 1992, pp. 225–256; Pierson, 'Social Policy and European Integration'.

31 George Kolankiewicz, 'The Breakdown of Welfare Regimes and the Problems for a Social Europe', in Hugh Miall (ed.), *Redefining Europe. New Patterns of Conflict and Cooperation*, London: Pinter Publishers, 1994, pp. 147–165.

32 *Eurobarometer. Public Opinion in the European Union*, 47, 1997, pp. 30-31. Such concerns are easily understandable in light of the loss of some five million jobs in the early 1990s, leaving EU unemployment over 10% in 1997. See *Employment, Industrial Relations and Social Affairs*, Brussels: European Commission, 1997.

33 Paul Krugman's characterisations of the Maastricht negotiations include: 'made no sense whatsoever', 'sheer nonsense', and 'absolutely no idea what they are talking about'. See *Peddling Prosperity. Economic Sense and Nonsense in the Age of Diminished Expectations*, New York: Norton, 1994, pp. 190–192. For some of the debate around the creation of a common currency, see the essays by Alan S. Milward, Tommaso Padoa-Schioppa, Sam Aaronovitch and John Grahl, and Edward Luttwak in Peter Gowan and Perry Anderson (eds), *The Question of Europe*, London: Verso, 1997.

34 Dieter Grimm, 'Does Europe Need a Constitution?', in Peter Gowan and Perry Anderson (eds), *The Question of Europe*, London: Verso, 1997, pp. 249-250. See also Jürgen Habermas, 'Reply to Grimm' in the same collection.

35 Gordon Smith describes the 'double conditionality' of entry: 'a reasonably well-functioning market system together with convincing evidence of democratic stability', in 'Can Liberal Democracy Span the European Divide?', in Hugh Miall (ed.), *Redefining Europe. New Patterns of Conflict and Cooperation*, London: Pinter Publishers, 1994, pp. 117–118.

36 Markoff, *The Great Wave*.

37 Thomas M. Franck, 'The Emerging Right to Democratic Governance', *American Journal of International Law*, 86, 1992, pp. 46–91. See also 'A Charter for Democracy', special issue of *World Affairs*, 153, 1990.

38 Although the Council of Ministers moved away from a rule of unanimity to a weighted majority system ('qualified majority') on many matters in 1966, it retained the tradition of aiming at unanimity. In combination with secrecy this tendency toward unanimity makes it very difficult for European publics to know what positions the representatives of their states have actually taken in negotiations (no doubt often different from whatever it is expedient for these representatives to claim in public).

39 See, for example, Paul Wapner, *Environmental Activism and World Civic Politics*, Albany: State University of New York Press, 1996.

40 The claims found below rest on data or analyses in the following: Sidney Tarrow, *Power in Movement. Social Movements and Contentious Politics*, Cambridge: Cambridge University Press, 1998, pp. 176–195 and 'Building a Composite Polity: Popular Contention in the European Union', Cornell University Institute for European Studies Working Paper 98.3, 1998; Jackie Smith, Charles Chatfield and Ron Pagnucco (eds), *Transnational Social Movements and Global Politics. Solidarity Beyond the State*, Syracuse: Syracuse University Press, 1997; Margaret Keck and Katherine Sikkink, *Activists Beyond Borders. Advocacy Networks in International Politics*, Ithaca, NY: Cornell University Press, 1998; John Markoff, *Waves of Democracy: Social Movements and Political Change*, Thousand Oaks, CA: Pine Forge Press, 1996, pp. 27-31.

41 Sidney Tarrow, 'Building a Composite Polity', pp. 18–20.

42 By way of imaginable analogy, a great deal of the mobilisations by French villagers during the revolutionary period involved long-familiar forms of action against local targets; nonetheless those mobilisations moved the national government to adopt some very nontraditional policies. See John Markoff, *The Abolition of Feudalism. Peasants, Lords and Legislators in the French Revolution*, University Park, PA: Pennsylvania State University Press, 1997.

43 Charles Tilly, *The Contentious French*, Cambridge: The Belknap Press of Harvard University Press, 1986, pp. 387–398.

44 For two different numerical attempts, see Smith on 'the transnational social movement sector' who finds growth 'just under 200 to more than 600 organizations' between 1972 and 1993; and Keck and Sikkink on 'transnational advocacy networks' who offer 102 in 1953 rising to 569 in 1993 (Jackie Smith, 'Characteristics of the Modern Transnational Social Movement Sector', in Smith, Chatfield, and Pagnucco (eds), *Transnational Social Movements*, p. 47; Keck and Sikkink, *Activists Beyond Borders*, p. 11).

45 On the Court's notion of 'fundamental rights' and 'essential procedural requirements' see Martin Shapiro, 'The European Court of Justice', in Sbragia, *Europolitics*, pp. 148–154.

46 Paul Pierson, 'Social Policy and European Integration', Andrew Moravcsik (ed.), *Centralization or Fragmentation? Europe Facing the Challenges of Deepening, Diversity and Democracy*, New York: Council on Foreign Relations, 1998, p. 135.

47 Yasemin Soysal raises some very important perspectives on rights issues in *Limits of Citizenship. Migrants and Postnational Membership in Europe*, Chicago: University of Chicago Press, 1994.

48 On the autonomy of the European Court of Justice produced by decision-making through secret majority vote, see Pierson, 'Social Policy and European Integration', p. 145.

49 Derek W. Urwin, *The Community of Europe. A History of European Integration Since 1945*, London: Longman, 1995, pp. 256–259.

50 te Brake, *Shaping History*; Charles Tilly, *Coercion, Capital, and European States, AD 900–1900*, Cambridge: Basil Blackwell, 1990.

51 For some reflections on the EU as a model of transnational organisation see Andrew Moravcsik, 'Europe's Integration at Century's End', in Andrew Moravcsik (ed.), *Centralization or Fragmentation? Europe Facing the Challenges of Deepening, Diversity and Democracy*, New York: Council on Foreign Relations, 1998, pp. 56–58.

52 But a national identity was running much stronger than a European one in 1997. 47% of respondents in EU countries claim to be of some nationality only, 46% claimed both nationality and Europeanness and 5% claimed only to be European (*Eurobarometer*, 47, p. 47). See also Sophie Duchesne and André-Paul Frognier, 'Is There a European Identity?', in Oskar Niedermayer and Richard Sinnott (eds), *Public Opinion and Internationalized Governance*, Oxford: Oxford University Press, 1995, pp. 193–226 and Anthony D. Smith, 'National Identity and the Idea of European Unity', in Peter Gowan and Perry Anderson (eds), *The Question of Europe*, London: Verso, 1997, pp. 318–342.

53 Curtin, *Postnational Democracy*, pp. 42–43. On the general theme of accountability, it is worth noting that in 1997 69% of EU adults wanted members of the Commission to depend on support in the European Parliament (see *Eurobarometer*, 4766, p. 27).

54 John Woolley summarises Italian policy goals in the 1980s: 'to make the liberalization of capital flows irreversible so as to tie the hands of any future parliament'. See his 'Policy Credibility and European Monetary Institutions', in Alberta Sbragia (ed.), *Euro-Politics. Institutions and Policymaking in the 'New' European Community*, Washington, DC: Brookings Institution, 1992, p. 169.

55 Curtin, *Postnational Democracy*, pp. 45–48.

Language, autonomy and national identity in Catalonia

Charlotte Hoffmann

El castellano es el español, y el catalán es español, un idioma español, uno de los idiomas españoles, con el castellano, el gallego y el vasco.

(Castilian Spanish is the Spanish language, and Catalan is also Spanish, that is, a language of Spain, one of the languages of Spain, together with Castilian Spanish, Galician and Basque.)

Camilo José Cela

Abstract

This chapter examines the role of language planning in the promotion of regional identity in Catalonia and discusses the factors that influence the sociolinguistic development of 'Catalonia's own language'. Issues of bilingualism, devolution and democracy in Spain's largest autonomous region, where a sizeable proportion of the population is of non-Catalan origin, have a bearing on the sense of national (both Spanish and Catalan) identity. It is argued that the time has come for a reassessment of Catalonia's language policies.

Introduction

In this contribution I will trace some of the main issues which have been at the heart of language policies in Catalonia since the late 1970s. As will become evident, the consensus which accompanied much of Catalonia's language planning efforts in the earlier period has worn thin for a variety of reasons which will be discussed. Political, economic, social and cultural conditions have changed so significantly over the last thirty years that traditional notions of autonomy, language and identity no longer afford solutions to present-day language problems.

Most Europeans may not be aware of the fact that Spain is one of the oldest economically developed multilingual states in the world. Among a considerable number of linguistic varieties, the four which today enjoy undisputed status as standardised languages are Castilian, Catalan, Galician and Basque. Catalonia's contribution to Spain's economic development and, indeed, to that of the whole Mediterranean region, undoubtedly has been of the first order. Yet the way in which Spain's history has been presented to the outside world and, for many years in the past, to her own population as well, has created the image of a united monolingual nation state. It was a state which during part of its imperialist history considered it paramount to combine colonisation with a holy duty to spread not only Christianity but also its language to the territories it had conquered, thus making Spanish today a world language with more than 300 million speakers—and growing fast. Yet, in various parts on the periphery of the Iberian Peninsula there have always been regions whose populations spoke their own language and defined their identity in terms of regional rather than national loyalties even during times of great pressure from the centre.

Two important themes in Spain's sociolinguistic history have thus emerged. On the one hand, the dominance of Castilian Spanish (enclosing a range of accents and dialects and spoken throughout Spain) which has been closely connected with the development of a centralised state promoting a strong national Spanish identity. On the other hand, the reaction by the regions to such centralist endeavours. During the four decades of Franco's dictatorship (1936–1975) monolingual Castilian language policies which emphasised the diglossic position of regional languages were rigorously pursued. This resulted in large-scale language shift and left all regional languages in a precarious situation in terms of numbers of people who could speak (and later teach) them and in terms of the linguistic state of the languages themselves. When it finally became possible to institute democracy in Spain it was generally accepted, within the whole of Spain, that the individual regions should be able to formulate their own linguistic policies and free to engage in measures aimed at recovering their languages. For the sociolinguist it has been quite fascinating to observe the sheer speed with which a large amount of language planning has been carried out and the commitment with which so many measures have been implemented and resulted in increased status for the languages and widespread use of them (Hoffmann, 1988, 1996a, 1996b). Naturally, the regional governments' language policies have also encountered opposition, especially in Catalonia, the first of the three autonomous regions to have approved its own language laws.

In post-Franco Spain, the language debate has intensified and become more polarised than it was ever before and it has become difficult to disentangle the linguistic and cultural from the parochial and political. It is becoming clear that certain fundamental questions have not been addressed yet, and until they are, tensions arising from different perceptions of linguistic rights and conflicting identities will continue. At the time of drawing up the 1978 Spanish constitution there were good reasons for devolving to the regions full responsibility for cultural, including linguistic, affairs. As a result, there is no national language policy, nor is there, at the national level, much evidence of a collective interest in maintaining and supporting Spain's multilingualism. Therefore, the question of the nature of the long-term relationship between the languages of Spain at national and regional level has not even been posed. But the debate about language policies (at times referred to in the press as a *diálogo de sordos*, dialogue of the deaf) has laid open the need to address this question and to reconsider certain cherished notions pertaining to language and to identity, now that Spain has settled into its role as a pluralist democratic member of the EU.

In the 1990s, as a consequence of Catalan politics and increasing Europeanisation which has affected Catalonia quite significantly, language has taken up centre stage in Catalan society, and it is an issue about which many Spaniards feel passionately. In Spain, the language debate touches upon questions of identity and power and their interrelationship on the regional, national and international level.

Sociolinguistic background

It is not uncommon to see Catalonia discussed in terms of a minority. After all, for much of its history it has shared a number of characteristics typical of minorities in a centralised state: in terms of self-identification and identification by others, the Principality's native inhabitants saw themselves as different in custom, tradition and language from the majority of Spaniards; and they resented being denied the recognition (and later the autonomous status) they aspired to. A number of traits, however, have contributed to making

Catalonia an atypical minority. For instance, between the twelfth and fifteenth centuries the region was an economically and politically powerful Mediterranean state with a flourishing cultural and literary output. This provided later generations of Catalans with a 'Glorious Past' (Fishman, 1971) lasting for well over 500 years for their language and culture to refer back to. Furthermore, Catalans remained the majority within their region so that they were only a minority *vis-à-vis* the whole of Spain. As such, Catalan society has a long history of stubborn resistance to political and cultural assimilation which successive central governments tried to enforce, often using extremely repressive measures. The leading role played by the middle classes in promoting Catalan language and culture, especially in the last hundred years or so, is another element which made Catalonia an unusual minority.

Of course nowadays Catalonia has outgrown her minority position. Within the democratic Spanish state Catalonia is one of the 17 *Comunidades Autónomas* and as one of the *comunidades históricas* (see later), that is regions with an historic claim to a separate identity with its own language and culture, she enjoys a particularly high degree of autonomy, with the power to exert considerable political influence in central government. Catalonia is also one of the economically most successful regions of Europe and benefited considerably from Spain's EU full membership since 1986.

The transition from dictatorship to democracy meant a return from official monolingualism to linguistic pluralism as the newly autonomous regions embarked on large-scale language planning policies aimed at recovering regional languages and giving them official status and currency in the respective regions. It is estimated that today approximately a quarter of all Spaniards speak a regional language in addition to the official language of the Spanish state, Castilian Spanish (Hoffmann, 1996b). Language planning is an ongoing process. It involves a large number of variables—historical, political, economic, social, cultural and linguistic—and since it touches the life of so many it never ceases to be in the public sphere. Of the three regions with their own separate language, Catalonia is the biggest, and it is the one that has embraced language planning most enthusiastically and whose language policies have gone further than any others.

The name of Catalonia as that of a political entity with its own identity and language exists at least since it was first recorded in 1176, and Catalan was its official language until 1716, after military defeat in the War of Spanish Succession where the Catalans had sided with the Austrians against the winning contender to the Spanish throne, Philip V of the House of Bourbon. The region then became subjected to Castilian laws and a series of repressive measures which included the suppression of the use of Catalan and the imposition of Castilian Spanish as the only language permitted for public use. As a result, the nobility, higher clergy, military and civil servants became completely Castilianised. The middle classes retained spoken Catalan for informal use and only the illiterate rural population remained monolingual Catalan. As a spoken variety, associated with rural backwardness, Catalan became stigmatised and the relationship between Castilian Spanish and Catalan one of diglossia.

One could have expected that, with the unfolding of the nation-state, the rise of the middle classes, urbanisation, improved communication and the beginning of universal education, language use would have shifted completely towards Castilian. However, in Catalonia the nineteenth century brought two developments which were to signify important advances for the Catalan language: large-scale industrial development and the emergence of Catalanism. The former led to the rise of a strong urban middle-class which was not only enterprising and liberal in outlook but also eager to invest and partake in cultural activities that found their expression in Catalan. The latter surfaced first as a Romantic movement known as the *Renaixença* (Catalan cultural Renaissance) which by the end of the century had provided the basis for the widespread use of Catalan not only in literary fields but also journalism and education. The linguistic status of Catalan was enhanced when the language became standardised. A new grammar and orthography rules together with dictionaries were published and a Catalan Academy founded. It was a time when, especially in Barcelona, major civic buildings were erected which were to become physical expressions of Catalan pride and confidence in their own culture.

Towards the end of the century Catalans began to embrace Catalanism as a political creed as well as a cultural one, as the movement demanding political independence from Madrid gathered momentum. The upper middle classes began to join the nationalist camp, although more cautiously. There were never any serious attempts to involve the lower groups in society, as the Catalan sociologist Salvador Giner (1984) points out. The rural population was, of course, fairly isolated and Catalan-speaking anyway. But the urban working classes, growing in number owing to urbanisation and immigration particularly from Andalusia and Galicia, were the

Castilian-speaking section of society and as such more open to social and political influences from outside Catalonia than from Catalan middle-class society. Even though the earlier immigrants adopted Catalan as a language of daily interaction in times when it was in public use, later waves of immigrants were so numerous that linguistic adaptation was no longer necessary. Today it is this section of Catalan society which poses the biggest challenge to Catalan language policies.

In the first part of the twentieth century Catalonia enjoyed two short periods of autonomy during which time Catalan was used in the public sphere such as administration, the media and education, first from 1914 to 1923, and then during the Second Republic from 1931 to 1936. During both periods cultural activities and education at all levels, often coupled with educationally progressive methods, were made priorities. This not only benefited the state of the language but also made it attractive for immigrants who saw it as the language for upward social mobility. Whereas the dictatorship of Primo de Rivera (1923–30) and its prohibition of the use of Catalan as an official language had struck a serious blow to Catalan, its fate was infinitely worse after the Spanish Civil War. For most of the forty years of Franco's rule Catalonia's language and culture were deprived of the recognition and independence previously enjoyed. The public use of Catalan was prohibited, its existence systematically eradicated and denied as names, toponyms, street signs, advertisements and publications in Catalan were banned and non-conformity punished. The language itself became stigmatised as a mere dialect and its speakers humiliated. Catalonia's autonomy was annulled and the region divided into four provinces which were administered from the central government in Madrid. The restrictive measures meted out to Catalonia are well documented by sociolinguists, Catalan as well as foreign (eg Vallverdú, 1973; Woolard, 1989; Hoffmann, 1991; Strubell i Trueta, 1993; Vidal-Folch, 1994; Hooper, 1995; Grugel and Rees, 1997) and there is no doubt that they left an indelible mark in the Catalan consciousness. Suppression breeds opposition, and there is a long history in Catalonia of protest and resistance to centralist policies which has helped to maintain Catalanism alive.

Centralist policies aimed at making Castilian Spanish the only recognised language used in the whole of the State had highly detrimental effects on Catalan. For instance, they reduced the number of those who could read and write the language as whole new generations were taught to become literate only in Castilian, they limited the scope of the use of Catalan, they prevented it from developing with the times, adapting to new situations and communicative requirements. But while the linguistic situation deteriorated, the status of the language as a symbol of Catalan identity became reinforced so that when the great political change came after the death of Franco in 1975 there was widespread support for the language policies of the new Catalan government, the *Generalitat*.

Autonomy and language

As the previous section shows, Catalanism is firmly rooted in Catalonia's middle classes. In fact, at one time the Catalan branch of the communist party made a point of avoiding the use of Catalan which they considered to be the language of the bourgeoisie. In all likelihood middle-class support has enabled Catalonia to pursue her goal of political self determination.

> The history of Catalunya is a history of land-owning farmers, of artisans, shopkeepers, workshop owners, . . . of merchants and industrialists, of a concern for the serious business of making money. Not only does Catalunya exhibit the basic defining characteristics of nationalism . . . she also perceives of herself as a nation. (Paulston, 1994: 56)

Others, too, have noted the importance of the concepts of nation and nationalism in the Catalan context where they refer to Catalonia and Catalanist sentiments rather than loyalty to the Spanish state. Woolard points out that whereas the term 'nationalism' is rarely defined, 'it is often invoked in debate and is a tremendously powerful concept for both supporters and opponents of Catalan nationhood' (1986: 34). Recent debate in Catalan society shows that this still holds true even though one might argue that previously held views on causal relationships between language, nationalism and autonomy have become less clear cut, more multifaceted.

The model of democratic state adopted by Spain in 1978 was that of a decentralised government based on devolution of powers, which the Spaniards call *el estado de la autonomías*. The justification for this model was that some of the *autonomías* (autonomous regions) had a generally recognised historical claim to their own separate identity based on the existence of their own language and cultural tradition. Other regions, it was felt, could also have a claim to autonomy but a weaker one than that of the *autonomías históricas*. For this reason the 1978 Constitution made provision for two different degrees of autonomy which one could refer to as full and partial autonomy (or first and second class, as critics would say). This fact has stayed in the forefront of the minds of Spaniards, influencing the debate about the nature and extent of regional independence and often souring the relationship between the centre and the periphery. It was not incidental that the Statutes of Autonomy of the 17 autonomous regions were approved in a chronological order which mirrored the strength of the respective claims to independence based on historical, cultural and linguistic distinctiveness. Catalonia's Statue was the first to be promulgated in 1979, followed by those of the Basque Country and then Galicia in 1980. The degree of autonomy enjoyed by the 17 autonomies, although variable, is high. The individual Statutes spell out the general remit of devolved regional powers, one of which is responsibility for educational, cultural and linguistic policies. Political and public debate in Spain, however, amply demonstrates that the meaning of autonomy is open to different interpretations. While for some it means decentralisation and devolution of power, others take it as a rightful expression of their separate identity which justifies pursuing a greater degree of autonomy. Such a demand can easily be used as a tactic for pressing central government for making more concessions on autonomy, but it can also cause public outcry and fuel suspicions on the part of those who feel threatened by regional policies. One such incident occurred in December 1989 when the Catalan parliament passed a motion affirming that 'the Catalan people do not renounce their right to national self-determination'. 'The meaning of autonomy', Brassloff (1996: 118) writes, 'is blurred at the edges and depends, like patriotism, on who is speaking, who is being addressed and when and in what circumstance, whether—for example—it is defined by those who simply "think Spain", or by regional nationalists for home consumption while negotiating with the national government and keeping half an eye on the other autonomous communities.' A feeling shared, and resented, by many Spaniards is that the Catalans, more than anybody else, demand special treatment, ie more self-determination.

The territoriality principle upon which Spain's pluralism is founded shows up major weaknesses when it comes to questions of language. Nowhere in Spain do administrative boundaries clearly coincide with linguistic ones. With regard to external boundaries it means that varieties related to Catalan are spoken in autonomies near Catalonia such as Valencia and the Balearic islands, which have their own agendas and linguistic policies, less ambitious than those of Catalonia, and who at times resent being included in Catalan claims. More importantly, the original internal linguistic cohesion of the Catalan region has become diluted as a result of prolonged and large-scale in-migration and population trends which show a higher birth rate among the immigrant communities, while figures for the Catalans are among the lowest in Europe.[1] Some even fear that while today only about half of Catalonia's six and a half million inhabitants are of Catalan descent, by the year 2040 there will be no 'pure' Catalans left at all (Hooper, 1995). Therefore, a linguistic 'territorial solution' which is the proclaimed aim of Catalonia's Statute of Autonomy, where Catalan is the region's dominant language and Castilian Spanish merely another language, may never be reached. So, by deciding not to opt for the 'personality principle', which gives linguistic rights to speakers of minority languages independently of the region in which they reside, the State has avoided conflict with the regions. But conflict does exist, as will become clear later, and the question arises of how long it will remain in the regional domain.

Language planning in Catalonia: the first 20 years

The legal basis for language planning was laid down in three different types of legislation: the Spanish Constitution, the Catalan Statute of of Autonomy and the Catalan Law of Linguistic Normalisation. The Constitution's Article 3 is considered the cornerstone of the state's linguistic policies as it declares Castilian to be the official language, making it both a duty for all Spaniards to know it and a right to use it, and furthermore declares that the other languages of Spain shall have official status in their respective Autonomous Communities. It is perhaps worth remarking that few national constitutions declare it to be a *duty* for citizens to know the nation's language, and clearly this provision was not the result of accident. Other aspects of linguistic and cultural rights, powers and responsibilities are laid down in other articles. Several commentators on the constitution have referred to the vagueness or ambivalence of its formulation of linguistic issues, a feature commonly seen as deliberate (eg Mar-Molinero and Stevenson, 1991; Hooper, 1995; England, 1993–94). It should not be forgotten that the backdrop to language policies in the late 70s and into the 80s was formed by the then still fresh memories of fascist linguistic repression and centralist thinking. Legislation at all levels had to tread a very careful path. In their discussion of the Constitution, Mar-Molinero and Stevenson (1991: 167) refer to the 'spirit of compromise which pervades each clause', while England (1993–94: 291) suggests that language legislation from that time 'has to be judged against the background of a climate of consensus and compromise between those seeking to promote regional languages and those whose instincts remained basically centralising, in line with the values of the old regime.'

Article 3 of the Statute of Autonomy constitutes the basis for the *Generalitat*'s language policy. It declares that Catalan is *la llengua pròpia de Catalunya*—*pròpia* could be translated both as 'own' and 'proper' although the exact meaning is fused in the minds of both Catalan and Spanish speakers. Official translations use 'own' in inverted commas, but to the ordinary citizen the connotation of 'the proper language' may often be present. The article spells out the co-official status of both Catalan and Spanish and asserts the *Generalitat*'s determination to ensure adequate knowledge of both languages and their normal and official use.

Language planning in Catalonia has always been driven by two forces. On the political side there was the desire for autonomy which would find expression in the use of the region's own culture and language. Official status for Catalan would be a powerful symbol of the region's independence. The other driving force was the realisation that Catalan, like the other regional languages of Spain, found itself in a precarious position after 40 years of suppression. Not only had the number of users fallen steadily and its transmission from older generations to the younger ones been jeopardised, the language itself had become Castilianised in various ways through grammatical interference and lexical borrowing as Catalans had become ever less familiar with the standard language. Language planning had thus become a crusade aimed at language recovery and it was supported by many who were otherwise less interested in Catalan politics.

Whereas the linguistic provisions of the national Constitution and the Statute of Autonomy recognise what is, in effect, widespread societal bilingualism, the aim of Catalonia's linguistic legislation has been to promote Catalan with a view to achieving a mainly Catalan-speaking region. In order to reach this objective, language planning had to embrace both status planning and corpus planning. As regards the former, measures were taken to promote the use of Catalan in all spheres of public life and special emphasis was laid on education. With respect to corpus planning, modern Catalan needed to be equipped linguistically so that it could be used appropriately (in terms of accepted standard pronunciation, grammar, lexis and register) for all written and spoken purposes. 'Linguistic normalisation' was the label chosen for the programme of language policies which had its legal basis in the Law of Linguistic Normalisation of 1983. The term expresses certain different, inter-linking aspects of status planning, namely the formulation of linguistic norms, the social extension of these for wider use, and the assertion that it should become 'normal' again to use Catalan.

The linguistic normalisation agenda was an extremely ambitious one as it had to take in a number of different areas (Hoffmann, 1996a). The 'restoration of Catalan to its rightful place' in itself involved a huge effort in terms of status planning as well as corpus planning. In order to establish Catalan as the normal vehicle in the sections of public use of language which were susceptible to government intervention—such as public administration, education and the media, language training for state employees, including teachers, and employees of radio and TV companies had to be organised; terminologies in a number of fields, teaching materials and other resources had to be produced; and free translations of public documents and materials, as well as interpretation and synchronisation of recorded material, had to be provided. The aim of making Catalan the 'normal' language to use for all public functions required a piece of linguistic engineering hitherto untried in any European context, namely overcoming the old diglossic situation (where Catalan had become the minoritised language) by means of government intervention to change linguistic perceptions, ie conferring high prestige to the variety that had traditionally had low status. In his discussion of reversing language shift Fishman (1991) refers to the above-mentioned measures as 'normalisation of the first kind'. 'Normalisation of the second kind' is the even more ambitious project of encouraging Castilian-speaking immigrants not only to feel at home among Catalans and identify with them, but also to use Catalan in both its spoken and written form.

The aims of normalisation policy were to promote Catalan in order to achieve full equality between Catalan and Castilian. There was never an explicit official policy of promotion of bilingualism, nor is societal bilingualism a long-term aim. Indeed, one could not help noticing from quite early on that the Catalan authorities avoided use of the term. In fact, the long-term goals of the *Generalitat*, although not laid down in law, started to become apparent long before the second round of linguistic legislation (which resulted in the 1998 law) when, in 1993, the then Director of Linguistic Policy of the *Generalitat* openly declared that the hope was to achieve a situation where Catalan was known by everyone and used as a first language just as Castilian was in Spain or French is in France. Catalan was to become the hegemonic and preferred language of Catalonia. Such pronouncements not only reveal what to many must seem an unrealistic aim, they also reflect a clear positioning of Catalonia as separate from Spain.

An important feature of the Catalan language policy has been its insistence on public acceptance and co-operation. It was said that the objectives of the normalisation policy were to be achieved voluntarily and gradually, over a period of time and involving several intermediate stages. Thus, the normalisation campaign of the early 80s with its slogan of *'el català, cosa de tots'* (Catalan is everyone's concern) was designed to encourage all Catalans to speak more and better Catalan, and to drive home the message that the future of the language lay in the hands of everyone. It is easy to see that the idea that Catalan should eventually become the language not only of public discourse but also of inter-group communication is not only ambitious but also controversial. Is it right, let alone feasible, to encourage roughly half of Catalonia's population to abandon their mother tongue much of the time in favour of Catalan? Not surprisingly, linguistic policy has met with the opposition of those who argue that Spanish speakers should be able to pursue their constitutional rights to use their own language, and to have their children educated in the language of their choice. Even before the Law of Linguistic Normalisation was promulgated in 1983 the 'Manifesto for the Equality of Language Rights' called for permanent and fully official bilingualism. A number of lobby groups and other associations, whose members come from inside as well as outside Catalonia and represent a variety of political and cultural backgrounds, have been founded since then as language issues have continued to be part of the public debate. It does seem, however, that there was a decrease in the fervour with which people debated such questions after the first round of implementation of measures resulting from the 1983 legislation, until it was rekindled in the years leading up to, and following, the second law of 1998. I shall return to some of the issues which dominated public controversy at a later point.

An assessment of normalisation

Normalisation has been most successful in the domain of public administration where Catalan is now the language used by all local official bodies, although Castilian Spanish can also be used if citizens chose to use it. All civil servants must sit examinations in Catalan and there are language classes provided by the School of Public Administration for those who move from other parts of Spain to take up posts in Catalonia. In the judicial services, however, it has proved very difficult to overcome the traditional practice of using Spanish and therefore the 1998 legislation has targeted this particular area. A concomitant of these policies has been that access to white-collar jobs has become perceived as being increasingly restricted to those with reasonable fluency in Catalan. This connection between language and social class has not gone unnoticed amid claims that this pushes disproportionately high numbers of non-Catalan speaking residents into low-status occupations.

Considerable advances in language promotion have also been achieved in education, although the sheer amount of effort and resources required to turn the entire system into using Catalan as the medium of instruction has necessitated a slower and gradual approach. Whereas earlier efforts were aimed at primary and adult education, later ones have turned their attention to the secondary sector and universities. Great care has gone into the design of immersion courses for children and training for teachers, even if a number of practical and other problems have meant that the implementation of legislation relating to education has varied considerably, in both quality and extent, throughout Catalonia. A major problem which is likely to take a generation or two of teachers to overcome, has been lack of staff who feel sufficiently competent to teach their subjects through the medium of Catalan. Because of the demographic distribution of Catalan and Spanish speakers, many schools outside the metropolitan area of Barcelona and one or two other industrial centres can be considered largely Catalan. This contrasts with children from Spanish-speaking homes in the industrial parts of Barcelona who have little opportunity of practising their Catalan with other children, either in school or outside. The situation is exacerbated by the presence of a large and influential private school sector (still dominated by Church-run schools), which attracts more children from Catalan-speaking families. The outcome of this situation has been a considerable concentration of chil-

dren from Catalan homes in private schools, leaving a disproportionate number of other children in the state schools who then have
fewer opportunities of mixing with their Catalan peers outside the
school context. When, in 1993, the *Generalitat* decided to introduce
Catalan-medium schools for primary pupils between 3 and 8 the
proposal was met with vociferous criticism from many Spanish-
speaking parents who considered this a threat to their children's
constitutional right to be educated in Castilian Spanish. However, it
should be said that there is clear evidence that the majority of
people in Catalonia, Catalan-speaking as well as of immigrant
background, support the *Generalitat*'s education policies, including
Catalan-medium instruction. The criticism that is levelled at education policies concerns the time and status schools afford to the language of the whole country, Spanish. Whether the education system
will succeed in turning Spanish-speaking children into Catalan citizens who will habitually use Catalan alongside Spanish will depend,
ultimately, on the success of the normalisation process in all
domains of public life.

When it comes to measuring the efficiency of these policies, census figures from 1986 and 1991 show that in these five years there
was a steady increase in the number of those who reported that they
could understand, speak, read and write Catalan. In the case of the
latter three categories the figures had doubled in relation to the 1986
figures, clearly as a result of education measures. In 1991 only 16.7
per cent claimed not to be able to understand Catalan. The 1991 figure for understanding was 83.23 per cent, but only half of those said
they could speak it (information from the Institut d'Estadística de
Catalunya, 1991). This is quite a low figure which may well worry
those who are concerned with language recovery. It reflects the gap
between knowledge of the language and active use of it and highlights the difficulty of persuading people to abandon their mother
tongue, which quite obviously fulfils all their communicative
requirements, in favour of another.

Inevitably, the increase in knowledge of Catalan has also affected
its use: it is used in a larger number of domains than before, and it
is widely used by Spanish speakers, most of whom are now bilingual
although with varying degrees of proficiency in and active use of
Catalan. But achievements with regard to language recovery have
been very unbalanced: in certain important areas of Catalonia such
as Barcelona, Castilian Spanish continues to dominate. Spanish
speakers are able to understand and speak Catalan but they do not
use it as frequently as Catalan speakers use Spanish. Rural areas

and many of the smaller towns, on the other hand, can be said to have become fully Catalanised. While an impressive amount of state-sponsored, and also independent, research has assessed individual aspects of Catalan language planning, such as knowledge and acquisition of Catalan and public attitudes towards it, studies of language use in terms of domains, interlocutor and frequency, for instance, have been few and far between. Perhaps it is still too delicate and potentially controversial an area of investigation.

Language and identity

An assessment of Catalan language policies thirty years after their inception must conclude that a considerable degree of success has been achieved. At least in part this can be attributed to the continued efforts by language planners to ensure consensus and popular support (a mark of post-Franco Catalan politics in general). Other factors have been influential as well, not least a strong tradition of acknowledging regional languages and cultures as part of Spain's national heritage and a belief that there exists a close bond between language and identity. Hooper (1995) suggests that there has always existed a hierarchy of loyalties ranging from local to regional to national which Spaniards themselves have felt at ease with but which have bedevilled attempts to build a strong unified state throughout Spanish history. This ability to spread one's loyalties in a pattern of concentric waves may, incidentally, be one of the reasons why Spaniards have found it much less problematic to embrace membership of the European Union than, for instance, the British.

Nowhere has this perceived bond between language and national identity been upheld more strongly than in Catalonia. Catalans have for a long time openly identified what they consider to be their national traits with their language. This combination of language and perceived national character constitutes the uniqueness, the '*fet diferencial*' (differential factor) of Catalonia and sets it apart from (some would even say above) the rest of Spain. Catalan self-identification has survived for centuries and it helps to explain why the assault on their language during the two dictatorships endured this century was considered to be not only socially unjust but also a direct insult to their proud cultural heritage (Green, 1993). It is within this context that the term used for their language, '*la llengua pròpia*', acquires its full meaning. Similarly, one cannot fail to appreciate how years of repression under Franco helped to focus people's desire for a democratic, pluralist system which would give regions a maximum degree of cultural and linguistic autonomy. Strubell i Trueta (1998: 156) draws attention to a further link between language and repression which emerged, referring to a 'belief that, among other things, Catalan gained an inner strength by being illegitimately suppressed. The suppression of democracy and Catalan culture and language gave them strong links in the public mind'. Whereas he accepts that it would be too simplistic to claim that all pro-democratic movements favoured Catalan and all dictatorial ones its repression, this century's Spanish history certainly offers evidence that there was some truth in this. But in today's Spain it would be dangerous to cling to what have now become historical impressions. Nationalist politics have moved away from the centre and are now an influential force in regional politics, often forcing the more progressively minded Spaniards to take up a national stance on issues such as autonomy and language policy.

As we have seen, the success of language planning in Catalonia can be attributed to a number of favourable circumstances, not the least important of which is the widely shared belief that regional autonomy should go hand in hand with the restoration of Catalan as a medium for national self-expression. But whereas in earlier times the equation 'being Catalan means speaking Catalan' may not have been challenged, the question today of who is and who is not Catalan is far less transparent. *La llengua pròpia* traditionally had enormous defining weight, but if one applied the criterion of just language today, then only about half the population of Catalonia would qualify, while the other half, mostly first or second generation immigrants from other parts of Spain, would not. This would clearly be unjust, as well as politically undesirable, since many of them consider Catalonia their home and the autonomous government depends on their support. Furthermore, too much insistence on the language and identity bond might also invite Spanish speakers to insist that their linguistic rights take precedence over Catalan self-ascription. A related thorny issue concerns the relationship between Spanish and Catalan identity, which is interpreted in widely differing ways. Politicians have long realised that there are no generally agreed criteria for defining Catalanness and have therefore adopted what Strubell i Trueta (1998: 151) refers to as 'an extremely open definition of Catalans . . . in order to avert the threat of a social and even political division along ethnolinguistic (and probably urban class) lines'. The official stance now appears to be that anyone who lives and works in Catalonia is regarded as Catalan. Nonetheless, language as part of national identity still figures strongly and is proclaimed to create national cohesion in the introduction of the 1998 law.

Europeanisation, language and identity in the 1990s

Since 1978 Catalonia (like the rest of the country) has benefited tremendously from Spain's democratic pluralist system. Catalonia has seen a consolidation of regional politics led by a centre-right government coalition of the *Convergència* and *Unió* parties (*Convergència i Unió*, *CiU*), since 1980 under the presidency of Jordi Pujol. Regional politics were strongly protective of regional industrial élites, no doubt in reaction to past centrist maladministration and corruption. Catalan industrial and bourgeois nationalism in turn provided strong support for the *Generalitat*'s economic and cultural policies. Since 1993 the *CiU* partnership has also been an influential actor in national politics, although its leaders are often perceived as somewhat opportunistic players of the Catalan nationalist card in return for their support of the central government on issues seen as less crucial to the Catalan cause.

Clearly, devolution has enabled the Catalans to promote their language wholeheartedly and the degree of success they have achieved has been of a very high order indeed, especially with respect to what Fishman calls normalisation of the first kind. However, some would argue that in their enthusiasm in applying language policies of their own design they have become fanatical and overbearing, whereas others would claim that not enough has been done to improve the precarious situation in which Catalan finds itself *vis-à-vis* Castilian Spanish.

The aim of language planning in the 1980s was to Catalanise public administration at regional and local level which meant that anyone occupying an official position was to be required to know and use Catalan. Obviously, this has given native speakers a natural advantage and it is they who are seen to be in power in Catalonia and the ones who can easily define their identity in terms of Catalan language. The non-autochthonous population have their linguistic and cultural roots elsewhere and they are more likely to define their identity in terms of Spain and the national language, while at the same time sharing some feelings of belonging to their new *patria chica* (inadequately translated as 'home'). In the context of the same territory, the conflict between personal effort to conform and what is perceived as official imposition can lead to resentment and, ultimately, to polarisation of positions. On the one hand there are those who claim greater autonomy for Catalonia and Catalan, and on the other those who do not primarily see themselves as Catalan, who may feel excluded from Catalan-dominated society and their linguistic rights threatened. The *Generalitat* has had to tread very carefully in its pursuance of a greater degree of autonomy in general and the implementation of its language policies in particular. In fact, in the face of opposition the originally proposed version of the second major piece of language legislation had to be watered down quite considerably before it could be passed.

Issues of language, identity and autonomy in Catalonia have further been influenced by the general social trends which have affected much of Europe in the latter part of the twentieth century. Since traditionally the bulk of incomers have been from other parts of Spain the effect on the linguistic situation has been to increase the number of Spanish speakers in an ethnolinguistically different region. The same applies to immigrants who have come from the former Spanish colonies which were all Spanish-speaking, but the numbers involved were small; in this Spain is, of course, quite different from countries like Britain or France with large immigrant communities. More recently, Catalonia has seen an influx of migrants from the Magreb, above all Morocco. However, it seems that no sociolinguistic investigation into language use by this group has yet been undertaken and that no special linguistic provision is made for their children by the education system. Nor is it clear to what extent, and by means of which language, they are integrated into Catalan society.

As one of Europe's most successful economic regions Catalonia has been drawn into globalisation trends as well. In economic and political terms globalisation has brought new methods of industrial production to the region, and this in turn has been accompanied by transfers of powers from the national to regional centres. The linguistic impact has been internationalisation and its concomitant spread of English. As elsewhere, there has been an upsurge in demand for English language tuition at all levels. English has replaced French as the first foreign language in the school curriculum throughout Spain, and it is offered at ever earlier stages. In Catalonia, the new situation has put English and Spanish in direct competition for teaching time in the bilingual education system which increasingly uses Catalan as medium of instruction, with the result that Spanish is often given the same time as English or even less. Reports that youngsters from Catalan and Castilian-speaking background alike feel that they leave their Catalan schools with insufficient competence in written Castilian and knowledge of Spanish literature are not missed by those who oppose further promotion of Catalan.

A third dimension that has come into play in Catalan society is Europeanisation. The whole of Spain, including Catalonia, has always had very positive attitudes towards Europe and been keen to play a full part in the EU. Spaniards have traditionally seen themselves as part of Europe but during the forty long years of fascist government they were rejected and felt looked down upon. Since she joined the EC in 1986 Spain has been a net economic gainer and for Catalonia in particular membership has brought a combination of financial and political advantages which have allowed her to circumvent national Spanish interest. As a result of direct lobbying for EC funds and political influence Catalonia has been successful in forging new supranational political and economic links with other influential EC regions. In 1994 the 'Committee of the Regions' (COR) which provides regions and municipalities with a consultative role of permanent standing within the EU structure was established. 'Significantly, Spanish interests have been well represented, with the emergence of leaders such as Jordi Pujol and Pasqual Maragall as leading actors on the committee' (Whitehead, 1996: 260). It is no coincidence that these two politicians are Catalan (Maragall is the leader of the Catalan socialist party and a former mayor of Barcelona). In fact, Pujol has been pushing for COR to be exclusively for the regions, perhaps in the hope that it may one day become a second chamber of the European Parliament.

Catalonia is also active in regional networks which promote the economic interests of its members and are designed to further economic and social cohesion within the EU. The most significant regional grouping is, according to Whitehead (1996) the one which has been dubbed 'the four motors', which includes Baden-Württemberg, Lombardy, Rhône Alpes and Catalonia. By comparison to their national neighbours these regions are 'substantially overdeveloped' (Whitehead, 1996: 264) and since the grouping is about mutual assistance and technology transfer, they will continue to benefit disproportionately. The gains are not only economic, since they confer political importance to regions which can be seen to be operating successfully without the need to go via national channels.

On the linguistic side, EU membership has given Spanish more prominence within Europe, whereas the Catalans have become very active members of a number of European institutions concerned with the promotion of minority languages and the protection of linguistic rights, while also trying to achieve greater prominence for the Catalan language in certain forums. Various resolutions passed by the European Parliament mention Catalan, for instance one of December 1990 dealing with the situation of languages in the Community, and the 1994 resolution on cultural and linguistic minorities in the (then) EC.

The language policy adopted in Maastricht in 1992 lends considerable support to linguistic diversity within the Union with its recommendation to make language learning a priority. Member states are encouraged to 'promote trilingualism; they are advised to make language qualifications desirable for entry into, and compulsory for exit from, higher education, and they are requested to give particular attention to the learning of minority languages' (Baetens Beardsmore, 1994: 94). The latter can be interpreted as meaning the regional languages of individual member states and also those EU languages which are not used for communication within the Union, for instance Greek, Portuguese and Danish. EU resolutions are rarely followed by increased funding for the courses they espouse, so one should probably not expect too much from this kind of positive language planning. But Catalonia is already fulfilling this European policy goal as the Catalan school curriculum offers two EU languages, Spanish and English. The acknowledgement of English as an international language, coupled with the acceptance of Catalan as the official language for Catalonia, has carried with it an implied sidelining of Castilian Spanish. In terms of identification, too, many Catalans will define their identity as Catalan and European, jumping the national Spanish identity. It can be no surprise that attitudes of this kind are resented by Castilian speakers both inside and outside Catalonia and have fuelled the debate about language planning in the 1990s.

The 1998 Law of the Catalan Language

The official name of the second major piece of language legislation is 'Act No. 1, of 7th January 1998 on Linguistic Policy', but it is generally referred to as the 'Law of Catalan'. It is more comprehensive in scope and more detailed with regard to specific measures than the

1983 Law of Linguistic Normalisation. For example, there are 39 Articles (as compared to 28 in the 1983 act), of which the first four outline the objectives, define the legal concepts of 'Catalonia's own language' and 'official languages', and deal with the linguistic rights of citizens. The Introduction, which is signed by the Director General of Linguistic Policy, states that the Law is to be regarded as a political message as it expresses the intention of the *Generalitat* to continue the process of language recovery and 'is a solemn pledge to the language of the country by the institutions of Catalonia' (p. 5). Furthermore, it is to be considered as a legislative improvement, consolidating and strengthening previous policies and ensuring the presence of Catalan in several social and cultural domains previously not included in normalisation legislation. The final sentence contains the affirmation that the Act on Linguistic policy represents a 'great step forward in the process of recovering the Catalan language . . . and is, at the same time, a great instrument for social cohesion' (p. 6 of the English translation).

This sentiment is repeated in the lengthy Introduction to the 1998 Act proper which sets out the aims of the act. These go beyond those of protecting Catalan stated in the 1983 Act, particularly in the third objective which aims at reaching equality regarding the linguistic rights and duties of citizens. The first part of the Act is the most interesting and it is headed 'The meaningfulness and situation of the Catalan language'. It contains some highly idealistic statements on the bond between language and national identity, while at the same time trying to be as inclusive as possible of all those who live in Catalonia: 'The Catalan language is an essential element in the national formation and character of Catalonia, a basic instrument for communication, integration and social cohesion of citizens, regardless of their geographic origin . . . ' (p. 7). The reader is then reminded that Catalan should also be seen as a link with other Catalan-speaking areas outside Catalonia (especially Valencia and the Balearics), thus emphasising the significance of the language beyond its national frontiers. The first paragraph concludes by stating that the language 'has borne witness to the loyalty of the Catalan people towards their land and their specific culture' (p. 7). This symbolic recognition of the phenomenon (and part of the *fet diferencial*) that even in times of adversity Catalans have maintained their language provides a moral obligation for the state to maintain it, too.

There follows a reference to historical and political events which have contributed to language shift, as well as present-day factors such as demographic changes and 'the restricted scope that the language has, similar to that of other official languages of Europe' (p. 7) where the trend is towards internationalisation. To the outsider this comparison with other European languages, presumably those of the smaller states such as Denmark or the Netherlands, seems curious in its self-confidence. Catalans do not compare their language to other regional minority languages but rather to national ones with similar numbers of speakers, it seems. The Law recognises that a language policy is required 'which effectively helps to achieve the normal use of Catalonia's own language and which at the same time guarantees a scrupulous respect of the linguistic rights of all citizens' (p.8). Appropriate though it may be, this statement indirectly spells out the dilemma of Catalan language policy: are these dual aims compatible when it comes to the implementation of language policies?

The Act contains a long catalogue of measures designed to promote the use of Catalan in a wide range of public and private institutional, cultural and economic enterprises such as the media, publishing, cinema, music and entertainment, computer science, advertising, employment and business, education at all levels including universities, and personal names/surnames and public denomination. Because of its numerous and detailed provisions, the Law will affect all citizens either directly or indirectly and for that reason reactions to it have come from many quarters of Catalan society.

Issues of identity, language and bilingualism in the debate about the 1998 law

The debate about the second round of language legislation involved, as was to be expected, the traditional issues of language, identity and autonomy and their attendant questions on immigration, minorities and linguistic rights. But it has also been much more polemical and politicised than previously as everybody appeared to join and take sides, and they seemed to be doing so out of the conviction that there was something significant to be gained. The forces at play were shown up quite clearly in the run up to the 1998 Act and provided for ample discussion material in the press and other media. For example, for some time the Barcelona-based *El Periódico* ran an almost daily analysis of the emerging debate, often under the heading of *La polémica lingüística*. Not only the political parties on the left and right representing nationalist Catalan or national Spanish interests were heard, other groups in Catalan society also entered into the debate such as the Church, lobby groups acting for immigrants or for the preservation of the Spanish language, and intellectuals—notably writers, philologists, linguists and would-be linguists. Noticeable, too, has been the increasing politicisation of Catalan sociolinguistic research itself.

As with previous language policy the governing *Convergència i Unió* coalition was keen to reach political consensus. But this time it was more difficult to attain. The *CiU* was accused of pursuing a hidden agenda of wanting to achieve Catalan monolingualism under the cloak of 'social normalisation' of Catalan, and their insistence on pushing through the Act was seen as being politically motivated. The *Partido Popular* (*PP*) which forms at present the national Spanish government but relies on the support of the *CiU* was similarly accused of political opportunism and of trying to make inroads among Spanish speakers in Catalonia—traditionally 'left voters'—with its insistence of free choice for parents to choose the language of education for their children. On the national level the Prime Minister, José Maria Aznar, declared that the fact that he had a political pact with the leader of the *CiU* did not commit him to supporting the *Generalitat*'s proposed legislation. However, the language question cut across traditional party lines as people from opposite sides of the political spectrum came together: for instance, the Catalan branch of the conservative national party *PP* and the Catalan left-wing nationalists *Esquerra Catalana* (*EC*) who both considered that the Law was dangerous, interventionist and likely to cause conflict. Tensions built up within coalitions, eg when some of the more ardent nationalist *Unió* spokesmen openly declared the Act's ultimate aim to be Catalan monolingualism—a position from which the party had to retract. It seems that in the course of the debate conventional political labels such as left-wing, right-wing and centre came to lose their significance to a large extent. Everyone apparently viewed the electorate in Catalonia as comprising just two groups, each about half of the whole: the 'ethnic' Catalans who define their identity as 'speakers of Catalan', and those who see themselves primarily as *castellanohablantes*, Spanish speakers. In this debate, in which *catalanistas* and *españolistas* (so called in the press) were often at loggerheads, identity was defined on the basis of who speaks what language. The facts that in reality all Catalans are equally competent in Spanish, and that Spanish speakers who wish to learn Catalan will find the task quite easy as they 'already have 80 per cent of the work done', as the Catalan journalist Arcadi Espada puts it (1997: 246), did not feature in the equation. Incidentally Espada's is an interesting and by no means isolated case: he claims he is one of many ethnic Catalan 'dissidents' who find themselves ostracised because of their support of Spanish in Catalonia and their doubts about the wisdom of Catalan cultural politics. Espada refers to the fifteen years preceding the publication of his book as *'una situación culturalmente anómala'* (p. 249). Catalan intellectuals who write for the Spanish-speaking public but live in Catalonia will recount stories that, in their view, indicate lack of support or even hostility towards them in their own land. Espada, who speaks and writes in both Spanish and Catalan, relates in his book (pp. 180–1) that after frequent appearances on TV3 (the Catalan-language local TV station) one day he expressed a sentiment against the main Barcelona football club (he had said he was glad they had lost a match). He was never again invited to take part in any programmes, and some time later one of the producers told him that this was because he was regarded as anti-Catalan—on the strength of the said comment. The well-known writer Ana María Matute, a native and lifelong resident of Barcelona, tells of her personal dissatisfaction when, on the occasion of being elected to the Royal Spanish Academy of the Language recently (the only woman member for the time being, incidentally) she was congratulated by the Presidents of sixteen *comunidades autónomas*—all, that is, except Catalonia, her view being that the reason could only be that she was not seen as sufficiently supportive of Catalan linguistic and cultural policies (personal communication).

The Catholic Church tried to avoid being drawn into the language debate but in view of its by now historic role in the Catalan cause this did not prove possible. Whereas at grassroots level some local parish publications demanded that all local churchgoers should learn Catalan, the position taken by the hierarchy has been one of advocating open and moderate Catalanism and cultural diversity. The Archbishop of Barcelona was at pains to point out that the majority of masses in his diocese were held in Spanish and that this situation reflected the Church's contribution to peaceful coexistence. This contrasted with the Papal Nuncio's protest that Spanish-speaking churchgoers in Catalonia were discriminated against as most church-services were offered only or mainly in Catalan. Increasingly, important members of the Church in Catalonia are ethnic Catalans and their promotion to higher positions is reported in the press as favourable to the promotion of Catalan identity.

71

Charlotte Hoffmann

The Church's involvement in Catalanism goes back a long time (see, for example, Brassloff, 1998) and has been described by Pi-Sunyer (1971: 130) as one of the three levels of ethnonationalist affirmation—the family and underground political parties being the other two. During the Franco dictatorship a number of groups and organisations ranging from folk dance groups and choral societies to literary associations and cinema clubs were run under the umbrella of the Catholic Church. They also 'contributed to the maintenance and transmission of Catalan identity' (Llovera, 1996: 193), as did certain events which have stayed in the collective memory and have become national days when Catalans celebrate and take pride in their identity publicly. Llovera describes two national days and their significance for Catalans and also refers to an event which took place in 1947 and which is seen by Llovera, as well as others, as the first occasion after the Spanish Civil War when Catalans had the opportunity to affirm their identity publicly. The occasion was the ceremonies of the enthronement of the Virgin of Monserrat, attended by more than 30,000 people, during which some speakers, for the first time in Franco's Spain, spoke in Catalan in public (to roaring applause) and the Catalan flag ('*la senyera*' which basically, and significantly, means 'the sign') was displayed in the presence of one of Franco's ministers—apparently because of a misunderstanding. It was also the first time that the dictator allowed the distribution of leaflets in both Catalan and Castilian, which was interpreted by some as an initial attempt at reconciliation between the winners and losers in the Civil War. In the public mind Monserrat later became a symbol of both the affirmation of Catalan identity and anti-Francoism. Whereas in the past this close association between Church and Catalanism did no harm to the former, the situation today is more delicate as the Church needs to be mindful of the social as well as linguistic composition of its congregation and can ill afford to be openly taking political sides. Thus, at the 50th anniversary of the April 1947 event (this time with a mere 10,000 present), the Abbott of Monserrat, formulating the official position of the Catalan Church today, declared that 'the diversity of our people is one of our main strengths'.

As mentioned earlier, bilingualism is a *de facto* phenomenon in Catalonia, both on the societal and the individual level, and since the democratic Constitution of Spain was proclaimed in 1978 it has been recognised *de jure*. It seems curious, however, that bilingualism as such is not promoted. Indeed the term is absent from virtually all official publications. What is more, in the linguistic debate *bil-*

ingüismo/bilingüe seem to have become loaded words, just as those who use them with a positive connotation are somewhat deprecatingly referred to as *bilingüistas*. In Spanish (and to a greater extent in Catalan) sociolinguistics, societal bilingualism has often been equated with diglossia and language shift as the coexistence of two languages for most of Spain's history carried the dominance of Castilian over Basque, Catalan and Galician with it. As it became necessary, or desirable, for speakers of regional languages to use Castilian, the local languages lost out linguistically as well as socially. The hidden fear therefore appears to be that promotion of bilingual policies will be a sure route of facilitating Catalan being replaced by Castilian.[2]

Conditions today have, of course, changed radically in relation to the past, in that linguistic policies have been successful in raising the status and widening the domains of use of regional languages. But even in Catalonia, where linguistic and cultural conditions have been favourable for the implementation of linguistic policies, Catalan and Spanish are openly perceived to be competing for territory, status and users. Catalan has gained a great deal in ethnolinguistic vitality and obviously it is far less threatened than it was twenty-five years ago. Nevertheless, neither linguistically nor sociolinguistically can the language be said to have been fully recovered: linguistic adaptation in terms of language choice and borrowing still tends to be one way only (from Catalan to Castilian Spanish) and demographic trends point towards a disproportionate increase of Spanish over Catalan speakers. Even non-nationalist sociolinguists agree that 'by any objective standards, Catalan is still a subordinate language in a process of "reverse shift", with a long way to go towards normalisation in key social areas' (Yates, 1998: 207).

The 'ethnic model', which was chosen for Catalonia and which allows two languages to co-exist officially in the same geographical space with equal status, works better in polities where each speech community has its own territory, or in a state such as Luxembourg where there is clear separation of function for each language and only one of them is tied to national identity. In order to safeguard the survival of their language, it seems clear that Catalans would prefer a 'territorial solution' with Catalan as the dominant language (*catalán hegemónico*). In this they are backed up by international sociolinguistic research that seems to imply that only aggressively monolingual policies such as for instance those pursued by the nationalist *québéquois* government, are likely to restore a threatened language. Fishman even goes as far as suggesting (when referring to the reversal of language shift in Catalonia) that 'perhaps, however, before the ultimate goal can be attained, a new "reverse diglossia" will have to be at least transitionally attained with Catalan H and Spanish L' (1991: 313) (the 'H' means 'High variety' ie dominant, and 'L' is the 'Low variety' or marginalised one). Ideas like these obviously ignore the composition and aspirations of modern society in Catalonia while at the same time highlighting the dilemma resulting from sociolinguistic expediency and social realities.

Conclusion

From a historical perspective, Spain's experience of democracy has been short, perhaps too short in order to judge the success of its constitutional arrangement. The system of devolved local government appears to have contributed to a successful, bloodless transition from centralised dictatorship to a democratic state with powers devolved to the regions, and it has tremendously facilitated Spain's fast pace of social and economic development, making it one of the EU members with the highest growth rates today. There is little doubt that a number of favourable circumstances have enabled Catalonia to achieve more gains than any other region, and this in turn has made it possible for the autonomous region to pursue highly ambitious, and costly, language policies which have gone quite a way towards recovering lost linguistic ground. In this, as in the achievements of their cultural policies in general, the Catalans have earned the admiration of many Spaniards and indeed Europeans.

We have seen that concepts of language and identity—territorial, linguistic and cultural—and their attendant issues play a considerable role in public discourse and that they are given conflicting interpretations. At one end of the spectrum are those people (for instance linguists like Gregorio Salvador) who view language primarily as a tool which becomes all the more powerful the higher the number of speakers who use it. At the other end are those for whom language is, above all, a powerful symbol of identity. Of course, both views are valid and can be said to apply simultaneously, but to differing degrees depending on the particular circumstances of a language. The conflict arises when languages are in competition with each other within the same territory and the inhabitants of that region do not agree on a common hierarchy of status. In Catalonia there are those who rank Catalan above Castilian, those who accept equal status for both, and those who see Castilian as the language with the highest status. The Spanish Constitution is ambiguously worded on the question of languages and therefore does not provide an objective reference point.

What is at the heart of the issue is that, as Cela says (see quotation above with his subtle distinction between (*el*) *español*, a noun, and *español*, an adjective), while Castilian Spanish is the Spanish language, Catalan is also Spanish as it is one of the languages of Spain. Castilian has the whole Spanish state behind it, which will always ensure its survival. In the case of Catalonia it is uncertain whether the '*estado de la autonomias*' model is sufficient for this purpose. Recent experience shows that the way to achieve survival is not by confrontational policies or by creating conflicts of allegiance in the minds of bilingual speakers. From a purely sociolinguistic perspective efforts to counteract language shift require 'affirmative action' or 'pro-active language policies' (Strubell i Trueta, 1998: 176), ie positive discrimination. However, language planning in Catalonia seems to have reached a point now where such action does not command general consensus any longer and a substantial proportion of the population are beginning to feel threatened. Attempts to go too far too fast down the 'normalisation' road can only backfire and it may well be that the Catalan government will have to rethink its language policies and lower its goals in the light of changed social circumstances.

As Catalonia enters the next century European preoccupations may take over (Catalan) nationalist ones and the population of Catalonia, mindful of its ethnic and linguistic mix, may come to view language differently. In this context one might also wish that the rather deprecatory term 'immigrants' were dropped from public, and sociolinguistic, discourse—the people concerned are, after all, fellow Spaniards and mobility within states and within Europe is a common enough feature of modern society. One could argue that it is no longer necessary to implement radical language policies in order to support Catalan identity—this identity is already quite well established. And, as has been shown above, the Catalan language no longer has the same defining character of Catalan identity it held in earlier times. Following present cultural trends everywhere in Europe, and being mindful of the fact that they live in a pluralist state, Catalans and non-Catalan Spaniards alike may learn to iden- tify with a variety of cultural national and supranational elements rather than continue to affirm their separateness. However, for this to happen the central government, too, would have to re-evaluate its policy of leaving cultural policies entirely to the regions. For cultural pluralism to work, and in order to ease the constant tension between the centre and the periphery which has been a hallmark of post-Franco Spanish politics, the Spanish government must be seen to be encouraging multilingualism and multiculturalism within all of Spain. Progressive stages of Europeanisation may encourage such moves.

Notes

1 In English, Spanish and Catalan publications the terms 'immigrants' and 'immigration' occur. It is worth pointing out that whereas many Europeans consider 'immigrants' to be people who have left their country of origin, often an ex-colony of their new host country, and are different in terms of language, culture and sometimes also ethnicity, in the Spanish context immigrants have traditionally been those who left a poorer region in Spain and settled in another, economically more prosperous. Because of many shared cultural and linguistic features, social integration has been relatively unproblematic. It seems that to continue now to call these people and their descendants 'immigrants' is to emphasise their 'otherness' unduly at a time when social mobility within states and the EU as a whole has become a widespread feature of modern society.
2 Catalan attitudes may be starting to change. On 28 March 1999 the Madrid daily *El País* published an extensive interview with the President of the *Generalitat*, Jordi Pujol, which contained the key phrase (and front page heading) *El bilingüismo nos va bien* (Bilingualism is fine for us). In the context of recent polls showing an increase of Catalan-Spanish speakers at the expense of monolingualism in both languages, Pujol was asked if he now accepted bilingualism as a component of the Catalonia of the future. He confirmed that he did, saying that bilingualism is a perfectly natural phenomenon and that Catalans were taking it in their stride – even if some local politicians were still nervous about it. He added that he hoped that (social) bilingual use would soon become a non issue.

References

Act No. 1, of 7th January 1998, on Linguistic Policy. Generalitat de Catalunya.
Baetens Beardsmore, H. (1994), 'Language policy and planning in Western European countries', in W. Grabe et al. (eds), *Annual Review of Applied Linguistics*, 14, New York: Cambridge University Press, 93–110.
Brassloff, A. (1996), 'Centre-periphery Communication in Spain: The politics of language and the language of politics', in C. Hoffmann (ed.), *Language, Culture and Communication in Contemporary Europe*, Clevedon: Multilingual Matters, 111–123.
Brassloff, A. (1998), *Religion and Politics in Spain*, London: Macmillan.
England, J. (1993–94), 'The debate on the languages of Spain: A *Diálogo de sordos?*' *Journal of Hispanic Research*, 2, 289–296.

Espada, A. (1997), *Contra Catalunya*, Barcelona: Flor del Viento Ediciones.

Fishman, J. (1971), 'National languages and languages in wider communication in the developing nations', in W. H. Whitley (ed.), *Language Use and Social Change. Problems of Multilingualism with Special Reference to Eastern Africa*, Oxford: Oxford University Press.

Fishman, J. A. (1991), *Reversing Language Shift*, Clevedon: Multilingual Matters.

Giner, S. (1984), *The Social Structure of Catalonia*, The Anglo-Catalan Society, Occasional Publications No. 1, London.

Green, J. N. (1993), 'Representations of Romance: Contact, bilingualism and diglossia', in R. Posner and J. N. Green (eds), *Trends in Romance Linguistics and Philology* (Bilingualism and Linguistic Conflict in Romance, vol. 5, Berlin: Mouton de Gruyter, 3–40.

Grugel, J. and Rees, T. (1997), *Franco's Spain*, London: Arnold.

Hoffmann, C. (1988), 'Linguistic normalisation in Catalonia: Catalan for the Catalans or Catalan for Catalonia?', in J. N. Jørgensen et al. (eds), *Bilingualism in Society and School*, Copenhagen Studies in Bilingualism, 5, Clevedon: Multilingual Matters.

Hoffmann, C. (1991), *Introduction to Bilingualism*, London: Longman.

Hoffmann, C. (1996a), 'Language Planning at the Crossroads: the Case of Contemporary Spain', in C. Hoffmann (ed.), *Language, Culture and Communication in Contemporary Europe*, Clevedon: Multilingual Matters, 111–123.

Hoffmann, C. (1996b), 'Monolingualism, Bilingualism, Cultural Pluralism and National Identity: twenty years of language planning in contemporary Spain', in S. Wright (ed.), *Monolingualism and Bilingualism: Lessons from Canada and Spain*, Clevedon: Multilingual Matters, 59–108.

Hooper, J. (1995), *The New Spaniards*, Harmondsworth: Penguin Books.

Llovera, J. (1996), 'The Role of Commemorations in (Ethno) Nation-Building. The Case of Catalonia', in C. Mar-Molinero and A. Smith (eds), *Nationalism and the Nation in the Iberian Peninsula*, Oxford: Berg, 191–206.

Mar-Molinero, C. and Stevenson, P. (1991), 'Language, geography and politics: The Territorial Imperative debate in the European context', *Language Problems and Language Planning*, 15 (2), 162–176.

Paulston, C. B. (1994), *Linguistic Minorities in Multilingual Settings*, Amsterdam: John Benjamins.

Pi-Sunyer, O. (1971), 'The Maintenance of Ethnic Identity in Catalonia', in O. Pi-Sunyer (ed.), *The Limits of Integration: Ethnicity and Nationalism in Modern Europe*, University of Massachusetts, Research Reports No. 9.

Salvador, G. (1987), *La lengua española y lenguas de España*, Barcelona: Ariel.

Strubell i Trueta, M. (1993) Catalan: Castilian. I. R. Posner and J. N. Green (eds), *Trends in Romance Linguistics and Philology* (Bilingualism and Linguistic Conflict, vol. 5, Berlin: Mouton de Gruyter, 175–207.

Strubell i Trueta, M. (1998), 'Language, Democracy and Devolution in Catalonia', *Current Issues in Language and Society*, 5 (3), 146–180.

Vallverdú, F. (1973), *El fet lingüistic com a fet social*, Barcelona: Ediciones 62.

Vidal-Folch, X. (1994) (ed.), *Los catalanes y el poder*, Madrid: Ediciones El Pais/Aguilar.

Whitehead, A. (1996), 'Spain, European Regions and City States', in C. Mar-Molinero and A. Smith (eds), *Nationalism and the Nation in the Iberian Peninsula*, Oxford: Berg, 255–270.

Charlotte Hoffmann

Woolard, K. A. (1986), 'The Crisis in the Concept of identity', in G. W. McDonough (ed.), *Conflict in Catalonia—Images of Urban Society*, Gainsville: University of Florida Press.

Woolard, K. A. (1989), *Double Talk: Bilingualism and the Politics of Ethnicity in Catalonia*, Stanford: Stanford University Press.

Yates, A. (1998), 'Language, Democracy and Devolution in Catalonia: A Response to Miquel Strubell', *Current Issues in Language and Society*, 5 (3), 204–209.

A community that can communicate?
The linguistic factor in European
integration

Sue Wright

Abstract

Language is an important but often neglected aspect of the political process. this chapter gives a brief overview of the main phases of the past thousand years of European history in terms of language choice and shift, showing how communities of communication developed in tandem with political power centres. This history reveals that all political associations develop the communication solutions which promote and serve their political ambition and that new ways of organising society are accompanied by new language practices. In this context it is unlikely that the European Union will prove an exception.

Europeanisation is not happening within a vacuum. Political power is also leaking away from state governments to relocate at global and regional level. The growing use of English as a global lingua franca and the renaissance of languages eclipsed in the period of nation building are further factors that affect the community of communication which is developing in Europe. Since the European project is developing in tandem with these other societal changes, the communication solutions it provokes will not be simple cause and effect relationships. Nonetheless, we can be sure that, if European integration progresses, new language practices will evolve to facilitate the circulation of information and ideas, the construction of democratic governance and individual access to centres of power. If they do not, then European integration will find itself halted at the level of a common market and a technocratic bureaucracy.

Language—the neglected factor

The question of European integration is usually discussed with little reference to the language factor. This is not surprising. Ignoring language difference is a very common practice. The histories of high politics in Europe recount the clashes of great dynasties, the rivalry of powerful nations, their wars and treaties, with little to say about channels of communication blocked or opened by the ability of the politicians to communicate with each other. Was Napoleon III predisposed to help Victor-Emmanuel because Cavour could argue the Italian case persuasively in French? Did the provisions of the Treaties of Versailles, Trianon and Sevres hold the germs of future conflict within them because Woodrow Wilson was swayed by those who could lobby in English?[1] One searches in vain for comment on the influence of lines of communication on political solutions. Little has been recorded. The same holds true for cultural histories. The scholarship which examines the development of the European Judaeo-Christian belief system, sometimes interweaving with Classical-Humanist philosophy and sometimes at loggerheads with it, has little to say about how ideas were shared and disseminated or obstructed and misrepresented because of the constraints of the great linguistic diversity of Europe. Even the historians of nationalism sometimes neglect language despite the evident use of linguistic unification in nation building, with knowledge and use of the national language coming to symbolise the speaker's loyalty to and identity with the nation.

In this essay I would like to take an unusual perspective and present certain aspects of European history in terms of language. This will be the story of how group formation—class or nation— is intimately linked to patterns of language use. The codes that are chosen and promoted by a society reflect actual social organisation and permit or hinder new relationships. Given a medium of exchange, groups can choose to be in contact, exchange information, influence each other or cooperate; without it they cannot. The periods when Europeans had 'voice' in each other's societies were times when it was possible to speak of pan-European classes, movements and events. During the era in which the Westphalian model dominated, boundaries between states became less permeable, national society more inward-looking. In this period the only response was 'exit' in the Hirschmanian sense;[2] action not discussion. Now we are in a period where contact and co-operation among Europeans is at a level not experienced for centuries. There has, however, been a lack of debate about how communication can be managed in an ever more integrated Europe. All the recent moves towards greater European integration (the Single European Act, the Treaty on European Union, Economic Monetary Union etc.) have taken place without any workable policy on how a multilingual polity will manage its multilingualism.[3] Communication is being achieved pragmatically, with individuals solving their own linguistic problems in a piecemeal way. The language factor is, however, central to the future of the European project whether this is admitted or not.

The lack of political will to confront this issue is understandable since language is not only a means of communication but also a badge of identity and a sign of membership of a community. The dismay that Europeans have expressed at the loss of their individual currencies, symbol of their economic sovereignty and wealth, would be overshadowed by their outrage were there to be any suggestion that their national languages take second place to a *lingua franca* within the European Union's institutions and for contact at interstate level. We are socialised into society through a language which then marks us as a member of our group. This is true for any society in any period, but became particularly salient in the age of high nationalism in Europe, when political élites manipulated this link between language and identity as one of the strategies for forging the nation. National governments set out to achieve the congruence of national languages with national borders and bring all those on the territory it controlled into a single nation. Other languages in competition with the single national language within state boundaries were actively discouraged and repressed. Education systems, conscription and melting pot strategies each helped the spread of the national language as well as promoting national identity. Thus the idea of one national language as 'badge of identity' for our national status has been propagated for at least two centuries and the rule of *un peuple, une langue, un Etat* is so highly developed within most European nation states, that many Europeans accept monolingualism in the national language as the norm and do not reflect on it. Loyalty to a single national language has been drummed into us as a patriotic duty and relatively few minority language communities have withstood the pressures from the central state apparatus. This explains the difficulties when we come to discuss how we should manage communication within the European Union. To permit the central role of the national language to be eclipsed in any domain of public life seems inconceivable and unpatriotic; to solve communication problems through personal bilingualism is an alien concept for many. The polyglot does exist in Europe but belongs either to a small cosmopolitan élite educated in a number of prestige languages or to a stubborn 'minority' which has refused to be totally assimilated in the national melting pot.

Monolingualism is the historical legacy that the member states bring to the European Union. The majority of governments in the nineteenth century tried to impose one single standardised national language within state borders. The goal was pursued along with varying amounts of vigour and enthusiasm. The governments of France, Spain and the United Kingdom tried very hard to eradicate linguistic difference among their nationals; the unification of Italy and Germany used the linguistic criterion as one of their organising principles and so produced countries with some linguistic homogeneity.[4]

Medieval Europe

Spain, France and the United Kingdom are among the longest established 'nation states'[5] in Europe. There is much debate over the date when one can begin to speak of a nation state as such,[6] for the medieval dynasties which established the frontiers of these states were only motivated to take land. They had no plan to group peoples of a similar cultural and linguistic heritage, nor to weld the disparate groups they conquered into a cohesive whole. The logic in the conquests, marriages and treaties which established the border between the territory of one monarch and the next was primarily the desire to have as much territory as possible together with defensible borders.[7]

The Capetian dynasty acquired the lands which were to become France by conquest, judicious marriage and diplomatic negotiation.[8] The United Kingdom was constructed through much the same mixture of conquest and inheritance,[9] although British monarchs could not boast the continuity of dynasty which the French royal house enjoyed until 1789. Spain achieved its borders through the unification of Aragon and Castile by marriage and the expulsion of the Moors from the Iberian peninsula in the late fifteenth century.[10] If there were any conformity imposed in the making of these states, it was religious: the Spanish Inquisition, the revoking of the Edict of Nantes, the establishment of the Anglican Church required subjects of the state to practise the religion of that state. This was the tradition of the early modern period expressed in the Peace of Augsburg in 1555, the principle of '*cuius regio eius religio*', that the ruled should accept that their religious allegiance would be dictated by the allegiance of their ruler.

Linguistic and cultural cohesion were, on the other hand, disregarded. It would be anachronistic to expect otherwise given how patterns of communication worked at the time. The medieval world was not organised primarily into territorial based linguistic communities. Feudal society had four components and the members of the three major groups had lines of communication which are quite alien to us today. The political class, the knights of Christendom, was a multilingual group. The personal linguistic repertoire of each individual was likely to be greater the higher he was positioned in the hierarchy. The reasons for this are clear. Firstly, at the highest level, marriages were arranged across linguistic and cultural divides to cement alliances and acquire territory. This meant that a relatively small group of families intermarried and between them ruled the kingdoms of Europe. Linguistically this had an extended effect as the brides brought their retinue with them to the new court, causing marriage and interaction to occur at less august levels too. The children of the class grew up in bilingual, if not multilingual, settings. Secondly, the feudal political system linked one man to another through the oath of allegiance. There was no stability in the constitution of political alliances; loyalty was to the man not to a single linguistic and cultural group, as it had been in earlier times and was to be again in the age of nationalism.[11] Death or dissension could cause a regrouping. This brought the ruling warrior class into contact with each other in changing patterns, with general disregard for linguistic division. Armies were multilingual; the feudal system caused those who owed fealty to the same suzerain to fight together. Thus boundaries were fluid, changing with marriage and inheritance; allegiance was not to a fixed centre. Where loyalty was not to the suzerain it was to God, and with a similar melting-pot effect. The Crusades in their pitting of Christendom against Islam created the possibility for the Christian knights to conceive of themselves as a European group fighting a common enemy and for contacts between them to be prolonged. Forces which fight together develop strategies for communicating. Multilingualism and the use of a *lingua franca* were the inevitable consequences of the medieval aristocratic world. Both were adopted as solutions.[12]

The Catholic Church was also pan-European and organised hierarchically with little regard for linguistic and cultural frontiers and secular political divisions. It had no difficulty in organising itself in this way since, in Church Latin, it had a ready-made *lingua franca*. The clergy used the sacred language for their ministry, for scholarship and for contact among themselves where no other language was available.

The peasantry in contrast was overwhelmingly monolingual, often in a dialect which had little currency outside a very limited area. This posed no problem to the individual who was unlikely to travel far and thus encounter the cleavages between the various dialect continua. These continua spanned Europe, unbroken. A traveller moving through the Southern Romance continuum could journey from the western seaboard of Portugal, through the Iberian peninsula, follow the Mediterranean coast from Perpignan to Nice, cross the Alps and go to the very south of Italy without finding two adjacent villages whose dialects were not mutually comprehensible. The same truth holds for the other dialect families, eg Celtic, Slavonic, Germanic. Of course the extremes of the continuum were very disparate but significant difference would be apparent only to the traveller, not to the speakers. Comprehension could always be achieved at adjacent points. Where it was withheld this would probably have been for reasons of a political nature not linguistic. It was only along the fault lines between the dialect continua and where there were pockets of linguistic singularity, eg the Basques, the Albanians, the Hungarians that there was no possibility at all of contact and comprehension without bilingualism.

The fourth group in medieval society, the artisan/trading class in the towns, was a small group in comparison. The rise of this class coincided with the end of the medieval world. The patterns of language use I have described disappeared along with it.

The desired congruence of nation and state

As power shifted away from the monarchy and aristocracy toward the middle class, and as literacy and scholarship were no longer the sole preserve of the Church, new patterns of governance and education inevitably brought about changes in language communities. In the first process, territorial boundaries became more stable, linked to peoples not to monarchs, and, with emerging democratic structures, the citizens had new rights and duties which caused a greater proportion of the population to take part in the political process and in the defence of the state. These activities had inevitable linguistic effect. In the second process, the sacred language lost its role as the language of scholarship; with secularisation and universal education the national languages supplanted Latin.

The case of France illustrates the first process clearly. As the French moved from absolute monarchy to republic, they debated the role of language in the process. Similar processes occurred in other countries including the United Kingdom and Spain but not in such a short time frame nor with such well recorded public consideration of how language could be harnessed to the nationalist project and the democratisation of the political process.

The French monarchy had not required all its subjects to speak French. In 1539 the Edict of Villers-Cotterêts had imposed French as the language in which laws would be given and enforced, but, in all other spheres, the state made no stipulation about the language to be employed. However, market forces exerted pressure. Those who spoke French had better access to political power and economic advantage in an increasingly centralised state.[13] From the reign of Philippe-Auguste onwards, culminating in the absolute power of the monarch in the seventeenth and eighteenth centuries, Paris dominated the country politically and commercially. The élites of territories incorporated into the French state made the personal decision to shift to French to retain some contact with power; the general population in these areas did not.[14]

The attraction of French was heightened because it also enjoyed international cultural and intellectual prestige and, by the seventeenth century, was beginning to replace Latin as a *lingua franca* for the élites of Europe.[15] This prestige stemmed in part from the cultural productions of the rich and glittering court of the French king, the most powerful monarch in Europe. The seventeenth century witnessed a golden age of literary creativity in French. Prestige continued in the eighteenth century because French gave access to new scientific thought, philosophical speculation and political ideas. French had become the language in which the certainties of absolutism and the *ancien régime* were being questioned. The Enlightenment was not merely a Parisian phenomenon it is true, but those who wrote in French, eg Diderot and the Encyclopaedists, Montesquieu, Voltaire and Rousseau, enjoyed widespread and profound influence.

Thus, those who learnt French were the ruling and aspiring middle class in France and the intellectual élite of Europe, with the result that at the time of the Revolution French had an established role as the second language of many of the most powerful in European society. It was, however, neither the first nor the second language of the great majority of the French.[16] This posed a problem for the revolutionaries. Whereas the French as subjects had had no overwhelming need to know French, as citizens they were called upon to participate in the political process. At first the revolutionaries organised translations of the tracts, papers and posters they sent out to the citizens, but soon revised this policy. French was the language of the revolution and the nation; it would be the vector of the ideals of the revolution and a unifying factor for the people. Disapproval of languages other than French was made clear:

> La monarchie avait des raisons de ressembler à la tour de Babel; dans la démocratie laisser les citoyens ignorants de la langue nationale, incapables de contrôler le pouvoir, c'est trahir la patrie, c'est méconnaître les bienfaits de l'imprimerie.[17]

The revolutionary government took steps to bring about a language shift within the population. Those who did not obey the new directives on use of the French language found themselves ranged against the revolutionaries and likely to be punished. The new generation was targeted as the best hope of change. Education through the medium of French was to be assured by the provision of a French-speaking teacher in every commune. In the short term, the Republic could not carry out its policies because of the lack of French speaking teachers as well the need to turn its attention and finances to the dangers from outside its borders. However, the wars of the Republic and the Empire effected to some extent the aims of the policies they had curtailed. The *levée de masse* which provided the soldiers for Napoleon brought young men together from all over France. In its scale, this *Grande Armée* was unlike any military adventure in the previous two centuries and was the first instance of the melting pot effect that conscription was to have for France.

When, at the end of the nineteenth century, the goal of free and obligatory schooling in French was finally achieved,[18] it increased the rate of language shift which conscription had started. Those children who resisted the change to French were reprimanded, humiliated, even punished physically. Both patterns of identity and patterns of language use were altered. From the Revolution onwards, French governments would pursue the policy of French for all citizens, in all domains. There was no official tolerance of the other languages[19] to be found within the borders of the French state.

The French republicans had identified the need for all members of a democratic polity to share a language in order for democratic debate to be possible: '*République une, langue une: la langue doit être une comme la République*'. It is true that the wishes of the majority are difficult to interpret unless the participants can articulate those wishes, debate and come to some consensus. Democracy is a language-borne process and requires a community with some

86

avenues of communication. The French revolutionaries were the first to articulate the problems that accompany multilingualism in the democratic process. Of course, the pragmatic needs of democracy were not the only motive for linguistic unification within the frontiers of state. In nation state building, language entered into a complex relationship with patriotism, and use and knowledge of the national language came to be seen as a demonstration of loyalty to the state.[20] Language was a means of achieving 'external distinction', differentiating France from the enemies that surrounded it.[21] A unified language was also a means of top down social control.[22]

The second process which led to a profound change in language practices is rooted in the Renaissance and Reformation. The religious dissension which led to the Reformation was expressed in the vernacular not in Latin. The Protestants rejected Latin along with some of the tenets of the Catholic Church. They translated the bible into their various vernaculars; new prayers and hymns were composed in the ordinary language of every day life. Literacy spread, fuelled by a desire to read the holy writ. This affected the Catholic regions as well and the bible was translated into the languages of the Catholic states. The desire to have access directly to the Scriptures was matched by technical invention. Religious texts, particularly the Bible, were published in great numbers as the introduction of the printing press into Europe took book production away from the copyists in the monasteries and allowed mass production. As Anderson[23] has argued, print capitalism had the effect of fixing the form of the language variety chosen as a print language and promoting it over a wide swathe of the adjacent dialect continuum. The entrepreneurial printer was not producing an expensive item for a single client as the copyist had done but a product where economies of scale were to be had if the language medium used could be understood by a large number of people. The print languages which were employed were the prestige dialects of the capitals, Paris, London and Spain, and of their political élites, and contributed to their expansion.

Almost contemporaneously with the rise of print capitalism, language academies were founded to oversee the standardisation process (Académie française 1635, Accademia della Crusca 1582, Royal Society for improving the English language 1664). With academies, language became an affair of the state with language planning in the sense of grammar and dictionary-making underpinning the market forces of print capitalism. Literacy continued to grow, fuelled by the advent of industrialisation and its need for a more educated work force than was required in the agricultural world.[24] Naturally, national education in the national standardised language affected the dialect continua. The frontiers fixed rather arbitrarily by conquest and annexation began to be linguistic boundaries as well. The people to the north of the Pyrenees were taught to be literate in French; the people to the south acquired Spanish.[25]

Other factors contributed to the high boundary fences between states. Commercially, each policy aspired to an economic self-sufficiency, using customs tariffs and import quotas to protect its own industry and agriculture. Trade within national boundaries was easy; trade across frontiers was not.[26] Administratively, the state involved itself more and more in the lives of its citizens and communicated with them through the national bureaucracy using the national language. Politically, the electoral process needed a nation-wide forum for debate and persuasion, as suffrage extended. First the written press, then the audio-visual media provided the possibility for interest groups to put their case to a national audience in the national language to affect events on the national stage. The media helped form national opinion and develop national consensus.

Each of these developments reinforced the status of national languages. Whether regional dialects and languages were actually banned or merely discouraged, the standardised national language was likely to spread in terms both of numbers of speakers and the numbers of domains where it was used, as members of minority language groups bowed to the pragmatic need to speak certain languages in order to be part of national society and to the patriotic demand to display loyalty by using the language of the nation. Thus states which had been linguistically diverse, such as France, Spain and the United Kingdom made some progress to linguistic uniformity—at least in public life. The idea of cultural and linguistic cohesion was central to the nationalist creed. The new states formed at the end of the First World War in the wake of the old empires grouped those from the same dialect continuum[27] and used the national education system to impose a standard form on all speakers. By the mid-twentieth century, language communities were vertically divided national communities. There might be a complex mosaic of language allegiance under the surface, but the public use of other languages on state territory had been actively discouraged in most states. Marginalised, denigrated, minority languages had been banished to the private domain, and under some regimes not tolerated even there.[28] Public life was overwhelmingly monolingual in the national language. State education meant that the monolingual minority language speaker had died out. National communities became homogenous as élites and middle and lower classes adopted closely related varieties of the same national language. The horizontal linguistic communities—the Latin speaking Catholic church and the pan-European aristocracy—had both been eclipsed by the national focus of religion, politics, economics and culture and defence and, in the case of the latter, the continuing growth of the middle class.

Globalisation and the spread of English

The autonomy and homogeneity of the nation state did not last long and it is the present breakdown that I would now like to examine. The inter-state system in its Westphalian model may still be a powerful idea,[29] but it is crumbling in a number of areas and all the indications suggest that this process will continue. In the economic domain, the global free market is gradually replacing the protectionist domestic economies of the sovereign state system. National governments can no longer protect their currencies or their financial markets. Trans-national corporations with turnover greater than some small states act in a context which takes little account of political boundaries. There is a convergence (in the developed world at least) in terms of consumption: products are designed, developed, produced and consumed in the context of a global market. The environmental problems of the industrial world also cross borders. Pollution of air and water or depletion of the ozone layer cannot be contained within state borders and so provoke international protest and demand international solutions, devised, agreed and implemented by transnational teams. The new issues of genetic modification and cloning lead to calls for global regulation. For a single state to legislate in isolation on new technologies now has little sense.

Politically, there has been an explosion in the number and power of international organisations and regime which challenge the sovereignty of national governments. There is a growing acceptance of external military intervention in the domestic affairs of the state when it is deemed to be acting against the norms set by the international community—whether this takes the form of aggression towards part of its own population or military threat to outsiders.[30] International forces under the flag of the UN, NATO, OSCE etc. enforce the will of the international community.[31] International courts supersede the authority of the national court in many areas and can hold national politicians to account for acts carried out on national territory.[32] Politics now demands global actors; little can be decided purely within national parliaments and governments.

The expansion of transnational relations is made possible by the new communication technologies. There has been a rapid expansion in the sources of information available to the individual. New technologies and techniques can be shared and disseminated instantaneously. News and opinion can circulate internationally; the state can no longer censor effectively[33] now that information from satellites and the Internet is so difficult to block; action and pressure can be concerted. Culture can be consumed globally with the Hollywood blockbuster showing simultaneously on all continents.

All this is very imperfect: many international peace initiatives are ill-conceived, under-funded, contested and follow the agenda of the powerful members of the UN Security Council; much of the news circulating on these global networks comes from a small number of global news agencies who dominate the market; the new global culture is often a lowest common denominator product designed to appeal to the greatest number and sometimes of little intellectual or artistic worth. In cataloguing the progressive internationalisation of human affairs I do not want to appear a naive positivist. It is clear that the process is problematic and the outcomes may be good and bad. What cannot be at issue, however, is that much political, economic and cultural life now takes place on a global stage. This being so, there must be linguistic effects.

Much of globalisation has happened in English and English has spread as a result of globalisation. It would, of course, be simplistic to believe that this is all that is happening; communication problems are solved in various ways. Transnational projects report a number of strategies to overcome linguistic difference. For example, the practice of participants from languages in the same dialect continuum each using their own language and developing their comprehension skills for the others has been reported from Mediterranean environmental protection groups and Dutch/German cross-border science parks.[34] Nor is it happening without furious reaction in some quarters—the Toubon Act of 1994 reiterated in a formal declaration that the language of the French Republic was French and attempted to halt the incursion of English loan words and the invasion of English in the public domain in France.[35] Of course, English is not the only foreign language learnt in the education systems of the world; the other 'languages of wider diffusion' or of economic importance (French, German, Spanish, Russian, Japanese, Hindi,

Chinese and Arabic etc.) are also taught. Nonetheless, English dominates. Despite attempts to find pragmatic alternative solutions, to limit the spread of English by law and to promote diversity in the education systems of the world, English continues to colonise more domains as the medium of communication. The numbers of situations in which it can be used and the numbers of people using it mean that the returns on learning the language are high. And with each extra individual who makes the personal decision to acquire the language, its usefulness is further confirmed.

The original reasons for the dominance of English were varied and numerous: the success of the Anglo-Saxons in the Second World War and their subsequent dominance of international politics in the post war world (eg in the United Nations Security Council, the IMF, the WTO); the eclipse of their main rival with the fall of communism and the apparent victory of the free market system in all parts of the world; the use of English as the *lingua franca* in which advances in science and technology are made known; the sheer numbers and wealth of US consumers which allow the film and television industry to recoup their costs on the domestic market and flood the world market with films and television programmes at a price that other national producers are unable to match; the legacy of the British Empire which left the English language with an official role in many post-colonial states; the international financial markets which look to US companies such as Standard and Poor or Moody's for credit ratings. The list could go on. Whatever the reasons, the process is so well advanced that the language now has a critical mass. No amount of policy making to restrict it can stem it nor can any other language challenge it—at least in the short term. In the long term, of course, any language change is possible; history teaches us that language practices change when the political situation changes. However, at the present time it is defensible to say that English has established itself as the *de facto lingua franca* of globalisation in the political, economic, defence, juridical and cultural domains.

Europe and its languages

European integration can be seen as part of the globalising process. Two quite disparate camps worked for its success: a group of visionaries believed the abolition of frontiers could attenuate the harmful nationalisms of Europe that had brought the world two major wars in this century; the business community saw the free movement of capital, people, goods and services as a means to prosperity. The European project can also be presented as an attempt to counter certain aspects of globalisation. Pre-1989, the idea attracted those who thought that a united Europe could provide an alternative to the two power blocs of the cold war. Post-1989, it appeals to those who want to counter US hegemony. In some ways the EU acts as an old-style state; in its commercial relationship with the outside world it continues to try to be protectionist and, although the boundaries between the member states have withered even more rapidly than has happened globally, the barriers between the EU and the outside world are high enough for the term 'Fortress Europe' to have some currency.

The European Union also acts as if it were a state in the political domain, even if it is a polity *sui generis*. It has many of the elements of a state: currency[36] and symbols, a parliament and an electorate,[37] taxes and redistribution of wealth,[38] laws, decided increasingly through majority voting, which take precedence over national law, a judiciary and an embryonic European defence force.[39] Each of these political developments has brought people into contact with each other and established communication needs which have to be met. In this way, Europeanisation resembles globalisation. However, European integration differs radically from the unplanned, piece-meal free market patterns of globalisation in that there is a formal political democratic process that has to be carried out at European level. Democracy needs a shared language. The populations of the fifteen member states which constitute the European electorate cannot constitute the European *demos* if there is no forum in which European public life can be played out in an exchange of views, persuasion and debate. The European Union is often accused of having a democratic deficit[40] and this is usually attributed to the lack of separation of political powers, to an overly secretive and unaccountable bureaucracy and to an executive which is not directly elected. The EU's lack of a democratic forum for debate is not often mentioned, but it is arguably one of the factors that differentiates the EU's political process from traditional democratic practice.

The great problem is, of course, that there is no language in which Europeans could decide to have a Europe-wide debate. The national solution, the imposition of a language top down, would not be tolerated within the Union. The states of the Union would never agree formally to the primacy of the language of one of its members. The founding treaty[41] stated that all the national languages are equal and with each enlargement this position has been maintained.[42] Nonetheless, meaningful citizenship and participation in the democratic life of a polity seem to demand forums for debate. This was one of the strongest arguments used by the governments of nation states as they centralised, imposing the national language at the expense of the idioms of the periphery. The argument that an electorate needs to communicate with itself as well as with the power centre is still valid.

What can be agreed to formally and what happens because of the pragmatic needs of communication are not the same thing. Even in the institutions of the Union, with their army of translators and interpreters, the commitment to a plurilingual regime has broken down under the strain of its complexity. The Commission uses French and English as its working languages; the Parliament and the Council of Ministers use all eleven official languages for formal sessions and key documents, but politicians admit that this rule is abandoned in less formal situations and again French and English dominate;[43] the European courts use French as their working language although the plaintiffs, defendants and witnesses have the right to use their national language. *De facto* French and English have become the *lingua francas* of the European institutions: French because the institutions are situated on French speaking territory and because of the prestige of France as the key founding member; English because of its role as a global *lingua franca*.

The European Union sets up networks, encourages contacts and funds journeys within its boundaries. The motivation for this is various. In some cases it is instrumental, as for example in the belief that transnational research groups funded at EU level are more likely to be able to compete on the global stage. In other cases it is in the service of integration, as in the example of the Socrates and Leonardo programmes through which young Europeans are funded to study and work in another member state. Europeans are now in contact across national borders to a far greater extent than was previously the case. And larger numbers of categories are touched by the phenomenon: small business people, local authority administrators, engineers, agricultural experts, workers in failing industries, workers in the new technologies are just some of the groups who have had EU financial help to meet, exchange ideas and work together. The long term effects of these contacts are likely to contribute to European integration. Anderson demonstrated the power of journeys to build new identities in new polities in his work on nationalism in south-east Asia.[44] It is likely that this process is at work in Europe.

In addition to the effacing of traditional boundaries, the EU has also conceived new ways of grouping Europeans. The Committee of the Regions has attempted to organise Europeans according to a geographical logic, bringing together those from the coastal regions of the Antarctic, the Mediterranean, the Baltic, the North Sea; the regions which share the Alps, the Pyrenees etc. This prompts Europeans to discuss their geographical concerns: climate, agriculture, pollution, fishing etc. and minimises their political differences. How far these contacts and networks will progress is not yet clear, but it is certain that these patterns are causing yet more Europeans to find ways to communicate across language divides. The evidence is necessarily anecdotal, but the incremental weight suggests that English is once again overwhelmingly employed as the language of contact for groups from disparate language backgrounds. Of course, other languages are employed, but none dominate in the same way.

Where clear and verifiable statistics do exist to measure the spread of English is in the various education systems of the member states. Records of who is learning what language show escalation in the number of learners of English at all levels. Where the choice of first foreign language is made at the level of the individual parent or student, decisions reveal that English is perceived at the most useful language to learn. This explains why, at the moment, despite all Commission efforts to promote diversity in foreign language learning through the Socrates and Lingua programmes, the education systems of the Member States are providing tuition in one foreign language to the virtual exclusion of all the others. In the school year 1996–97 89 per cent of all EU secondary school children were reported to be learning English (Eurydice, 1998). This showed an increase on the 1992–93 figure of 88 per cent (Eurydice, 1996), which was itself a jump from the 83 per cent recorded in 1991–92 (Eurostat, 1994). In addition the 1998 report shows that 26 per cent of non-anglophone pupils at primary level are now learning English.[45]

The trend towards English as the first foreign language is illustrated most graphically by the Spanish case. Here there has been a remarkable and unexpected shift from French to English. In 1985–86, 28.5 per cent of Spanish secondary pupils were learning French (reported in Calvet, 1993). The 1998 Eurydice report shows that this figure has now dropped to 8 per cent. This mirrors the rise in English from 71.1 per cent (reported in Calvet, 1993) to over 90 per cent (Eurydice, 1996). Thus, even in the education systems of southern Europe where French was traditionally the first foreign language, English now dominates.

The dominance of English has caused some resentment, particularly among the French where the eclipse of French as the European *lingua franca* has not been welcomed. Initiatives to counter the slide to English within the EU come in large measure from the Francophone community,[46] supported by those who are unhappy at the prospect of boring uniformity. If the global context was not so politically and economically significant, the EU could solve its communication needs by adopting a planned language such as Esperanto which would not advantage one constituent group more than the others. This is most unlikely to happen because the Europeans are not acting in a vacuum; they live in the globalising world in which English has an increasingly important role. However, the EU cannot recognise this formally; the residue of nationalism and inter-state competition makes it difficult to adopt the language of any individual state for general use. And in this case the situation is compounded by the fact that the biggest group of English speakers, the British, remain the least enthusiastic and committed Europeans. So a market led and pragmatic adoption of English as a *lingua franca* is happening against an official commitment to diversity.

The renaissance of 'regional' languages

Before concluding, there is another phenomenon—political and linguistic—that I would like to consider briefly. The success of unificatory nationalist policies has proved to be transient in Europe and a centrifugal force is at work in many states. In every corner of Europe we can find examples: the 1994 Belgian constitution makes Belgium 'a federal state consisting of communities and regions'; a group in Northern Italy calls for an independent Padania; in Central Europe, Czechoslovakia has split into the Czech Republic and Slovakia; further east the Baltic Republics, Ukraine and Belarus have regained their independence; the fissiparous tendencies in the Balkans have dominated the news for nearly a decade. These political situations are disparate and some more advanced than others, but the tendency is clear.

In the case of the three countries, France, the United Kingdom and Spain, which I cited as examples of long established 'nation states' at the beginning of this paper, it is only in France that these strong centrifugal forces are having little effect.[47] In Spain, the 1978 constitution acknowledged the existence of other 'nationalities' (*nacionalidades*) within the one and indivisible spanish 'nation' (*nación*) and the Spanish state decentralised to give significant power to seventeen Autonomous Communities. In three of these, Catalonia, the Basque Country and Galicia, political autonomy was accompanied by the return of the local language to the public domain and as a medium for the political process. In the UK, the Scottish and Welsh voted for devolution in referenda in September 1997 and those the delegates for their assembles in May 1999.[48] In 1998, the Good Friday agreement proposed a solution to 'the Troubles' which would devolve some power to a new Northern Ireland Assembly and set it in a complex powersharing arrangement with both London and Dublin. In Wales, the devolution of political power has also brought about developments on the linguistic front and Welsh is moving into a number of domains from which it had long been banished.[49]

Ultimately, it seems, the nationalist policies for linguistic unification devised in the ministries and cabinet rooms of London and Madrid were unable to eradicate the other languages present on national territory. In the case of Wales and Catalonia in particular, apparent linguistic unity appears to have been as transitory and lightly rooted as political unity. The linguistic renaissance is, of course, a mirror of the relocation of political power. Welsh and Catalan have not simply enjoyed a revival and a reaffirmation of the potency of the language as a badge of identity for the group, they have regained ground because they are the languages of power in the new situation of devolution and autonomy. People do not learn them simply as a way of showing allegiance to an ancestral group; they learn them in an instrumental way to have access to power and economic advantage. Because of this the two languages are likely to continue to expand in terms of number of speakers in the two territories and in terms of domains.

Conclusion: the new medievalism?

Political power is clearly relocating, moving away from its concentration within national government to new loci at subnational and at inter- or supernational levels. A number of scholars[50] have termed this phenomenon the new medievalism, arguing that trends suggest that Europe is returning to a form of political organisation similar to that which existed in medieval Europe, the essential characteristics of which were overlapping authority and divided loyalty. The following quote from Bull encapsulates the argument:

In Western Christendom in the Middle Ages . . . no ruler or state was sovereign in the sense of being supreme over a given territory and a given segment of the Christian population; each had to share authority with vassals below, and with the Pope and (in Germany and Italy) the Holy Roman Emperor above . . . If modern states were to come to share their authority over their citizens, and their ability to command their loyalties, on the one hand with regional and world authorities, and on the other with sub-state or sub-national authorities, to such an extent that the concept of sovereignty ceased to be applicable, then a neo-medieval form of universal political order might be said to have emerged. (Bull, 1977: 254–255 in Held, 1995: 137)

The consequence of such political development would be that the nation state would be weakened as a power base even if it did not disappear. Of course it would be foolish to overstate the case; power may be moving out of the capitals, but we should not exaggerate the extent of the process.[51] The capitals—Madrid, London, Rome, Paris etc.—are still by far the most influential seats of power, even if the periphery, the provincial cities and the regions now have more autonomy and room for action and if the sovereignty of the state has withered in the context of globalisation.

The linguistic consequences of such a new political arrangement, were it to develop further, would be twofold: the first a greater use of a *lingua franca* where power is increasingly exercised at the super- or international level; the second the renaissance of regional languages in the areas which reclaim the right to govern and administer at the local level. Of course we should exercise the same caution here too; the national languages will not disappear although they may cease to play such an exclusive role in the various national spaces. As before language practices are likely to follow political developments. Both linguistically and politically we may need to accustom ourselves to plurality: an acceptance of multi-layered political identities and affiliations and personal bi- or multi-lingualism which will allow us to be actors at all the levels where power is exercised.

Finally, I would like to stress three things. Firstly, I subscribe to no essentialist arguments. Language is a carrier of identity but our language practices can be the carriers of the identities we choose. Renan, in his seminal essay '*Qu'est-ce qu'une langue?*' made the important point that language is inclusive. No-one is predestined to be a member of a language community. In the context of nationalism, enormous numbers accepted language shift in order to join a particular nation. The European project does not require so much; the acquisition of an auxiliary language alongside the language of the smaller community of which one is a member would be enough to allow a European democratic space to develop.

It may well be that the *lingua franca* that could create a *demos* for the European political process and permit networks and information flows among all Europeans, not simply the élite, has already started to exist through the incremental weight of the choices made by individuals. English appears to many to facilitate access to political power, economic advantage and the new information society and they have accepted the pragmatic need to acquire it. It seems rather dishonest to continue with the fiction that the European Union is proudly plurilingual and accords equal place to all its official languages. This has ceased to be true in any but the most formal of settings. Moreover, the large numbers of citizens who have a mother tongue other than the eleven official languages are not overly interested in this support for diversity which excludes them. Accepting that the linguistic competence and skills to survive in and profit from the European project depends primarily on individual initiative seems excessively neo-liberal, but it may be more acceptable than any alternative based on planning and direction which would be viewed as fundamentally undemocratic by European citizens and anathema to their governments. To submit to linguistic market forces may be no less undemocratic but it has the virtue of not being imposed.

Thirdly, I am not *personally* advocating English as this auxiliary language, the *lingua franca* for Europe; I am merely trying to foresee what linguistic effects there may be when the 350,000,000 citizens of the European Union exercise their democratic rights together in one democratic polity, use their rights of freedom of movement and residence within the Member States and travel and meet in the networks and teams fostered by European grants and policies. Since European integration will not occur within a vacuum, globalisation and devolution will also affect how Europeans communicate across boundaries. The causal relationships among these processes will be neither simple nor unidirectional, but, even if we cannot be certain how the situation will eventually stabilise, we can be reasonably sure that new language practices will evolve to facilitate the circulation of information and ideas, the construction of democratic governance and individual access to centres of power. If in the unlikely event that they do not, then language will prove one of the main barriers to European integration. If it continues to lack the community of communication necessary for democratic political development, the EU will find itself halted at the level of a common market administered top down by a patrician technocracy.

Notes

1 For example, the success of the Czechs as consummate lobbyists is usually left unexplored. Benes and the Czechoslovak National Council in Paris and Masaryk in Washington ensured that the Czechs would dominate in the new Czechoslovakian state. The Slovak politicians, less cosmopolitan, less fluent in French and English, less able to foster relations and put their case, were included in the Czech plans. See A. Klima, 'The Czechs', in M. Teich and R. Porter (eds), *The National Question in Europe*, Cambridge: CUP, 1993, and R. Lansing, *The Peace Negotiations: A Personal Narrative*, Boston: Houghton Mifflin, 1921.

2 A. Hirschman, *Exit, Voice and Loyalty*, Cambridge: Harvard University Press.

3 The EU supports 'unity in diversity'. All the official languages of the Member States are also official languages of the Community (Article 217 of the EEC Treaty). See below. All treaties and laws are published in all languages. Within the institutions all the official national languages are also working languages, although this may be more theory than practice. The Treaty on European Union (1992) included the protection of cultural diversity in its preamble.

4 There are many dialects in both Germany and Italy, but they all come from a single dialect continuum in each case, with the exception of very small communities of Greek speakers and Croatian speakers in the Italian state, and Sorb speakers in the German state.

5 These three countries are not nation states in the strict sense of the word—a polity with a cohesive population in terms of tradition, language and culture. There are, of course, very few states where this rigorous definition applies.

6 For a discussion of this see L. Greenfeld, *Nationalism—Five roads to modernity*, Cambridge, Mass.: Harvard University Press, 1992.

7 :Louis XIV, Louis XV and Napoleon I were eager to secure geographical frontiers. L'Abbé Grégoire's report on the Alps gives the French view (Abbé de Grégoire, *Rapport présenté à la Convention nationale au nom des Commissaires envoyés par elle pour organiser les départements du Mont-blanc et des Alpes maritimes*, Nice: Cougnet, 1793).

8 French historians treat the conquest of Clovis and Charlemagne as the founding events of the French nation (F. Braudel, *L'identité de la France*, Paris: Loisirs, 1986; G. Duby, *Le Moyen Age*, Paris: Hachette, 1987, etc.). However, the political conditions of neither the sixth nor the ninth centuries would allow continued control and administration of the territories conquered, and most gains were swiftly lost in further conflict. It seems more defensible to date the creation of the present French state to the successes of the Capetian monarchy from the thirteenth century onwards. Philipps-Auguste defeated a coalition of northern barons and neighbouring kings at Bouvines in 1214 and a coalition of southern nobles and princes at Muret in 1213. The defeat of the Anglo-Normans at the end of the 100 Years War secured the south west. The border was drawn along the

Pyrenees in the treaty ending the Franco-Spanish war (1659). Provence became French after the death of its count, le bon roi René, with no direct heir. Corsica was acquired from Genoa in 1768. Nice and Savoy were ceded in exchange for France's help in the unification of Italy. Brittany came into the state by marriage at the end of the fifteenth century. The northern and eastern frontiers were extended by campaigns during the reigns of Louis XIV (1648 Alsace; 1667–8 Flanders; 1672–8 Franche-Comté; 1681 Strasbourg) and Louis XV (1766 Lorraine), although much had to be ceded to the Prussians in 1871 after the French defeat in the Franco-Prussian war.

9 Wales was conquered by Edward I (1277–84). Henry VIII attached it formally to the English state by the statutes of 1536 and 1542. Scotland and England fought several wars in the twelfth century ending in the Treaty of Northampton 1328 which recognised Scottish independence. James VI of Scotland inherited the English throne on the death of Elizabeth I in 1603. This was a union of states without a union of laws which did not come until the two countries were joined by the Act of Union in 1707, a step which ensured the centralisation of the United Kingdom and the dominance of London (C. Russell, 'Composite monarchies in early modern Europe', in A. Grant and K. Stringer (eds), *Uniting the Kingdom*, London: Routledge, 1995). The English had attempted to take Ireland from the eleventh century onwards, only achieving the complete conquest of the island in the sixteenth century. In the late nineteenth century and early twentieth century the Irish independence movement grew in strength. After several years of war Ireland was partitioned: the south gained independence; the north remained part of the United Kingdom. Other small islands in the area are also part of the UK: Scilly Isles, Channel Islands, Isle of Man.

10 The Moors (an Arab/Berber force) conquered the Iberian peninsula except for the northern provinces in 611–14. In 1212, Pedro II of Barcelona launched the Reconquista. It took until 1492 and the fall of Grenada for the 'reconquest' to be complete. Spain in its present form dates from the alliance through marriage of Aragon (which included Catalonia) and Castile. Charles V completed the unification of Spain which then included Portugal. Spain was an absolute monarchy, whose king also held the title of Holy Roman Emperor and which was the first of the European colonising powers.

11 See C. Clausewitz, *On War*, Hertfordshire: Wordsworth, 1997, for a discussion of the concept of loyalty and total war.

12 The personal multilingualism is apparent from the biographies of key Crusaders. See, for example, J.-L. Déjean, *Les Comtes de Toulouse*, Paris: Fayard, 1988. The *lingua franca* tended to be sabir rather than Latin, a pidgin produced by the Romance languages in contact with Arabic.

13 J. Richard, 'L'Ecole et les dialectes', in E. Berthert, *et al.* (ed.), *Langue dominante, Langues dominées*, Paris: Edilio, 1982; D. Ager, *Identity, Insecurity and Image: France and Language*, Clevedon: Multilingual Matters, 1999.

14 Ibid.

15 And beyond. See A. Sauvageot, *Français d'hier ou français de demain*, Paris: Nathan, 1978, for a discussion of knowledge of French at the Ottoman court and P. Rickard, *A History of the French Language*, London: Hutchinson, 1974, for a discussion of the acceptance of French as the language of international diplomacy in the eighteenth century.

16 In the language census he undertook in 1792 the Abbé Grégoire established that less than a third of the population spoke French or even had some understanding

of it. Abbé de Grégoire, *Rapport sur la nécessité et les moyens d'anéantir le patois, et d'universaliser l'usage de la langue française*, Paris: Instruction publique, 1794.

17 B. Barère, quoted in Lodge, op. cit., p. 215.

18 Education became free, secular and obligatory in France in 1881 and 1882.

19 Breton, Flemish, dialects of German, dialects of Occitan, Franco-Provençal, Bacque, Catalan, Corsican.

20 See D. Conversi, *The Basques, the Catalans and Spain*, London: Hurst, 1997 and M. Strubell, 'Language, Democracy and Devolution in Catalonia', in *Current Issues in Language and Society*, vol. 5, no. 3, 1998, for a discussion of this in the context of Catalonia under Franco.

21 See A. Lodge, *French: from dialect to standard*, London: Routledge, 1993.

22 For a discussion of language as social control see M. Foucault, *Discipline and Punish: the birth of the prison*, London: Allen Lane, 1997 (trs Sheridan).

23 B. Anderson, *Imagined Communities*, London: Verso, 1983.

24 See E. Gellner, *Nations and Nationalism*, Oxford: Blackwell, 1983, for a discussion of this.

25 This point is more nuanced for Spain since Catalan played a role as language of education in some periods. The point holds for the Basque country. Basque élites were mostly literate in Spanish. See Conversi, op. cit.

26 Smaller states have always been forced to come to terms with bilingualism in the need to communicate across borders, since they were too small in economic terms to survive as self-sufficient units. The Netherlands, as a small trading nation has always had a proportion of citizens whose linguistic repertoire was more than the national language.

27 The Treaty of Versailles also set out to punish the defeated. Mostly this coincided with Woodrow Wilson's 14 principles. Where it did not, it overruled them. Thus Hungarian-speakers were incorporated into Romania and Czechoslovakia. In Hobsbawm's assessment 'the new succession states, whether carved out of Russia or the Habsburg Empire, were no less multinational than their predecessors' (E. Hobsbawm, *Age of Extremes*, London: Abacus, 1995, p. 33).

28 For a discussion of the treatment of the minority languages of France see G. Vermes, *Vingt-cinq Communautés françaises*, Paris: L'Harmattan, 1988. For the Celtic languages and the British government see W. Ferguson, *The Identity of the Scottish Nation*, Edinburgh: Edinburgh University Press, 1998; D. Sharp, *Language in Bilingual Communities*, London: Edward Arnold, 1973, etc. For the Spanish situation see Conversi, op. cit., Strubell, op. cit. The French Republics achieved the most complete success. From a situation in the 1790s where only a third (at best) of the population spoke French, there is now a very high level of linguistic cohesion in the state and none of the other languages of France has any official role in the public domain. In the United Kingdom, the rigorous attempt to eradicate the Celtic languages has resulted in the disappearance of Cornish and Manx, Gaelic is in regression. Welsh, however, survived and is now in a period of expansion. In Spain, the efforts of Madrid to root out Basque, Galician and Catalan—whether under the monarchy or the Franco dictatorship, were singularly unsuccessful. During the repression the languages retreated into the private domain, remaining a symbol of resistance and resurfacing to become official languages in three Autonomies under the new Constitution.

29 A point of view expressed by A. Milward, *The European Rescue of the Nation-State*, London: Routledge, 1994 and A. Amin and J. Tomaney, *Behind the Myth of the European Union*, London: Routledge, 1995.

30 The year of writing (1998–99) witnessed the US and a number of European states bombing Serbia to stop Serbian military action in Kosovo, a province recognised as within Serbian state borders; the US and the UK bombed Iraq in order to force it to comply with the demands of the UN weapons' inspectorate to investigate freely within the country.

31 The will of the international community is dominated by the biggest states, which means of course that it is not international in the pure sense. Moreover, the most powerful states can ignore international pressures. However, this does not invalidate the argument that national boundaries are generally breaking down.

32 In 1999 there was a world wide debate over whether General Pinochet could be tried by the international community for crimes committed within Chile.

33 For example, the governments of China and Singapore have both tried to limit the information supplied by the Internet. The Internet was developed by the US military to survive attack in the Cold War and so is multi-centred and non-hierarchical. This makes it almost impossible to control. Satellite TV is also difficult to regulate since signals cannot be easily jammed.

34 For a full discussion of these strategies see S. Wright, *Community and Communication*, Multilingual Matters, in press.

35 See D. Ager, op. cit. for a full discussion of events and attitudes in France.

36 From 1 January 1999 eleven EU member states shared a currency.

37 The EU has a parliament; citizens can vote in local and European elections wherever they are resident.

38 The EU collects taxes directly and indirectly and redistributes wealth to aid its weaker regions and sectors through its structural funds, the European Regional Development Fund and the Social Development Fund, through the Cohesion Fund and through the Common Agricultural Policy.

39 In the Amsterdam Treaty, the EU considered the establishment of common defence and foreign affairs policies, which would extend the various bi- and multilateral initiatives which already exist. See H. Wallace and W. Wallace (eds), *Policy-making in the European Union*, Oxford University Press, 1996; J. Peterson and H. Sjursen (eds), *A Common Foreign Policy for Europe*, London: Routledge, 1998n for further discussion.

40 In both the academic literature, eg R. Bellamy, V. Bufacchi and D. Castiglione, *Democracy and Constitutional Culture*, Lothian Foundation Press, 1995, and the media eg *The Guardian*, 30/07/1993, 'A democratic deficit but don't tell the people: interview with Mark Jorna'.

41 The basic text concerning the use of language in the institutions of the EU is Article 217 of the EEC which made the language regime of the Community the affair of the Council 'acting unanimously'. Under this article, the Council adopted Regulation No. 1 on 15 April 1958 which made the official national languages of the Member States the official languages of the EEC. This resulted in four official languages (French, Dutch, German and Italian).

42 Following the accession of Denmark, the UK, Ireland, Spain, Portugal, Greece, Finland, Sweden and Austria, there are now eleven official languages. An official language must be the language of the state as a whole, and so Catalan has been refused official language status.

43 For details of how this has happened see N. Labrie, *La construction linguistique de la Communauté européenne*, Genève: Champion, 1993; S. Wright, 'Language policy and planning in Europe', *Language Teaching*, July 1995, pp. 148–160 and

M. Schlossmacher, 'Die Arbeitssprachen in den Organen der Europäishen Gemeindschaft', *Sociolinguistica*, 8, 1994, pp. 101–122.

44 B. Anderson, op. cit.

45 The dominance of English is strongest in the countries in the Germanic continuum/in the north of the continent. The 1992–93 figures show that 100% of Swedish secondary school children were learning English. The figure was over 90% in Denmark, Germany and Finland, over 80% in the Netherlands and Austria. The percentages fell to 71% in Belgium, 66% in Italy and Luxembourg, 64% in Greece and 52% in Portugal. From the southern, Romance continuum, only Spain and France reported that more than 90% of their secondary pupils were learning English. In the primary sector Finland led the English-learning league with 64% of pupils with Spain second at 63% (Eurydice, 1998). The Eurydice report noting the dominance of English remarks that: 'The other official languages of the EU feature less in the curriculum and are selected less often by pupils' (Eurydice, 1998).

French is the only real rival for English, with 32% of non-Francophone EU secondary school pupils learning it in 1996–97 (Eurydice, 1998). This percentage has remained constant since 1992–93. The statistics break down as follows: Luxembourg 100% of secondary school children learn French, as do 98% of Dutch-speaking Belgians, 70% of Irish pupils, 44% of Greek and 44% of Portuguese. No data was available from the UK for that year.

In only four countries were there significant numbers learning German: Denmark 67%, Luxembourg 100%, Dutch 61% and Sweden 42%. Only the French had a significant number of secondary school pupils learning Spanish (29%) (Eurydice, 1996).

46 For the polemical debate on this see D. Noguez, *La colonisation douce*, Paris: Rocher, 1991; C. Hagège, *le français et les siècles*, Paris: Odile Jacob, 1987; E. Venouvrier, *Naître en français*, Paris: Larousse, 1986; G. de Broglie, *Le français pour qu'il vive*, Paris: Gallimard, 1986.

47 Although even here there are some small groups agitating for devolution/autonomy/independence in Corsica, the French Basque Country and Brittany.

48 This development came in the wake of the 1997 Labour victory. The previous Conservative government had presided over a period of intense centralisation.

49 For full details see S. Wright, 'The renaissance of Catalan and Welsh: political causes and effects', in K. de Bot, S. Kroon, P. Nelde and H. van de Velde (eds), *Contributions to a Language Policy*, Nederlandse Taalunie, forthcoming.

50 H. Bull, *The Anarchical Society: a study of order in world politics*, London: Macmillan, 1977; D. Held, *Democracy and the Global Order*, Cambridge: Polity Press, 1995; T. McGrew, 'A Global Society', in S. Hall, D. Held and T. McGrew (eds), *Modernity and its Futures*, Cambridge: polity Press, 1992; P. Schlesinger, 'Europeanness: a new cultural battlefield?', in *Innovation*, 5/1, 1992, pp. 12–22 and W. Wallace, *The Transformation of Western Europe*, London: Pinter, 1990.

51 A. Milward, op. cit.

Third country nationals as European citizens: the case defended

Andreas Føllesdal

Abstract

The Amsterdam Treaty bolsters Union citizenship in order to bring the European Union closer to the citizens of Europe.[1] Inadvertently, this strategy gives citizens of non-EU states an inferior status in the European Union, even though they may be semi-permanent residents in a Member State. Union citizenship increases the social and political exclusion of third country nationals, in violation of the basic democratic principle that those affected by social institutions should also enjoy political levers of influence. This chapter first briefly sketches a Liberal Contractualist defence for awarding this group full citizenship in the relevant Member State, arguing in particular for three somewhat contested issues: that third country nationals should not only enjoy Union citizenship, but also be given national citizenship in the Member State of residence; that Member States may impose conditions, oaths etc. on such prospective citizens; and that Member States may withhold some privileges from those resident third country nationals who refuse to be naturalised. The chapter goes on to present and discuss, only to dismiss, the most plausible arguments offered in defence of current practice within the context of a Europe of open borders for Member State citizens. These arguments seek to deny citizenship to third country nationals in order to: protect national and locally endorsed values ensuring social homogeneity of the community; exclude people with non-liberal values; ensure commitment to a shared future which warrants democratic rights in the first place; avoid instability caused by citizens with conflicting multiple loyalties; ensure and foster the ideal of active political participation, impossible for dual citizens; and avoid backlash problems among current EU citizens which threaten the stability of welfare policies of member States and the EU.

Introduction

When asking 'whose Europe?', 10 million inhabitants are not part of the answer. They are 'third country nationals': nationals of non-EU states, residing lawfully in the EU. They have no right to move within the Union, nor can they vote in municipal or European Parliamentary elections, unlike citizens of Member States who also enjoy 'Union citizenship'. Ironically, 'Union citizenship' was established with the aim of bringing the Union closer to its citizens. But by putting citizens first, Union citizenship treats these third country nationals as second class.

The European Union Migrants' Forum puts the challenge eloquently: 'the present situation undermines the Union's expressed commitment to the elimination of racial discrimination, racism and xenophobia, and the integration of settled migrants.' Discrimination and xenophobia is evidenced by the hesitant response to such new categories as 'Islamic Europeans', and more urgently, racially motivated attacks on 'guest workers' in many Member States. What it is to be a European must be reconsidered.

Third country nationals, nearly three per cent of the EU population (Eurostat, 1998), must be part of the answer to the question 'whose Europe?' This is in line with the European Commission, which recognises that 'integration policies must be directed in a meaningful way towards improving the situation of third country nationals legally resident within the Union by taking steps which will go further towards strengthening their rights relative to those citizens of the member states' (1994).

The important question is how third country nationals should be included. This chapter defends the position that third country nationals must be offered citizenship in their country of residence. These countries include Germany, which hosts many from Central European countries and from Turkey; France with large Moroccan and Algerian populations; as well as the Netherlands, Belgium and the United Kingdom. The liberalisation of naturalisation criteria recently announced in Germany is an example to be applauded. The solution of offering Union citizenship is not enough, as this citizenship supervenes on citizenship proper, and is not enough to ensure the standing of third country nationals as equals.

Section 1 provides a brief historical overview, focussing on the upshot of the Amsterdam Treaty. Section 2 focuses on the normative case for citizenship generally. Section 3 presents the normative case for a particular treatment of third country nationals. Three somewhat contested issues are addressed. Third country nationals should not only enjoy Union citizenship, but also be given national citizenship in the Member State of residence. Member States may impose conditions such as oaths on such prospective citizens. Thirdly, Member State may withhold some privileges from those resident third country nationals who refuse to be naturalised. Section 4 considers and rebuts objections to this position.

Historical backdrop and the outcome of Amsterdam

Union citizenship is a bundle of legal rights and powers, most prominently including the right to move and reside freely within the Member States, the right to vote and run in European Parliament elections from the country of residence, and to run for and vote in municipal elections where one resides (Art. 8).

Three reasons are often cited in favour of Union citizenship: the perceived need to facilitate free movement, first for workers, by removing the negative effects of being foreigners (Preuss, 1996: 139); the need to foster some sense of European identity; and the need to cultivate a shared sense of the normative legitimacy of the European order, as consistent with central norms and ideals of European democracies.

The Amsterdam Treaty (Art. 81) furthers these aims by awarding individuals rights and powers over Community institutions, thus fostering trans-border options and interdependencies (Preuss, 1995: 280; Breton, 1995; Laffan, 1996: 97; Guild, 1996). By its choice of the term 'citizenship' the Treaty clearly joins the tradition of state building, where civil, economic and social citizenship has been used to further perceived legitimacy (Closa, 1992; Welsh, 1993; Mouffe, 1992: 17).

The Amsterdam Treaty makes efforts on several fronts to further these goals. It seeks to reduce the so-called 'democratic deficit' by increasing the powers of the European Parliament; it strengthens the rule of law in granting the European Court of Justice jurisdiction over Art. F(2) TEU regarding compliance with the European Convention for the protection of Human Rights. And the Amsterdam Treaty seeks to increase citizens' opportunities for comprehension and control of Union institutions, thus bolstering the significance of European citizenship (for overviews cf Nentwich and Falkner, 1997; Petit, 1998).

Several of these measures seek to enhance stability and compliance among citizens. However, these measures also threaten long-term stability, since third country nationals are ignored. EU law solidifies the cleavage between European voters and the non-European, non-voting residents of the EU (Weil, 1996). The perceived need is to build shared interests, identity and support among Member State citizens. Therefore the scope of persons accorded Union citizenship is not expanded: Article 8 was only changed to stress that 'Citizenship of the Union shall complement and not replace national citizenship'. Several proposals for reform have been suggested (Wiener, 1997; Kostakopoulou, 1997: 16–18), exploring and expanding the notion of citizenship in different ways.

The general case for citizenship

Citizenship is important and widely held in democracies, and rights of political participation are in the core of powers it accords. This is one of the main reasons why the Amsterdam Treaty relies on the concept of Union citizenship. Citizenship is a practice which regulates the relationship of individuals to the bodies of governance to which they are subject. The bundles of rules which shape such practices of citizenship specify the powers, liabilities, rights and immunities which hold between the two. Citizens should enjoy roughly equal institutionalised influence over policy formulation and implementation.

The normative justification of these political rights rests on two normative claims as found eg within the tradition of liberal contractualism (John Rawls, 1971; Charles Beitz, 1989). Firstly, a commitment to equal respect requires that social institutions can be justified in in terms of their effects on all affected parties—on citizens and non-citizens alike.

Secondly, one of our important interests is to influence the institutions and culture which in turn shape us. The value of this interest is paramount within modern states, where some individuals enjoy centralised control over the basic institutional frameworks under central control, and where, historically, the social institutions have been inescapable.

The focus on formal rights in this chapter should not be taken to deny importance of belonging and 'access' (see Wiener and Della Sala, 1997). Rather, rights are important background conditions which frame individuals' perceptions of belonging and opportunities for common projects and future.

The political rights of citizenship gives expression to the general norm that those affected by the use of public power should also be in a position to influence that use. Moreover, as persons equally worthy of respect, the individuals subject to public rule should also have an equal say in how they should be ruled. Without such political rights, individuals remain subjects.

With increased migration and exit options the value for individuals of such controls might be on the wane. However, the condition of permanently resident non-nationals point to a fundamental inconsistency in current citizenship practice both within many states and within the European Union as a whole (Bauböck, 1994: 220; Meehan, 1993).

The inconsistency between practice and central liberal values may be regarded as most obvious relative to universal human rights norms (Soysal, 1994: 159, 1996: 18), or relative to national norms and practices of membership (Carens, 1989). Either way, the commitment to equal respect, combined with a recognition of the pervasive impact of social institutions, is incompatible with the current legal status of third country nationals of the European Union.

Third country nationals enjoy human rights protections within each Member State and often enjoy local voting rights as a matter of national legislation. Yet they are not included in the scope of individuals acknowledged as full Union Citizens by the treaties of the Union—while they are often as profoundly affected by the European political order as any Member State citizens. Invisible in the eyes of the European polity, they are socially dead in the political order of the European Union.[2]

Some details in the normative case

Permanent resident non-European nationals are drastically affected by the institutions they live under, yet they are not allowed to influence the institutions through voting rights. They are a class of permanent residents in the European Union prevented from obtaining equal legal status as other permanent inhabitants—a position which is in no way reconcilable with the liberal contractualist commitment to equal respect.

The policy regarding third country nationals that I wish to defend shares with several others an insistence that legal long-time residents should have the right of optional naturalisation to become national citizens—and hence Union citizens—under certain conditions, eg along the lines of US practice (Hammar, 1990; Walzer, 1981, 1983; Carens, 1989; Bauböck, 1997).[3] However, it has some features which distinguish it from some other suggested alternatives. Three aspects require some attention before considering objections to such practices.

Union citizenship and national citizenship

Only a combination of national and Union citizenship provides individuals with satisfactory control over the social conditions which shape their lives. Permanent residents must therefore be offered the same combination of citizenships. This is because both national citizenship and Union citizenship will endure, as underscored by Article 8(1) of the Treaty on European Union: 'Citizenship of the Union shall complement and not replace national citizenship.'

To be sure, Union citizenship may gradually replace the emotional, legal and cultural significance of national citizenship—for better or worse. It may lead to an organic European identity (Weiler and Mayer, 1995: 15; Weiler, 1996), and may prevent harmonisation of national traditions (Bauböck, 1997). Until then, both national and Union citizenship must be available to third country nationals.

The European Migrants' Forum has argued otherwise. They have maintained that extending Union citizenship 'to lawfully resident third country nationals would provide true equality of treatment in the fundamental areas of application of Community law' (1996). Their view partly stems from the realisation that naturalisation to Member States may be politically more difficult. However, the recent liberalisation in Germany indicates that policies may change. And providing third country nationals with Union citizenship is simply not enough, as long as that bundle of powers is designed to supplement Member State citizenship.

Member states may impose conditions such as oaths

The case for granting political rights rests on two assumptions: that the resident alien intends to remain in the territory over a long period, and that she shares a commitment to a limited and specifiable set of civic values. These values include democratic decision-making and 'constitutional patriotism', regarded as general compliance with and endorsement of certain procedural principles (Habermas, 1992).

Liberal contractualism allows a state to require not only a commitment to formal decision-making procedures, but also a commitment to substantive principles of distributive justice for the European polity (Føllesdal, 1997). Thus it may be reasonable to ask prospective citizens to give public expression to their willingness to be guided by their sense of justice: compliance with law and furtherance of the common good as they see it, where appropriate. Thus oaths of allegiance, or other evidence of socialisation may be in order. France, for instance, requires a five-year residence, and knowledge of the French language (Weil, 1996: 76). Germany requires a 'commitment' to German culture as well as knowledge of the language (Fulbrook, 1996: 94). But details of the common weal are contested, so for this reason oaths promising to further the interests of the new nation state should be relatively vague. The reason why it may be legitimate to require such an oath, is that resident aliens may not have been socialised into the requisite sense of justice, while for those born in the territory, such socialisation presumably occurs through schools and civic society.

In light of the need for indicators of socialisation, it seems insufficient to award citizenship on the basis of domicile alone, as Kostakopoulou has maintained (1997: 9). The difference is background between resident aliens and others would warrant oaths, some evidence of good character and the like, eg as discussed by O'Keefe (1994: 105, criticised by Kostakopoulou, 1997). Insofar as such conditions can be justified on the basis of relevant differences regarding the likely socialisation, these conditions cannot be dismissed as expressing qualified respect.

A commitment on behalf of third country nationals to remain in the territory, however, seems unwarranted. We must bear in mind that with free movement this is not a condition generally expected of other citizens of Member States. Satisfactory blocks against serial and opportunistic changes in citizenship—by resident aliens as well as others—may still be appropriate.

Member States may withhold some privileges from those able but unwilling to be naturalised

From the perspective of liberal contractualism it may be accepted that Member States withhold some privileges, such as political rights tied to national parliaments, from those resident third country nationals who refuse to be naturalised.

Rainer Bauböck (1994) appears to hold a different view, namely that all foreigners should enjoy all political rights as soon as they satisfy residence requirements (227). Choosing naturalisation, then, has virtually no legal implications, though it has important symbolic significance. The basis for Bauböck's view is a particular conception of consent taken to be central to contractualist views. The concern seems to be that foreigners should not be faced with a choice between giving up their existing citizenship which provides meaning to their life project, and on the other hand living their lives as aliens under social institutions beyond their influence. Too much is at stake either way. It is not clear why these alternatives place individuals in a bind which makes choice among them illegitimate— in particular given the plausibility of insisting that those who have power to control the shaping of common institutions and policies must be committed (in some modest way) to a common national weal and future.

Objections considered

This part of the chapter presents and discusses, only to dismiss, the most plausible arguments offered against allowing third country nationals to become citizens, within the context of a Europe of open borders for Member State citizens.

Protect national and locally endorsed values ensuring social homogeneity of the community

Existing common values, culture or mores are sometimes claimed to be worth maintaining 'for their own sake', and including resident aliens as full citizens is regarded as a threat to the maintenance of such national cultural homogeneity (Woodward, 1992: 82). Similar arguments may be offered against permitting third country nationals into the community of European states, which are alleged to

111

share certain liberal, democratic or Christian values incompatible with the values of the third country nationals.

As a blanket justification for excluding third country nationals such 'communitarian' arguments are open to three general charges: two empirical, and one normative. Firstly, the empirical claim that there is, in each state, exactly one dominant set of norms and values which is generally held and accepted, and which includes norms of exclusion of others, seems dubious to say the least—and even more so at the European level. Individuals within a Member State hold competing conceptions of the good, each of which is often internally inconsistent. Moreover, many of these conceptions, as well as the dominant cultures in such democracies, are committed to human rights, including norms of toleration of cultural variation.

Secondly, let's assume for the sake of the argument that diversity among inhabitants might become a threat to internal homogeneity. It still seems blatantly implausible to hold that letting third country nationals enjoy voting rights poses such a risk, while intra-EU mobility of persons, which is accepted by all Member States, is no reason for concern. The EU Member States already include many citizens of non-Christian faiths, and respect for religious minorities within European states has been embedded—at least in principle— since the Peace of Westphalia. Thus, third country nationals with non-Christian or otherwise different world views do not signal anything completely new, but rather draw attention to some pre-existing tensions in the liberal heritage of Europe.

The third, normative objection is that cultural homogeneity or survival of a culture in the abstract cannot plausibly be granted much value in arguments about a just political order maintained by force. This is not because liberalism in general dismisses culture, understood as shared practices, values or beliefs. Such an interpretation seems blatantly at odds with much recent liberal thought (including Rawls, 1998; Macedo, 1990; Gutmann, 1985; Buchanan, 1989; Føllesdal, 1998). The point is instead that liberal contractualism is committed to normative individualism—that it is only interests of individuals which can form the basis for claims on such issues. Relevant interests can, of course, include interests in joint projects, and in developing interests in interaction with others— there is no atomistic inclination in this view (contrary to criticism by, eg Taylor, 1979). Maintaining cultural homogeneity must thus be defended in terms of its importance for individuals. Why, then, is culture important? Culture, understood as the background pattern of practices and beliefs, makes life projects possible and worthwhile, and enables us to form and pursue expectations. Citizenship rights and duties are aspects of some such practices. A plausible case against abrupt institutional and cultural change can be made on the basis of our interest in controlling cultural change to maintain legitimate expectations, and thus give meaning to our life (Barry, 1991).

This should lead us to agree that knowledge of local culture and traditions is important because changes must accommodate expectations built on such existing practices. But this hardly suffices to rule out all claims of others which may lead to cultural and institutional changes over time (Føllesdal, 1996). Furthermore, the normative standing of an existing culture depends on whether its substantive content satisfies certain minimum standards of legitimacy.

It seems incompatible with liberal contractualism to require of one another more than a commitment to shared civic values and a sense of justice—to comply with and further just institutions, domestically and at the European level. Commitment to the 'national culture' or 'the European social model', specified as an extensive set of social rights, would be too strict and controversial a condition to impose (Wiener and Della Sala, 1997: 610), attractive as it might seem from the Liberal Contractualist perspective (Føllesdal, 1997). Moreover, no shared culture can be protected against all democratically induced change.

We move on, therefore, to consider two arguments offered in favour of maintaining a more circumscribed domain of existing culture and institutions, based on the need for social stability.

Exclude people with non-liberal views

Immigration is sometimes regarded as a threat to stability. Reasons of national security would warrant the exclusion of subversives who reject the fundamental political virtues and social solidarity characteristic of Western democracies. This worry may fuel the unease in many Member States about Islamic resident aliens, reminiscent of the scepticism facing Jews and Catholics in 18th- and 19th-century England (Cesarani, 1996: 60), and in many conflicts in Europe since.

The need for general compliance with legitimate social institutions seems unobjectionable, as is the need for broad acceptance of a limited set of civic virtues such as commitment to democratic procedures for conflict resolution, respect for the rule of law and the law of the land, compliance with human rights norms, and a sense of justice. Some such condition is compatible with liberal contractualism (Macedo, 1990)—contrary to communitarian critics who at times doubt that liberals can insist on the need for any broadly shared values or commitment (Mulhall and Swift, 1996; Føllesdal, 1998). But the liberal contractualist view insists that the set of such shared goals is strictly limited.

We should also bear the dynamic aspects of EU legislation in mind: the requisite shared commitments to the common goals of the state and the EU are likely to develop and be shaped by the institutions and policies (Preuss, 1995: 277–78).

It is difficult to see how this legitimate concern should lead us to deny citizenship rights to third country nationals in the EU. They have lived in a Member State for a long period of time, during which presumably any serious contempt for fundamental values is uncovered; they may be required to take an oath of upholding civic values, and their children will presumably also be socialised into the proper civil values. It is therefore unclear why third country nationals seeking citizenship should be regarded as more of a threat to public order and stability than other foreigners—such as intra-EU migrants.

Moreover, as Carens notes, such restrictions would only apply if there was a real danger that the political order would be threatened—were a critical mass of non-liberal minded individuals likely to form (Carens, 1992: 29).

A final observation regarding this objection concerns the alleged 'clash of cultures' sometimes assumed, for instance when tensions are suggested between Islamic and Christian world views. There are shared values across 'civilisations', and disagreements within them, sufficient to question whether conflicts about human rights, democracy or liberalism are due to a 'Clash of Civilizations' (*pace* Huntington, 1996). Some deplorable Western traditions have dismissed human rights well into this century, and there are strands and components of theories of human rights in many non-western normative traditions. For instance, a long-standing and broadly shared view on the responsible use of state power is that it must be used for the common good, understood as the good of present and future individual members of society. Such accounts are found in the Western natural law tradition (Finnis, 1980: 168), but similar strands were also developed by the Islamic philosophers Ibn Abi-al-Rabi (9th century), Al-Farabi and Ibn Khaldun (1332–1406) (see Ahmad, 1965; An-Na'im, 1990).

Ensure commitment to shared future

Some have argued that members of a political system must have not only ethnic and civil attachments to the community, but a long term commitment (discussed by Laffan, 1996: 89–90). Transient workers lack this commitment, and should therefore not enjoy political rights.

A charitable interpretation and elaboration of this objection may point to the preconditions justifying democratic rule in the first place: that those permanently affected by social institutions should also be able to influence them according to their conception of the common good and sense of justice. Insofar as some individuals are transient residents, they are unlikely to be subject to the rules they impose on others. Thus their claim to a share of power is likely to be unjustified. Here what is problematic is transience, rather than the lack of shared values.

This argument does not hold in particular against third country nationals. Transience and divergent culture are not characteristics unique to them. Citizenship rights may well be extended conditional on renunciation of other citizenships, and a common policy of denying repatriation may also be introduced, to prevent serial citizenships. Moreover, citizenship may well be offered after a period of residence, possibly with a knowledge test, to ensure some acquaintance with the culture of the Member State.

Rainer Bauböck holds otherwise, that individuals may well be so tied to their country of origin that it is unfair to require such renunciation in order to obtain political rights in the new country. The contractualist approach developed here, however, suggests that this interest cannot reasonably be said to override the competing interest of citizens of the receiving country, to be assured that those sharing political power are wielding that power for the common good. We should also bear in mind that many naturalised immigrants may pursue projects tied to their old national identity regardless of whether they maintain that legal citizenship.

Moreover, these considerations cannot be decisive. Within a state, citizens typically enjoy local voting rights regardless of whether they intend to stay in a municipality during the rest of their life, thus permanence and shared values do not always seem to be relevant. Similarly, intra-EU citizens enjoy rights of free movement and Union citizenship rights, without regard to permanence and shared values. Mutual commitment and shared future hardly seems plausible for this group, yet intra-EU movement is an intended effect of much EU legislation. This aspect of Europeanisation indeed challenges traditional democratic theory: how can we ensure that the electorate apply the proper long-term perspective on voting, when we can no longer assume that the electorate themselves will be affected by these laws? Increased travel between Member States may suggest that decisions should not be made at the local level, but rather at the level within which travel is likely. Be this as it may, the exclusion of third country nationals from citizenship rights seems arbitrary.

Another interpretation of this argument may hold that third country nationals lack the requisite affective attachments with the European polity and its inhabitants. However, this interpretation rests on several contested assumptions about 1) the legitimate role of such attachments as a condition for political rights, since only a 'thinner' commitment to civic virtues and justice is appropriate as a condition for citizenship; 2) the need for such attachments among Europeans in the future; and 3) whether immigrants—and their children—are less likely to foster such attachments than are others.

Avoid conflicting loyalties

Third country nationals who become citizens of a Member State may experience dilemmas of multiple loyalties, since they can hardly be expected to abolish old ties and cultural values.

Some writers actually regard the possibilities for multiple political membership as positive. Thus Meehan notes that Union citizenship offers us 'the opportunity to act on the fact that we have more identities than our nationality' (Meehan, 1993: 155). However, others recognise that non-exclusive political memberships create dilemmas (Weiler, 1995: 219; discussed by Shaw, 1997). But note that such dilemmas are not unique to third country nationals: similar dilemmas occur for resident aliens who enjoy voting rights in municipal elections—as is the case for all resident aliens in the Netherlands, Austria, Sweden, Denmark and elsewhere. Moreover, related challenges occur for all citizens of Member States, since they must juggle Member State citizenship and Union citizenship.

In what sense is dual citizenship a threat to state sovereignty? Rainer Bauböck points to four objections to multiple citizenship: conflicting loyalties, incompatibility of legal norms, evasion of citizen duties, and diminishing of citizen rights (Bauböck, 1997: section 1:3). However, it would appear that conflicting loyalties and incompatible legislation, as well as loopholes leading to evasion, can be regulated and avoided through better co-ordination among states and clarification of the powers of the EU. These tasks must be performed in any case, and solutions may well suit the plight of third country nationals as well. The general public may fear third country nationals' instability less if the most glaring dilemmas are removed, and once there are measures which ensure against serial citizenship.

Foster active political participation

A related objection focuses on the difficulty of being politically active in more than one political community. This drawback is lamented from the point of view of some civic republicans—who would also criticise the statement of Union citizenship for exclusively focussing on rights and ignoring citizenship duties.[4]

In response, note that granting citizenship in a Member State may well be made conditional on renouncing all other citizenships. However, active citizenship in the sense entertained by this objection seems inappropriate as an ideal within liberal contractualism. The view that lives are stunted in the absence of political engagement is contested and unsuitable as the basis for how the political order should be constructed.[5] Moreover, this worry holds as much against intra-EU migrants as against third country nationals.

Avoid backlash among current Union citizens

One politically important objection against letting third country nationals become citizens is that the current population may feel threatened. The newcomers may be perceived as competitors for scarce resources, or as threats to established transfer schemes of social welfare. This is no doubt one cause of the social unrest and so-called 'xenophobic' reactions and political movements in Member States. Immigrants challenge the expectations and established life styles of the settled populations. The challenge, as Adrian Favell notes, is to maintain the social capital among citizens, in order to live securely among multiple cultures (Favell, 1996: 12).

This is an important concern, and one which a publicly shared conception of the just European order could help address. It is not at all clear, however, that this fear will stem primarily from third country nationals—nor that withholding citizenship from this particular group reduces the fear. Intra-EU mobility of workers poses an equally dire threat to livelihood and established mores. Part of the policy response may be to highlight naturalisation procedures and thus convey to the general public that resident aliens are seeking full integration, and taking on the burdens entailed by full citizenship.

Concluding remarks

This chapter has sketched a defence for offering citizenship to third country nationals, and has argued against several frequently voiced objections against this position.

This defence does not eliminate the practical problems of co-ordination, risks of free riding, cultural conflicts, or xenophobic harassment of the new citizens. The main claim is more limited, that policy changes must aim at offering them citizenship. A general policy of allowing naturalisation to third country nationals entails large adjustments and co-ordination among national legislations and policies to avoid conflicts. But drastic changes are forced upon Member States, in any case, dealing with increased intra-EU migration and common immigration policies. The challenges of third country nationals are best met by co-operation and harmonisation among states, rather than by preventing citizenship (see Bauböck, 1997).

The case of third country nationals is politically urgent, and illustrates how the developing European polity poses central challenges to received normative political and democratic theory. The fragmented past provides an insufficient normative basis for a stable and legitimate order under the new circumstances of open European borders.

No comprehensive agreement among all affected parties can be expected regarding shared values, shared history or shared future in Europe. Several centuries ago, conflicting conceptions of the good life in Europe led to the emergence of liberalism. Liberal thought may be developed further, to address the new challenges facing Europe. We must determine more clearly what Europeans must expect of one another in order to maintain stable nation states, within a stable and just European political order. Granting third country nationals citizenship is an important start.

Notes

1 An earlier version of this chapter was presented at a Workshop on Migrants, Minorities and new forms of Citizenship in the European Union, European University Institute, Florence, March 1998. Support is gratefully acknowledged

from ARENA—a programme of Advanced Research on the Europeanisation of the Nation State, under the Research Council of Norway, and from EU TSER program (SOE 2973056) on European Citizenship and the Social and Political Integration of the European Union.

2 For social death see Patterson, 1982 and Rawls, 1993: 33

3 I shall not here address the package of powers, privileges and obligations of those who choose to remain aliens—eg of Euro denizens, see Hammar, 1990; Bauböck, 1997.

4 For a clarifying discussion see Kymlicka and Norman, 1994.

5 Note that this is a different point than that made eg by Machiavelli, that stability of the political order requires politically vigilant citizens. See Skinner, 1984, who holds that Machiavelli offers an instrumental defence of public spiritedness among citizens to guarantee negative liberties.

Bibliography

Ahmad, I. (1965), *Sovereignty Islamic and Modern: Conception of Sovereignty in Islam*, Karachi: The Allies Book Corporation.

An-Na'im, A. A. (1990a), *Toward an Islamic Reformation: Civil Liberties, Human Rights and International Law*, Syracuse: Syracuse University Press.

Barry, B. (1991), 'Self-government Revisited', in *Democracy and Power, Essays in Political Theory I*, Oxford: Oxford University Press, 156–86.

Bauböck, R. (1995), 'Changing the Boundaries of Citizenship', in *From Aliens to Citizens*, ed. Rainer Bauböck, Avebury: Aldershot, 201–32.

Bauböck, R. (1997), 'Citizenship and National Identities in the European Union', Harvard Jean Monnet Chair Working Papers, 4/1997.

Beitz, C. (1989), *Political Equality*, Princeton: Princeton University Press.

Breton, R. (1995), *Rethinking Federalism: Citizens, Markets, and Governments in a Changing World*, eds Karen Knop, Sylvia Ostry, Richard Simeon, and Katherine Swingon, Vancouver: British Columbia Press, 40–58.

Buchanan, A. E. (1989), 'Assessing the communitarian critique of liberalism', *Ethics* 99 (4), 852–882.

Carens, J. H. (1989), 'Membership and Morality: Admission to Citizenship in Liberal Democratic States', in William Rogers Brubaker (ed.), *Immigration and the Politics of Citizenship in France and North America*, German Marshall Fund of America, Lanham, Md.: University Press of America, 31–49.

Carens, J. H. (1992), 'Migration and Morality: A Liberal Egalitarian Perspective', in Brian Barry and Robert E. Goodin (eds), *Free Movement. Ethical Issues in the Transnational Migration of People and of Money*, New York: Harvester Wheatsheaf, 25–47.

Cesarani, D. (1996), 'Citizenship and Nationality in Britain', in David Cesarani and Mary Fulbrook (eds), *Citizenship, Nationality and Migration in Europe*, London: Routledge, 57–73.

Closa, C. (1992), 'The Concept of Citizenship in the Treaty on European Union', *Common Market Law Review*, 29, 1137–69.

European Commission (1994), *White Paper on European Social Policy*, COM (94) 33 of 27.7.1994.

European Union Migrants' Forum (1995), *Proposals for the Revision of the Treaty on*

European Union at the Intergovernmental Conference of 1996, enlagenda/igc-home linstdoc/ngo/migrant.htm.

Eurostat (1998), '1.3% of EU population: EU has nearly 5 million people from "med 12"', Eurostat memo 0498, 16 April 1998.

Favell, A. (1996), 'Rethinking Applied Normative Political Theory: An Institutionalist Approach to the Problem of Multicultural Citizenship', APSA Paper.

Finnis, J. (1980), *Natural Law and Natural Rights*, Clarendon Law Series, Oxford: Oxford University Press, Clarendon.

Fulbrook, M. (1996), 'Germany for the Germans?' in David Cesarani and Mary Fulbrook (eds), *Citizenship, Nationality and Migration in Europe*, 88–105, London: Routledge.

Føllesdal, A. (1996), 'Minority Rights: A Liberal Contractualist Case', in Juha Raikka (ed.), *Do We Need Minority Rights? Conceptual Issues*, The Hague/London/Boston: Kluwer Academic Publisher/Kluwer Law International, 59–83.

Føllesdal, A. (1997), 'Do Welfare Obligations End at the Boundaries of the Nation State?' in Peter Koslowski and Andreas Føllesdal (eds), *The Welfare State Under Siege: Ethical Issues of Social Policy*, Studies in Economic Ethics and Philosophy, Springer, 145–63.

Føllesdal, A. (1998), 'Communitarian Criticisms of Liberal Contractualism: An Account and a Defense', in Frank Brinkhuis and Sasha Talmor (eds), *Memory, History and Critique: European Identity at the Millennium*, Cambridge, Mass.: MIT, CDROM.

Guild, E. (1996), 'The Legal Framework of Citizenship of the European Union', in David Cesarani and Mary Fulbrook (eds), *Citizenship, Nationality and Migration in Europe*, Routledge, 30–54.

Gutmann, A. (1988), 'Communitarian critics of liberalism', *Philosophy and Public Affairs*, 14 (3), 308–322.

Habermas, J. (1992), 'Citizenship and national identity: some reflections on the future of Europe', *Praxis International*, 12 (1), 1–19.

Hammar, T. (1990), *Democracy and the Nation-State: Aliens, Denizens and Citizens in a World of International Migration*, Aldershot: Avery.

Huntington, S. P. (1996), *The Clash of Civilizations and the Remaking of World Order*, New York: Simon and Shuster.

Kostakopoulou, D. (1997), 'European Citizenship as a model of Citizenship Beyond the Nation-state: Possibilities and Limits', unpublished paper, ARENA Conference, December.

Kymlicka, W. and Wayne Nonnan (1994), 'Return of the Citizen: A Survey of Recent Work on Citizenship Theory', *Ethics*, 104 (January), 352–81.

Laffan, B. (1996), 'The Politics of Identity and Political Order in Europe', *Journal of Common Market Studies*, 34 (1), 81–102.

Macedo, S. (1990), *Liberal Virtues: Citizenship, Virtue, and Community in Liberal Constitutionalism*, Oxford: Clarendon Press.

Marshall, T. H. (1949), 'Citizenship and Social Class', reprinted in *Class, Citizenship and Social Development*, Chicago University Press, 1963, in *The Marshall Lectures, Cambridge University*, Cambridge: Cambridge University Press, 70–146.

Meehan, E. (1993), *Citizenship and the European Community*, London: Sage.

Mouffe, C. (ed.) (1992), *Dimensions of Radical Democracy*, London: Verso.

Mulhall, S. and Adam Swift (1996), *Liberals and Communitarians*, revised version, Oxford: Blackwell.

Nentwich, M. and Gerda Falkner (1997), 'The Treaty of Amsterdam: Towards a New Institutional balance', *European Integration Online Papers*, vol. 1, no. 15.

O'Keeffe, D. (1994), 'Union citizenship', in O'Keeffe and Twomey (eds), *Legal Issues of the Maastricht Treaty*, West Sussex: Wiley.

Patterson, O. (1982), *Slavery and Social Death*, Cambridge, Mass.: Harvard University Press.

Petit, M. (1998), 'The Treaty of Amsterdam', Harvard Jean Monnet Chair Working Paper, Series 2/1998.

Preuss, U. K. (1995), 'Problem of a Concept of European Citizenship', *European Law Journal*, 1 (3), 267–81.

Preuss, U. K. (1996), 'Two Challenges to European Citizenship', in Richard Bellamy and Dario Castiglione (eds), *Constitutionalism in Transformation: European and Theoretical Perspectives*, Oxford: Blackwell, 122–40.

Rawls, J. (1971), *A Theory of Justice*, Cambridge, Mass.: Harvard University Press.

Rawls, J. (1988), 'The priority of right and ideas of the good', *Philosophy and Public Affairs*, 17 (4), 251–276.

Rawls, J. (1993), *Political Liberalism*, New York: Columbia University Press.

Shaw, J. (1997a), 'Citizenship of the Union: Towards Post-national Citizenship?' Harvard Jean Monnet Chair, Paper 6/97.

Shaw, J. (1997b), 'European Citizenship: The IGC and Beyond', *European Integration Online Papers*, vol. 1, no. 3.

Skinner, Q. (1984), 'The Idea of Negative Liberty. Philosophical and Historical Perspectives', in Richard Rorty, Quentin Skinner, and Jerome B. Schneewind (eds), *Philosophy in History: Essays on the Historiography of Philosophy*, Cambridge: Cambridge University Press, 204–19.

Soysal, Y. (1994), *Limits of Citizenship. Migrants and Postnational Membership in Europe*, Chicago: University of Chicago.

Soysal, Y. (1996), 'Changing Citizenship in Europe: Remarks on Postnational Membership and the National State', in David Cesarani and Mary Fulbrook (eds), *Citizenship, Nationality and Migration in Europe*, Routledge, 17– .

Taylor, C. ([1979] 1985), 'Atomism', in *Philosophical Papers*, vol. 2, Cambridge: Cambridge University Press, 187–210.

Walzer, K. (1981), 'The Distribution of Membership', in Peter G. Brown and Henry Shue (eds), *Boundaries: National Autonomy and its Limits*, Totowa, NJ: Rowman and Allanhead, 1–35.

Walzer, K. (1983), *Spheres of Justice: A Defense of Pluralism and Equality*, New York: Basic.

Weil, P. (1996), 'The Lessons of the French Experience', in David Cesarani and Mary Fulbrook (eds), *Citizenship, Nationality and Migration in Europe*, London: Routledge, 74–87.

Weiler, J. H. H. (1995), 'Does Europe Need a Constitution? Reflections on Demos, Telos and the German Maastricht Decision', *European Law Journal*, 1.

Weiler, J. H. H. (1996), 'European Neo-constitutionalism: In Search of Foundations for the European Constitutional Order', in Richard Bellamy and Dario Castiglione (eds), *Constitutionalism in Transformation: European and Theoretical Perspectives*, Oxford: Blackwell, 105–21.

Weiler, J. H. H. with Haltern Ulrich and Franz Mayer (1995), 'European Democracy and Its Critique: Five Uneasy Pieces', EUI Working Paper, RSC No. 95/11, and Harvard Jean Monnet Working Paper, 1/1995, Badia Fiesolana, Dan Domenico, Italy: EUI.

Welsh, J. (1993), 'A People's Europe? European Citizenship and European Identity', Working Paper, ECS No. 93/2, European University Institute, Florence.

Wiener, A. (1997), 'Assessing the Constructive Potential of Union Citizenship—A Socio-Historical Perspective', EIOP Paper.

Wiener, A. and Vincent Della Sala (1997), 'Constitution-making and Citizenship Practice—Bridging the Democracy Gap in the EU?' *Journal of Common Market Studies*, 35 (4).

Bridges

The European public sphere and the deficit of democracy

Reiner Grundmann

Abstract

This chapter explores a threefold European deficit: a democratic deficit, a deficit in European identity, and a deficit in the European public sphere. It argues that although interests such as social movements have most leverage at the national level, since this is the level at which the media are largely organised, the emergence of distinctively 'European' issues such as BSE means that national cycles of media attention are becoming increasingly synchronised. This makes it more likely that a homogenisation of issues and opinion will occur at the European level. This would favour the eventual emergence of a supranational identity. The creation of a European public sphere through the synchronisation and homogenisation of cycles of media attention on contentious 'European' issues is a more realistic prospect than direct attempts to create a 'new European' identity through public education or the legal system.

Introduction

As several authors have remarked, the European Union suffers from a lack of democracy. It has also been noted that an important requirement for a European democracy would be the emergence of a European public. Today both requirements are absent. In this chapter I analyse the conditions under which a European public sphere could emerge. The chapter starts from the premise that a supra-national European government will not be a real option in the near future. As in the past, European integration will mean a cumbersome process entailing progress and backlash. Moves towards a supranationalist state are likely, but will be thwarted by tendencies opposing a further and substantial dissolution of national sovereignty. Main reasons for the problems of the supra-nationalist project are the strength of national identities and the weakness of a European identity, the deficit of democracy within the EU and the corresponding lack of legitimation for European institutions. Under these conditions it is easy for enemies of further integration ('Eurosceptics') to mobilise public concern about a bureaucratic superstate located in Brussels.

European integration theory has been largely dominated by intergovernmental and international relations approaches. The fascinating question for some scholars in this speciality was and still is whether European integration can be best described as a supranational (federal) state or as a result of intergovernmental bargaining. Others see the European Union as an institution *sui generis* which combines intergovernmentalism with supranationalism. Recent developments have recast this debate. The Maastricht referenda in France and Denmark, the discussion about a European Central Bank, and, closely connected to it, the introduction of a single European currency (the Euro) have raised crucial questions like: will European integration go any further? How is the deficit of democracy to be overcome? How can Europe gain in legitimacy? How is European citizenship to be defined? How is Europe to be defined? And, what does it mean to be a European?

As the 'old-fashioned problems of democracy and identity' (Picht, 1993) are returning, even taking centre stage, the concerns of international relations appear to be less salient. It seems appropriate to shift the focus of attention to frameworks developed in sociology and comparative public policy. The history of European integration and the institutional arrangements which have been created so far explain why we have a problem of democratic legitimation. And the dynamics of integration which involve more and more nations giving up more and more parts of their sovereignty to Europe pose the question of what sort of polity should replace the nation states.

In this chapter I shall review the European integration literature with reference to democratic legitimation, questions of identity and the public sphere. There is a deficit in all of the mentioned fields and I shall comment on all of them. However, in terms of identifying remedies, I shall limit myself to the exploration of the public sphere. Here I offer some speculations about the conditions under which a European public sphere could emerge. Data from a pilot study on the media discourse in three EU member states are presented. The hypothesis (or, rather, the speculation) is that pan-European issues will lead to a synchronisation of public attention across member states which is seen as a precondition for a homogenous European public sphere and hence for a European polity. The premise behind this reasoning is that the main task of European unification is the creation of a legitimate leadership. A basic wisdom of political theory says that only those governments that can be thrown out of power by the electorate are legitimate. A homogenous public sphere is one of the main preconditions for this to happen.[1] The mass media have a crucial place in the process of political agenda setting (Iyengar, 1987). Political issues are mainly defined through mass media and public opinion is to a large degree influenced by the mass media. They are the mediating link between the citizens and the politicians in power. However, there are no European-wide mass media which inform all the European public simultaneously about the same issues as there are on the national level.

The history of European integration is marked by an increase in the competence of European institutions but this is not paralleled by an equal increase in legitimation granted to them by the voters: there are no parties with a European wide range, there are no (or only a few) European political figures, and there is no European public sphere. To be sure, there are national public spheres (as there are national political parties (Bardi, 1996)) within Europe, but they remain segmented. A single European public sphere would have the function of selecting from among the multiplicity of possible political issues for Europe. Only under this condition could citizens choose political answers to these issues and, on this basis, elect their leaders (Reif, 1997). In the final analysis it is the voters who decide whether to confirm a government in power or whether to drive it out of power. I will tackle these issues in the following way. First, I outline the historical roots of the current problem of democratic deficit within the EU. next, I will pay some attention to the research on 'European identity', discussing two main concepts and their implications, demos and ethnos. I will then single out the public sphere as the analytical level on which the problem will be located. Democratic participation leading to informed choices depends crucially on the interest, knowledgeability, and motivation of citizens. If they are not informed about specific political issues, this may result in a general lack of interest which borders on political apathy. If they are informed about, but not particularly interested in, these issues, they might well lend their diffuse support to politicians in power—for some time. However, this unconditional support may turn abruptly into specific opposition and thereby create severe crises. These crises are of a different and more hazardous nature than those on the national level:

Whereas a national political system does not usually run into trouble when a government policy is disliked (it will at most result in the election of a new government), the EU as a whole comes under fire and is at risk of legitimacy crisis if a particular policy is perceived to be ineffective or wasteful. (Leonard, 1998: 30).

Democracy

It seems to be commonplace to note that the European Union suffers from a lack of democracy (Grimm, 1996; Lepsius, 1991; Reif, 1992; Scharpf, 1996; Weidenfeld, 1990). Somewhat more contentious is the issue of identifying prerequisites of a European democracy. Some see it in a common identity of their citizens, others in the emergence of a European public (see Deflem and Pampel, 1996; deLange, 1995; Delanty, 1995; Gerhards, 1993; Habermas, 1996; Reese-Schäfer, 1997; Smith, 1996; Taylor, 1996). Today both requirements are absent. The state of democratic legitimation could be characterised by three factors:

1. The history of European integration is marked by a technocratic approach which was mainly set into motion by an élite. 'It was born in an era when public approval mattered relatively little and when the wider geo-political agenda was utterly dominated by the Cold War.' It has been described by the same author as a 'benign technocratic conspiracy designed to bring about irreversible integration' (Leonard, 1998: 17–18). The genesis of this process is closely associated with Jean Monnet. Without exaggeration, Monnet can be described as one of the architects of the European Community. Hence, a 'certain saintliness' has been conferred upon him by advocates of European unity (Milward, 1984). Monnet proposed a specific method of integration, and set it into practice with the 'High Authority' of the European Coal and Steel Community (ECSC). It has been remarked that the institutions of the European Community are remarkably similar to those designed in 1950 for the ECSC (Pinder, 1985–6; Featherstone, 1994). It has also been noted that we are still today paying for his false departure of technocracy and élitism. In any case, the Commission today suffers from a weak and fragile democratic legitimacy.

   Monnet was committed to the idea of supranationalism and the principle of a High Authority reflected this view. In addition, Monnet adopted specific principles of public policy, as developed in France where the technocratic approach had always been strong (compared to countries like Britain). The High Authority was also operated in a corporatist style, 'a process marked by *engrenage*, involving networks of outside producer and interest groups. Specifically, it was the practice of consulting representatives of industry to work out the details of policy' (Featherstone, 1994: 115).[2] 'In a sense, Monnet considered the High Authority as the repository of the European General Will, with the evil governments merely the spokesmen for the selfish political wills. The Treaty, as administered by the High Authority, *is* the basic European consensus for progress, peace and federation', as Haas (1958: 456, orig. emph.) put it. To be sure, the Commission is not the exact copy of the High Authority. But it follows the same logic in that it is the driving force of integration. Monnet thought it 'wrong to consult the peoples of Europe about the structure of a Community of which they had no practical experience' (quoted in Featherstone, 1994: 159). He proposed to insert some democratic accountability, but the assembly he envisaged was rather weak. His plan did not foresee the Council of Ministers which clearly, for his taste, would have had too much power. 'In sum, for Monnet technocrats had to build Europe first, before the politicians and the people could get their hands on it' (Featherstone, 1994: 160).

2. The history of European integration is also marked by a permissive consensus or diffuse support (Almond, 1950; Easton, 1965; Key, 1961; Lindberg/Scheingold, 1970). Diffuse support denotes 'a reservoir of goodwill' and a commitment to an institution that is not contingent upon short-term satisfaction with policy outputs ('specific support') (Gibson and Caldeira, 1998: 67).[3] The notion captures the fact that the general public is rarely attentive to, or informed about, the arcane details of highly technical and complex issues. But if the public becomes dissatisfied with the outcome of EU policies and blames their government for these EU policies, citizens can 'throw the scoundrels out': 'If the EU is blamed for economic conditions, excessive bureaucracy or extravagant agricultural spending, all governments may sink or swim together (Norris, 1997: 275).[4] In the beginning of the 1990s, the permissive consensus was eroded, as illustrated by the referendum of 1992 in Denmark which rejected the ratification of the Maastricht treaty and the referendum in France in the same year which accepted it only by a tiny majority.

3. The EU is also unpopular. It took quite some time for social

scientists to realise that this is the case; they were surprised by the 'fury of Maastricht' (Gibson/Caldeira, 1998: 63). Among others, Leonard (1998) has given three interconnected reasons for the low popularity of the EU. Firstly, he notices that the EU's institutions are detached from people's everyday experience. Secondly, he sees that the priorities of EU policy-making are not those of most voters. Whereas they want jobs, less crime and protection for the environment, EU officials dedicate most of the time and money to EMU and Common Agricultural Policy.[5] Thirdly, the benefits of the EU are spread unevenly within the member states. Most of the direct benefits go to minority groups such as farmers, declining industries and underdeveloped regions. There are also marked differences between how the benefits of the EU are perceived by EU officials and ordinary people, with variations between different social strata. The EU is perceived as a club in which more highly educated, professional people have more interest than other social strata (Leonard, 1998: 26–7).

> According to its original conception, the Commission was not supposed to enjoy democratic legitimacy: this was not seen as essential to the task at hand. However, with the process of integration, it is increasingly apparent that the Commission's role is undermined by this lack of public legitimacy. This affects its ability to exercise leadership on behalf of European unity. (Featherstone, 1994: 163)

The prospects for transnational European democracy therefore appear dim. How could more democratic control and legitimation be brought about? One could turn to the classic model of division of powers between legislative and executive or to direct election to the European Commission from the mass electorate. Or one could envisage the European Parliament having more power, electing and dismissing members to the Commission. However, in all cases, the prerequisite for accountability and transparency seems to be a politicisation of the decision-making process which at present is suffocated by a rationale of consensus. Simply providing more information will not do for two reasons. First, uninteresting information will not remedy the lack of transparency.[6] Providing more of the same leads to information overload. This may create openness without transparency. Second, 'filling an alleged information deficit will not necessarily restore confidence among people who mistrust political processes, for whatever reason' (Lodge, 1994:

361). There are some quite sophisticated proposals in this respect, for example, Weiler's European public square ('Lexcalibur') which is a marketplace of information, placing the entire decision-making process of the Community on the Internet. This is not meant to introduce virtual government but to enhance the power of all actors by giving them more information: 'The most immediate direct beneficiaries of Euro governance on the Internet would in fact be the media, interested pressure groups, non-governmental organisations, and the like' (Weiler, 1997: 515). Realistically, this instrument is not open to ordinary citizens since most of the information will consist of tedious technical detail. It is up to the Euro-experts to select relevant pieces of information and make them public through the mass media.

The public is unable to identify and recognise political leaders in the Commission. What is more, the public seems less concerned with the balance of power *within* European institutions (between the Commission, the Council and the Parliament) than between national governments and 'Brussels'. This is an important point to keep in mind. It has potentially far-reaching implications when applied to the search for solutions to the legitimacy crisis. I shall return to this point.

For several reasons, the solution to this problem cannot be the replica of the nation states' solution on a larger scale (Delanty, 1998). The institutional design of the European Union does not allow for this simple and most obvious solution. The European Parliament does not have the powers of a national parliament and will not get them in the near future.[7] The EP does not control European politicians, nor the budget, nor does it have legislative functions.[8] The members of the Commission and the Council are not directly accountable to European voters. However, they are accountable to their national electorates. This provides the important link between Brussels and the voters in different member states. As Tarrow (1995) has shown in the case of social movements, these are important political actors seeking change who mainly pressurise their national governments. There is a well-known difference between the representation of diffuse and concentrated interests (Olson, 1965; Wilson, 1980; Vogel, 1993). While the latter are well organised by lobbying organisations represented in Brussels (Coen, 1998), the former are often not. They tend to use the 'tried and true techniques of domestic pressure and social protest.' For these groups, 'peripheral protest becomes the functional equivalent of European interest representation. Therefore, . . . the national state becomes a mediator between domestic constituents and European policy makers' (Tarrow, 1995: 243). It can be added that even in cases where there is interest representation at the European level (as is the case with environmentalist groups), direct protest still has an important place in political mobilisation.

Since national channels of influence are still important and may, paradoxically, become even more important with more efforts at supranational integration, it is interesting to look at different institutional designs in different European countries in order to identify different opportunities for democratic control. Germany and the UK are quite distinct in this respect. In Germany, EU policy is enacted behind closed doors, mainly on the cabinet level. The parliament does not discuss these matters in a prominent way, although the second chamber (the representation of the *Länder*) seems to be more sensitive to the issue. In the UK, there is a special parliamentary commission which receives every European law-making proposal within 48 hours. Government has to comment on it within ten days. In many cases the responsible minister is invited in front of the parliamentary commission and instructed how to vote in Brussels (Schauer, 1992: 7; Senger/Etterlin, 1992). In Germany there is no systematic control of how parliamentary recommendations fare in Brussels. This might be read as a particular example of the permissive consensus which prevailed in Germany in the Kohl era.

These examples all point to the importance of the national level. It seems as if in the absence of a powerful and functioning ('proper') European Parliament, democratic control has to be exercised by powerful institutions in the member states (parliaments, mass media). Different institutional designs on the national level can make a decisive difference on the European level.

After the deficit of European democracy, I turn now to the second big deficit, the European deficit of identity.

Identity

There are two different concepts of the nation state which have been labelled 'Western' and 'Eastern' (Smith, 1997) and which correspond to the distinction between *demos* and *ethnos*. The Western concept stresses national territory, common institutions and a political community which binds citizens together (*ius soli*). The Eastern model is more focused on ethnic descent and cultural ties. Here, the element of folk culture, customs, rituals and religion are much more

important (Smith, 1997: 324). Sometimes, the element of blood relationship is added on to this view (*ius sanguinis*). If we were to go
through this list, we might ask ourselves if there is a European territory, or a European political community, if there exist common customs, a common language or a common religion. Obviously, the
elements of the 'Eastern' notion of nationhood are clearly lacking in
the European Union.[9] But what about the Western notion? What
about a common territory and a common political community?
'Europe is not a continent—as in the ancient geographers' dream—
but a sub-continent: a peninsula of the Eurasian land-mass', as
Pocock (1997: 306) aptly observed. This raises thorny questions
about demarcation and definition of political communities. Who is
to be considered a European? Where should the limits of the
Eastern extension of the EU lie? According to Anthony Smith,
'national identifications possess distinct advantages over the idea of
a unified European identity. They are vivid, accessible, well established, long popularised, and still widely believed . . . In each of
these respects, "Europe" is deficient both as idea and as process.
Above all, it lacks a pre-modern past—a "prehistory" which can
provide it with emotional sustenance and historical depth' (Smith,
1997: 325). Smith expects strong ethnic sentiments to persist in
many parts of the sub-continent, along with periodic revival of
national identities, 'fuelled by the quest for ethnic traditions and
cultural heritages of distinctive myths, memories and symbols'
(Smith, 1997: 327).

One of the main reasons for the re-emergence of nationalist
movements in post-industrial societies is the growing importance of
means of communication and information. The mass media,
telecommunications and computerised information lead, paradoxically, to the emergence of smaller and denser networks made up of
homogenous ethno-linguistic groups (Anderson, 1983). If applied to
the European Union this would mean that because of its many linguistic and cultural differences a homogenous identity will not
come forth (I will come back to the question if and how the concept
of an 'imagined community' can be applied to Europe).

Demarcations are vital to identity formation.[10] But this is clearly
a very contested and dangerous undertaking.[11] Applied to Europe
as a whole, the creation of 'the other', of out-groups or outsiders, ie
the negative definition of Europeanness (not Jewish, not Black, not
Orthodox, not Muslim—but what about Greece and Turkey?) may
well replace the more cumbersome process of building a positive
European identity.[12] And there are some worrying examples from

the recent past which point in this direction. Immigrants and guest-workers have been the target of intolerant and/or racist attacks. But where could Europe turn in order to create popular European myths and symbols? Common standards in education could be employed to this end, but only to a certain degree. They would differ markedly as soon as one enters historiography. It is indeed hard to imagine a common European identity looking back at 'itself', writing its own, common history (Pocock, 1997). Again, it becomes plain that the variety of national identities remains a strong barrier towards further integration. 'As long as educational systems remain different in Europe and resist standardisation—which is not only highly probable in the foreseeable future, but also a declared intention of the Maastricht Treaty—Europeans will differ in basic forms of thinking and behaviour. This variety certainly constitutes a major difficulty for European cooperation, where the intercultural problems of communication are often underestimated . . . ' writes Picht convincingly (1993: 87). Picht proposes another solution, in which he envisages the emergence of a *New European* which 'has to be as sophisticated as the merchants and courtiers of the Renaissance or the multinational and multilingual inhabitants of Central and Eastern Europe before Hitler and Stalin . . . He has to know foreign languages beyond the superficial and unreliable *koiné* . . . ' (Picht, 1993: 87). This seems rather an exaggerated aspiration, overburdening the European citizen, possibly leading to an ever more pronounced élitism across Europe. The humanistic ideal of intercultural training is certainly valuable, especially with the aim of not rejecting one's own identity but confronting other identities in a fruitful fashion—as is Picht's intention. But this is an evaluative question which depends also on the degree of optimism one has. One could, with Anthony Smith, ask the rhetorical question: 'Has the long-standing German love affair with Italy made any difference to the intensity of German nationalism, in this or the last century? Or shall we rather agree with Karl Kautsky that the railways are the greatest breeder of national hatreds?' (Smith, 1997: 335).

Leaving the *ethnos* strand of thought and entering the realm of *demos* gives us perhaps more possibilities in thinking about a European identity. These possibilities may be better in tune with the values of our time. First of all, it is obvious that the European 'project' is attractive for the young and mobile. The very notion of the 'project' makes this clear: it is a journey to an unknown destination and unknown ways of getting there (Weiler, 1993). Such an outlook resonates very much with prevalent ideas about a post-modern society. In fact, as Pocock has said, 'Europe'; could become 'the ideo-logy of a post-historical culture, in which varyingly affluent and vary-ingly alienated masses . . . float from one environment to another with no awareness of moving from one past, and one commitment to it, to another . . . The affluent populations wander as tourists—which is to say consumers of images—from one former historical culture to another, delightfully free from the need to commit themselves to any, and free to criticise while determining for themselves the extent of their responsibility' (Pocock, 1997: 303–4, 312).

The second reason is that people may have multiple identities. They can move between them according to different needs and con-texts. Sometimes these identities may be conflictual, but they may also be compatible with each other. Smith uses the term 'concentric identities' to describe the Catalan who is also a Spaniard and a European, or the Scot who is also British and European. Joseph Weiler criticised this notion on the grounds that it conceives of a European citizenship in the same way as we understand our national citizenship. He offers another version of multiple *demoi*, but one with several qualifications. First, individuals are—as in Smith's version—invited to see themselves as belonging to two *demoi*. Second, the member state nationality and European citizen-ship are seen as interdependent: 'One cannot, conceptually and psy-chologically (let alone legally), be a European citizen without being a member state national.' And third, Weiler sees a civilisatory dimension in this: 'It is the acceptance by its members that, in a range of areas of public life, one will accept the legitimacy and authority of decisions adopted by fellow European citizens in the realisation that in these areas preference is given to choices made by the outreaching, non-organic, *demos*, rather than by the inreaching one' (Weiler, 1997: 510). That this position advocates a more ambiguous notion of 'concentric identities' than Smith's is evident. However, one can have similar qualms about this proposal as about Picht's. Weiler's proposal, it appears to me, expects too much of citi-zens and thus runs the danger of overburdening them. However, Weiler is aware of this danger when he stresses the continuing signif-icance of the national level: 'Nationals of the member states are European citizens, not the other way round. Europe is "not yet" a demos in the organic national-cultural sense and should never become one' (Weiler, 1997: 511).

In the next section, I finally address the last of the three areas of deficit: the public sphere.

The public sphere

As has been emphasised by many authors, there is a remoteness, opaqueness and inaccessibility on European governance. 'The drama lies in the fact that no one accountable public authority has a handle on these regulatory processes—not the European Parliament, not the Commission, not even the governments. The press and other media, a vital estate in our democracies, are equally hampered' (Weiler, 1997: 512). In line with this view, the argument will be advanced that a homogenous European public sphere would be the precondition for a European polity, since it is the public which has the agenda setting function in a democracy and it is the voters that can throw a government out of office. It is therefore the public which selects politically relevant problems. There exist different national public spheres, but no common European political agenda and hence no requirement for politicians to perform according to the expectation of a 'European' constituency.

My argument is based on the distinction between two avenues for the strengthening of the public sphere in Europe: on the one hand, the Europeanisation of national public spheres, and on the other hand the emergence of a transnational European public. The first amounts to a synchronisation, the second to a homogenisation of the national public spheres. The second is more ambitious and would probably follow a period after which national public spheres have become synchronised with regard to key political issues. This distinction would provide a tool which can be made operational for investigating empirical examples of transnational communication processes.

Despite the increasing technical possibilities, there is no common European media system and it is doubtful if it can ever be established. The obstacles presented by heterogeneity of culture and language are too big (de Swaan, 1991; Große-Peclum, 1990). However, even the more modest synchronisation and homogenisation of national public spheres is thwarted in many ways. One reason is to be found in the fact that news correspondents in Brussels, Strasbourg, and Luxembourg have a primary interest in reporting for their home market. They thus select topics which relate mainly to the domestic policy questions in their home countries. These journalists are aligned nationally and not according to transnational political options (eg, left/right; pro-EU/contra-EU, market liberalisation/protectionism, ecology/economy). As a consequence, a special type of information is selected from within the European power centre which then structures topics and evaluations within the public spheres of the member states. This information is regarded as relevant on the *domestic* policy agenda (Gerhards, 1993). It is questionable whether the reporting of politics can engender a specifically European identity (Bakir, 1996: 191). As the example of international news agencies shows, they place greater emphasis on their own domestic market even when selling these stories to foreign clients (Boyd-Barrett, 1981). Here we have yet another example of the importance of the domestic policy arena.

On the level of the member states a similar process can be observed. Every member state pursues a national line even and especially where European policy is an issue in the national public debate. This factor together with the specific working of the correspondence system in Brussels (see last paragraph) seems to operate in a self-reinforcing manner. Both strengthen *national* discourses about Europe. What is more, every member state looks at Brussels ('at the EU') but no one sees her neighbouring country. There is no 'crossing of social circles' (Simmel). Apart from the élites, the broad public in the member states knows little or nothing about the public debates in the other member countries. Political issues which are sensitive to voting behaviour and which enter the agenda of all member states simultaneously could provide an opportunity to cross cut social circles. Only issues which are related to voting behaviour on the national level will make any impact on politicians acting in Brussels. National political party mobilisation is still paramount. As Paul Taylor in his book on the EU, presenting evidence from poll data, has observed: 'The basis of political power in the European Union remained the national parties and the national constituency: there was no European-level constituency' (Taylor, 1996: 148). And Taggart wrote in the summary of his recent article on Euroscepticism: 'When parties compete on a European level, it is clear that domestic considerations take precedence over European ones' (Taggart, 1998: 384).

The introduction of the single currency and the BSE crisis are topics which have a transnational, European dimension and are still at the centre of debate within the member states. I suggest that such pan-European issues will lead to a synchronisation of national public spheres and thereby strengthen the transnational public sphere. It is in this sense that the coming of a European imagined community could be perceived.[13]

Empirical illustrations

In what follows, I shall present some results of a small research project on transnational European media communication, as exemplified in the BSE crisis and the introductory steps towards a common European currency. I am interested in the question of how national publics perceive salient political issues in other member states. These issues are partly national in character in that they have a more immediate impact in one country compared to another. But they are also European in that they are subject to decision-making on the European level. Both dimensions make them an appropriate topic for news reporting and hence for an analysis of transnational communication patterns. However, a caveat seems in order. This exercise is purely illustrative, supposed to support my speculation about the development of the European public sphere. It should not be seen as an empirical test of hypotheses.

Method

I conducted a database research in the CD-Rom version of the *Financial Times*, *Le Monde*, and *Frankfurter Allgemeine Zeitung* (*FAZ*) for the years 1995–1998. The first search was for 'BSE' in the headlines of articles. In the case of the *Financial Times*, the terms 'BSE', 'CJD' and 'mad cow' were used, in the case of the *FAZ* 'BSE', 'Creutzfeld' and 'Rinderwahnsinn'. In the case of *Le Monde*, the equivalent 'ESB' had to be replaced since there it is used as an acronym for a business organisation. The search was performed by using the terms 'vache folle' and 'Creutzfeld'. The second search was for '*Euro*' in the headlines of articles in all three papers, excluding hits for the 1996 Euro football tournament, other Euro-sport events and 'Euro-Disney'.

Results (see Fig. 1 and 2)

a) BSE

During 1995, the topic BSE attracted scarcely any attention except for about eight articles per month at the end of 1995 in the *Financial Times*. An explosion of interest occurred in March 1996 in all three countries. Significant is the much higher level of attention in France where *Le Monde* had about sixty articles, compared to eleven and nineteen in Germany and the UK respectively. In April 1996, attention increased even further in France (reaching the level of one hundred articles, a record in the period under investigation) while Germany and the UK remained below twenty. In May, attention receded somewhat, in France to fifty, in the UK to eighteen, in Germany below five. June saw another peak in Germany (20) and France (98) while the UK reached the peak in September with 24 articles. By that time, *Le Monde* had dropped to the same number (24) while Germany had levelled off to six. Since then, attention has constantly decreased until the end of 1997. Britain shows a peak in the spring of 1998 stirred by the launch of the BSE Inquiry.

b) Euro

Despite the many peaks and valleys, there is a clear increase in attention which culminates in the summer of 1997, followed by another peak in spring 1998. Outstanding interest was shown in Germany in June 1997 (75 articles) and in France in April 1998 (107 articles) and in the UK in November and December 1998 (102 and 100 articles). What the data also shows is an increase in average attention, ranging from 4 articles per month (in all countries) in 1995, to 13 in 1996, to 30 in 1997, and to 48 in 1998.

Discussion

Both examples show an interesting pattern. There is a parallel rise in the level of attention across the three countries examined which we may describe generally as synchronisation. This synchronisation can take three forms, tight coupling, loose coupling, and hysteria. Tight coupling describes a common path of development, loose coupling denotes a delay or anticipation of the trend in the other two countries. Hysteria indicates a conspicuous overreaction of one country compared to the other two.

a) *Tight coupling.* The line graph in Figure 1 (BSE from 1995 to 1998) shows a peak in attention which occurs in all three countries in the period from March to September 1996. Figure 2 (Euro 1995–1998) clearly shows a constant rise from January 1995 to December 1998 although there is an overall lower interest in the UK in 1997 (which could be explained by the fact that the UK will not join the Euro in the first round and therefore sees less urgency in the topic). There are two periods of peak attention in June 1997 and April–May 1998. Both peaks are coinciding in all

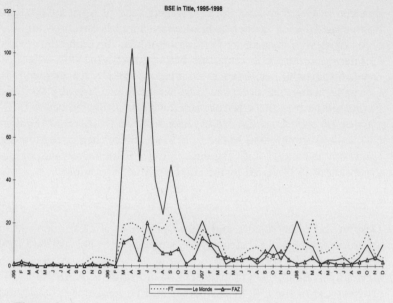

Figure 1

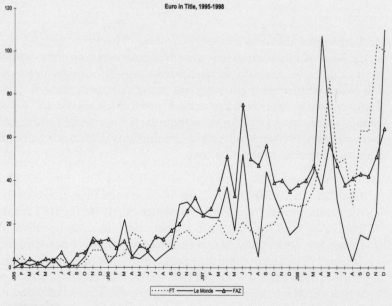

Figure 2

three countries in a very clear manner as are the downward trends in August 1997 and July 1998. Other points of upward convergence occur in April and June 1997 and in April and December 1998.

b) *Loose coupling.* The UK anticipates the other countries' public attention to the BSE crisis by three months (December 1995) which seems hardly surprising given the central role of this country. This is also seen in the somewhat more pronounced reaction of the *FT* when compared to the *FAZ*. There are also instances where attention goes up in one country while going down in the other two, as seen in September 1996, August 1997, and March 1998 (*FT* vs. *FAZ* and *Le Monde* on BSE).

c) *Hysteria.* An interesting phenomenon occurs in periods of synchronisation where one of the three countries gives an unusual high priority to the relevant issue compared to the other two. For example, in Spring 1996 in France, there was an exceptional high attention to the BSE issue which was more than fivefold of that of the UK.

What are the implications of these findings?

First, the expectation of a synchronisation of public attention in the three countries was confirmed. However, there is an interesting cross-national attention cycle. France was especially interested in the BSE crisis in the UK, maybe because of her high dependence on British beef. And Britain became highly interested in the discussion about the Euro during the period of election of the first president of the European Central Bank in May 1998 where the two candidates (Duiseuberg and Trichet) stood for two distinct monetary policies (strong Euro vs. public spending). Since his term will last until a possible joining of the UK, the increased British interest in this debate seems natural. It even outplays the German attention in 1998. Second, it is not clear if there was a homogenisation in the attention cycle. This would only be verifiable by a content analysis of the articles. The analysis of this process lies beyond the scope of this article, it is the object of further research.[14]

Conclusion

In this article I have examined a threefold European deficit, a democratic deficit, a deficit in European identity and a deficit in a European public sphere. All three are interlinked but they can be separated for analytical reasons. While I think that a common European identity is the least likely to emerge in the medium term, given all we know about cultural inertia, there is some potential with proposals regarding democratic reform. My own contribution has examined the prospects of a European public sphere. The starting point was that the national level is still the place where diffuse interests have most leverage, mainly because the media are still geared very much to national political attention. The next step in the argument was that the synchronisation of national cycles of attention is a precondition for their homogenisation. Seen from the perspective of the potential development of the European public sphere, the issues of democracy and identity can be reframed. Whereas a synchronised European public will facilitate legitimate decisions on a European level, a homogenised European public would favour the emergence of a supranational identity. This approach does not invoke problematic strategies of overburdening citizens as is likely if one attempts the creation of a *New European* or tries to oblige them to obey supranational law. The problem with the former is that it relies on romantic ideals of human development, the problem with the latter that it presupposes a universally informed citizenry which acts in an enlightened way. Both assumptions are unrealistic. We must not forget that the main facet of democracy is that it gives the electorate the power to drive the existing government out of power. This will always happen with respect to selected and salient issues which command the attention of large proportions of the population, no matter how well educated or how well informed they are on every detail of the political process. Therefore, it seems that the process of further integration and simultaneous attempts to reduce the above mentioned deficits can best be achieved by the transformation of the public sphere. However, this is a process which can be influenced only marginally from above (from 'Brussels').[15] Institutional constraints and opportunities on the national level should not be underestimated. To be sure, political reforms within the EU, from above, may well make a difference. The extension of powers of the Presidency of the Commission is such a possibility.[16] However, it seems likely that such a move, too, will become one of the contested political goals which rises to prominence in the public spheres—thus fuelling the debate and controversy over the future of Europe. But in this process of open debate, more and more parts of the electorate in different member countries could come to see this debate as their common debate. In this sense they could imagine a European c/Community.

Notes

1 By homogenous I mean a public sphere in which the same issues are debated at the same time with a view to the same political decision process.

2 This technocratic approach was reflected by early scholarship on European Unification represented by Haas or Schmitter (Haas, 1958; Haas and Schmitter, 1964). Only later did they come to recognise the relevance of public participation (see Reif, 1993).

3 This attitude might be connected to the experience of the two great wars of this century. One of the major initial motivations for the founding of European institutions was to exclude such a development in the future. As people with direct wartime experience become fewer, this motive recedes.

4 It was perhaps for this reason that the European Parliament was not courageous enough to dismiss the Commission in its first motion of mistrust in January 1999. It did so, however, on the second occasion.

5 According to official EU surveys, 92% see fighting unemployment as a priority, 89% poverty and social exclusion, 88% maintaining peace and security, 85% protecting the environment (Eurobarometer, 48, quoted in Leonard, 1998: 66 fn 6).

6 Grønbech-Jensen (1998) distinguishes between three dimensions of transparency: decision-preparation, decision-taking and decision implementation. According to him the EU is not deficient in decision-preparation. As regards decision-taking, the EU is less transparent than the legislative bodies of the member states. And as regards decision implementation, 'the Community remains closed, at least compared to the Scandinavian member states' (Grønbech-Jensen, 1998: 198).

7 At the time of writing, it is not clear how much power the EP will have after the resignation of the Commission.

8 Lodge distinguishes between inter-institutional relations and the position of the Council. Her argument is that the Council accepted too much mainly unjustified criticism. 'The Commission became the usual scapegoat for government's wanton disregard of the fact that together, acting as the Council, they acted as the EC's legislature but not in a manner of the presumed openness characteristic of liberal democratic parliamentary regimes but of a closed, secretive, unaccountable system' (Lodge, 1994: 346). In Lodge's view, it is thus the Council, not the Commission, which is to blame. While this argument makes some valid points about the structure of the problem and the political motivations for blaming the Commission, it underestimates the Commission's role as a driving force in further unification.

9 It is noteworthy that Germany adheres to an Eastern conception of citizenship. However, at the time of writing, new legislation is being proposed.

10 'Each human being shares often highly contradictory identities and social roles as a member of his family, or rather his families, or his locality, of his professional, social political and religious adherences, of his region, of his nation and possibly by virtue of transnational links . . . They are bound together by the physical continuity of life, by individual biographies . . . ' (Picht, 1993: 84).

11 'If the last 50 years of European history have taught us anything, it is the danger of searching for an identity against the "other", either within or outside European territory' (Leonard, 1998: 37).

12 'Christianity cannot occupy an exclusive place at the heart of a European identity both because large numbers of Europeans are not Christian, and because more

than half of all Europeans think that formal religion no longer plays an important role in society' (Leonard, 1998: 38).

13 There are some signs that previous judgements which saw no mass media potential in EU topics, apart from snide comments (Gerhards, 1993), are obsolete. On the contrary, one would expect that the issue will be high on the political agenda in the years to come. It goes without saying that Eurosceptics will always be fond of sneering about such things as the famous standard for the shape of bananas, allegedly made obligatory by Brussels.

14 It will have to address the question of the degree to which different audiences interpret events, information, and messages in different ways.

15 'Given that it is extremely difficult for the media to create meaningful EU symbols, and to disseminate these over the EU region, it must be concluded that the media will fail in this mission unless there are strong social forces in the real world that are already working towards this goal. In other words, if a European identity is to emerge, it must do so in an evolutionary manner. It is not something that can be constructed' (Bakir, 1996: 194).

16 *The Guardian*, 4 Jan. 1999, p. 12: 'Delors plans new federalist coup'.

Bibliography

Anderson, B. (1983), *Imagined Communities. Reflections on the Origin and Spread of Nationalism*, London: Verso.

Bakir, V. (1996), 'An Identity for Europe? The Role of the Media', in M. Wintle (ed.), *Culture and Identity in Europe*, Aldershot: Avebury, 177–200.

Bardi, L. (1996), 'Transnational Trends in European Parties and the 1994 Elections of the European Parliament', *Party Politics*, 2 (1), 99–114.

Boyd-Barrett, O. (1981), *The International News Agencies*, London: Constable.

Coen, D. (1998), 'The European Business Interest and the Nation State: Large-firm Lobbying in the European Union and Member States', *Journal of Public Policy*, 18: 75–100.

de Lange, R. (1995), 'Paradoxes of European Citizenship', in Peter Fitzpatrick (ed.), *Nationalism, Racism and the Rule of Law*, Aldershot: Dartmouth, 97–115.

Deflem, M. and Fred C. Pampel (1996), 'The Myth of Postnational Identity: Popular Support for European Unification', *Social Forces*, 75 (1), 119–143.

Delanty, G. (1998), 'Social Theory and European Transformation: Is there a European Society?' *Sociological Research Online*, vol. 3, no. 1., <http://www.socre sonline.org.uk/socresonline/3/1/1.html>

Easton, D. (1965), *A Systems Analysis of Political Life*, New York: Wiley.

Featherstone, K. (1994), 'Jean Monnet and the "Democratic Deficit" in the European Union', *Journal of Common Market Studies*, 32, 149–170.

Gerhards, J. (1993), 'Westeuropäische Integration und die Schwierigkeiten der Entstehung einer europäischen Öffentlichkeit', *Zeitschrift für Soziologie*, 22, 96–110.

Gibson, J. L. and Caldeira, G. A. (1998), 'Changes in the Legitimacy of the European Court of Justice: A Post-Maastricht Analysis', *British Journal of Political Science*, 28, 63–91.

Giesen, B. (1993), 'Intellektuelle, Politiker und Experten: Probleme der Konstruktion einer europäischen Identität', in Bernhard Schäfers (ed.), *Lebensverhältnisse und soziale Konflikte im neuen Europa, Verhandlungen des 26. Deutschen Soziologentags*, Frankfurt am Main: Campus, 492–504.

Grimm, D. (1995), 'Does Europe need a Constitution?' in P. Gower and P. Anderson, *The Question of Europe*, London: Verso, 239–258.

Grønbech-Jensen, C. (1998), 'The Scandinavian tradition of open government and the European Union: problems of compatibility?' *Journal of European Public Policy*, 5, 185–199.

Große-Peclum, M.-L. (1990), 'Gibt es den europäischen Zuschauer?' *Zeitschrift für Kulturaustausch*, 40, 185–194.

Haas, E. B. and Schmitter, P. (1964), 'Economics and differential patterns of political integration: projections about unity in Latin America', *International Organization*, 18, 705–37.

Haas, E. B. (1958), *The Uniting of Europe*, Stanford: Stanford University Press.

Habermas, J. (1996), 'Reply to Grimm', in P. Gower and P. Anderson, *The Question of Europe*, London: Verso, 259–264.

Iyengar, S. (1987), 'Television News and Citizens' Explanations of National Affairs', *American Political Science Review*, 81, 815–831.

Key, V. O. Jr. (1961), *Public Opinion and American Democracy*, New York: Knopf.

Leonard, M. (1998), *Rediscovering Europe*, London: Demos.

Lepsius, M. R. (1991), 'Nationalstaat oder Nationalitätenstaat als Modell für die Weiterentwicklung der europäischen Gemeinschaft', in Rudolf Wildenmann (ed.), *Staatswerdung Europas?* Baden-Baden: Nomos, 19–40.

Lindberg, L. and Scheingold, Stuart A. (1980), *Europe's Would-be Policy: Pattern of Change in the European Community*, Englewood Cliffs, NJ: Prentice Hall.

Lodge, J. (1994), 'Transparency and democratic legitimacy', *Journal of Common Market Studies*, 32, 343–368.

Milward, A. (1984), *The Reconstruction of Western Europe*, London: Methuen.

Norris, P. (1997), 'Representation and the democratic deficit', *European Journal of Political Research*, 32, 273–282.

Olson, M. Jr. (1965), *The Logic of Collective Action*, Cambridge, MA: Harvard University Press.

Picht, R. (1993), 'Disturbed Identities: Social and Cultural Mutations in Contemporary Europe', in S. Garcia (ed.), *European Identity and the Search for Legitimacy*, London: Pinter, 81–94.

Pinder, J. (1985–6), 'European Community and Nation-State: A Case for Neofederalism?' *International Affairs*, 62.

Reese-Schäfer, W. (1997), 'Supranational or transnational identity—Two models of cultural integration in Europe', *Politische Vierteljahresschrift*, 38 (2), 318–329.

Reif, K. (1997), 'European elections as member state second-order elections revisited', *European Journal of Political Research*, 31 (1–2), 115–124.

Reif, K. (1993), 'Cultural Convergence and Cultural Diversity as Factors in European Identity', in S. Garcia (ed.), *European Identity and the Search for Legitimacy*, London: Pinter, 131–153.

Reif, K. (1992), 'Wahlen, Wähler und Demokratie in der EG. Die drei Dimensionen des demokratischen Defizits., *Aus Politik und Zeitgeschichte*, B19/92, 43–52.

Richmond, A. (1984), 'Ethnic Nationalism and Post-Industrialism', *Ethnic and Racial Studies*, 7, 4–18.

Scharpf, F. W. (1996), 'Democracy in transnational politics', *Internationale Politik*, 51 (12), 11–20.

Schauer, H. (1992), 'Wir brauchen eine neue Europapolitik', *Aus Politik und Zeitgeschichte*, B42/92, 3–15.

Senger und Etterlin, S. von (1992), 'Das Europa der Eurokraten', *Aus Politik und Zeitgeschichte*, B42/92, 16–27.

Smith, A. D. (1995), 'National Identity and the Idea of European Unity', in P. Gower and P. Anderson, *The Question of Europe*, London: Verso, 318–342.

Swaan, A. de (1991), 'Notes on the emerging global language system—regional, national and supranational', *Media Culture & Society*, 13 (3), 309–323.

Taggart, P. (1998), 'A touchstone of dissent: Euroscepticism in contemporary Western European party systems', *European Journal of Political Research*, 33, 363–388.

Tarrow, S. (1995), 'The Europeanization of Conflict: Reflections from a Social Movement Perspective', *West European Politics*, 18, 223–251.

Taylor, P. (1996), *The European Union in the 1990s*, Oxford: Oxford University Press.

Vogel, D. (1993), 'Representing Diffuse Interests in Environmental Policymaking', in R. Kent Weaver and Bert A. Rockman (eds), *Do Institutions Matter? Government Capabilities in the United States and Abroad*, Washington, DC: The Brookings Institution, 237–271.

Weidenfeld, W. (ed) (1990) *Wie Europa verfaßt sein soll*, Gütersloh: Bertelsmann Stiftung.

Weiler, J. H. H. (1993), 'A Journey to an Unknown Destination: A Retrospective and Prospective of the European Court of Justice in the Area of Political Integration', *Journal of Common Market Studies*, 31: 417–46.

Weiler, J. H. H. (1997), 'To be a European Citizen—Eros and civilization', *Journal of European Public Policy*, 4, 495–519.

Wilson, J. Q. (1980), 'The Politics of Regulation', in J. Q. Wilson (ed.), *The Politics of Regulation*, New York.

Extending ethnolinguistic democracy in Europe: the case of Wales

Stephen May

Abstract

The recent establishment of political devolution in Scotland and Wales would appear to herald far greater national, and eventually regional autonomy within a British state long dominated by England. However, support for devolution in Wales remains, at best, ambivalent; in contrast to Scotland where devolution is far more strongly supported. Much of this can be explained by the fact that Wales, unlike Scotland, is almost indistinguishable from England with respect to its institutional structure. As such, Wales has historically sought a distinctive identity from England principally through the promotion and retention of Welsh language and culture *within* rather than outside these shared institutional arrangements. This, in turn, has led in recent years to a significantly increased role for the Welsh language in the public domain in Wales, after centuries of proscription, and the emergence of a nascent Welsh bilingual state. The prospect of greater self-government is likely to solidify these developments. However, it can be argued that the contribution of Wales is most significant here not as an example of political devolution but as a model of ethnolinguistic democracy. In this latter respect, Wales provides us with a democratic model that specifically accommodates and promotes bilingualism and minority language rights while, in so doing, redefining the traditional role of language(s) in the nation-state. Both these aspects offer important lessons for the rest of Europe's nation-states which, despite moves to greater political devolution and regionalism, often remain reluctant to protect, let alone foster the minority languages still spoken within their borders.

Introduction

Since its landslide victory in May 1997, the present Labour government in Britain, led by Tony Blair, has embarked upon an ambitious and wide ranging process of constitutional reform of the British state. The first stage of this reform, which was trailed early in Labour's election manifesto, has been the granting of greater political (and, to a lesser extent, economic) devolution for Scotland and Wales. This process of devolution was implemented almost immediately Labour came to power with the publication of government white papers outlining the plans for Scottish and Welsh devolution. There followed referenda in Scotland and Wales on the establishment of a Scottish Parliament and a Welsh Assembly, respectively, with a strong endorsement in the Scottish referendum and an extremely narrow endorsement in Wales. The closeness of the Welsh referendum notwithstanding, both institutions were formally established in May 1999. They were also elected by proportional representation, at least in part; another first in a British electoral system which has until now been based exclusively on the Westminster 'first past the post' system.

These developments ostensibly pave the way for far greater national, and eventually regional autonomy within a British state long dominated by England and, in particular, its south eastern metropolitan core in and around London. From a broader European perspective, they also appear consonant with moves towards greater political devolution and regional control within European Union member states, something which again Britain had, until these developments, resolutely resisted (Keating and Jones, 1995).

However, the closeness of the Welsh referendum vote raises some important issues, most notably the ongoing ambivalence of many in Wales to the prospect of greater self-government. Much of this can be explained by the fact that Wales, unlike Scotland, is almost indistinguishable from England with respect to its institutional structure. This is reflected in the administrative term 'England and Wales' which is employed to describe a wide range of shared institutions and programmes. As such, Wales has historically sought a distinctive identity from England principally through the promotion and retention of Welsh language and culture *within* rather than outside these shared institutional arrangements. This process, which may be described as 'cultural nationalism' (Hutchinson, 1994), emphasises 'cultural continuity' and collective memory and does not necessarily extend to an advocacy for self government or secession.

The consequence has been that much of the nationalist activity in Wales has concentrated on issues of language and culture. It is not possible in this chapter to explore more fully the social and political influence of Welsh nationalism, its tendency to historical romanticism and, at least until the most recent elections to the new Welsh Assembly, its limited electoral success (see Borland *et al.*, 1992; C. Williams, 1994; G. A. Williams, 1985).[1] However, what is of principal interest here is that, despite this unpromising background, the pressure exerted by nationalist groups on the British state has led in recent years to a significantly increased role for the Welsh language in the public domain in Wales, after centuries of proscription, and the emergence of a nascent Welsh bilingual state.

The prospect of greater self-government is likely to solidify these developments. However, it can be argued that the contribution of Wales is most significant here not as an example of devolution but as a model of ethnolinguistic democracy. In this latter respect, the development of an emergent bilingual state administration is predicated on the linguistic rights of minority Welsh speakers and effected by the legitimation and institutionalisation of the Welsh language, alongside English, in the civic realm. As such, Wales provides us with a democratic model that specifically accommodates and promotes bilingualism and minority language rights while, in so doing, redefining the traditional role of language(s) in the nation-state. Both these aspects offer important lessons for the rest of Europe's nation-states which, despite moves to greater political devolution and regionalism, often remain reluctant to protect, let alone foster the minority languages still spoken within their borders (Nelde *et al.*, 1996).

Welsh devolution and its discontents

On 18 September 1997, the Welsh electorate voted in a national referendum in favour of a devolved Welsh Assembly. The result constitutes an unprecedented development in the history of Wales. For the first time since the (1536) Act of Union, Wales—or Cymru, to give it its Welsh name—will have a formalised degree of self government, however limited, within the British state.

But only just, since the vote for devolution was achieved by the narrowest of margins—50.3 per cent to 49.7 per cent, an actual majority of less than 6000. Indeed, the contest was so close that it came to hinge on the result from the last of the twenty-two Welsh counties to declare, Carmarthenshire. This predominantly Welsh-speaking area in west Wales voted in favour in sufficient numbers to allow the 'yes campaign' which, until that time had been trailing, to win through at the last. Even so, the final 'yes vote' comprised only

149

25.2 per cent of the total electorate in Wales of 2.2 million people. Moreover, clear regional differences were evident between the more anglicised east and north-east of Wales bordering England, whose counties voted no, and the more Welsh-speaking west and north-west of Wales who, allied with the Labour heartlands in the southern Welsh valleys, voted yes. As many media commentators observed at the time, Wales seemed a nation divided.[2]

The degree of surprise surrounding the closeness of the Welsh vote, voiced by these same commentators, was at one level understandable. After all, the referendum had been instigated by the newly elected Labour government in Britain as part of a wider package of constitutional reform, devolving power to the constituent nations and regions of Britain. The constitutional reform programme had been widely trailed and had formed a central feature of the Labour party's election policy in May of that year. In that election, Labour had won an unprecedented 179 seat majority over their main rivals, the British Conservative Party, decisively ending the latter's eighteen uninterrupted years in power. Such was the scale of Labour's victory that in Wales—admittedly, a traditional Labour stronghold anyway—the Tories had lost all their parliamentary seats. This, in itself, should have augured well for a comfortable endorsement of devolution in Wales for what, after all, was a central Labour policy. And if this was somehow not enough, as many pro-devolutionists indeed feared (see below), the example of Scotland should also have acted as a strong precedent. Just the week before, the Scottish electorate in a parallel referendum for a fully fledged Scottish Parliament, had delivered a decisive vote in favour of devolution at 74.3 per cent to 25.7 per cent. Given that 60.1 per cent of the Scottish electorate voted in the referendum this also constituted an endorsement by 45 per cent of that electorate.

And yet at another level, the closeness of the vote, or the fact that Welsh devolution succeeded at all, was not so surprising. Objections were consistently raised in the campaign, for example, about the inadequacies of the Welsh devolution package itself. In contrast to Scotland's 129 seat Parliament—with its ability to enact primary legislation and vary taxes—the Welsh were only to have a 60 seat Assembly, with all that the difference in nomenclature implies. The Welsh Assembly, once it is elected in May 1999, will assume responsibility for the administrative powers currently exercised by the Welsh Secretary in the British Parliament in Westminster, London—a not insignificant development since it involves direct control of an annual budget presently estimated at £7 billion.

However, it will also have no legislative and tax varying powers beyond the enactment of secondary legislation. This clear disparity between the Scottish and Welsh devolution proposals led to the criticism, effectively employed by the anti-devolution campaign in Wales, that the Welsh Assembly would be a 'mere talking shop', and thus an expensive and unnecessary economic and administrative burden. This charge could never have been made successfully against the proposed Scottish Parliament.

The disparity between the Scottish and Welsh devolution proposals also points to another, more crucial reason for the close result of the 1997 Devolution Referendum in Wales. Historically, there has always been a much greater ambivalence in Wales towards self government than in Scotland—ironically, most notably in the Labour Party itself, the dominant political party in Wales since early this century. This is graphically illustrated by the result of the only other instance of a Devolution Referendum—in 1979, under the previous Labour administration—when the Welsh electorate convincingly rejected devolution, by over four to one.

Indeed, one of the most notable features of the 1979 campaign was the vociferous opposition to devolution from within the Welsh Labour party itself. In effect, this group contended that a Welsh Assembly would be 'a sellout to nationalism' and the first step onto the 'slippery slope to separatism' (Davies, 1989), arguing instead for the primacy of British class-based interests. As G. A. Williams comments, this group 'played largely on the fears of the Welsh language and (rather oddly) of corruption, fears of being taken over by north Walian Welsh speakers with double-barrelled names, [and] fears of losing hold on Britain' (1985: 294). Ironically, many in the Welsh-speaking heartland of north and west Wales, *y fro Gymraeg*, voted against devolution because of the opposite fear—that any subsequent Assembly would be dominated by the interests of the more populous industrialised and anglicised south (Osmond, 1989). When these two trends combined, the overwhelming defeat of Welsh devolution became inevitable—confirming, it seemed, the principal allegiance of the Welsh electorate to *British* interests (G. A. Williams, 1985). As Balsom *et al.* conclude in a survey of public attitudes in Wales at the time: 'There is almost a complete lack of political will for self-determination' (1982: 19; see also Butt Philip, 1975: 125–129). In contrast, the parallel Scottish Referendum in 1979 saw a narrow vote in favour (52 per cent) although at only 33 per cent of the total electorate this still fell short of the 40 per cent threshold required for change at the time.

Given this background, it is not so surprising perhaps that devolution in Wales was not so warmly endorsed in the 1997 referendum as many had expected. Again, some Welsh Labour MPs publicly opposed devolution, although not to the same extent as in 1979. Moreover, in the campaign, and in the government's white paper itself, *A Voice for Wales* (Stationery Office, 1997a), almost no mention was made of Welsh national identity as a basis for supporting devolution. Instead, the stress was placed on the economic and administrative benefits of devolution and its proposed effect in redressing the 'democratic deficit' in Wales (Adonis, 1997; Freedland, 1997; Thomas, 1997). *Scotland's Parliament* (Stationery Office, 1997b), the equivalent white paper for Scotland, was markedly different in this respect. As with the Scottish referendum campaign more broadly, the case for devolution was underpinned at all times by the question of Scottish national identity—framed principally in relation to Scotland's claim to historical nationhood—and the political rights attendant on it (*The Times Higher*, 12 September 1997: 7). Concomitantly, the charge that devolution would lead inexorably to the 'breakup of Britain' had little purchase in the Scottish campaign, in contrast to Wales where this fear was more effectively mobilised by anti-devolutionists.

What lies behind these clear differences between Wales and Scotland—with respect both to enthusiasm for devolution itself, and to the status and powers ascribed to their respective legislative bodies? To answer these questions we need to examine briefly the historical antecedents which have shaped the Welsh political and cultural context and its relationship to the British state.

The institutional incorporation of Wales

Unlike Scotland, which was united by treaty with England in 1707, and which has since retained intact much of its civil society (including its own legal, church, and education systems), Wales has a much longer and more assimilative relationship with its dominant neighbour, England. A brief history is instructive here. Wales was brought increasingly into the ambit of English rule from the time of Edward I (1239–1307). The subsequent colonisation of Wales by England in the fourteenth and fifteenth centuries led to the area's increasing anglicisation, particularly with respect to trade (Kearney, 1989). Relatedly, while much of Wales continued to speak Welsh—a language spoken since the sixth century and for which written records exist from the eighth century—Welsh/English bilingualism became an increasing feature in these areas (P. Jenkins, 1992). These developments were the prelude to the area's formal incorporation within the British state in the sixteenth century. The (1536) Act of Union, and the related act of 1542, instigated by Henry VIII (1491–1547), firmly situated Wales within the political, legal and administrative jurisdiction of the British Crown and Parliament. As a result of these acts, the Welsh language was proscribed from the courts, and from all official domains, in favour of English, while virtually all separate Welsh institutions were eliminated.

The instructions of the Act of Union directly affected only a small number of Welsh élite—those who held or sought property or position. However, with the dismantling of any separate institutional focus, the establishment of a political norm soon became a powerful social norm as well (Butt Philip, 1975). As Iris Marion Young observes, if particular groups 'have greater economic, political or social power, their group-related experiences, points of view, or cultural assumptions will tend to become the norm, biasing the standards or procedures of achievement and inclusion that govern social, political and economic institutions' (1993: 133). This describes well the English/Welsh relationship. In effect, the Welsh élite became assimilated into the English class and political system—eventually adopting both the latter's mores and language (C. Williams, 1982). Concomitantly, Welsh language and culture—still strongly evident among the peasantry (*y werin*)—were deemed of little value, both by the Welsh élite themselves and by the English political system to which they were increasingly beholden. As the Welsh historian, Kenneth Morgan, concludes: 'Wales continued to be regarded as a remote tribal backwater, economically backward, adhering obstinately to its antique language in the face of the "march of intellect"' (1995: 198).

It was not until the rise of religious Nonconformity[3] in the early half of the nineteenth century, and the industrialisation of Wales in the latter half, that this state of affairs was to change significantly. These two developments provided the basis for a new Welsh national (and nationalist) movement—a movement whose characteristics have been much discussed elsewhere (see Morgan, 1995; G. A. Williams, 1985). For the purposes of this present discussion, it is enough to point out that an important consequence of the rise of nineteenth century nationalism in Wales was the *re-establishment* of separate Welsh institutions and legislative measures. These were primarily cultural, religious and educational—reflecting the particular emphases of the nationalist movement of the time. Legislation specific to Wales included the (1881) Welsh Sunday Closing Act, the (1888) Local Government Act and the (1889) Welsh Intermediate Education Act.[4] More significantly perhaps, a range of national institutions were created over this period, including the University of Wales (1883), the Board of Education, a national library and a national museum (all 1907), and a Department of Agriculture (1912).

Yet, despite these advances, the basic political and social organisation of Wales remained largely indistinguishable from England's. For example, it was not until 1956 that a Welsh capital (Cardiff) was officially designated. Indeed, it was only after the Second World War that a specifically Welsh institutional framework was to emerge. As Charlotte Aull Davies (1989) argues, this development was tied principally to the expansion of the British welfare system which saw many government departments reorganised on a regional basis. In most cases, Wales came to be treated as a single administrative unit, resulting in the steady growth of Welsh bureaucracy and, for the first time, a coordinated degree of economic planning in Wales—although such developments still fell well short of the idea of regional government in the wider European sense (Keating and Jones, 1995).

Easily the most prominent of the newly emergent regional organisations was the Welsh Office, established in 1964 and headed by a Welsh Secretary of State. Even this development, though, indicated the limited and belated nature of such reforms in Wales since its counterpart in Scotland—the Scottish Office—had been in existence since 1886. Moreover, upon its establishment under Harold Wilson's Labour government, the role of the Welsh Office was initially envisaged as being largely symbolic since the Labour government's own political interests at the time continued to be resolutely British and centralist (G. A. Williams, 1985). However, and this is the crucial point, once established, the Welsh Office gradually began to accumulate power (Davies, 1989). This gradual enlargement of the Welsh Office's administrative responsibilities led, in turn, to the introduction of a range of legislative measures specific to Wales and, in particular, the Welsh language. These measures, which began to lay the basis for a bilingual state (Williams and Raybould, 1991), included: the (1967) Welsh Language Act, offering 'equal validity' for English and Welsh in Wales; the (1988) Education Reform Act which incorporated a specifically Welsh (and Welsh language) dimension into the newly established National Curriculum of

England and Wales; and the (1993) Welsh Language Act which extended the 1967 Act considerably in its support for Welsh in the public domain.

I will outline in more detail below the specific nature of these developments. Suffice it to say at this point, that the institutional infrastructure administered by the Welsh Office came to be increasingly identified with the re-emergence of the Welsh language into the public or civic realm, after years of proscription and neglect. It must be said though that these developments were also to some extent the result of the strong political pressure exerted by the Welsh language movement in the 1960s and 1970s. This movement coalesced around *Cymdeithas yr Iaith Gymraeg* (the Welsh Language Society) which was established in 1962 as an organisation committed to direct non-violent action on behalf of the Welsh language. Their programme of direct action contributed, at least in some measure, to the establishment of Welsh-medium language schools, Welsh language media (notably, the Welsh language television channel, *Sianel Pedwar Cymru* [S4C]), the Welsh Language Board, and to an increasing demand for public services available in Welsh. It led the now late Gwyn Williams—himself, no great fan of the Welsh language movement—to conclude:

> The consequences have been extraordinary. In response to a militant campaign whose hunger has been insatiable, the British state, ruling a largely indifferent or hostile Welsh population, has in a manner which has few parallels outside the [former] Soviet Union, countenanced and indeed subsidised Welsh cultural nationalism. *Wales is now officially, visibly and audibly a bilingual country.* The equal status of Welsh is nearing achievement. Whole Welsh language structures, serviced by an effective training and supply apparatus, exist in education, administrative life and the media. The issue of the Welsh language, in many fields of Welsh action, blots out all other political considerations. (G. A. Williams, 1985: 292–293; my emphasis)

The emasculation of the Welsh language

The recent re-emergence of the Welsh language into the public domain is all the more remarkable in light of the long history of anglicisation in Wales. Indeed, the process of anglicisation—by which the Welsh people became increasingly assimilated into an

English-dominated cultural and ideological system (C. Williams, 1990)—is perhaps the most prominent aspect of its history. In this respect, it is not so much the *spread* of English which has been crucial in anglicising Wales, at least not up until this century. Indeed, Wales remained 90 per cent Welsh-speaking in the sixteenth and seventeenth centuries (P. Jenkins, 1992) and as late as 1880, three out of four Welsh people still spoke the Welsh language by choice (Morgan, 1981). Rather, it has been the diminution of the *status* of Welsh and its *restriction* to private, low-status language domains which has proved to be more debilitating historically.

The cumulative effect of these processes has seen a rapid decline of the Welsh language over the course of this century. The once strong Welsh-speaking heartland (*y fro Gymraeg*) has retreated in the face of English into the western and northern rural margins of Wales. This retreat is also reflected in the overall percentage of Welsh speakers in Wales, which has diminished from 43.5 per cent of the population in 1911 to only 18.7 per cent at the time of the 1991 census—approximately 600,000 speakers. Not only that, Welsh monolingual speakers—who, in 1911, still constituted 8.5 per cent of the population—have now all but disappeared. Put simply, virtually all Welsh speakers today are bilingual in English as well (Aitchison and Carter, 1994).

To many the decline of Welsh was viewed as a positive trend— English was perceived as the language of progress, equality, opportunity, the media and mass entertainment (C. Williams, 1990). Even today, the practice of unfavourably comparing the utility and status of Welsh to English remains commonplace. In effect, the English language has come to be seen by many Welsh as a form of cultural and linguistic capital, an escape from primitivism, and a demonstration of having embraced the 'modern' way of life (Miles, 1996). Concomitantly, the Welsh language was increasingly regarded as having little cultural, social and economic value.

Given the long historical vitiation of Welsh, that so many adopted this latter option is perhaps not surprising. What *is* surprising is that it took so long for them to do so, and that despite it all, Welsh remains a living language, still spoken today as a language of everyday life by nearly 20 per cent of the Welsh population. Moreover, in the 1991 census, this decline has for the first time this century been, if not reversed, at least abated (Aitchison and Carter, 1994). It is to these counter-trends, and their institutional basis, that I now want to turn.

Building a bilingual state: the legitimation and institutionalisation of Welsh

Since 1991 we have seen in Wales the development of a number of striking counter-trends to the long history of anglicisation and associated Welsh language loss. Not only has Welsh language decline begun to be reversed, albeit still tentatively, but there is now also a growing urban base for the Welsh language. Most notable here is the role and influence of the capital city, Cardiff, which has become the administrative centre for the Welsh language. The growing urbanisation of the Welsh language thus highlights the significance of the institutionalisation of Welsh, particularly in the public sector where the ability to speak Welsh is viewed increasingly as a form of linguistic and cultural capital. To this end, Aitchison and Carter observe that while the long demonstrated detraction of the language is still extant, 'it is by no means as powerful as it was, and there is [now] a widespread awareness of the advantages of a knowledge of Welsh, especially in public employment' (1994: 115). These developments also present us with a central irony, since the decline of the traditional Welsh-speaking heartland, so long associated with the fate of the language, is continuing apace at the same time as the language is being regenerated in urban contexts. This fascinating dualism between a declining heartland and a resurgent periphery constitutes the present core of contemporary Welsh life (C. Williams, 1995).

Also significant is the fact that the most rapid growth in the Welsh language can be found in the 3–15 year age group. The burgeoning use of the Welsh language in this age group—which now constitutes 22 per cent of the Welsh-speaking population—is largely attributable to the influence of Welsh-medium education, particularly in the anglicised areas of south and north-east Wales where it has been widely promoted in recent times (see below). Accordingly, many of these speakers are second language learners of Welsh, a feature that is increasingly evident in the adult population as well, where language courses for adult learners are growing in popularity.

There are some caveats to be made here. One is that the dominance of the public sector, at least to date, in fostering the renaissance of the Welsh language may tie it too closely to a particular, class-based bilingual élite—as, for example, happened historically in Ireland. Another is the potential backlash that such an association may generate among English speakers. Indeed, this is already evident in charges of 'reverse discrimination' and even 'racism', at recruitment policies which give preference to bilinguals within the public sector (see below). A third caveat has to do with the efficacy of Welsh-medium education. While it has proved crucial in promoting Welsh/English bilingualism, especially in the anglicised areas of Wales, it does not ensure that those for whom Welsh is principally a school language will continue to speak the language in other social contexts (Baker, 1992; Jones, 1995; C. Williams, 1994, 1995). I will return to each of these concerns in due course. Meanwhile, it is still possible to state that the prospects for the Welsh language itself, and the possibilities of successfully developing a bilingual Welsh state, have never looked better. A recent national survey on attitudes to the language, for example, found widespread support across Wales (71 per cent) for the use of Welsh. Similarly strong support (75 per cent) was found for making Welsh co-equal in status with English in Wales, while almost nine out of ten (88 per cent) agreed that the Welsh language is something to be proud of (NOP, 1995). This remarkable turn around in the fortunes of the Welsh language, and for the prospects of state bilingualism, are underpinned by recent legislation in Wales—notably, the (1993) Welsh Language Act and the (1988) Education Reform Act—and by the rapid expansion, and widely acknowledged success of Welsh-medium education.

The Welsh Language Act

Colin Williams has argued, in relation to Wales, that 'if a fully functional bilingual society [is to be achieved], where choice and opportunity are the twin pillars of individual language rights, then clearly that possibility has to be constructed through both the promotional and regulatory powers of the state' (1994: 162). A significant step in establishing such rights in Wales occurred in October 1993, when a new Welsh Language Act (*Mesur yr Iaith Gymraeg*) passed into law. The Act replaced its more limited 1967 predecessor and repealed all previous legislation to do with the Welsh language, including the original Acts of Union. The new Act's genesis, under the then Conservative government, was the result of a more sympathetic approach to Wales and the Welsh language by the British government in general (Thomas, 1997), and of the cumulative influence of the Welsh language lobby in particular. While still limited in some respects, as we shall see, it nonetheless clearly reflects the significant advances made on behalf of the Welsh language in recent times.

In the Act, Welsh is treated for the first time as having 'a basis of equality' with English within Wales although it qualifies this equality as being that which is appropriate within the circumstances and 'reasonable practicable'. To this end, the new Act provides for the right to use Welsh in courts, given suitable notice, and also states that public documents in Welsh should carry the same legal weight as those in English. However, perhaps its most significant feature is the *statutory* recognition provided to *Bwrdd yr Iaith Gymraeg* (the Welsh Language Board). *Bwrdd yr Iaith* had originally been established in July 1988, although merely as an advisory body on the language, with little status and power. In this respect, it was not too dissimilar initially to its Irish equivalent, *Bord na Gaelige* (Irish Language Board). Under the Act's aegis, however, *Bwrdd yr Iaith* is now authorised not only to promote and facilitate the use of the Welsh language but also to ensure its adoption within the public sector. The latter is to be achieved via formal language schemes formulated by public organisations and submitted to the Board. These schemes are to specify the measures each organisation aims to take in order to provide effective bilingual services in Wales. Again, there is the caveat invoked that such bilingual services will be provided 'so far as is both appropriate in the circumstances and reasonably practical'. However, as the subsequent Draft Guidelines for implementation of the Act outline, it is *Bwrdd yr Iaith*, crucially, not the organisations, which determines the parameters of reasonableness and practicality: 'It will not be acceptable for those preparing schemes to adopt a highly subjective and restricted view of what is appropriate in their circumstances or reasonably practicable' (Welsh Language Board, 1995: 6). Likewise, the Draft Guidelines stipulate that organisations should not rely on the *current* demand for services in Welsh as a basis for their schemes, on the premise that once more effective bilingual services become available so too will demand increase:

> It is acknowledged that, in the past, many Welsh speakers turned to English in dealing with public organisations because they were not certain what services were available in Welsh. Some were also concerned that using Welsh could lead to delay or a lower standard of service. Therefore, *whatever their experience to date*, organisations should plan for an increase in demand and respond accordingly. (1995: 5; my emphasis)

The end result envisaged for each organisation is that public service provision through Welsh should be a natural, integral part of the planning and delivery of that service. For this to occur, a sufficient number of Welsh-speaking staff is required, particularly in regional areas where the number of Welsh speakers from which to draw has been traditionally low. This, in turn, will require the active recruitment of Welsh-speaking staff. As the Guidelines again state: 'Organisations may need to adopt positive action strategies which publicise the fact that job applications from Welsh speakers are welcomed. This will reflect the fact that Welsh will increasingly be a regular part of public life—especially as organisations implement the requirements of the Welsh Language Act through their individual Welsh language schemes' (1995: 24). Moreover, in the context of the language schemes, if an organisation concludes that it cannot reasonably meet its obligations under the Act without having Welsh speakers in certain posts 'then, as a general rule, appointing persons able to speak Welsh to these posts will be justifiable' (1995: 24).

As one might perhaps expect, this position is not entirely uncontroversial. Indeed, the question of whether a knowledge of Welsh can be stipulated as a requirement of employment has faced a number of legal challenges in Wales. In one prominent case in 1985, *Jones v. Gwynedd County Council,* Gwynedd county council was taken to court by two disgruntled English-speaking applicants when they failed to secure a council position working with senior citizens (many of whom were Welsh-speaking). They argued that the Welsh language requirement for the position was discriminatory under the British (1976) Race Relations Act. The initial Industrial Tribunal upheld the complaint on the basis that Welsh speakers formed a 'sub-ethnic' group—thus suggesting that differentiation on the basis of ethnicity had occurred. However, this was later overturned on appeal. In this latter ruling (in 1986) it was concluded that language differences within an ethnic group were not applicable under the Race Relations Act.

The Welsh Language Board Draft Guidelines also specifically adopt this position, stating that 'distinguishing between Welsh people on the grounds of their ability or inability to speak Welsh does not . . . amount to racial discrimination' (1995: 24). The Guidelines further assert that 'under the law of the European Union, it will not be discriminatory to insist that a post-holder should be able to speak a specific language if linguistic knowledge is required to fulfil the duties of the post' (1995: 24). In other words, language qualifications in the labour market are no more or less restrictive than other professional qualifications required for specific forms of employment and are entirely applicable, and defensible, when bilingualism and/or multilingualism are a functional necessity.

Levelling charges of 'racism' with regard to such language requirements can thus be seen as a manifestation of narrow monolingualism rather than a legitimate argument (Glyn Williams, 1994).

That said, there remain limitations in the scope of the Welsh Language Act and in the related remit of *Bwrdd yr Iaith*. For example, in contrast to two equivalent private members bills on the Welsh language, tabled unsuccessfully to the British parliament in the 1980s, the Act does not accord official status to Welsh. This omission, along with the various caveats evident in the Act, suggest that the status of the Welsh language remains subsidiary to English. Conspicuously, the Welsh Language Board's remit also does not extend to the private business sector—unlike in Québec, for example (see C. Williams, 1994). This means that businesses may, if they choose, remain largely untouched by Welsh language requirements. While many are beginning to respond positively to such requirements, often as the result of local pressure, the opposition to the mandatory use of Welsh by industry and business on grounds of practicality and profitability remains strong and consistent (Aitchison and Carter, 1994). Moreover, even in the state sector, the Board only has the right to investigate organisations which fail demonstrably to meet the requirements outlined under the Act and, subsequently, to *recommend* remedial action. There is also no general clause which *guarantees* an individual the right to use the Welsh language in their interactions with any public body, or to insist on a Welsh-medium education for their children.

Nonetheless, the significance of the Welsh Language Act and the functions of *Bwrdd yr Iaith Gymraeg* should not be underestimated. As Colin Williams argues, 'the reconstituted Welsh Language Board looks set to become the most critical government agency yet in the social history of Wales' (1995: 65). In effect, *Bwrdd yr Iaith* is in the vanguard of a new approach to language planning in Wales which now centres increasingly on the *re*legitimation of Welsh in a specifically *bilingual* context. To this end also, the language focus in Wales has broadened beyond the needs and interests of Welsh speakers, with the exclusive overtones that this preoccupation necessarily suggests, to include a more systematic recognition of the needs of second language learners and non-Welsh speakers. Williams concludes that the increasing professionalisation, or institutionalisation of the Welsh language 'has severed the intimate link between language promotion and the nationalist programme and offers a more promising basis for Welsh development precisely because it has been embraced by a wide spectrum of public and political agencies in Wales' (1994: 142).

Welsh-medium education

This more inclusive approach to Welsh language planning is also clearly evident in the rapid growth of, and associated burgeoning support for Welsh-medium education—that is, an education where pupils are taught wholly or partly through the medium of Welsh. For example, the greatest growth of Welsh-medium education—and, by extension, of Welsh speakers—has occurred in the historically anglicised areas of Wales. Thus, Welsh-medium education has been crucial in providing an expanding base of Welsh-speakers in these anglicised areas and, more broadly, in contributing to the abatement of the long history of Welsh language decline. The increasingly widespread support for Welsh-medium education—among both English- and Welsh-speaking parents, many of whom are middle-class—also has much to do with the educational success of the movement (Lyon and Ellis, 1991; Packer and Campbell, 1993). In short, Welsh-medium education has shown that academic success and the retention of a minority language are not incompatible aims. In so doing, it has also demonstrated more broadly how the legitimation and institutionalisation of Welsh can be successfully achieved within the public or civic realm.

The result is that Welsh-medium education is now an established, and prominent, feature of contemporary Welsh life only some 50 years after the first Welsh-medium school was actually established. Indeed, the actual growth of Welsh-medium education, particularly in recent years, can be regarded as nothing short of spectacular. *Cylchoedd meithrin* (nursery groups), for example, have seen a growth throughout Wales from a base of 67 in 1971 to 617 in 1992. In 1992, these groups reached over 10,000 children, 60 per cent of whom came from non-Welsh-speaking backgrounds (PDAG, 1993a). Similarly, in 1993 there were 538 Welsh-medium primary schools, constituting 33.3 per cent of the total number of primary schools in Wales and 19.8 per cent of the total primary school population (PDAG, 1993b).[5] Moreover, the majority of pupils being educated in these Welsh-medium schools (59 per cent) actually spoke English at home (PDAG, 1994). A similar story is evident in secondary education where 58 secondary schools (25.5 per cent of the total number of secondary schools) are designated as Welsh-medium schools (PDAG, 1993b). Welsh-medium education is also increasingly available at tertiary level, albeit still in a limited capacity, while there is special provision for training teachers through the medium of Welsh at designated teachers colleges.

However, there remain limits to both the influence and efficacy of Welsh-medium education. One limitation relates to the extent to which education can influence wider language use. Thus, while the rapid growth of Welsh-medium education has clearly had a mitigating effect on Welsh language decline, it has not been able to halt, let alone reverse this decline as yet. Part of this can be explained by the largely piecemeal development of Welsh-medium education which has resulted in considerable variation of provision from region to region (Rawkins, 1979, 1987). Add to this the fact that even now Welsh-medium education only reaches approximately 20 per cent of the school population and it is not hard to see the limits of its reach and influence. In short, the majority of children in Wales are still educated through the medium of English, a point that should not be forgotten.

For those pupils from English-speaking homes who learn Welsh through school, and even for first language speakers of Welsh, there is the additional question of whether they will continue to use the language once they have left school. Numerous language attitude surveys in Wales (Baker, 1985, 1992; Lewis, 1975; Sharp *et al.*, 1973), and wider sociolinguistic research (Edwards, 1985; Fishman, 1991; Gardner and Lambert, 1972; Harley, 1993), suggest that education by itself is not enough to maintain minority language use. This is particularly so for Welsh-medium schools in anglicised areas. Such schools may well have contributed to the creation of a new generation of Welsh speakers in the post-war period. However, they also epitomise the fragmentation of the wider bilingual community within Wales since these schools often provide the only significant domain where a predominantly Welsh-medium milieu can be experienced (C. Williams, 1995).

The increasing institutionalisation of Welsh in the public domain is a key here to providing more opportunities and incentives to maintain the use of Welsh after school. However, even this has limitations. The institutionalisation of Welsh does not extend as yet to the corporate sector and, along with the genesis of Welsh-medium education, it also tends to reinforce the perception that a knowledge and use of Welsh is a peculiarly middle-class preoccupation. The latter perception arises to some extent from the close historical association of the middle-classes with Welsh-medium education. This association is further reflected in the growing development of a bilingual élite within the public sector—a Welsh 'taffia' as it is sometimes called. To this end, Colin Williams cautions that because the growth in the educational sector has outpaced concomitant developments in the world of work and social interaction:

we are faced with a generation of bilingual school leavers who have been socialised into believing that their bilingualism is prized by a society, which on examination turns out to be a rather narrowly constructed, middle-class public sector society, which rewards its own as purveyors of information and knowledge. There are clear class implications in the development of an administrative bureaucracy which is both the principal agency for change and the principal net beneficiary of [such] change. (1994: 168)

Williams suggests that there may be no other way forward but nonetheless argues that too great a reliance on the public sector may be detrimental to the language in the long term. As such, much of the present advocacy of Welsh language planning is directed towards extending the use of Welsh into other domains (Aitchison and Carter, 1994; C. Williams, 1994, 1995; Jones, 1995; see also Baker, 1992). The central premise of this new approach is encapsulated by Williams: 'although great strides have been made . . . within the "Welsh schools" system, we now need to refocus our central goal as language planners from *bilingual education in Wales* to *education for a bilingual Wales*' (1994: 143).

While much of the educational interest in Wales has centred then on Welsh-medium education, these caveats point to the need for an educational approach with concerns that are broader than just language. Crucially, this is also now beginning to occur in Wales, principally as a result of the (1988) Education Reform Act and its subsequent impact on the organisational and curricular development of Welsh education.

The Education Reform Act

For all the significance of developments relating to Welsh-medium education, what remained lacking was a *formal* distinction between the English and Welsh education systems. Welsh-medium education may have established a significant niche for itself, and generated a related educational bureaucracy. However, distinct educational provision in Wales was still primarily dependent on internal advocacy from parents and educationalists and, more crucially, external largesse from the British government (Jones, 1997). In this respect, the control and direction of Welsh education continued to reflect the wider incorporation of Wales within a British state dominated by England. The (1988) Education Reform Act was to change all this, albeit accidentally.

The Act, a centrepiece of the Conservative Thatcher administration, established a National (sic) Curriculum for England and Wales. The deliberate qualification in the title of the 'National' Curriculum is important here. Like all previous major educational reform affecting 'England and Wales', the whole thrust of the Act was actually concerned with the needs of the English (national) curriculum (Jones, 1997). Ironically, as it turns out, this is perhaps where it has been least successful. The New Right ideology underpinning the Act—an unwieldy combination of *laissez faire* economics and social conservatism—led on the one hand to an emphasis on the increased marketisation and commodification of education and, on the other hand, to the promotion of a centralised, highly prescriptive, 'traditional' curriculum. This dual emphasis, and its sometimes conflicting demands, resulted in both considerable controversy about, and active opposition to the subsequent implementation of the National Curriculum within England (see Ball, 1990; Flude and Hammer, 1990; Lingard *et al.*, 1993).

In marked contrast, the Act has been received in Wales with considerably more enthusiasm. Many of its more controversial New Right elements have simply been disregarded in Wales, thus avoiding the controversies apparent in England, while debates about curriculum content have also proved less problematic (Daugherty, 1993; Reynolds, 1994). More crucially, the Act has achieved what no other previous major legislation had come near to doing—the establishment of a Welsh education system *in its own right*. That this development was not envisaged by its original proponents makes the end result even more remarkable.

In short, the 1988 Act has accomplished a fundamental transformation of Welsh education within the last decade. This is most evident in the curriculum where the Welsh language is now not only formally recognised as a principal language of instruction within Welsh-medium schools, but also as a *national* language that should be taught *as of right* to *all* pupils within Wales. Despite recommendations from previous educational reports along these lines, little actual progress had been made prior to the Act in this latter regard.

The formal recognition of Welsh throughout all schools in Wales occurred because at the time of the drafting of the National Curriculum in the mid-1980s there were a sufficient number of Welsh-medium schools to ensure that the government of the day could not define the core language component of the National Curriculum (at least in Wales) as solely English. Conceding that Welsh was now the language of instruction and initial study for a significant minority of schools in Wales meant that Welsh had to be recognised as a 'core subject' in these schools under the Act (Williams and Raybould, 1991). Following from this, Welsh has also been given the status of a 'foundation subject' within all other schools in Wales, to be *compulsorily* studied by all non-Welsh-speaking children as a subject (National Language Forum, 1991). As an official report on the place of Welsh within the National Curriculum summarised it at the time: 'Our objective is to ensure that non-Welsh-speaking pupils in Wales, by the end of their compulsory schooling at 16, will have had the opportunity to learn sufficient Welsh to enable them to use it in their everyday life and to feel part of a bilingual society' (cited in Edwards, 1993: 264).

There remain ongoing concerns about whether there will be a sufficient number of teachers and resources to staff and support such a wide ranging language-based programme (Williams and Raybould, 1991; PDAG, 1993c). The requirement that Welsh be studied to Stage 4 of the National Curriculum—that is, up to GCSE level at 16 years—has also since been downgraded to Stage 3 (14 years); the result of an amendment to the Act in 1993. The latter legislation can be regarded as yet another example where the needs of the English curriculum have detrimentally affected Wales (Jones, 1997), since the amendment was itself a response to an official review, headed by Sir Ron Dearing, on the many difficulties encountered in the original implementation of the National Curriculum *in England*. Nonetheless, the key feature of the Education Reform Act, at least with regard to the language, remains intact—for the first time, Welsh has been established as a compulsory element of the curriculum within all schools in Wales. In contrast, the earlier advances of Welsh-medium education, important though they were, remained dependent on sufficient local parental demand and/or the beneficence of individual local head-teachers for their successful enactment (Rawkins, 1979, 1987; Baker, 1995).

Conclusions

In a recent report on the current situation of 48 minority language groups in the European Union, Nelde *et al.* found that 'the demographic size of a language group is no guarantee of the group's [linguistic] vitality, with the existence of some of Europe's largest language groups being severely threatened' (1996: Executive Summary). Two other variables were identified as far more influential in their analysis:

1) the low status of many minority groups and their often related social, cultural and economic marginalisation; and
2) the degree to which minority languages were recognised by the state *and* supported within civil society—what Nelde *et al.* have termed the processes of 'legitimation' and 'institutionalisation'.

The development of a nascent bilingual state in Wales clearly demonstrates the importance of the latter process. In effect, the example of Wales shows us how an historic, but currently minority language can be effectively legitimated and institutionalised within the public domain—albeit alongside its dominant partner, English—after centuries of proscription, derogation and neglect. In so doing, the principle of political democracy—so often predicated on the cultural and linguistic practices of a dominant ethnic group (see May, forthcoming)—comes to include greater *ethnolinguistic* democracy as well.[6]

Moreover, the concept of ethnolinguistic democracy has particular pertinence to the European Union as a whole. After all, in this age of increasing globalisation, and with the burgeoning spread of English as the current world language, the EU has been much concerned of late with the question of retaining cultural and linguistic distinctiveness—at least at national levels—in its formal operations (see Wright, this volume). Thus, the European Parliament reaffirmed in December 1990 the 'principle of complete multilingualism . . . consistent with the respect which is owed to the dignity of all languages which reflect and express the cultures of the different peoples who make up the [EU]' (cited in Fishman, 1995: 49). The central principle involved here is the widely held recognition of state languages as a symbolic reflection of the people who speak it. However, it does not take much to see that this principle can be applied equally to *intra*-state languages as to *inter*-state languages, something which many members of the EU are still reluctant to even countenance, let alone act upon (Nelde *et al.*, 1996).

Furthermore, the extension of ethnolinguistic democracy to the intra-state level need not result necessarily in the resurgence of romantic nationalism, and its attendant processes of cultural and linguistic reification. As Bhikhu Parekh has observed, 'a community's identity is subject to constant change . . . Every community must wrestle with it as best it can, and find ways of reconstituting its identity in a manner that is both deeply sensitive to its history and traditions and fully alive to its present and future needs' (1995: 267). Such a process, which John Hutchinson (1994) describes as 'cultural nationalism' is, at its best, a nationalism principally concerned not so much with tradition *per se* but with the modernisation of national communities *from within*, thereby enabling socio-political development on more indigenous lines.

This position appears to encapsulate what is currently occurring in Wales with the recent development of a formal bilingual state. A bilingual Wales, based on a new set of urban Welsh identities (C. Williams, 1995), offers an alternative both to a narrow language-based conception of Welshness *and* to its opposite, the disavowal of any public role for Welsh within contemporary Wales. The result, as Fiona Bowie outlines, is that

> Wales in increasingly looking out, towards Europe, as well as within, at its own mixed population, its bilingualism, and its cultural roots. I perceive a new confidence and determination by Welsh-speakers, incomers and English-speaking people alike, to forge a Welsh identity which builds on all these disparate groups and experiences. It will be different from the Wales of the imagination and from the Wales of the past, but it will also be distinctively and assertively Welsh. (1993: 191)

Finally, these developments in Wales illustrate that moves to greater regional autonomy need not inevitably lead to a greater emphasis on devolution and independence at the expense of culturalist emphases. Indeed, it can be argued that the European Union's increasing emphasis on regional autonomy has strengthened rather than weakened the tenets of some cultural nationalist movements. Certainly, this is the case in Wales where, despite an ongoing ambivalence to greater political devolution, we are seeing the (re)emergence of an historic language within the civic realm. It is my view that this latter process offers not only Wales, but also the rest of Europe, a useful model for the future—one that acknowledges more fully the ongoing role and influence of minority ethno-cultural groups, and the languages they speak, within the formal workings of modern democratic nation-states.

Notes

1 In the election for the Welsh Assembly in May 1999, the principal Welsh nationalist party, *Plaid Cymru* (The Party of Wales), gained 17 out of the total of 60 available seats, becoming the 'official opposition' in the Assembly, and denying the Labour Party, which has dominated Welsh politics for much of this century, its

expected outright majority. This result is by far the most successful outcome for *Plaid* in any election, since its previous electoral impact has been largely minimal. The 'first past the post' electoral system for British elections has clearly disadvantaged *Plaid* in this respect, and is likely to continue to do so, at least in that forum. However, the long-standing marginal impact of Welsh nationalist politics also has had much to do with the close association of Welsh nationalism with a particular form of Welsh identity—Welsh-speaking, rural, and religiously Nonconformist—that has had little resonance with the increasingly anglicised industrial areas of Wales. Since the 1970s, *Plaid* has attempted to shed many of its prior associations with a narrow language-based nationalism, placing emphasis instead on an inclusive notion of Welsh citizenship, although one that respects the language and cultural traditions of Wales (Borland *et al.*, 1992). Nonetheless, the party has been unable to convince the wider electorate of its changed intentions until this most recent election for the Welsh Assembly. Even here though, the result should not be overstated since it appears to be based primarily on a combination of a very low electoral turnout (with proportionately more *Plaid* supporters actually voting), and a protest vote against both the inept local administration of many Labour-controlled councils and the perceived centralism of Labour party policy towards Wales. The close result of the preceding referendum for a Welsh Assembly, which I will proceed to discuss in some detail, indicates the ongoing tenuousness of the political influence of Welsh nationalism within Wales.

2 In employing the term 'nation' to describe Wales, I am not wanting to commit the sin of retrospective nationalism. In this sense, I readily accept that if Wales is a nation, it has only come to think of itself in these terms within the last two centuries. Moreover, it is only quite recently that Wales has been perceived as a nation by others within the British state. Indeed, it was only after the Irish Home Rule crisis in 1885–86 that the British ruling class formally recognised the existence of a distinct Welsh nation—the last of the present constituent nations of Britain so to be recognised (Morgan, 1995; E. Williams, 1989). Nonetheless, what we now know as Wales has a long territorial and linguistic history, dating back to the first millennium, upon which aspects of modern Welsh national identity have clearly been built (Kearney, 1989).

3 Religious Nonconformity in Wales was based on evangelical Protestantism and its principal expression was the culture of the chapel. Calvinistic Methodism was the most prominent of these groups although Independents and Baptists were also significant. The influence of Nonconformity was felt extensively in both industrial and rural areas of Wales and was increasingly contrasted with the established (British) state Anglican church (see Glanmor Williams, 1979).

4 These three acts all strengthened a distinct Welsh identity within Britain. The Welsh Sunday Closing Act reflected the strength of Nonconformity in Wales by enforcing the closure of public houses on Sunday. The Local Government Act created new county councils for Wales, thus formalising a cohesive administrative identity, while the Intermediate Act likewise created a network of Welsh 'county schools' (see Morgan, 1995).

5 This discrepancy is a consequence of the large numbers of Welsh speakers in small rural schools (PDAG, 1993b).

6 It is important to note here that greater ethnolinguistic democracy does not necessarily entail ethnolinguistic equality (see May, forthcoming). This is clearly the case in Wales, for example, since English remains the dominant language in most public (and many private) domains.

Stephen May

Bibliography

Adonis, A. (1997), 'Hear the new voice from the valleys, *The Observer*, 24 August 1997, 23.

Aitchison, J. and Carter, H. (1994), *A Geography of the Welsh Language 1961–1991*, Cardiff: University of Wales Press.

Baker, C. (1985), *Aspects of Bilingualism in Wales*, Clevedon: Multilingual Matters.

Baker, C. (1992), *Attitudes and Language*, Clevedon: Multilingual Matters.

Baker, C. (1995), 'Bilingual education and assessment', in B. M. Jones and P. Singh Ghuman (eds), *Bilingualism, Education and Identity*, Cardiff: University of Wales Press, 130–158.

Ball, S. (1990), *Politics and Policy Making in Education*, London: Routledge.

Balsom, D., Madgwick, P., and Van Mechelen, D. (1982), *The Political Consequences of Welsh Identity*, Glasgow: Centre for the Study of Public Policy, University of Strathclyde.

Borland, J., Fevre, R., and Denney, D. (1992), 'Nationalism and community in north west Wales', *The Sociological Review*, 40, 49–72.

Bowie, F. (1993), 'Wales from within: conflicting interpretations of Welsh identity', in S. Macdonald (ed.), *Inside European Identities: ethnography in Western Europe*, Oxford: Berg Publishers, 167–193.

Butt Philip, A. (1975), *The Welsh Question: nationalism in Welsh politics, 1945–1970*, Cardiff: University of Wales Press.

Daugherty, R. (1993), 'Why policies must be made in Wales', *The Times Educational Supplement*, 22 October 1993, 18.

Davies, C. (1989), *Welsh Nationalism in the Twentieth Century: the ethnic option and the modern state*, London: Praeger.

Edwards, D. (1993), 'Education and Welsh language planning', *Language, Culture and Curriculum*, 6, 257–273.

Edwards, J. (1985), *Language, Society and Identity*, Oxford: Basil Blackwell.

Fishman, J. (1991), *Reversing Language Shift: theoretical and empirical foundations of assistance to threatened languages*, Clevedon: Multilingual Matters.

Fishman, J. (1995), 'On the limits of ethnolinguistic democracy', in T. Skutnabb-Kangas and R. Phillipson (eds), *Linguistic Human Rights: overcoming linguistic discrimination*, Berlin: Mouton de Gruyter, 49–61.

Flude, M. and Hammer, M. (eds) (1990), *The Education Reform Act, 1998: its origins and implications*, London: Falmer Press.

Freedland, J. (1997), 'A kinder, more gentle nationalism for Wales', *The Guardian*, 8 September 1997, 7.

Gardner, R. and Lambert, W. (1972), *Attitudes and Motivation in Second-Language Learning*, Rowley, Ma.: Newbury House.

Harley, B. (1993), 'After immersion: maintaining the momentum', *Journal of Multilingual and Multicultural Development*, 15, 229–244.

Hutchinson, J. (1994), *Modern Nationalism*, London: Fontana.

Jenkins, P. (1992), *A History of Modern Wales, 1536–1900*, London: Longman.

Jenkins, R. (1991), 'Violence, language and politics: nationalism in Northern Ireland and Wales', *North Atlantic Studies*, 3, 31–40.

Jones, B. (1995), 'Schools and speech communities in a bilingual setting', in B. M. Jones and P. A. Singh Ghuman (eds), *Bilingualism, Education and Identity*, Cardiff: University of Wales Press, 79–107.

Jones, G. (1997), *The Education of a Nation*, Cardiff: University of Wales Press.

Lewis, E. (1975), 'Attitude to language among bilingual children and adults in Wales', *International Journal of the Sociology of Language*, 4, 103–121.

Lingard, B., Knight, J., and Porter, P. (eds) (1993), *Schooling Reform for Hard Times*, London: Falmer Press.

Lyon, J. and Ellis, N. (1991), 'Parental attitudes towards the Welsh language', *Journal of Multilingual and Multicultural Development*, 12, 239–251.

Kearney, H. (1989), *The British Isles: a history of four nations*, Cambridge: Cambridge University Press.

Keating, M. and Jones, B. (1995), 'Nations, regions, and Europe: the UK experience', in M. Keating and B. Jones (eds), *The European Union and the Regions*, Oxford: Clarendon Press, 89–113.

May, S. (forthcoming), *Language, Education and Minority Rights*, London: Longman.

Miles, R. (1996), 'Racism and nationalism in the United Kingdom: a view from the periphery', in R. Barot (ed.), *The Racism Problematic: contemporary sociological debates on race and ethnicity*, Lampeter: Edward Mellen Press, 231–255.

Morgan, K. (1981), *Rebirth of a Nation: Wales 1880–1980*, Oxford: Clarendon Press.

Morgan, K. (1995), 'Welsh nationalism: the historical background', in K. Morgan, *Modern Wales: politics, places and people*, Cardiff: University of Wales Press, 197–213.

National Language Forum (1991), *Language Strategy—1991–2001*, Caernarfon: National Language Forum.

Nelde, P., Strubell, M., and Williams, G. (1996), *Euromosaic: the production and reproduction of the minority language groups in the European Union*, Luxembourg: Office for Official Publications of the European Communities.

NOP (1995), *Public Attitudes to the Welsh Language*, London: NOP Social and Political.

Osmond, J. (1989), 'The modernisation of Wales', in N. Evans (ed.), *National Identity in the British Isles*, Harlech, Gwynedd: Coleg Harlech, 73–89.

Packer, A. and Campbell, C. (1993), 'The reasons for parental choice of Welsh-medium education', paper presented to the *Fifth National Conference on Minority Languages*, University of Wales, Cardiff, July 1993.

Parekh, B. (1995), 'The concept of national identity', *New Community*, 21, 255–268.

PDAG (1993a), *Welsh and the Early Years*, Cardiff: PDAG.

PDAG (1993b), *Welsh Language Education*, Cardiff: PDAG.

PDAG (1993c), *Welsh Medium Resources: future funding needs*, Cardiff: PDAG.

PDAG (1994), *Development of Welsh Medium Education—1977–1992*, Cardiff: PDAG.

Rawkins, P. (1979), *The Implementation of Language Policy in the Schools of Wales*, Centre for the Study of Public Policy, University of Strathclyde.

Rawkins, P. (1987), 'The politics of benign neglect: education, public policy, and the mediation of linguistic conflict in Wales', *International Journal of the Sociology of Language*, 66, 27–48.

Reynolds, D. (1994), 'Education in Wales 1978–1994: from problems to policies?' in W. Bellin, J. Osmond, and D. Reynolds (eds), *Towards an Educational Policy in Wales*, Cardiff: The Institute of Welsh Affairs, 4–10.

Sharp, D., Thomas, B., Price, E., Francis, G., and Davies, I. (1973), *Attitudes to Welsh and English in the Schools of Wales*, London: Macmillan.

Stationery Office (1997a), *A Voice for Wales*, Norwich: Stationery Office.

Stationery Office (1997b), *Scotland's Parliament*, Norwich: Stationery Office.

Thomas, A. (1997), 'Language policy and nationalism in Wales: a comparative analysis', *Nations and Nationalism*, 3, 333–344.

Welsh Language Board (1995), *Draft Guidelines as to the Form and Content of Schemes*, Cardiff: Welsh Language Board.

Williams, C. (1982), 'Separatism and the mobilisation of Welsh national identity', in C. Williams (ed.), *National Separatism*, Cardiff: University of Wales Press, 145–201.

Williams, C. (1990), 'The anglicisation of Wales', in N. Coupland (ed.), *English in Wales: diversity, conflict and change*, Clevedon: Multilingual Matters, 19–47.

Williams, C. (1994), *Called Unto Liberty: on language and nationalism*, Clevedon: Multilingual Matters.

Williams, C. (1995), 'Questions concerning the development of bilingual Wales', in B. M. Jones and P. Singh Ghuman (eds), *Bilingualism, Education and Identity*, Cardiff: University of Wales Press, 47–78.

Williams, C. and Raybould, W. (1991), *Welsh Language Planning. Opportunities and constraints*, Cardiff: PDAG.

Williams, E. (1989), 'The dynamic of Welsh identity', in N. Evans (ed.), *National Identity in the British Isles*, Harlech, Gwynedd: Coleg Harlech, 46–59.

Williams, Glanmor (1979), *Religion, Language and Nationality in Wales*, Cardiff: University of Cardiff Press.

Williams, Glyn (1994), 'Discourses on "nation" and "race"', *Contemporary Wales*, 6, 87–103.

Williams, Gwyn A. (1985), *When was Wales?* London: Penguin.

Young, I. (1993), 'Together in Difference: transforming the logic of group political conflict', in J. Squires (ed.), *Principled Positions: postmodernism and the rediscovery of value*, London: Lawrence and Wishart, 121–150.

Towards a post-national polity: the emergence of the Network Society in Europe

Barrie Axford and Richard Huggins

Abstract

This chapter explores the prospects for a postnational polity in Europe where the territorial base of power is replaced by a system of networks and flows in which the principal resource is knowledge. The argument depicts a united Europe as a space of flows rather than as a super- or supra-statist entity. Tensions that arise between a Europe of networks and spaces and a Europe of places are examined, partly through a study of the burgeoning European Information Society Project which attempts to harness these developing networks in the service of European integration. Issues relating to the democratic nature of governance without government in the network polity are highlighted to exemplify the difficulties of re-imagining Europe. The rhetoric surrounding the European Information Society expresses the ambivalence within a programme that foresees Europe as a web of discursive spaces while continuing to acknowledge the power of the old imagined communities based upon territory and ethnicity.

Introduction

At the millennium, the idea of a united Europe remains elusive, even when applied narrowly to the European Union, which, depending on your point of view, either stands as the most audacious experiment in post-territorial governance in the modern world, or just a tribute to advanced multi-lateralism. This elusiveness stems in part from the vagaries of what is still an immanently partisan enterprise, the product of political agendas which continue to spawn different visions of European unity. In part it springs from the liminal qualities of the wider European and global environments after 1989. But it also demonstrates the fact that the assumed logics of European integration have been problematised by major changes taking place in world-wide rationalistic culture where, until recently, territoriality was the most powerful constitutive rule (Axford and Huggins, 1998; Meyer *et al.*, 1997; Anderson, 1996). These changes are conveniently summarised as the impact of globalisation upon nation-state autonomy and upon national definitions of value, but also—and this is critical—upon the prospects for super or supra-statist models of regional integration, where these are still rooted in territorialist assumptions about the nature of rule. In this chapter we will examine the prospects for a European network polity, which is de-spatialised, multi-layered and multi-nodal, and based upon networks of interaction which are local, regional, national, European and global in scope. We look to exemplify these developments in the emergence of a European Information Society, a paradigm case of the issues involved in (de)constructing Europe.

What Europe?

As part of a renewed interest in 're-imagining' a united Europe, some commentators (Anderson, 1996; Ruggie, 1993) have revisited Hedley Bull's reflections on the prospects for a 'new medievalism' (1977) in which the concept of territorial sovereignty has little meaning and where authority is exercised jointly and severally by states, by regional and world authorities and by a host of formal and informal global, trans-state and sub-state actors. In such a political order, loyalty is shared rather than exclusive and identities are either multiple or hybrid. There is also a growing willingness to describe some developments in transnational politics as auguries of non- or post-territorial governance, thereby conjuring the image of a postmodern state or polity in Europe. Other less exotic, but possibly more idealistic interpretations, refer to the prospects for a post-Westphalian, or a cosmopolitan model or European governance, and this too is non-statist and participatory (Goodman, 1998). All such imagery is appropriate in a world where modern institutions and cultural practices are everywhere under challenge, but, as we shall see, the idea of a post-modern polity, or of governance without territorial government, leaves moot important questions about what sort of polity and what kind of identities can subsist in a post-territorial, post-modern 'space of flows'. In other words, the social morphology of the post-national polity in Europe is far from clear.

Yet, in his well-known analysis of the 'unbundling' of statist sovereignty in Europe, John Ruggie intimates that the EU may be the world's first post-modern form of transnational governance (1993). Ruggie's interpretation of the EU as a 'space of flows' rather than a territory to be governed or regulated in the conventional sense of these terms was a timely reminder not to confuse the construction of de-spatialised networks and communities or neo-communities with the processes of nation and state-building characteristic of the transition from pre-modern to modern societies. A strong reading of Ruggie's account depicts Europe—'united' Europe—as a space created and reproduced through transnational, regional and local networks of interaction, involving, for example, cultural, commercial, scientific, financial and educational actors and interests. The same model of radical interdependence across borders is glimpsed in Manuel Castells's rather allusive discussion of the 'network state' in Europe (1998), while for Michael Mann (1998: 184–207), 'Euro', as he puts it, is really just a web of interaction networks, composed of multiple, overlapping and intersecting networks of technical specialists, Euromanagers, businesses, Socrates exchange students, even football hooligans. Euro lacks overall internal cohesion of the sort standard in many territorial states and it also lacks external closure.

One need not agree fully with any of these accounts to recognise that new forms of spatial practice are emerging to interrogate received definitions of and prescriptions for the organisation of political, economic and cultural space. In practical terms these forms are part of a dynamic re-shaping of world-society through the opportunities they provide for re-imagining and re-enacting the scale of social organisation, and because of the scope they offer for re-defining the behaviour and possible the identity of various actors. All of which is quite liberating, because it provides a means of questioning further the hackneyed antinomy between *intergovernmentalist* and *integrationist* visions of a united Europe. In this antinomy, Europe is still relatively ordered politically and emotionally through the competing claims of national and European or supranational jurisdictions, competences and identities, while the whole debate is contained intellectually by the still dominant imagery and 'inarticulate major premises' of territorial rule. These premises, as james Caporaso says (1996) have acted as a conceptual grid informing both theoretical and practitioner discourse on European integration. At the same time it is important to remember that even if it is possible to define Europe as an intersubjective web of connections and reciprocities tying the continent together in complex fashion, it is not, and probably never can be, just that. Let us carry this point a little further, as a way of demonstrating the complexities of re-imagining Europe.

The processes of globalisation and of European integration have relativised identities by penetrating or dissolving the boundaries around relatively closed systems, and by creating trans-societal and post-territorial discursive spaces and networks of relationships along the time-space edges of existence. Along the way, important transformations may be in train; for example, in existing categories of social stratification, in signifiers such as locality, and in the key associations of citizenship and nationality (Axford, 1999). Because of these shifts, it is now less clear what constitutes a political community, and what factors define various statuses under it. A more prosaic, but no less powerful reminder of this putative transformation in the architecture of governance and the conduct of democratic politics, is provided by James Rosenau (1998: 30). He too is exercised by the notion that legitimate systems of rule can be exerted and maintained even in the absence of established legal and political authority, and across, even regardless of, conventional borders. In his account, what musters as global governance is highly disaggregated, with multiple centres of authority and a growing number of skilful and well-resourced players (Rosenau and Fagen, 1997). Rosenau's model of global governance is, of course, cognate with more nuanced accounts of the EU as a 'multi-level' and multi-agency polity or one characterised by the 'new governance', both of which trade on the greater pluralism and relative statelessness of the EU (Hix, 1998; Marks, 1993). Of course, it is still unclear whether any version of 'governance without government' amounts to, or should be considered as a simulacrum of democratic polity and civil society; issues we take up below. When it comes to the crunch, such descriptions may be no more than convenient metaphors for a world in turmoil, but they do emphasise the fragility of territorial boundaries and identities and the burgeoning forces of both localism and globalism.

In fact, very few treatments of European unity from within the established political science paradigm, do more than flirt with the notion of a post-modern polity. Those which do tend to adopt a robust neo-liberal interpretation of the boundary dissolving power of economic transactions—also seen in the pristine logic of the Single European Act—or just skirt the issue of transformation, preferring to see 'post-modern' features as instrumentalities. More thorough-going postmodernist accounts abjure any holistic idea of

'Europe' at all, purporting to see the world in general 'branching into fractal nets' (Luke, 1995). For example, Tim Luke's work on post-modern geographies and on the impact of new technologies upon sovereign spaces consists of a sustained anti-realist diatribe in which various denationalised agents are prime movers in the creation of 'neo-world orders', each made from rearranged glocal space. The upshot is a more dynamic, more interconnected, yet more fragmented and fluid milieu for enacting authority and managing flows of influence from multiple sources, than can be contained by the Euclidean geometry and identity spaces of territorialised or super-territorialised modernity. To reiterate, in these radical positions a 'united' Europe would be no more than a 'space of flows', *pace* Ruggie, or a de-territorialised space where the logic of market opportunity, to quote Richard Falk (1998: 6) no longer coincides with the logic of territorial loyalty. Ruggie is suitably cautious on the prospects for a de-territorialised politics and a de-territorialised governance, describing a Europe deconstructing into a non-territorial *space of flows*, which also subsists with the more conventional *space of places*.

In a fully-fledged post-modern discourse, many of the problems which attend the construction and maintenance of a functioning polity are conveniently sidestepped or rendered nugatory. Concerns about identity, or the charge of being seen as inauthentic in some way or other, are hardly salient in an environment where identities are no more than the sum of shifting preferences or whim. Governance now appears as the management of mutable expressions of interest and of difference. Borders too, so crucial to the political and cultural landscapes of the modern world, 'melt into air' to borrow a phrase, and 'habitats of meaning' (Baumann, 1992: 190) owe more to Sony than to soil. As Philip Schlesinger and Nancy Morris opine, one might easily draw the conclusion that the spaces of most collective identities have already become 'deterritorialised', due to migration and the creation of electronic communities, and that borders—to taste and imagination, as well as around jurisdictions—are all relativised (1997: 23). But in Europe, as elsewhere in the world, borders continue to matter. Ethno-territorial disputes, even civilisational conflicts, have proliferated in the wrack of Soviet hegemony and there is a growing commitment to orthodoxies which celebrate exclusion and appeal to the secureness of closed communities against the depredations of any number of demonised *others*, or of mere strangers. Even within the post-historical core of 'Euroland' a good many Germans lament the passing of the Deutschmark as a symbol of *national* potency, and Austrians rehearse the politics of exclusion in their growing support for the Freedom Party, which advocates the deportation of unemployed and welfare dependent migrants.

So places and borders count, along with the identities and symbolism attached to them. When discussing the appropriateness of labels like post-national or post-modern in relation to the political and cultural morphology of Europe and European unity, it is as well to remember that we should not reduce places (localities, any territories) simply to spaces through which meanings flow. Many people, including those already routinely engaged in transnational flows and networks—Euro-lobbyists, Green activists, commodity brokers, even jobbing academics—may enact intense and visceral identities as locals and nationals and continue to behave as though 'real' culture is fully the property of particular territories and bounded societies (Axford, 1999). Hence, the more grainy reality is that older frameworks of collective identity continue to exist alongside new, deterritorialised spaces and flows, including trans-national mediascapes, finanscapes and ethnoscapes (Appadurai, 1996). The tortuous processes of European integration, as Schlesinger and Norris argue, produce 'dislocations in these diverse modes of collective being—older and newer—bringing about new problems of socio-cultural coherence, as well as ushering in new opportunities for affiliation' (1997: 23).

In other respects the idea of or prospects for a post-modern, post-territorial polity in Europe run up against issues which go to the heart of the democratic project; issues which are central to this book. First is the objection that the anti-categorical flavour of post-modernism is inimical to the 'imaginary presuppositions' of liberal democracy itself (McLennan, 1995: 93). The argument here is that a *demos*, even a collective entity known as 'the people' can not subsist in a post-territorial space of governance, where the emphasis is on shifting identities and difference, and there is no sense of belonging to a common endeavour, nor, in Europe, the moral currency and cultural capital with which to build one. Second, the claims that the networked Europe might constitute a post-national space of governance leaves some commentators lamenting the alleged loss of community that results at a national level, a loss that subverts both liberal democracy and strains of communitarian democracy. The 'thin' but universalist political identities of liberal democracy and the 'thick' particularisms of communitarian ideology are said to be compromised where there is no community of fate or affect, no jumble of meanings that tie people to a particular place and a particular culture. In other words, undone by the very rootlessness of a de-spatialised, networked polity. Third, the prospects for active and practical citizenship, central to republican traditions of democracy, are held to be undermined because of the logistical and resource problems of ensuring effective participation by non-élites in post-national politics; and fourth, even in the fluid and mutable world of networks, difficulties remain about criteria for inclusion and exclusion and about the directionality of flows of influence across them. In other words, in a network polity, it is impossible to abrogate questions of resources and power.

As we noted earlier, all these questions are germane to the subject matter of this book, the more so because they arise from a quite radical way of imagining Europe. They will be taken up again in the conclusion, but now we will look in greater detail at the idea of a post-national network polity in Europe, outlining the advantages of a network approach to post-territorial governance. We will then explore the morphology of the network polity in Europe through an examination of aspects of the European Information Society, which offers a general prescription for, and maybe an augury of, a 'united' Europe (or rather, Europes) made up of transnational networks, some virtual, others phenomenal and, in one version at any rate, consisting only of digital borderlands. Because of the conflicting policy prescriptions and contradictory logics of integration which are contributing to its development, the idea of an informational network society usefully expresses all the tensions associated with the construction of Europe. In the final section of the chapter we will explore those issues which, on some accounts, render any kind of a network polity morally weightless and devoid of referential grounding and legitimacy. These issues clearly bear on the viability of a post-national polity in Europe.

The idea of a post-national, post-territorial polity in Europe

Very few current treatments of European unity have much truck with realism, where the ontology of actors is given and the world ordered through the rational and self-interested motivations and behaviour of autonomous state actors. In such accounts, integration is the product of enduringly *intergovernmental* relations between independent states, whose collective behaviour corresponds to a kind of rational anarchy. But in a recent *tour-de-force*, Hirst and

Thompson (1996) have recourse to neo and micro-realist arguments to shore up the idea of the independent nation-state surviving the pressures of the worldwide culture and practice of economic neo-liberalism. Confusingly they also adopt what is really a macro-realist stance on the location of the EU as somewhere between a supra-territorialist entity and a dense network of transactions and interdependencies among still powerful state actors. Variations on the realist theme found, for example, in liberal intergovernmentalism (Moravscik, 1993) also continue to stress the importance of key state actors to the integration process, through their bargaining strategies and in respect of convergence in key areas of policy, such as market liberalisation. In all such accounts territoriality remains the dominant discourse. By contrast, neoliberal variants and functionalist and neo-functionalist approaches to European integration (Keohane and Hoffman, 1991) stress 'low politics' as an important dynamic of international relations. The 'low politics' of European integration is predicated on the power of economic and functional integration to effect ever-closer union, against the 'high politics' of state autonomy and sovereignty. The 'spillover' from pragmatic accommodations by various actors to shifts in the locus of decision-making, or to the growing density of routine communications and other transactions across borders leads to a community of interest *and* affect based on strengthened European institutions and a greater sense of European identity. Curiously, 'low politics' in the guise of citizen action has been hard to find in the constitutive account of *actually existing integration* in the EU and its predecessors, which is almost a text book case of top-down bureaucratic élitism and high politics. There is some evidence that this situation is changing, and that forms of sub-politics, from localities, citizen groups, social movements and more assertive expressions of public opinion, such as occurred in Denmark in the first referendum on the Maastricht Treaty, are beginning to enact a European polity 'from below'. Following the Maastricht Treaty on European Union, neo-functionalist reasoning has achieved something of a comeback, despite the fact that it is deterministic, with 'spillover' providing the evolutionary logic for an integration process nonetheless reliant, in the real world, on the motivations of actors to make it work. The neglect of agency in neo-functionalist accounts is a besetting weakness.

With the possible exception of some neo-functionalist positions and those labelled 'transactionalist' (Deutsch, 1953), all the preceding models work within a territorialist paradigm, even where they advocate or predict a European entity which is above the nation-state. Of late, the study of European integration and of the European Union in particular has taken a rather different slant, where the conceit is to depict the EU as an interesting variant of the genus *state*, complete with a functioning political system, albeit one which is only relatively institutionalised, centralised and differenti-ated, by comparison with the classical models of the recent European past (Badie and Birnbaum, 1983; and see Hix, 1998 for an extended discussion of recent theorising). For Majone (1996) this relatively stateless entity is best understood as a form of 'regulatory state', probably federal in demeanour and best typified by the United States in the days before the New Deal.

More in line with our position is the widely canvassed treatment of the EU as a form of 'new governance' (Marks, 1993; Marks, Hooghe and Blank, 1996). In this 'new orthodoxy' (Hix, 1998: 41) the EU has become a unique system of 'multi-level governance' (Marks, 1993). The use of the term governance again underlines the lack of any necessary relation to the state, while still implying the existence of robust political and policy processes in which state, non-state, sub-state and trans-state actors all play a part. But the real charge in the new model of European unity is that governance rather than government becomes the definitive feature of the new polity. Both territorial and functional interests and constituencies operate through more-or-less open policy communities and net-works, and the regulation of the borderless economic space created by the internal market in Europe provides the dynamic for a more 'polycentric and non-hierarchical' form of governance (Jachten-fuchs, 1997: 40 and 1995). As Hix notes (1998: 40), 'with no clear hierarchy of power and competence anywhere in this process, this is "governance without government"' (Rosenau and Czempiel, 1992).

And so it is, primarily because, as Rosenau says (1998: 40–47) in de-territorialised spaces of governance, it is possible to discern func-tional equivalents for those institutions and practices characteristic of territorial polities and democracies. These are visible in the decentralization of power and decision-making authority to intra-state regions and localities; in the kind of transnational private interest government exercised by NGOs; in the scope for the emer-gence of global and European publics through the activities of social movements and epistemic communities; through the network-ing of localities and 'natural' economic zones across borders (see Ohmae, 1992 for a more radical account of cross-border regions) and in the capacity for electronic communications to both compress the world and enlarge the scope for citizen interaction and participation. Equivalent it may be, but this sort of governance is quite unlike any state-centric, hierarchical and compliance driven model of rule. Most telling of all, it does signal the ways in which a post-territorial state or polity (Caporaso, 1996) might not just subsist, but prosper as a democratic endeavour.

The difficulty with imagining a postnational polity is that much of the evidence currently available is not systematic, although this is beginning to change (see, for example, Kohler, 1998 and Boli and Thomas, 1997) to the extent that there are now available some proper intimations. First, is the sense that, however defined, borders can no longer be seen as enclosures which are effectively policed by nation-states. This much is common currency: the state as the guardian of defence and guarantor of societal values and collective identity, has been hollowed out, in the much worn, but apposite, expression, and many of its functions extra-territorialised. Because of this there is no reason to believe that a European Union made in the image of a territorialised state would be any more successful in policing its borders, leaving aside the vexed question of where these would be located (especially in the context of a 'wider' Europe) and (in the case of culture) how they might be defined. Second, much power, especially in the form of capital, *flows* across borders and through places (Castells, 1996). In the European Union, it would be a simplification, but still a recognisable truth, that the economy and some aspects of economic law have become Europeanised, but con-stitutional law remains largely national (Jachtenfuchs, 1997: 6). According to Baumann (1998: 9) power has become 'emancipated from politics', which in many respects still looks resolutely national. While this dichotomy is plausible, it is over-simplified. A more com-plex rendering of the impact of regional and global integration on the political community that is the nation state, would be to argue that the growing salience of transnational relations and institutions is weakening or, at least, altering the meaning of citizenship within states (Falk, 1998). This is an interesting argument, one predicated on the decline of national traditions of citizenship as a direct result of the increase in bonds of interest and solidarity across borders, and on the loss of social capital and hence of motivation, within them (Putnam, 1995; Boyte, 1996). Of course an alternative reading is that loss of energy at national levels may be compensated by transnational action and by the creation of cosmopolitans, if not world or European citizens, where the notion of citizenship refers to the sense of belonging to a political community rather than just for-mal rights of inclusion.

Elites in general are more and more likely to create links and solidarities across borders as well as, maybe rather than, within them, which sometimes fuels the claim that cosmopolitanism is the designer chic of a transnational ruling class (Sklair, 1998). Yet other citizens, concerned either to resist or augment the effects of Europeanisation and globalisation increasingly follow suit, organising locally, nationally and transnationally. Arguably, political and economic élites are able to act more effectively at the European level, while this is much less true of social movements, some organised interests, such as trade unions and consumer groups, and various public interest groups. In either case, it is vital to avoid slippage into neo-functionalist determinism and retain the sense that these are negotiated and contingent adjustments on the part of reflexive actors. Third, the construction of a non-state citizenship is being effected through EU policy and treaty provisions (Soysal, 1995; Wiener, 1997). This remains a contested area, one, which captures the tensions in the national-postnational dichotomy. Citizenship of the EU is granted to those who hold the nationality of a member state. However, the rights attached to the status of Citizen of the European Union, which extend to local voting rights based on residence, are rights irrespective of nationality, and thus exemplify the principles of extra-territoriality (certainly) and postnationality (possibly). From the standpoint of migrant groups (but also from those of other constituencies), the emergence of transnational networks of activists of the sort canvassed by Richard Falk, point up the tensions between the claims of citizenship and those of nationality, and between the notion of a procedural citizenship based on rights and the substance of a citizenship based on participation—low politics again (Delanty, 1998: 4.3). Networks also contribute to the formation of transnational public spaces and the prospects at least, for a form of transnational discursive citizenship, although here too it could be argued that the gap between deliberation in the form of communicative rationality and the purposive discourse which denotes a practical citizenship, may be wider in the post-national polity than in bounded national systems. Paradoxically, organised transnationalisation is often fuelled by enduring concerns with the protection of particular identities which may be local or national, as well as ethnic in origin (Kastoryano, 1998). Fourth, there has been what Sidney Tarrow calls a marked 'Europeanisation of conflict' (1995) through the agency of Euro-groups and transnational movements, where the locus of conflict is shifted to the Community level. For example, in Italy, a growing concern with immigration from

North Africa is perceived as a European, rather than an Italian problem, stemming from EU policies that have turned Europe into a world space. Resolution is sought at the European level of governance, not elsewhere. By the same token the scope for transnational governance in the shape of policy networks and communities is enhanced greatly by the willingness of corporate and other actors to engage with European institutions as regulators and major allocators of value. The question remains as to how far this engagement Europeanises actors, and what this means, as opposed to simply altering their behaviour. Finally, and most germane to this chapter is the space and time devouring capacities of electronic communications and networks and the opportunities they provide to imagine new spaces of governance and sociality. Castells's monumental exegesis on the 'network society' (1996, 1997 and 1998) is perhaps the most complete statement on the importance of information technologies in the spread of networks throughout the entire social structures of bounded societies and beyond, but the thesis is also common currency among those who discern 'post-modern geographies' in the networks and flows of the information age (O'Tuathail, 1998). In O'Tuathail's wonderfully polemical account of the demise of territorialist narratives, 'telemetricality' has remade the 'bonds, boundaries and subjectivities of actors, societies and polities, as they have unfolded across global space' (1998: 6). How do these ideas play in the European context?

The network polity in Europe

The deterritorialisation of the functions of governance and the growth of trans-border communities and networks in Europe point towards a post-national polity. This emergent polity displays elements of new governance, but its most characteristic feature is that it is a post-modern space of flows, of communities without unity, increasingly pluralistic, open and founded on networks. Interest in networks is now widespread across the social sciences and beyond. There is no complete agreement on what constitutes a network, although it is understood that a network is an open structure, sometimes with a set of relatively stable relationships, but sometimes not. These relationships are of a non-hierarchical and interdependent nature. Networks have no common or central principle of organisation and they are not reliant on functional integration for their survival. Participants in networks typically share a common interest and perhaps a common identity. Castells notes that networks have nodes and not centres and peripheries, and these can be linked through both symmetrical and asymmetrical relationships. In other words, networks are very post-modern.

In the study of European integration much of the work done by political scientists has centred on the phenomenon of policy networks. Within this genre a divide exists between those studies which treat network analysis as a gloss on the study of interest mediation, or which see policy networks as a functional solution to the co-ordination problems of modern societies, and those which see networks as a new form of governance much akin to the 'governance without government' perspective (for a summary and analysis of these positions see Borzel, 1997). As Borzel indicates, this latter approach is not exercised by whether the nation-state is getting stronger or weaker, but with the transformation and the 'Europeanisation' of the state, in which it commutes from actor to arena. The Europeanisation of the territorial state is seen as a process which de-borders action and fragments the state. In this process, policy networks are seminal actors (Kenis and Schneider, 1991).

As a model for contemporary governance in Europe, the policy network model captures the indeterminate nature of the European Union as a system of rule. However, we need to traffic beyond even the more radical model outlined above in order to grasp the utility of the network model as a metaphor for a post-national polity. In part this is a matter of widening the scope of inquiry, of recognising the ubiquity of networks in European and global space. But it is also necessary to consider networks as collective actors rather than simply arenas in which action takes place. They are potential contexts for the transformation of identities, expressive as well as instrumental.

The network metaphor and postnationalisation

Processes of Europeanisation and globalisation move through the negotiated and often contingent articulation between local subjects and more encompassing flows and structures. The growing complexity of these articulations intimates the possibility of disorder, rather than functional closure, since the connections reveal new sites for potential conflict and new opportunities for structuration and transformation. Tim Luke has it that 'moving from place to flow, terrains to streams, introduces non-perspectival, anti-hierarchical and disorganisational elements into traditional spatial/industrial/ national notions of sovereignty' (1995: 127). So notions of a united Europe, or of the EU as a web of interconnectedness do not, can not describe a featureless, anodyne field. Rather, we can discern multiple configurations or several Europes (Axford, 1999) which, at least for the present, co-exist. United Europe partakes of some elements of state-centred co-ordination, a whiff of supranationalism and a growing amount of non-hierarchical, cross-border networking.

The latter Europe is seen particularly in the growing reach and density of networks and flows: of goods between nations, through migration, business and tourism (Ash, 1998) as well as in the post-national politics of INGOs and the cyborg cultures of 'organisationless' transnational corporations which, through strategic networking, show a 'single face' to the world. Such interconnections connect Europe in a visible and measurable way, but do so more profoundly because they are redefining the experiences and perceptions of more and more actors. Thus the taxonomic status of a 'European' company may lie more in its management style and corporate culture than it does in objective measures of Europeanness, such as the proportion of its operations and employees abroad. At all events, Europe now becomes the cognitive frame of reference for many actors in many domains, although it remains less so in matters of culture and morality.

The networked Europe created out of the intersection and entwining of these multiple configurations is disordered, perhaps chaotic in the sense suggested by Jonathan Friedman (1997). In it, ontological certainties are themselves relativised, and as we have argued, constitutive rules, even hegemonic scripts like that of territoriality are increasingly challenged through the transformative capacities of trans or denationalised agency. As a metaphor for such a world, the imagery of transnational networks is entirely appropriate.

So the advantages of network analysis for reimagining Europe are obvious. For one thing, it affords a more systematic picture of the organisation of social relations than is possible in any purely postmodernist account, where only the discursive practices of individual actors are deemed relevant. In network analysis, both the frames of meaning used by actors and the circumstances in and on which they act are admissible. This admissibility involves understanding the reflexive relationships between the actor and a notionally external world, which is both natural and social. We say 'notional' to emphasise the point that actors enact their environments, but as suggested above, this does not mean that the external world is simply a mirror of 'internal' identity or consciousness, as in autopoietic systems.

Ulf Hannerz says that the global ecumene is a network of networks where individuals and groups are drawn into 'a more globalised existence' (1992: 47) and the morphology of networks facilitates this shift. Arguably, but without any trace of neo-functionalist determinism, the same is happening in Europe. In the first place, networks can be intra and inter as well as trans-organisational, and can cut across more conventional units of analysis to clarify linkages which exist between different personal and institutional domains (Axford, 1995: 78–82). Most appropriate to the European and global setting, networks can structure social relationships without constraint of place or the need for co-presence. Much of the recent work done by cultural anthropologists addresses the ways in which local and global social relationships are articulated and either reproduced or transformed by sustained or fleeting encounters. By contrast, in the field of International Relations the interest in networks, most pronounced in the study of international regimes, has stemmed largely from a concern with the problems of co-operation in a world still governed by the rational anarchy of the international system of states. More recent and theoretically impertinent work does look to explore the ways in which global instabilities are challenging the bordered world of states, having regard for the burgeoning number of 'postnational mobilisations' (Shapiro and Alker: 1995) that are both the product of that instability and which subvent it.

The network perspective draws attention to those increasingly widespread and diverse forms of transnational mobilisation found in networks, whether of business men and women, of exchange students, or of pen pals and diasporas, whose relationships (*pace* Hannerz) may be either long-distance or involve a mixture of presence and absence, of coming together and moving apart, of brief encounters on the telephone, or extended dialogues, or many-to-many exchanges on the Net. The strength of the network metaphor is that it captures the openness of social relationships which do not involve just economic or market exchanges, and are not just governed by administrative rules, the systematic use of power, or the constraints of place. In this it shares some of the anti-categorical fervour of postmodernist positions. The ideal network has many of the attributes of an ideal community: complementarity, commitment, accommodation between participants, reciprocity and trust.

In reality, power and conflict are unlikely to be absent from net-worked relations, which are rarely entirely pacific. Doreen Massey (1995) cautions the need to be aware of the power-geometry present in de-spatialised social relations, and this is a pertinent reminder that the organisation of diversity, in the networked polity, is often quite brutal, attesting to great asymmetries of power. This noted, the network metaphor affords insights into a Europe becoming more integrated, while acknowledging that the processes of integra-tion are 'more pluralistic, decentralised and mutable' (Marcus and Fisher, quoted in Hannerz, 1992: 36) than is often assumed. Network analysis portrays a looseness and diversity which go some way to capture the inchoate character of current Europeanisation and globalisation, and offers a glimpse of the diverse contexts through which a more acute consciousness of Europe and the world is occurring for many people.

Indeed, the very looseness and inchoateness of the globalised, post-hegemonic world itself accelerates the dissolution of bounded and autonomous nation-states and territorial geo-politics. The post-modern feel of this liminal environment is palpable, as the borders between the domestic, the international and the global implode, to reveal 'configurations of people, place and heritage (which) lose all sense of isomorphism', to quote Appadurai (1996: 46). Geography, according to Latour (1997), now becomes a matter of association and connectivity, not space. For him the globalised world is made up of 'actor-networks' consisting of collectives of humans, cyborgs and technologies, which quite confound received wisdom about ter-ritories and the subjects and objects under their dominion. We now turn to consider the European Information Society as a prototype, or perhaps a laboratory for the network polity in Europe.

The European Information Society as a network polity

Despite the central importance of the information society to European Union policy makers and visionaries there exists a rela-tive lack of detailed studies of the policy process in this area (Wallace and Wallace, 1996; George, 1996) and a relative dearth of work on the construction and functioning of networks established under the information society rubric. Nevertheless, we shall attempt a preliminary analysis of the emergence of a European informa-tional space, which, we believe is a paradigm case of new structures of governance and new patterns of connectivity.

In a speech made on 18 September 1997, the then European Union Commissioner Martin Bangemann stated that: 'As society is propelled from industrial to information age by the dual forces of converging digital technologies and globalisation, governments are finding it difficult to keep pace with change and define the appropriate policy response'. Since the early 1990s the European Union has embarked on a highly self-conscious attempt to create a 'new' Europe through the application of information technology to all aspects of life. The creation of a European Information Society offers an insight into the reconfiguration of the cultural, social, economic and political landscapes in Europe. The transformative potential of the information society and attendant technologies is a significant challenge to all forms of usual politics and those strains of civil society characteristic of modernity.

Images of the information society abound in the late twentieth century as the advances in digital technology accelerate and as information and communications technologies (ICTs) are applied more systematically. The exact nature of the information society is far from clear[1] but many actors, local, national and supranational adopt its rhetoric and advocate its implementation as a strategy for dealing with a fast-moving world.

The argument runs roughly as follows. The rapid proliferation and convergence of computer and communication technologies coupled with the routine application of such technologies to every aspect of public and private life is rapidly transforming the organisation of our societies. The 'digital revolution' (seen by some as equal in importance to the industrial revolution of the eighteenth century)[2] whose technologies facilitate the storage, transmission and processing of large quantities of data without reference to spatial or temporal constraints, is a seminal process, impacting on the order, structure and spatiality of our societies and on social practices.[3]

Unlike earlier shifts in the technology of information, at the end of the twentieth century a significant structural change is in train. This change is the convergence of media, communications and computer technologies, that is, the effective merging of hitherto distinct technologies. Convergence of technologies is a feature of the information society's technical infrastructure and will facilitate routine and widespread use. The routine use of information technologies is itself a feature of the emergence of media cultures (Stevenson, 1995; Fiske, 1995; Kellner, 1995; Poster, 1995) which bring more and more aspects of social life and more and more actors 'within the frame of the media' (Castells, 1997).

The EU is engaged in a detailed and extensive programme of constructing a 'European' Information Society. Indeed, it might not be overstating the case to suggest that the creation of an information society is one of the most important policy areas of the whole European project, involving an increasing number of Directorates-General (DGI, DGIII, DGIV, DGX, DGXIII, DGXV), specialist groups, state-actors, NGOs, corporate and public bodies in the formulation, implementation and review of polity. In itself this complex policy network is a paradigm for the creation of a networked European space, of governance without government. The EU Framework programmes have increasingly stressed the centrality of the Information Society project and under *Framework Five*, 3.6 billion Euro has been made available for the Information Society project. In fact the 1990s have seen a flurry of information society related policy prescriptions and we can usefully date the present interest[4] from the 1993 white paper on *Growth, Competitiveness and Employment*. Since then the construction of an information society has been pursued avidly and there have been a series of policy initiatives, opinions and reports.[5] A brief overview of information society policy allows us to analyse the direction of policy and examine specific applications. It also allows us to explore the inherent tensions which characterise European policy in this area (Axford and Huggins, 1996).

The European Union's interest in the Information Society ranges across three principal areas. First, the Union and its member states are committed to the idea that the application of advanced information technology will lead to significant economic gain and competitive renewal within the economies of member states. (It is also true that this conviction is enhanced by the perceived costs of past failures to exploit the competitive advantage of the early take-up of information technology). Second, the EU argues that the creation of an information society—through both virtual and phenomenal transnational networks—will enhance the projected integration of European member states. Third, the information society will (through the application of ICTs to 'solve' specific difficulties of groups, regions and individuals) encourage greater cohesion within the EU.

The sort of European Information Society prescribed in the policy statements outlined in this chapter is one which, as Kevin Robins (1994) suggests, looks to promote the 're-imagination of community and identity in Europe'.[6] In this it is in accord with Jean Monnet's conception of European unity and how to achieve it through a top down engineering of a European communications space and the social practices that will characterise it, mediated and regulated by the Brussels quasi-state. But as with so much of Community policy, this prescription suffers because it is the child of separate 'logics' which may not be compatible. The first is the liberalising ethos of the internal market in Europe where the creation of the European information society is seen as an integral part of the opening up of a de-regulated, transnational economic space. In prospect, the logic of the single market carries the liberal ideology of de-regulation to the point where not only is there a 'formal devaluation of the vast political resources which have come to be organised in and around the nation-state', as Schmitter and Streeck (1991) maintain but also (and this is crucial) a potential redefinition of the very idea of a European polity and civil society, as a space created and recreated by networks of interaction (Axford, 1995).

But the second logic to some extent confounds the first, and it derives from the marked tendency to imagine and prescribe a European 'unity' or model of 'Europeanness' which is, as Robins (1994) states, 'a national community writ large' (see also, Delanty, 1995 and 1998). This model, shared by many state-centric theorists of the integration process, owes much to the overwhelming influence in Europe of the Westphalian model of governance (Held, 1992; Rosamond, 1996). This model laid down the principles of the modern European state system and began to establish the state as the ontological centre of modern identity formation. Such a model prescribes a European information space which, in contrast to the market logic, is decidedly élitist, much more regulated, and defensive in regard to the allegedly pernicious influence of Americanised 'global' cultures and big players in the information society. Not to be coy, the policy thrust displays many of the features of the processes of nation-state modernisation, in which modernising élites have generally sought to create an 'isomorphism of people, territory and culture' (Collins, 1990).

An accommodation between these two logics, or at least a convenient squaring of the circle, has been achieved through a kind of neo-functionalist wishful thinking, wherein the growth of the information society is seen as contributing to the creation of truly Europeanised publics, who in turn and in time will, as Robins (1994) says, begin to 'imagine the new community of Europe'. Quite how this will be achieved is not all that clear since neo-functionalist reasoning—with its reliance on 'spillover' from economic interconnections to produce a community of affect—also makes the mistake of confusing changes in behaviour with changes in identity. As we have noted above, it also relegates agency to the rim of social explanation.

In recent years, the policy direction of the EU in the area of the information society has begun to emerge with more clarity and direction. The 1993 white paper identified the need to create a 'common information area' within the EU to allow a fuller realisation of the opportunities offered by the information society.

But the clearest statement of European Union policy in the area of the information society is the 1994 *Europe and the Global Information Society: Recommendations to the European Council* or the Bangemann Report, as it is often known. This report stressed the urgent need for EU action in the area of the information society and emphasised its potential for economic gain as well as its transformative potential socially and culturally. The report argues that the application of advanced ICTs creates a revolution, and that 'this revolution adds huge new capacities to human intelligence and . . . changes the way we work together and the way we live together' (Bangemann, 1994: 3). Furthermore the 'information society has the potential to improve the quality of life of Europe's citizens, the efficiency of our social and economic organisation and to reinforce cohesion' (Bangemann, 1994: 5).

The Union's claim that the search for greater social cohesion and accelerated integration can be furthered by the creation of an information society is problematic, although strongly held. The first difficulty resides in the apparent belief that information society technologies can be used instrumentally to achieve affective ends, greater interconnectivity of course, but also a more profound sense of European identity. The second is that the desired goals of greater cohesion and integration are couched in terms of some super or supra statist entity in Europe, but these aims are not compatible with, nor are they likely to contain, the post-modern character of 'technologies of miracles and dreams', whose social and cultural impact is likely to be disaggregative and dangerous to any sort of meta-narrative.

Following the publication of the Bangemann report, the Commission published a communication entitled *Europe's Way to the Information Society: An Action Plan* also in 1994. This report identifies the significance of the information society and the possible direction of policy initiatives needed to create such a society. In particular the report identifies ten priority application areas in which specific policy directives should be undertaken. These are, teleworking, distance learning, a network of universities and research centres, telematic services for small and medium enterprises, road traffic management, air traffic control, healthcare networks, a trans-European public administration network, electronic tendering and city information highways.

Where the Bangemann Report outlines a vision of Europe's path to the information society and its subsequent location within a global information order, *Europe's Way to the Information Society: An Action Plan*, is a statement of policy on how best to proceed. The report is also notable for the way it tries to juggle the Communities' concern to maintain a market-led stance on innovation, product design and infrastructure, with the perceived need to provide an over-arching goal for the creation of a European communications area.

The plan identifies four specific lines for action by the Community. First is the creation of a regulatory and legal framework covering telecommunications infrastructure and services, copyright and intellectual property rights, privacy, media concentration and the free movement of audio-visual products. Second is the construction of trans-European networks, services, applications and content. Third are social, societal and cultural aspects, including the linguistic and cultural dimensions of the information society. The fourth line of action is the promotion of the information society and the crucial task of 'Preparing Europeans for the advent of the information society' (Bangemann, 1994). The Information Society Project Office (ISPO) provides an interface between industry and users and aims to promote the idea of an information society.

In 1996 the policy proposals of the EU were reviewed and further refined with the publication of the Commission communication *Europe at the Forefront of the Global Information Society: A Rolling Action Plan*. Whilst maintaining the basic premise of earlier policy proposals this plan places significantly more emphasis on the business environment stressing the need for greater liberalisation of the telecommunications industries and the increased application of advanced technology to working and business practice. In addition this plan identifies the need for greater application of the information society initiatives to educational structures and practices. The Rolling Action plan also places greater emphasis on the potential impact of the information society on the everyday life of European citizens. Finally the 1996 Action Plan, in recognising the huge cost of creating a European information society charges the Fifth Framework proposals with greater responsibility for encouraging end-user orientated research and development funding.

As the idea of the information society has taken hold within the European Union a number of research and action programmes have developed which ultimately will shape the nature and extent of the information society. These include the Telematics Programme, ACTS,[7] ESPRIT,[8] RACE,[9] INFO2000,[10] MLIS,[11] TEN-TELECOM.[12] The outcome of these initiatives to date has been more than 400 accomplished, on-going and forthcoming actions related to the information society project (Goldberg, Prosser, Verhulst, 1998). More recently, a High Level Group of Experts have been charged with assessing the social impact of the information society[13] along with various other discussion and advisory groups, including the European Internet Forum and the Information Society Forum. As the information society project has mushroomed, a growing number of diverse actors have become involved in the policy process thereby widening the scope of participation.

The European Union has created a policy framework through which it seeks to create an information society, which is fundamentally reliant on networks that are often transnational in organisation and membership. Characteristic of all the programmes and actions initiated under the umbrella policy of the information society project are high levels of inter-action and networking between European level agencies, state, provincial and local governments, NGOs, business and corporate actors, educational organisations, research institutes and a variety of user-groups. These networks give substance to the intention to transnationalise because they encourage, even require the setting up of deliberative and collaborative groups across nation-state boundaries. For example, successful bidding for European funding under information society projects is tied, in part, to the creation of genuinely transnational networks of actors. Moreover, the problems that the information society tries to solve, whether drug-abuse or care of the elderly, and the policy outcomes pursued in terms of cohesion, sociality and economic regeneration are re-identified as *European* rather than national.

The networks being formed display some of the characteristics of a network polity. These networks are often of indeterminate duration and scope, multi-layered, cross-sectoral, and built upon public-private partnerships with considerable end-user orientation. Crucially, for the issue of governance without government, the European Information Society is not heavily institutionalised but resembles more a fluid space of social, cultural and economic activity in which significant decisions about the 'shape' of Europe are being taken.

Two further examples of information society projects are apposite. First, in 1993 the Manchester Telecities Declaration launched a system of digital networking between 13 European cities.[14] Since then the network has grown, with 70 cities involved by the time of the 1996 Antwerp Declaration. This network has the express aim of promoting economic regeneration and improving the life of citizens through the application of telematics. The Antwerp declaration stresses the importance of co-operation between cities in achieving economic and life-quality goals and in furthering the aims of the information society. This project is a good example of the characteristics of transnational, virtual networking between situated actors and of the way in which, through the uses of technology, such networking breaks with more conventional modes of political and civic association.

A further example is an experiment in local democratic communication originating in the London Borough of Lewisham and spreading out to other parts of Europe. Funded (in part) under the telematics programme, the London Borough of Lewisham is a key member of a network involving Bologna in Italy, Ronneby in Sweden and the Information Society Project Office of the European Union. The latter is responsible for funding a large scale programme entitled *Dialogue* which is designed to involve local communities in decision-making, and in promoting cross-national deliberation of common issues. The project involves the use of a wide range of techniques and strategies including on and off-line citizens panels, a junior citizens technology project called 'tellytalk', focus groups and a range of issue-based community forums. These forums are used to increase citizen participation in local government and the data generated by them are reported to Lewisham Council and other agencies, with a view to inform subsequent decisions. This example points up the construction of transnational networks, but also suggests that deliberative and practical citizenship can be encouraged through the use of information technologies. Presumably the concerns of the residents of Lewisham, Bologna and Ronneby are, by and large, local. Yet their interconnection as participants in a trans-national virtual forum intimates the potential for postnational practical citizenship based on information and deliberation.

Conceived of as an informational space, the European Union looks more like a network than a tree, as Castells says (1997). Information Society projects orientated to the end-user offer the prospects for a rejuvenation of the European project itself, because as Castells states, the 'real process of religitimization of Europe appears to be taking place in the burgeoning of local and regional initiatives, in economic development, as well as cultural expressions, and social rights, which link up horizontally with each other, while also linking up with European programs directly or through their respective national governments' (1997: 331).

Keohane and Hoffman clearly have the same idea in mind when they say that the European Union is 'essentially organized as a network that involves the pooling and sharing of sovereignty rather than the transfer of sovereignty to a higher level' (1991: 13). As we noted earlier in the chapter, in such a conception the European Union reveals some of the characteristics of medieval institutions in which there are a multitude of overlapping authorities, and only a diffuse form of state. Castells, somewhat confusingly, uses the expression 'network state' to describe this state of affairs, where 'authority is shared along a network' (1997: 332) but what he is describing is a form of network polity.

The notion that the European Union is or will become a network polity has a number of implications for both theory and practice. For one thing it demonstrates that attempting to imagine the future of Europe in terms of a nation-state 'writ large' is not appropriate and that more conventional notions of Europe as a political or cultural community do not fit with the current state of European integration. For another, it is necessary to recognise that networks, even virtual networks can function as actors and as contexts wherein identities are made and re-made. Ulf Hannerz argues that what is primary and has the feeling of intimacy is not always restricted in space (1996: 98). If one accepts this, the idea of a transnational network as a community is not a contradiction in terms. To imagine a network polity in Europe, this recognition is a necessary first step, although it requires quite a leap of faith, and not a little empirical research. What seems more likely is that the information society project will create a 'virtual' Europe in which 'society' will be constituted as a discursive framework rather than a system of values, as 'thin' rather than 'thick' (Delanty, 1998). In the final section of this chapter we consider some of the issues raised by the idea of a network polity for democratic practice.

Conclusion: issues in the formation of a network polity in Europe

In this chapter we have argued that transnational networks and flows are an augury of a postnational polity in Europe, where borders of various sorts are less and less relevant to the conduct of governance and, more contentiously, to definitions of political community and civil society. Lest this seem too radical or utopian/dystopian, we have been concerned to point out that for the foreseeable future such developments do not mean the death of the territorial state, nor of those associations and identities tied to it. Rather, the postnational polity will subsist both as a post-modern *space of flows* and a modern *space of places*, in Ruggie's terms. It is also worth noting Mike Featherstone's useful insight to the effect that new non spatial networks and communities of interest are 'third cultures' (1990) consisting of people in policy networks, diasporas, social movements and so on, which all afford opportunities for new allegiances and identities, but without the necessary concomitant of the destruction of older ones. This insight beggars more conventional and linear models of social change because it is not evolutionary and, through its willingness to espouse the possibility of multiple identities and a pluralism of content and consciousness, is very post-modern.

The networks and flows of the emergent Information Society in Europe provide an insight into how such a polity might subsist, although a good deal more empirical work into the construction and functioning of networks needs to be done in order to give substance to the arguments we have offered here. As a model for a new social morphology in Europe, reference to the networks of the European Information Society project may strike some commentators as misplaced, or the analysis premature, but the field seems to us to express the changing nature of political reality apparent in: i) the de-territorialisation of social relations and governance; ii) the decentralsation and fragmentation of the state; iii) the transnationalisation of what used to be called domestic politics; iv) the privatisation of governance, especially in areas such as the regulation of capital markets; v) the blurring of public and private domains; vi) the proliferation of actors in any and all policy areas; and vii) the growing importance of information in all areas of life, as a resource and in terms of the capacities that arise from new forms of interaction and connectivity (see Kenis and Schneider, 1991 for a discussion of these features; Axford and Huggins, forthcoming 2000; Pal, 1997).

A good deal of work on the modernisation of governance is happy to adopt the network metaphor. The instantiation of an Information Society in Europe pushes the analogy further because even though its very conception is rooted in different models of a united Europe (put crudely, super-statist versus regionalist and localist) its logic, tied to the development of digital-electronic-telecommunications, is markedly post-modern. Which is to say that it promotes difference, affords opportunities for cultural and consumer niches, enables the mobilisation of governance, politics and sociality regardless of borders and encourages the setting up of virtual networks and organisations, freed from both time and space.

Using electronic networks as a model for governance in post-territorial Europe is obviously a radical step. Networks are more fluid and variable than the institutions of conventional governance and reflect a growing number of policy-relevant actors, complex forms of knowledge and complex patterns of connectivity and interaction. But networked forms of governance are one thing, a networked politics in a networked democracy may be quite another. Let us return briefly to the issues posed above and examine the potential for a democratic network polity in Europe, bearing in mind that there has been a chronic concern with the EU's 'democratic deficit', and that questions of democracy and legitimacy also dog intergovernmentalist, super and supra-statist models of EU government and governance.

Of overarching concern is the notion that a post-modern polity is injurious to the 'imaginary presuppositions of democracy', because the EU (however conceived) is not, and never can be, a nation-state. As such, it does not possess a *demos*. Politics and the very idea of 'a' people who have a shared commitment to national definitions of value and a part to play in how values are allocated, are still rooted in the territorial state and the bounded society. In the absence of a *demos*, runs the argument, there can be no transference of a national model of liberal, majoritarian democracy to the EU (Jachtenfuchs, 1997). Gerard Delanty (1998: 4.2–4.6) warms to this theme, arguing: i) that the further fragmentation of sovereignty and the deployment of multi-level governance in the EU makes the prospects for a unitary European demos even more remote; (ii) that legitimation needs can not be met in a system where there is so little direct input from the mass of citizens, leaving aside iii) that citizenship in the EU is necessarily codified in terms of transnational rights which often override national citizenship. There is also a notable absence of what he calls a 'participation dimension' to EU citizenship, and while this is also a feature of liberal conceptions of citizenship *per se*, in the absence of a European equivalent of national identity, the upshot is the aforementioned democratic deficit and possibly a legitimation deficit as well.

These concerns are voiced about rather less radical models of the EU polity than the one we have outlined in this chapter, and they are all 'implicitly linked to the model of the state' as the container for a democratic polity (Jachtenfuchs and Kohler-Koch, 1997: 15). Used in a critique of the network polity, do they carry still more weight? Proponents of the EU as a *sui generis* model of rule, have sought a way around such difficulties, suggesting that the EU policy process could be made more transparent and accessible by placing it on the Internet (Weiler, 1997); by increasing the participation of functional rather than territorial constituencies through the use of weighted voting systems (Schmitter, 1996) and by playing down the salience of 'thick' national and ethnic ties in favour of 'thinner', but more general civic rights and obligations (Wiener, 1997). In addition, proponents of the new governance have emphasised the changing nature of EU decision-processes and decision-outcomes, which are increasingly about efficiency of throughput and output, not the representation of constituencies; consensual problem-solving not bargaining and conflict, and regulation not redistribution. In such an environment, legitimacy is secured through the openness of the policy process and because of the positive-sum nature of the outcomes. As a result, legitimacy as the cornerstone of democratic governance is retained, but along the way the sense of what actually constitutes a democratic system of rule has become more anodyne.

Even in a post-modern polity, it would be hard to dispense with the legacies of modernist rule entirely. National citizens, increasingly accustomed to judging élites by performance, are also prone to use more abstract and demanding criteria when asked to judge the democratic credentials of the personnel and institutions of governance. Would it be any different if systems of rule were established across borders as a matter of routine, or if political mobilisation and participation were to be facilitated through e-mail, list-servers and the Web? In truth it might, but in order to dispense with the norms and rules framing modernist discourses of democracy, postmodern forms and practices would have to be accompanied by changes in consciousness and culture, which reposes the problem of how to foster the legitimacy of a European polity not tied to territory, and this raises the question of active citizenship.

In trying to address the question of legitimacy, the new governance motif deals with only one side of the issue (Hix, 1998: 51), namely the efficiency and fairness of policy outputs. The other side, less anodyne and more visceral, is the matter of citizens' participation in the policy process. The limited amount of indirect participation allowed to EU citizens at present is in marked contrast to the plethora of formal rules establishing their rights. For there to be effective citizen participation in a postnational European polity, there would have to be a feisty low politics in existence, complete with warring transnational political parties as agents of mobilisation and representation, and citizens who felt they had a stake in the new community. The new governance perspective, in some ways attuned to the postnational form of the EU polity, downplays the possibility of anything resembling a competitive democratic politics with blood on the carpet, because this is the province of the state, and the EU can never be a state. But the imperative to recreate a territorialist politics in a post-territorial space, in order to secure its democratic credentials, ignores the growing volume of research and evidence which identifies in transnational space, functional equivalents for territorial institutions and practices (Rosenau, 1998) and also discerns an 'innovative and variegated type of politics' (Falk, 1996: 8) in the activities of social movements and networks.

Many analysts of information and communications technologies argue that the mobilisation of interests and other expressions of active citizenship are potentially easier through the use of ICTs, although, as ever, questions remain about availability, access and skills. The competence of citizens in a post-territorial polity, and possibly their sense of efficacy too, would depend on them acquiring these attributes through forms of communicative action (Habermas, 1996). Communicative action implies both the socialisation of members of a discursive community and the potential for purposive concerted action through deliberation and reflexivity. Clearly there are difficulties with this prescription in a post-territorial polity, but while the idea of discursive competence may be easier to achieve than actual involvement in routine decision-making, the bracketing of deliberation and reflexivity to the life-world runs the risk of reducing the active citizen to a 'judicious spectator' or 'outside protestor' (Boyte, 1996).

In addition, it would be difficult, if not unthinkable, to envision a postnational, democratic polity without a framework of democratic public law entrenched across borders, and a respect for eminently liberal notions about equal rights and equal obligations, in circumstances where individuals can freely adjudge their common conditions of association (Held, 1995, 1998). Although it is hardly the whole Kantian package of universal, trans-cultural authority, David Held calls this state of affairs a cosmopolitan or radicalised democracy, complete with overlapping and spatially variable sovereignties and multiple communities and citizenships. Others, less convinced of the power of transnational networks to fashion a European civil society, cleave to the idea that a transnational politics, even one protected by general but weak rights, is no more than the politics of the relatively powerless faced with the trans-territorial power of corporations and producer networks. Even if this were true, it still leaves such a politics as networked, pluralistic, countervailing and to that extent, democratising. Networks of governance and networks of activists realise a European sub-politics (Beck, 1996) and transnationalise key areas of public policy and citizen activity. As a result they give substance to and normalise the idea of postnational public spaces (Kohler, 1998). But it may be that there are problems with labelling all such activity postnational, even where it crosses boundaries. Sidney Tarrow (1996) suggests that what are often discussed as trans and postnational social movements are just instances of the diffusion of nationally based collective action, forms of transnational exchange between actors fully rooted in national contexts or transnational issue networks. These strictures are helpful in establishing a working typology of social movements, and in pointing out the messy imbrication of national and postnational actors and issues, but they do not weaken the claim that neither democracy nor community can be limited to the territoriality of contiguous space.

Of course, having abjured or severely qualified the still powerful spatial paradigm of territoriality, we are obliged to step outside liberal discourses on the idea of a political community and neo-Tocquevillian assumptions about the natural spaces of civic association (Shapiro, 1997). Assimilationist accounts of community, such as those seen in different strains of communitarian thinking (Rorty, 1989) with their emphasis on strong democracy (Barber, 1984) rooted in thick models of community, where local and traditional attachments are peremptory and absolute, have little grip on the realities of a post-modern, postnational Europe. Of course they still influence the cultural imagination of many nationals and some denizens of the European space, and thus have political consequence. If the idea of a European community of fate has any purchase at all in this more liminal environment, it does not lie in the idea of a super-territorial European demos, or in some richer fantasy of a pan-European cultural identity. Delanty rightly points to the fact that, implicitly at least, policy makers in the EU have already shifted to a model of community which recognises pluralities of interest and identity and the irrepressible flow of communications, thereby deconstructing Europe and re-creating it as a web of discursive spaces, joined by networks and those who people them (1998: 5.2). But the uncomfortable fact is that the Information Society project tables all these versions of European unity as viable and compatible. In itself, this is witness enough to the ambivalence and ambiguity that informs millennial discourses on European unity. Perceiving a different sort of European unity in the networks and flows of the information society is also a reminder of the staying power of old imaginaries and older fictions.

Notes

1 For a discussion of the concept of the information society see F. Webster (1995), *Theories of the Information Society*, London: Routledge; F. Webster (1996), 'The Information Society: Conceptions and Critique', in *Encyclopedia of Library and Information Science*, 58 (21), 74–112; F. Webster and K. Robbins (1998), 'The Iron Cage of the Information Society', in *Information, Communication and Society*, 1, 1, 23–45.

2 Not least the EU itself.

3 For example, see *Green Paper on the Convergence of the Telecommunications, Media and Information Technology Sectors, and the Implications for Regulation: Towards an Information Society Approach*, COM(97)623 (1997) or *The Digital Age: European Audiovisual Policy* (1998).

4 It is tempting, but inaccurate, to conceive of the interest in 'Information Societies' as a recent development. The concept has a long history and the transformative impact of information technologies has been trumpeted on many occasions—to no avail.

5 For example see *Europe and the Global Information Society: Recommendations to the European Council* (Bangemann Report) 1994, *Europe's Way to the Information Society. An Action Plan* (1994), *Europe at the Forefront of the Global Information Society: Rolling Action Plan* (1996), *Building the European Information Society for Us All* (1997).

6 For an extended version of the argument produced in the next few paragraphs, see B. Axford and R. Huggins, 'Media Without Boundaries: Fear and Loathing on the Road to Eurotrash or Transformation in the European Cultural Economy?' *Innovation*, 9, 2, 1996, 175–186.

7 Advanced Communications Technologies and Services.

8 The European Union's information technologies programme.

9 A European Research Programme.

10 A Multimedia programme for the Information Society.

11 Multilingual Information Society.

12 Trans-European Telecommunications Networks.

13 See *Building the European Information Society for Us All* (1997).

14 Amsterdam, Barcelona, Birmingham, Bologna, Den Haag, Hull, Koln, Leeds, Lille, Manchester, Nantes, Nice, Nottingham.

Bibliography

Albrow, M. (1996), *The Global Age*, Cambridge: Polity Press.

Amin, A. (1997), 'Tracing Globalization', *Theory, Culture and Society*, 14 (2), 123–37.

Anderson, J. (1996), 'The Shifting Stage of Politics: New Medieval and Postmodern Territorialities', *Environment and Planning D: Society and Space*, 14, 133–53.

Appadurai, A. (1990), 'Disjuncture and Difference in the Global Cultural Economy', in M. Featherstone (ed.), *Global Culture: Nationalism, Globalization and Modernity*, London: Sage.

Appadurai, A. (1996), *Modernity at Large: Cultural Dimensions of Globalization*, Minneapolis: University of Minneapolis Press.

Archibugi, D., D. Held, and M. Kohler, *Re-Imagining Political Community: Studies in Cosmopolitan Democracy*, Cambridge: Polity.

Axford, B. (1995), *The Global System: Economics, Politics and Culture*, Cambridge: Polity Press.

Axford, B. and R. Huggins (1996), 'Media Without Boundaries: Fear and Loathing on the Road to Eurotrash or Transformation in the European Cultural Economy?' in *Innovation: the European Journal of Social Science*, 9 (2), 175–84.

Axford, B. and R. Huggins (1998), 'European Identity and the Information Society', in F. Brinkhuis and S. Talmor (eds), *Memory, History and Critique: European Identities at the Millenium*, New Haven, MIT Press/ISSEI (CD-ROM).

Axford, B. and R. Huggins (eds), (2000), *New Media and Politics*, London: Sage.

Axford, B. (1999), 'Enacting Globalization: Transnational Networks and the Deterritorialisation of Social Relationships', *Protosociology, An International Journal of Interdisciplinary Research*.

Badie, B. and P. Birnbaum. (1983), *The Sociology of the State*, Chicago: University of Chicago Press.

Balandier, G. (1992), *Le Pouvoir sur Scènes*, Paris: Balland.

Barber, B. (1984), *Strong Democracy: Participatory Politics for a New Age*, Los Angeles: University of California Press.

Bauman, Z. (1992), *Intimations of Modernity*, London: Routledge.

Bauman, Z. (1998), *Europe of Strangers*, ESRC Transnational Communities Programme Seminar Series, 24.

Beck, U. (1992), *Risk Society*, Cambridge: Polity Press.

Bellah, R. *et al.* (1985), *Habits of the Heart*, Berkeley, CA: University of California Press.

Boli, J. and G. Thomas (1997), 'World Culture and the World Polity: A Century of International Non-Governmental Organisation', *American Sociological Review*, 62, 171–90.

Boyte, H. (1996), *Beyond Deliberation: Citizenship as a Public Work*, Chicago: PEGS Conference, 11–12 February.

Caporaso, J. (1996), 'The European Union and Forms of State', *Journal of Common Market Studies*, 34 (1), 29–52.

Castells, M. (1996), *The Rise of the Network Society*, vol. 1, Oxford: Blackwells.

Castells, M. (1997), *The Power of Identity*, vol. 2, Oxford: Blackwells.

Collins, R. (1990), 'National Culture: A Contradiction in Terms?' in Richard Collins (ed.), *Television, Policy and Culture*, London: Unwin Hyman.

Commission of the European Communities (1993a), *Growth, Competitiveness, Employment: The Challenges and Ways Forward into the 21st Century*, COM (93) 700 FINAL.

Commission of the European Communities (1994), *Europe's Way to the Information Society: An Action Plan*, COM (94) 347.

Commission of the European Communities (1994), *Europe and the Global Information Society: Recommendations to the EC* (Bangemann Report), Brussels.

Commission of the European Communities (1996), *Europe at the Forefront of the Global Information Society: Rolling Action Plan*.

Commission of the European Communities (1997), *Building the European Information Society for Us All*.

Commission of the European Communities (1997), *Green Paper on the Convergence of Telecommunications, Media and Information Technologies*, COM (97) 623.

Commission of the European Communities (1998), *The Digital Age: European Audiovisual Policy*.

Deutsch, K. (1953), *Nationalism and Social Communications: an Inquiry into the Foundations of Nationality*, Cambridge, MA: MIT Press.

Falk, R. (1998), *The Decline of Citizenship in an Era of Globalization*, The Transnational Foundation for Peace and Future Research Forum: Meeting Point.

Featherstone, M. (1990), 'Global Culture: An Introduction', *Theory, Culture and Society*, 7, 2–3.

Featherstone, M. (1995), *Undoing Culture: Globalization, Postmodernism and Identity*, London: Sage.

Featherstone, M. (ed.) (1990), *Global Culture: Nationalism, Globalization and Modernity*, London: Sage.

Featherstone, M. (1991), *Consumer Culture and Postmodernism*, London: Sage.

Fiske, J. (1995), *Media Matters: Everyday Culture and Political Change*, Minneapolis: University of Minnesota Press.

Friedman, J. (1996), *Transnationalization, Socio-Political Disorder and Ethnification As Expressions of Declining Global Hegemony*, <http:www//creepy.soc.lu.se/san/papers/transnateth.html.>

George, S. (1996), *Politics and Policy in the European Union* (3rd edn), Oxford: OUP.

Giddens, A. (1994), *Beyond Left and Right*, Cambridge: Polity.

Goldberg, David, Tony Prosser, and Stefan Verhulst (1998), *Regulating the Changing Media: A Comparative Study*, Oxford: Clarendon Press.

Goodman, J. (1998), 'The European Union: Reconstituting Democracy beyond the Nation-State', in A. McGrew (ed.), *The Transformation of Democracy*, Cambridge: Polity/The Open University, 171–182.

Habermas, J. (1996), *Between Facts and Norms: Contributions to a Discourse Theory of Law and Democracy*, Cambridge, MA: MIT Press.

Hannerz, U. (1992), 'The Global Ecumene as a Network of Networks', in A. Kuper (ed.), *Conceptualising Society*, London: Routledge.

Hannerz, U. (1996), *Transnational Connections*, London: Routledge.

Held, D. (1992), 'From City States to a Cosmopolitan Order', *Political Studies*, 42 (special issue), 10–40.

Held, D. (1995), *Democracy and the Global Order*, Cambridge: Polity.

Held, D. (1998), 'Democracy and Globalization', in D. Archibugi, D. Held, and M. Kohler, *Re-Imagining Political Community: Studies in Cosmopolitan Democracy*, Cambridge: Polity.

Hix, S. (1998), 'The Study of the European Union: The "New Governance" Agenda and its Rival', *European Journal of Public Policy*, 5 (1), 38–65.

Jachtenfuchs, M. and B. Kohler-Koch (1996), 'Einleitung: Regieren im Dynamischen

Mehrebensystem', in Jachtenfuchs and Kohler-Koch (eds), *Europaische Integration*, Opladen: Leske und Budrich, 15–44.

Jaques, M. (1993), 'Battleground of Europe's Future', *Sunday Times*, 27 March.

Kastoryano, R. (1998), *Transnational Participation and Citizenship: Immigrants in the European Union*, WPTC-98-12.

Kellner, D. (1995), *Media Cultures*, London: Routledge.

Kenis, P. and V. Schneider (1991), 'Policy Networks and Policy Analysis: Scrutinising a New Analytical Toolbox', in B. Marin and R. Mayntz (eds), *Policy Networks: Empirical Evidence and Theoretical Considerations*, Frankfurt AM: Campus Verlag, 25–59.

Keohane, R. and S. Hoffman (1991), *The New European Community: Decision-Making and Institutional Change*, Boulder: Westview Press.

Kohler, M. (ed.) (1998), *Re-imagining Political Community*, Cambridge: Polity.

Laffan, B. (1996), 'The Politics of Identity and Political Order in Europe', *Journal of Common Market Studies*, 34 (1), 81–102.

Lash, S. and J. Urry (1994), *Economies of Signs and Space*, London: Sage.

Latour, B. (1993), *On Actor Network Theory: A Few Clarifications*, http://www.keele.cstt.latour.html

Luke, T. (1996), 'Governmentality and Contragovernmentality: Rethinking Sovereignty and Territoriality after the Cold War', *Political Geography*, 15 (6/7), 491–507.

Luke, T. (1995), 'World Order or Neo-World Orders. Power, Politics and Ideology in Informationalizing Glocalities', in M. Featherstone, S. Lash, and R. Robertson, *Global Modernities*, London: Sage.

Majone, G. (1996), 'A European Regulatory State?' in J. Richardson (ed.), *European Union: Power and Policy-Making*, London: Routledge.

Mann, M. (1998), 'Is There a Society Called Euro?' in R. Axtmann (ed.), *Globalization and Europe*, London: Pinter.

Marks, G. (1993), 'Structural Policy and Multilevel Governance in the European Community', in A. Cafruny and G. Rosenthal (eds), *The State of the European Community 11: The Maastricht Debates and Beyond*, Boulder: Lynne Rienner, 391–410.

Marks, G., L. Hooghe, and K. Blank (1996), 'European Integration in the 1980s: State-Centric v Multi-Level Governance', *Journal of Common Market Studies*, 34, 341–78.

Marks, G. *et al.* (1993), 'Structural Policy and Multi-Level Governance in the EC', in A. W. Cafruny and G. G. Rosenthal, Boulder: Lynne Reiner.

Massey, D. (1995), 'A Global Sense of Place', in D. Massey, *Space, Place and Gender*, Cambridge: Polity.

McGrew, A. (ed.), *The Transformation of Democracy*, Cambridge: Polity/The Open University.

McLennan, G. (1995), *Pluralism*, Buckingham: Open University Press.

Meyer, J. W., J. Boli, F. Ramirez, and G. Thomas (1997), 'World Society in the Age of Globalization: The US Latina/o–Latin American Case', *Cultural Studies*, 103 (1), 144–81.

Morley, D. and Kevin Robins (1994), *Spaces of Identity*, London: Routledge.

O'Tuathail (1998), *Re-Thinking Geopolitics*, London: Routledge.

Ohmae, K. (1992), 'The Rise of the Region-State', *Foreign Affairs*, Spring, 79–87.

Poster, M. (1995), *The Second Media Age*, Cambridge: Polity Press.

Putnam, R. (1995), 'Bowling Alone: America's Declining Social Capital', *Journal of Politics*, 6 (1), 65–78.

Rabinow, P. (1993), *A Critical Curiosity: Reflections on Hypermodern Places*, mimeo.

Reise, U. (1992), 'Postmodern Culture: Symptom, Critique or Solution to the Crisis of Modernity?—An East German Perspective', *New German Critique*, 57 (Fall), 157–70.

Robins, K. (1994), 'The Politics of Silence: The Meaning of Community and the Uses of Media in the New Europe', *New Formations*, vol. 21, 80–102.

Rorty, R. (1989), *Contingency, Irony, Solidarity*, Cambridge: Cambridge University Press.

Rosamond, B. (1996), 'Understanding European Unity: The Limits of Nation State-Centric Integration Theory', *History of European Ideas*.

Rosenau, J. N. and E. O. Czempiel (1992), *Governance without Government: Order and Change in World Politics*, Cambridge: Cambridge University Press.

Rosenau, J. (1998), 'Governance and Democracy in a Globalizing World', in D. Archibugi, D. Held, and M. Kohler, *Re-Imagining Political Community: Studies in Cosmopolitan Democracy*, Cambridge: Polity.

Rosenau, P. and H. Bredemeier (1993), 'Modern and Postmodern Conceptions of Social Order', *Social Research*, 60 (2), 337–62.

Ruggie, J. (1993), 'Territoriality and Beyond: Problematising Modernity in International Relations', *International Organisation*, 47 (1), 149–74.

Schmitter, P. (1991), *The European Community as an Emergent and Novel Form of Political Domination*, Working Paper No. 26, Madrid: Juan March Institute.

Shapiro, M. and H. Alker (eds), *Challenging Boundaries: Global Flows, Territorial Identities*, Minneapolis: University of Minnesota Press.

Sklair, L. (1998), *Transnational Practices and the Analysis of the Global System*, ESRC Transnational Communities Programme Seminar Series, 22.

Soysal, Y. (1994), *The Limits of Citizenship in the Contemporary Nation-State System*, Chicago: University of Chicago Press.

Stevenson, N. (1995), *Understanding Media Cultures: Social Theory and Mass Communication*, London: Sage.

Tarrow, S. (1995), 'The Europeanization of Conflict: Reflections from a Social Movement Perspective', *West European Politics*, 18 (2), 223–51.

Tarrow, S. (1996), 'Fishnets, Internets and Catnets: Globalization and Transnational Collective Action', *Estudios Working Paper*, 78.

Taylor, P. (1996), *The European Union in the 1990s*, Oxford: OUP.

Wallace, H. and W. Wallace (1996), *Policy-Making in the European Union* (3rd edn), Oxford: OUP.

Webster, F. and K. Robins (1998), 'The Iron Cage of the Information Society', *Information, Communication and Society*, 1 (1), 23–45.

Webster, F. (1995), *Theories of the Information Society*, London: Routledge.

Webster, F. (1996), 'The Information Society: Conceptions and Critique', *Encyclopedia of Library and Information Science*, 58 (21), 74–112.

Weiner, A. (1997), *European Citizenship Practice: Building Institutions of a Nation-State*, New York: HarperCollins.

Citizenship and human rights— particular and universal worlds and the prospects for European citizenship

David Jary

Abstract

This chapter* makes the argument that the concept of universal citizenship rights based on human need is compatible with a recognition that particularistic identity (eg specific nationalities) exist. Following Habermas, Jary makes the case that diversity is essential to the discourse of human culture. In the first part of the paper, Jary discusses the work of Feyerabend, Habermas, Turner, Doyal and Gough in order to establish the position that universal rights preserve the conditions for cultural diversification and autonomous action while also enabling a search for social solidarity and integration between different groups. In the second part of the chapter, on the historically substantive prospects for European Union citizenship, Jary draws on Habermas, Held, Linklater and others to show that an inclusionary, cosmopolitan emancipatory citizenship may develop within a post-national civil state.

Aims and outline of this chapter

Citizenship is double-edged, both 'inclusive' and 'exclusive'. The close association between citizenship and forms of ethnic nationalism grounded in particular cultures and languages emphasises citizenship's exclusive features. The co-existence of many such cultures, languages and ethnicities is sometimes taken to provide support for a relativistic approach. In this chapter, I take issue with current conceptions of 'culture' and 'cultural boundedness' which have recourse in an uncritical way to conceptions of 'relativism'. I intend to marshal arguments in support of the claim that universalistic conceptions of 'truth' and 'citizenship rights' based on 'human need' remain viable once they have been reworked to take due account of nationalism.

It is helpful to distinguish between two conceptions of culture and language: (i) culture and language as diversity and relative meanings ['culture-1'], and (ii) culture and language as a universal requirement for human existence ['culture-2']. While relativist arguments emphasise the first conception, the second preserves the possibility of universals grounded in a concept of human needs and rights. This latter possibility is always capable of being realised, given the 'unfinished' but culturally improvable nature of the human animal (Gehlen, cited in Turner, 1993).[1]

In fact, these two conceptions of culture and language are *complementary*. A number of theorists, notably Jürgen Habermas, have sought to move beyond a simple dichotomy between universalism and relativism. In the first sections of the chapter I will argue that the work of the iconoclastic Austrian philosopher, Paul Feyerabend, often seen as dangerously 'relativist', also points in this direction. Feyerabend's 'Millian' conception of 'two argumentative chains' ('relativist' and 'realist') will be outlined and similarities noted with Habermas's conceptions of truth, justice, and his 'discourse ethics'. Taken together, Feyerabend and Habermas confirm the view that citizen rights are ultimately universal human needs and rights, the crucial component of our humanity. Later in the chapter, I draw upon the work of Bryan Turner (1993), Len Doyal and Ian Gough (1991), David Held (1992 and 1995) and Andrew Linklater (1998).[2]

The particular and universal will be presented not as the 'dualism' proposed in much contemporary social and cultural theory but as a 'duality', a complementary pair in which the pursuit of universalism requires a respect for separate 'traditions'. Particularistic characteristics such as nationality and gender, which are part of our individuality and identity, are essential to the continuing discourse that is human culture. However, this discourse depends upon universalism. A further point is that human needs and rights are closely related to our knowledge-creating activities. The two things—truth/knowledge and human rights/needs—are inherently entwined and mutually reinforcing.

In the light of this discussion, the chapter then also considers the prospects for 'civic nationalism' and a European Federal State, especially in view of the deficit with respect to democracy and rights which characterises many European institutions. I also examine the implications of immigration for 'exclusionary' notions of nationality and citizenship based on 'blood' ties or cultural homogeneity.

Feyerabend's Millian philosophy and two 'argumentative chains'

Feyerabend is often seen as a relativist. However, his intention was to create space for a more realistic ('flesh and blood') understanding of the possibilities and limits of science and universalism, once relativism was taken fully into account. Feyerabend was adamant that he was not a relativist in any ultimate sense of the term.[3] He defines 'philosophical relativism' as 'the doctrine that all traditions, theories, ideas, are equally true or equally false, . . . that any distribution of truth values over traditions is acceptable' (*Science in Free Society*, 1978: 83).[4] This form of relativism is nowhere defended in his work. Rather his 'relativism' is: 'of precisely the kind that seems to have been defended by Protagoras . . . ' (SFS: 82). It is 'civilised and reasonable'; 'because it pays attention to the pluralism of traditions and values' (SFS: 28). In science it allows for the incorporation of elements of earlier 'rejected' theories. In social life it allows learning from the study of alien cultures. And it allows members of minority traditions of all kinds to either protect their own world views or to move beyond them. In the spirit of doing justice to complexity, Feyerabend acknowledges the possible merit of traditions rejected by western science, such as 'folk' medicine, for example. Feyerabend's opposition to orthodox 'rationalist' methodology gives proper respect to particular forms of life. It stands for 'learning from the comparison of practices', for 'dialectical growth of knowledge', for 'reason' as well as 'experience'. We will find this position useful in our consideration of the particular and universal worlds of citizenship.

The Millian view

Feyerabend's well-known strictures 'against method' are a celebration of the intellectual and social openness advocated by John Stuart Mill in *On Liberty*.[5] Mill's ideas, which were very much influenced by his contacts with feminist thought, connect directly with the conceptions of truth, citizenship and human needs and rights I wish to advance.

Two argumentative chains

Feyerabend identifies 'two argumentative chains' which, he suggests, represent two ever-present, competing modes of discourse. In the first of these:[6] 'accepting a form of life L we reject a universal criticism and the realistic interpretation of theories not in agreement with L' (*Rationalism, Realism and Scientific Method*, 1981: xi)[7] (see Figure 1).

First chain: L (form of life) ⟶ Criticism ⟶ Realism_L

Second chain: Criticism ⟶ Proliferation ⟶ Realism

Figure 1 *Feyerabend's two argumentative chains*

In terms of the Kuhnian 'scientific paradigm', this first chain represents the closed world of 'normal science' which is language- and theory-relative. As Kuhn pointed out, successful scientific paradigms derive strength from their closed character. More generally, this first argumentative chain represents the closed world of *any other* bounded culture (in Wittgenstein terms, any 'form of life', or any particular practice). Feyerabend insists that such forms of life are in many cases knowledge-enhancing and life-enhancing. As Alisdair MacIntyre (1981: 244) asserts, what matters 'is the construction of local forms of community within which civility and moral life can be sustained'.[8]

One of Kuhn's definitions of a scientific paradigm was a 'universally recognised scientific achievement that . . . provides model problems and *solutions* for a *community* of practitioners' (Kuhn, 1970: vii, emphasis added).[9] In the absence of any theory-neutral language (of the kind sought, for example, by logical Positivists), paradigms will often appear 'disjoint' or 'incommensurable'. Relativism and the idea of herme[neu]tically-sealed cultures is, of course, central to many versions of phenomenology, structuralism and poststructuralism. The 'linguistic turn' in philosophy and social science is also a *'cultural* turn', placing all the emphasis upon diversity and relative meanings.[10] Feyerabend accepts the very real benefits associated with this first argumentative chain. However, he recognises that another argumentative chain is possible which overcomes its restrictions.

In the second chain (see Figure 1), 'criticism' means that: 'we do not simply accept the phenomenon, processes, institutions that surround us but we examine these and try to change them' (*RRSM*: ix). 'Proliferation' means that 'we use a plurality of theories (systems of thought, institutional frameworks) from the very beginning'. In contrast with the first chain, we do not restrict ourselves to working with 'a single theory, system of thought, institutional framework until circumstances force us to modify it or to give it up' (*RRSM*: ix). The arrows in this model do not 'express a well-defined connection such as logical implication', but rather indicate: 'that starting from the left hand side and adding physical principles, psychological assumptions, plausible cosmological conjectures, absurd guesses and plain common-sense views, a *dialectical* debate will eventually arrive at the right hand side' (*RRSM*: x).

It is the ever present possibility of both these two chains which led Kuhn to refer to the 'essential tension between tradition and innovation' in science (Kuhn, 1977).[11] Their co-existence also provides a basis on which all kinds of movements of 'counter-expertise'—for example, on environmental or medical issues—can contest with 'scientific orthodoxies' within a democratic public sphere. Most crucially, it is also the basis on which a cultural or moral community can expand its horizons from a particular to a different or more general frame of reference.

Feyerabend and Habermas

Turning to questions of truth and knowledge in relation to citizen rights, I now want to note some important similarities between Feyerabend and Jürgen Habermas. The latter's conception of discursively grounded claims to 'truth', resting on general conceptions of 'communicative competence' and 'human interests' has been much criticised in its details. However, this statement remains the best we have. Once its author has dropped his more grandiose 'transcendental' claims,[12] it is also consistent with Feyerabend's view.

For Habermas, 'experience supports the truth claim(s) of assertion . . . But a claim can be redeemed only through argumentation' (Habermas, *Legitimation Crisis*, 1957: xvi).[13] The 'will to truth' is implicit in the very structure of the 'speech act':

> Truth is not the fact that a consensus is realised but rather that at
> all times at any place, if we enter into a discussion a consensus
> can be realised under conditions that recognise it as a justified
> consensus. 'Truth' means warranted assertability . . . 'Truth'
> cannot be analysed independently of 'freedom' and 'justice'.
> (Habermas, *LC*: xvi–xvii)

For Habermas, 'all participants must have the same chance to initiate and perpetuate discourse . . . to give reasons for and against statements, to express attitudes, feelings, intentions and the life' (Habermas, *LC*, 1976: xvii). And for Feyerabend too: 'The debates settling the structures of a free society are open debates . . . solutions will not be imposed but will emerge only where people solve particular problems in a spirit of collaboration . . . a free society is a society in which all traditions are given equal rights, equal access to education and other positions of power' (*SFSI*: 30).

Feyerabend and Habermas jointly support the case that basic citizenship and human rights are the crucial component of knowledge-creation and the search for truth. Given the assaults by post-structuralism and post-modernists on the continued viability of the second chain, support for the existence of both chains has been made to seem outmoded. However, once the mediating effects of language and the provisionality of all claims in either chain are acknowledged, I can see no epistemological or ontological barriers to using Feyerabend's or Habermas's principles as a basis for claims about 'reality' and 'morality'.[14] Indeed, there would appear no alternative but to do so. To deny this step, while seeking to generalise 'relativism', would be paradoxical.

The frontiers of forms of life are never absolute; any discourse soon involves 'reality claims' that can only be redeemed discursively and trans-culturally. Of course there are many problems—eg conflicts of rights or values, between individuals or between nations—which are not automatically readily resolved by a Habermasian formula such as 'the regulation of the effects of social practices on each in the light of the freely expressed interests of all concerned'. Compromise or 'agreement to differ' as well as consensus can be the outcome of a Millian or a Habermasian discourse. The point remains, however, that issues can only be addressed 'realistically' in discursive contexts. To suggest in principle that particular classes of issue can never be resolved or even addressed realistically—rejecting dialogue—is simply to proceed by assertion.

Contrary to the claims of Lyotard, Foucault and other critics,[15] universalism does not aim to resolve every issue. Nor does it involve eliminating the plurality of ways of living. On the contrary, a variety of ways of life and a plurality of viewpoints are highly significant in any context of knowledge-seeking or attempting to resolve political and ethical disputes. This is a major reason for choosing to highlight Feyerabend's two chains alongside Habermas's more familiar models. A central element of the justification of universal rights is that such rights preserve the possibility for autonomous action and for individual diversity[16] while also enhancing the possibility for social solidarity and integration on new terms within modern or post-modern societies.

As Dews confirms in his introduction to Habermas's *Autonomy and Solidarity* (1992: 22),[17] 'Habermas's theory of consensus has nothing to do with the homogenization of language-games or the supremacy of one language-game', but expressly relates to 'the condition of possibility of plurality'.[18] Discourse ethics takes account of several factors, including[19] (i) the complexity and 'hermeneutic sensitivity' of any application of universal moral principles within particular contexts; (ii) the fact that people's acquisition of identity and 'conceptions of the good life' arise from their particular cultural and gendered locations and cannot therefore be expected to arise simply via a 'discourse ethics'; (iii) the continuation of manifest inequalities of economic and political power which 'distort' access to discourse; and (iv) the fact that the conditions for the operation of a universal morality require the prior establishment of conducive personality structures and social structures.

Habermas and those like him remain acutely aware of the barriers in practice to the full expression of political rights which arise, above all, from the operation of administrative power and capitalism—seen as a politically anonymous form of 'systems integration' that by-passes the 'social integration' associated with the consciousness of actors and the operation of 'values, norms and the processes of reaching understanding'. However, Habermas claims that the 'ideal' conception of discourse provides a vantage point on moral issues. He argues that the introduction of freedom of speech and the franchise assists a learning process in which modern life worlds are increasingly favoured. This is bound up with Habermas's much discussed and much criticised (but, I will argue, still tenable) 'evolutionary' or developmental sociological argument about human rights.[20] I explore this evolutionary and developmental argument in sociological thinking in more concrete terms in the final two sections of this chapter.

Citizenship, human needs and universal human rights

Following the widespread retreat from evolutionary theory and the partial eclipse of Marxism, talk of human needs and human rights has become largely unfashionable in sociology. Nevertheless, the relation between citizenship, human rights and human needs in 'evolutionary' or developmental terms has been addressed by a number of sociologists and philosophers; for example, by Bryan Turner in his 'Outline of a theory of human rights' (1993) and by Len Doyal and Ian Gough in their powerful book, *A Theory of Human Need* (1991).

Turner, like many other British sociologists who discuss citizenship, begins with T. H. Marshall's (1963) classic treatment. Marshall identified three sets of citizen rights—civil, political and social—as historically decisive and outlined a linear development from the first to the third of these.[21] Any account of the basis for truth, justice and the exploration of ways of living, must recognise the interdependence of these three rights. Some commentators, for instance Anthony Giddens,[22] have been critical of Marshall's 'evolutionary' view. However, recognising historical 'non-linearity' and 'contingency' is not a barrier to evolutionary analysis.[23]

Bryan Turner urges a movement 'from citizenship to human rights' and urges far greater sociological attention to human rights and needs. He argues that all three areas of citizen rights identified by Marshall constitute universal human rights that can be demonstrated as grounded in universal human needs. Turner explicitly couches his argument in terms of the conception of 'culture as the universal requirement of the "unfinished" human being'; in other words, the second meaning of culture set out at the start of this chapter. It is the 'unfinished', open, fluid capacity of human beings that gives rise to the expansion of human knowledge, including the fusion of cultural horizons. This capacity also fosters the expansion of human sympathies and the universalisation of human values.

Turner notes that the idea of universal rights has been largely unconsidered or else directly repudiated by much of contemporary mainstream sociology. However, he insists that the 'existing conceptualisation of citizenship requires the supplement of rights theory' (Turner, 1993: 489).

At the heart of Turner's argument, which has resemblances to the thinking of Barrington Moore,[24] is the assertion that 'sociology must and can ground the analysis of human rights in a concept of [universal] human frailty, especially the vulnerability of the body, in the idea of the precariousness of social institutions, and in a theory of moral sympathy'. Ironically, in making his case, Turner refers to specific features of human societies—uncertainty, risk, globalisation, environmental threats, etc.—that are identified by other theorists, such as Giddens or Beck,[25] who are far more sceptical about the utility of evolutionary and developmental arguments. Against a one-sided emphasis on the 'social construction' of selves, bodies,

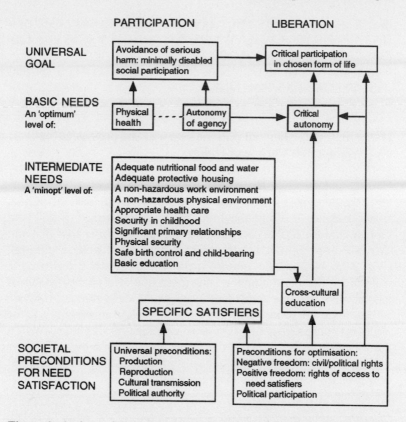

Figure 2 *Outline of Doyal and Gough's Framework*, from A Theory of Human Need, Macmillan Press Ltd. (1991: 170)

and social structures, Turner argues for the addition of biological and environmental dimensions to be more fully included in an 'embodied', ecologically and globally-conscious social theory. Globalisation in particular, especially in an increasingly technological world, also highlights the actual or the potential interdependence of everything.

Len Doyal and Ian Gough's *A Theory of Human Need* also elaborates the human needs-rights relation (see Figure 2). Their approach is consistent with what Turner wishes to achieve, the grounding of rights in needs. These authors take direct issue with subjectivist and relativist approaches. They, too, insist that all human beings have basic needs that cannot be reduced to cultural preferences. For example, personal health and autonomy are presented as essential preconditions for participation in wider social and political life and thus as universal needs. Their approach operationalises needs, providing a realistic critique of particular social and political conditions for rights.

It is now possible to turn more directly to the question of citizenship within the European Union.

Habermas and others on nationalism and the prospects for citizenship in the European Union

I would maintain that there is far greater scope than has been generally accepted for a sociological exploration of the basis of human rights and needs along the lines pursued by Turner, Doyal and Gough, and Held. The latter identifies seven categories of rights and sites of power grounded in this way: health, social welfare, cultural, civic, economic, pacific, and political. He argues that they are the basis for a 'democratic public law', a critique of class and gendered inequalities, and an immanent critique of democracy. However, rather than pursuing such potential ways of underpinning the Habermasian programme, I want to continue my argument with a more explicit exploration of the immediate historically substantive prospects for citizenship and human rights, including pressing questions of nationalism, within contemporary Europe.

'Identity' within the 'post-national' civil state

Habermas has emphasised the possible emergence of a 'post-national' identity formation in which new forms of citizenship and novel political forms begin to prevail.[26] he believes this may occur in association with globalisation of which European integration is an element. The underlying general model which underpins Habermas's formulation assumes a sequence of development as follows: pre political nations; empires composed of subject nations; nation-states of citizens; and more complex forms of multiple citizenship within 'post national' cosmopolitan civil states and an emerging international law.

Habermas argues that this developmental sequence arises explicitly from 'a spreading awareness that there is no longer any alternative to universalistic value orientations'. This tendency is heightened by a 'world-wide sensitivity to violations of human rights, to exploitation, hunger, misery and the demands of national liberation movements' (*A&S*, 1992: 240). In the light of our argument for the ever-present coexistence of two argumentative chains, it is interesting that the place for ethnic nationalism or other traditional bases of national-historical identity formation in this new context is questioned by Habermas, but not wholly repudiated, on the grounds that 'the universalist principles of democratic states need an anchoring in the political culture of each country' (*C&NI*: 11).

Habermas accepts that identity, including some pre-existing national identity, is essential to 'who we are' as well as 'what we wish to be'. This identity cannot be detached from the history of our particular nations. But, and especially for the Germans, he believes that a 'constitutional patriotism'—including pride in the rule of law and the overcoming of racism—can replace traditional forms of nationalism. In the case of constitutional patriotism, forms of nationalism and citizenship the universalisation of rights become increasingly central. In these circumstances, participation in postnational structures and the adoption of post national identities can also flourish.

It is vital to recognise—again in line with the existence of two argumentative chains—that such a universalism can have, as Habermas puts it, 'a thoroughly cosmopolitan (or multi-cultural) meaning' (*A&S*, 2: 401). In other words, the same universalistic content can be located within a variety of cultural forms of life. May there not be conflicts between such cosmopolitanism and the life of particular states? Habermas's answer is that ultimately 'the order of precedence between the political duties of the citizen and the moral duties of the human being' are simply different from those in an earlier age of absolute sovereignty of states. This formulation still ignores many practical political difficulties and appears utopian in part. However, I believe that, as Habermas suggests, it is in harmony with important global tendencies. This is so, in spite of the apparent counter-examples in Europe, Africa, and elsewhere, and the renewed visibility of racist movements, not least since reunification, within Germany itself.[27] Even writers such as Tom Nairn, who suggests that 'Nationalism is the mainstream, and it's time we recognised the fact', agree that it is a 'civic' nationalism, a community of patriotic equal citizens without ethnic basis, that provides the only sustainable nationalism within the new global culture. For Habermas, much as for Feyerabend or Turner, the key thing is that our sensitivity towards other human beings 'can generate a reflective distance from', and ambivalence towards, our own traditions. Though we do not 'pick and choose our own traditions', we can choose how we develop them.

Germany today

How viable is Habermas's viewpoint in the light of current problems of a reunified Germany? Aren't these viewpoints and projections simply impossibly utopian? David Cesarani and Mary Fulbrook have examined the general issues in their *Citizenship, Nationality and Migration in Europe*.[28] Like others, they note the major differences in form and substance between three bases of national identity: the principle of *jus sanguinis* (nationality of descent, of blood) which until today has been the basis of German citizenship; the British mixture of *jus sanguinis* and *jus soli* (nationality of birth); and the more 'active' and open, non-ethnic French conception, inclusive of all those who accept the principles of the French Revolution (and perhaps also French culture). To some extent, these variants seem likely to be replaced (in Germany at least and in all probability more widely within Europe) by more inclusive national conceptions of citizenship as well as by wider pan-European conceptions.

West German incorporation of East Germany occurred on the grounds of 'blood ties'. The EU has so far allowed member states to determine their own nationality laws which risks enshrining a more entrenched ethnic citizenship further bolstered by right-wing defensive action of the kind described by Cesarani and Fulbrook. However, the counter tendencies to such an outcome remain strong. In Germany, the exclusion from citizenship status of *Gastarbeiter* and other 'non-German' 'immigrants' (even if German-born) while refugee ethnic Germans are admitted, has been widely identified as anomalous and indefensible. Constitutional reform is being promoted by the Schroeder government. This will reform the citizen laws to grant citizenship to categories previously excluded or admitted only on condition that they met strict criteria of 'integration and affiliation'. 'Second generation' immigrants will receive citizenship if their parents meet residency criteria. Under certain conditions 'dual citizenship' will also be available, thus severing citizenship from cultural conformity. Although this is already provoking a further 'backlash' reaction, fuelled by the media,[29] it seems likely that under the Schroeder government these constitutional reforms will stick and become part of a wider trend to a more inclusive citizenship within Europe.

Perry Anderson[30] has recently reflected on the pattern of political support in the new post-unification Germany. He emphasises the extraordinary speed and magnitude of change, and the trauma of the West's virtual annexation of the East. Anderson also notes the presence of a right-wing backlash and the fact that two thirds of previous East Germans report themselves as not yet feeling 'citizens of their own country'. However, he celebrates the vibrancy and pluralism of electoral allegiance in the new Germany, including the basis for a Centre-Left/Red-Green initiatives on work and welfare. Against this background, Anderson regards the potential admission under the revised constitutional arrangements of more than four million new German citizens as 'an unambiguous act of emancipation' (p. 12).

The trend from culture-1 to culture-2 within Europe: is this the way forward?

It is important to recognise the 'intrinsic mutability of national traditions' and their actual mutability historically. As Fulbrook and Cesarani remark in the 'Conclusion' to their volume, there is no 'essential' citizenship. This being so, we can look forward to a severing of the mythical one-to-one link between citizenship and ethnicity, between citizenship and culture (ie culture-1) within nation-states. Weil, for example, argues that it would be helpful if the EU 'were to create a genuine European nationality with a common citizenship carrying common rights' that was also accessible to non-Europeans.[31]

Prospects and problems for a European state

How does Habermas propose that we respond to the opportunities and dilemmas presented by the prospect of a European state, especially with respect to possible ways in which individual identities, cultures, and previous sovereign states might inter-relate?

When asked what are the prospects for the European Union becoming the Federal Republic of Europe, Habermas gives guarded though ultimately optimistic answers. He is clear that any European super/supra state would require a basis of identity, but recognises that:

In a future Federal Republic of European States, the same legal principles would also have to be interpreted from the vantage point of different national traditions and histories. One's own national tradition [would], in each case, have to be appropriated

219

in such a manner that it is related to and relativized by the vantage points of the other national cultures. (*C&NI*: 11)

At the same time these national traditions would: 'be connected with the overlapping consensus of a common, supranationally shared political culture of the European Community'. And: a 'particularist anchoring of this sort' need in no way impair the universalist meaning of popular sovereignty and human rights' (*C&NI*: 11).

Habermas recognises that these would be major steps, not least because European institutions have not as yet been associated with sufficient civil, especially participatory, 'democratic' rights. Furthermore, any ready attainment of such Europe-wide democracy is made problematic given Europe's lack of linguistic unity. As a large multi-cultural state, the USA has succeeded to some degree but has done so with the advantage, till now at least, of the 'melting pot' provided by a dominant language.[32]

The development of the European Community has also highlighted a particular 'tension between democracy and capitalism' a 'vertical divide between the systemic integration of economy and administration at the supranational level' and a 'political integration that thus far works only at the level of the nation-state' (*C&NI*: 13). Thus, as Habermas expresses it, the 'technocratic shape' taken by the European Community—not least by the Commission with its bureaucracy and mode of legislation—may have reinforced suspicions that in this the prospect of democratic citizenship may have always been 'a mere illusion' since 'the exacting concept of the citizenship is at best suited for the less-complex relations within an ethnically and culturally homogeneous community' (*C&NI*: 13).

For Habermas, this also raises the issue of whether the orientation towards economic criteria of rationality in Brussels is part of a wider tendency also affecting nation-states whereby 'politics has gradually become a matter of the administration' in a way that undermines citizenship (*C&NI*: 15). As far as Habermas is concerned, the existence of 'citizenship reduced to the interests of client or customer becomes all the more probable, the more the economy and the state apparatus . . . develop a systemic autonomy and pushes citizens into the periphery of organizational membership' (*C&NI*: 17). When money and power become the dominant imperatives, it is difficult to maintain the model of a self-directed community of citizens.

Habermas is not sure whether patriotism can survive, either in existing nation-states or in the new Europe, if participatory self-rule

220

is marginalised. In his view, identification with a historical community is an insufficient basis if citizens are denied core freedoms. In spite of these considerations, Habermas displays guarded optimism about a new European order. He envisages:

> a networking of different communication flows . . . organized in such a way that they can be supposed to bind the public administration to more or less rational premises and in this way to enforce social and ecological discipline on the economic system without impinging on its intrinsic logic. This provides a model of a deliberative democracy that no longer hinges on the assumption of macro-subjects like the 'people' of 'the' community but on anonymously interlinked discourses or flows of communication. The model shifts the brunt of fulfilling normative expectations to the infrastructure of a political public sphere that is fuelled from spontaneous sources. Citizenship can today only be enacted in the paradoxical sense of compliance with the procedural rationality of a political will-formation, the more or less discursive character of which depends on the vitality of the informal circuit of public communication. (*C&NI*: 18)

Habermas maintains that today an 'inclusive public sphere' depends centrally on the 'stabilizing context' of a wider 'liberal and egalitarian political culture'. This pluralistic setting for communication can only be effective as a form of participatory democracy if decision-making bodies are open and sensitive, responsive to a wide range of contributions from their informal environments. Without this 'interplay between institutionalised processes of opinion and will formation and those informal networks of public communication', citizenship will become no more than 'an aggregation of pre-political individual interests and the passive enjoyment of rights bestowed upon the individual by the paternalistic authority of the state' (*C&NI*: 18).

Habermas accepts that within a dynamic multi-cultural single market there will be 'social tensions'. However, he argues that if those tensions are managed in a productive way this will encourage 'the new endogenous type of new social movements' (*C&NI*: 18) concerned with peace, women's issues and the environment. This would make public issues more relevant to the life-world. For many of the relevant problems solutions have to be European, a fact that will lead to the strengthening of European-wide communications networks. This, in turn, will improve contacts between regional parliamentary bodies and enhance the influence of the European Parliament.

Habermas envisages both a common political culture and particular national traditions in art, literature, and so on. A common 'European constitutional patriotism' would grow from diverse interpretations with shared 'universalist rights and constitutional principles' taking their place 'in the context of different national histories' (*C&NI*: 19). This would be a Europe that did not look backwards to the Middle Ages but forward towards the 21st century. Europe would operate 'under changed premises' aimed at 'reaching understanding with and learning from other cultures' (*C&NI*: 20).

In fact, European unification as it has been practised combined internationalism and a reduced emphasis on descent or on culture *within* Europe with an increasingly 'fortress Europe' mentality in regard to the rest of the world. This mentality is heightened by the scare tactics of the right and the timidity of the centre left, factors that led to the revoking of German asylum laws in 1993. These aspects of European unification disturb Habermas. It seems that European citizenship is likely to remain 'exclusionary', perhaps even become more exclusionary, *vis-à-vis* the external world.

In Anderson's view,[33] the experience of East Germany's annexation and integration demonstrates the rapacious dominance of market logic and throws doubts on the proposition that rapid enlargement of the EU would prove 'emancipatory', at least in the short term, for Eastern Europe. Anderson emphasises that the problems facing the new Europe often 'pose much more dramatic dilemmas than generally imagined' (p. 127). In view of these considerations, it may be that the goal of a more inclusionary, cosmopolitan emancipatory citizenship would be most effectively pursued not via an ever expanding European federal state but, rather, via improved international institutions. However, none of this undermines the validity of a viewpoint that sees European citizenship on Habermas's proposed new terms. This is compatible with a vision of Europe playing its part in the establishment of new international institutions moving beyond previous state forms. This could be the way forward.

Held and Linklater on new global political institutions

The work of David Held in *Democracy and the Global Order* and elsewhere and Andrew Linklater in *The Transformation of Political*

Community indicate how new institutions might emerge. They also underline the significance of global trends. Held emphasises three overlapping elements of globalisation: (i) the loss of regulatory effectiveness by individual states, (ii) the way local groups and movements are challenging the nation-state as a representative and accountable power and (iii) new patterns of global interconnectedness in political decision making among states and citizens. Held suggests that, as a consequence of the increasing two-way 'globalising' interlinkage of the local and the global, the 'meaning and place of democratic politics' have 'to be rethought in relation to a series of overlapping local, regional and global processes and structures' (1992: 33). A repair of the democratic deficit is likely to involve plural and multi-level conceptions of citizenship. As a result, citizenship might involve multiple levels of allegiances and rights, as follows: within localities; in regions within states; within national states; in (new) federal multi-states; arising in relation to other international (regional and global) institutions, including the rulings of international law; and within organisations and social and political movements that may operate at any or all these levels.

Held sees a strong constitutional basis as essential to any move towards more cosmopolitan forms of citizenship and democracy. The European Union in association with the European courts is seen as potentially playing an increasingly important part in providing legitimation for such institutions.

Linklater recognises the dangers of privileging one foundation but is 'unapologetically universalistic' and Habermasian in his vision of a 'triple transformation of political community'. He wants 'greater respect for cultural differences', a commitment to 'the reduction of material inequalities' and resistance to all 'pressures to contract the boundaries of community; (1998: 3). He wants to combine the universal and 'difference' within emerging forms of political community. He sees three ways of doing this: 'pluralist international society of states'; 'a more solidarist international society of states and peoples'; and a future European society which avoids either the dispersal of identities into a multiplicity of self-enclosed idioms and petty nationalisms or a monopolisation by central authority.

Linklater stresses that normative and sociological accounts of practical possibilities are both required. He uses the work of Michael Mann,[34] Giddens and others to establish the limits and possibilities of political development. 'Progress' is not guaranteed, but following Habermas he argues that 'accumulated moral resources' exist that can support a widening of the boundaries of the dialogic community; especially in Europe. Linklater argues that significant transfers of power are possible within Europe, both sub-nationally and trans-nationally.

Conclusions—towards an expanded 'post-national' conception of citizenship

Undoubtedly ours is a sceptical and often culturally pessimistic age. There exist many strong reasons why pessimism so often prevails. These include 'concrete exigencies', many knowledge-induced fail-ures of 'reflexive' control of 'risk' of the kind identified especially by Beck and Giddens, the re-emergence of intolerant forms of nation-alism and the rise of fundamentalist religious ideologies. However, let us acknowledge these concrete reasons, and the possibility of overcoming them, rather than retreating to the forms of epistemo-logical or ontological impossibilism suggested by post-structuralist and postmodernist thinkers.

Post-structuralist and post-modernist vocabulary and accounts of society express powerfully some of the difficulties in respect of indi-vidual identity and autonomy, social solidarity, and so on, that arise from a linguistically fluid, libidinally expressive, often 'disembed-ded', consumption dominated, media dominated, 'runaway', con-temporary world. Furthermore, major 'crises' have occurred in 'received epistemology' and scientific Marxism. However, on the positive side, these intellectual crises provide a liberation from dogma and the potential for a new openness to dialogic resolution of issues of fact and value.

In his *Representative Government*, John Stuart Mill suggested that cultural homogeneity is a requirement for stable democratic govern-ment.[35] However, I have suggested that a more cosmopolitan civic nationalism that recognises diversity is potentially attainable. This vision is more consistent with the Mill of *On Liberty*. As has been seen, a number of theorists are prepared to argue that a civil nation-alism recognising cultural diversity provides, morally, the best way forward. Compared with the undoubted risks of a new exclusionary irredentism, Habermas, Held and Linklater outline the possibilities of international institutions and new 'post national' state forms that 'go beyond' culturally homogenised unified nation states. They envisage a 'civic nationalism' that recognises diversity and post-national multinationalist states and/or international institutions providing for complex multi-level and multi-national citizen identities.

In 1995, in an interesting and revealing debate, Habermas sharply opposed Dieter Grimm (1995)[36] on the issue of whether cultural homogenisation is a requirement for further political integration and viable European constitutional statehood. Pluralism (in terms of institutions and levels of state activity) and multiculturalism (including multi-citizenship) are not just compatible with but implied by a discourse ethics.

Like Grimm, Habermas recognises the problems of the 'democratic deficit' within existing European institutions and obviously has no wish to accelerate tendencies towards the 'automisation of bureaucratized politics' (1997: 260). However, for Habermas, unlike Grimm, cultural homogenisation is not seen as a prerequisite for this: the democratic deficit must be tackled directly and this can be done only if Europe moves forward constitutionally. Habermas notes that Grimm wishes to 'distance' himself from the extremes of the Schmittian *völkischen* definitions of homogeneous community. Habermas counters such definitions with the declaration that 'democratic citizenship establishes an abstract, legally mediated solidarity among strangers': 'What unifies a nation of citizens as opposed to a *Volksnation* is not some primordial substrate but rather an intersubjectively shared context of possible understanding' (p. 262). 'There can be no European federal state worthy of the name of a democratic Europe unless a Europe-wide, integrated public sphere develops', 'a civil society with interest associations; non-governmental organizations; citizens' movements', and so on together with 'a party system appropriate to a European arena', 'a public communication that transcends . . . the until now limited national public spheres' (p. 263).

Habermas does not take the ethical and political understandings of citizens in a democratic community as a 'historical-cultural *a priori* that makes democratic will-formation possible' (p. 264) but sees it as the outcome of communication between those citizens. Appropriate European institutions would help this communication occur and also provide the 'shared historical experience' of overcoming nationalism. European identity would combine this shared experience with continuing national diversity.

The Maastricht Treaty has brought into being for the first time an explicitly trans-European citizenship (see O'Leary, 1996),[37] specifically including rights of European-wide residence, the right to vote in municipal and European elections in the place of residence, the right to diplomatic protection in third countries, the right to petition the European parliament, and the right to utilise the European Ombudsman. These were added to the rights already embedded in earlier frameworks such as the Community Charter of the Fundamental Social Rights of Workers, rights that include protection from discrimination on grounds of nationality or gender, and rights to economic free movement.

It must, of course, be acknowledged that this move to a European citizenship remains very much the outcome of a compromise between states which remain sovereign, but these steps do have the explicit objective of fostering European identity. They still fail to provide automatic citizen rights to nine million residents who are not European nationals, with the entitlement to citizenship remaining determined by the definitions of citizenship of individual member states. As O'Leary among others has suggested this bears relatively little relation to a European social reality in which immigration has been central.[38] Clearly there are still obvious rights deficits, including restricted rights to social welfare benefits, framed at present to inhibit economic migration, electoral rights that are not fully portable, courts of justice with limited jurisdiction and rights with less than binding force within individual states and dependent still on international conventions, and limitations on the rights of third country nationals. Thus there remains obvious scope for an expansion of rights in all these areas.

For all such shortcomings, however, the potential is there for Europe to be the first political community transformed by peace rather than war. As Habermas argues, 'only regionally comprehensive regimes like the European Union can still affect the global system' and be capable of maintaining the welfare state and combating the further segmentations and deprivations of the underclass and 'the moral erosions of community' that will continue if nothing is done. Both Habermas and Held point to the possibility of building outwards from Europe to achieve a greater regulation of the international economy: 'a post Bretton Woods' resolution and a defence of the welfare/social state.

Arguably, therefore, Europe remains the best location and more general stimulus for future development of 'post state' forms, even if there are immediate limitations and changes have to continue at a relatively slow pace.[39] Europe's internal diversity is not a disadvantage in this context. As Anthony Giddens (1994: 81)[40] asserts, far from a process of simple homogenisation, globalisation often leads 'to an insistence on diversity, a search to recover lost local traditions, and an emphasis on local cultural identity', one aspect of which has been a renewal of local nationalisms and ethnicities. 'The famously Janus-faced character of nationalism' Giddens (1994: 131–2) continues, 'comes from the fact that it straddles the divide between civil association and the conception of the state as a community with its own "personality". It isn't surprising, therefore, that in a post traditional age nationalism [sometimes] stands close to aggressive fundamentalisms, embraced by neo-fascist groups as well as by other sorts of movements or collectivities'.

Giddens emphasises the positive 'pluralism' represented by nationalism as well as its negative aspects. He notes that fundamentalism is usually brought in the long run to submit to dialogic justifications, despite initial resistance. So much does Giddens now embrace this view that we find him prepared to argue that we can 'speak of the emergence of universal values'—not least because of the real world 'collective threats which humanity has created for itself' (Giddens, 1994: 20). As John Hall[41] suggests, such universal values above all consist of a shared framework 'within which differences can exist: if this option is under attack inside the West but can be shown both 'morally superior and sociologically possible, a responsibility rests on us to lend it our support'. We must not lose confidence.

Notes

* This chapter draws on papers presented at the Citizenship and Cultural Frontiers Conference, at Staffordshire University, April 1994 and the Second European Sociology Conference: 'European Societies: Fusion or Fission', Budapest, August/September, 1995.

1 B. Turner (1993), 'Outline of a theory of human rights', *Sociology*, 27 (3), 489–512.

2 Turner, op. cit.; L. Doyal and I. Gough (1991), *A Theory of Human Need*, London: Macmillan; D. Held (1995), *Democracy and the Global Order*, Cambridge: Polity Press; Held (1992), 'Democracy: From city-states to a cosmopolitan order?' *Political Studies*, Special Issue, 40, 10–39; and A. Linklater (1998), *The Transformation of Political Community*, Cambridge: Polity Press.

3 Undoubtedly Feyerabend's self-declared 'Dadaism' and his many polemical flights misled many critics into misreading his intentions and implications of his thinking. In fact, Feyerabend's writings were sometimes deliberately intended to mislead, by showing how easy it was for the supporters of methodical forms of rationalism to be misled by their own intolerant 'rationalistic' readings of others who did not share their particular versions of 'rationalism'. Beneath such appearances and such traps, however, Feyerabend's ideas always involve a 'serious playfulness', and the aim of enhancing human fulfilment and understanding and not

at all a one-sided celebration of relativism and 'irrationalism'. His (in)famous statement in *Against Method* 'anything goes' is in fact a reply to Lakatos: if you insist on a single rule of method, then, 'anything goes'.

4 P. Feyerabend (1978), *Science in Free Society*, London: New Left Books (SFS).

5 As against the far more principled, but stilted, terms of Karl Popper's argument for an 'open society', I have discussed in detail elsewhere in ways relevant to the argument of the present paper the terms of Feyerabend's repudiation of Popper's philosophy—see D. Jary (1991), 'Beyond objectivity and relativism: Feyerabend's "two argumentative chains" and sociology', *Poznan Studies in the Philosophy of the Social Sciences and Humanities*, 22, 39–58.

6 For the particular purposes of this paper I have reversed the order in which these appear in Feyerabend's own account.

7 P. Feyerabend (1981), *Rationalism, Realism and Scientific Method*, Cambridge: Cambridge University Press (*RRSM*).

8 See A. MacIntyre (1988), *Whose Justice, Which Morality?* Paris: University of Notre Dame Press.

9 T. Kuhn (1970), *The Structure of Scientific Revolutions*, University of Chicago Press.

10 The classic, much analysed 'sociological' statement in these terms is, of course, Peter Winch (1958), *The Idea of a Social Science*, London: Routledge.

11 T. Kuhn (1977), *The Essential Tension*, University of Chicago Press.

12 While Habermas, like Feyerabend, gives up the search for final foundations, assumptions about the presuppositions of language remain crucial. Based on the universal sociality of language he expressly 'steers a path between the formal (and individualistic) and the communitarian traditions in ethical thought'. As Linklater (1998) makes clear, while a 'transcendental' basis is rejected a 'procedural' focus remains decisive. Compared with the transcendentalism and individualism of classical Kantian or liberal contract approaches it is the social interactional context that is emphasised. For Linklater, in this Habermas moves beyond Kant or Marx while retaining some of the advantageous features of their approach. In *Democracy and the Global Order* (166–7) Held distances his own position from Habermas's, saying that it is misleading to think of the latter's methodological assumptions as ultimately grounded in all discourse since there can be no such thing as the final and correct understanding. It is not clear that this extra caution adds up to a substantial difference of approach. In any event, Held along with Habermas, Linklater and Doyal and Gough all share in the importance of the establishment of an understanding of the general conditions for democratic dialogue and make use of this as a vantage point.

13 J. Habermas (1957), *Legitimation Crisis*, London: Heinemann (*LC*).

14 For the moment, the term 'moral' is used here to demarcate a category of truth or validity claim apart from the factual assertorial. It should be noted however, that Habermas also makes careful distinctions between the 'moral', 'ethical' and 'political'—see Habermas (1989), *Moral Consciousness and Communicative Action* and Habermas (1996), *Between Fact and Norm*. In particular, 'morality' (including 'justice') is distinguished by Habermas from individual 'ethics'. These are usefully discussed in W. Outhwaite (1996), *A Habermas Reader*, Cambridge: Polity Press. An awareness of these distinctions will be important later in framing the precise terms in which Habermas grounds his case for greater European integration.

15 I would argue that in some at least of their writing and political stances these post-structuralist and post-modernist thinkers can be seen as comparable with a

'Millian' view. However, it is beyond the scope of this chapter to argue this further.

16 It is utterly central to Habermas's overall argument that individuality and self identity depends crucially on shared language capacities, and mutual respect.

17 J. Habermas (1992), *Autonomy and Solidarity*, London: Verso (*A&S*).

18 Significantly, his position, and especially Feyerabend's and the Millian position generally is, I would argue, also compatible with a varied basis for, for example, feminist epistemologies and feminist conceptions of citizenship. As a Habermasian, Linklater, for example, accepts the dangers of privileging one foundation but also notes the limits of post-modernism—Rorty, Foucault, Derrida, Lyotard, and so on—its contradictory relativism and 'implicit universalism' grounded in human sympathies. He accepts the importance—especially following Gilligan's feminist critique of Kohlberg (C. Gilligan (1993), *In a Different Voice*, Cambridge: Polity Press)—of recognising particularistic 'care' as well as universalistic 'justice', but he also notes that Habermas sees the two as related (Linklater, 1998: 94). In this manner, taking on board aspects of post modernism, radical feminism and the contemporary politics of difference, Linklater underlines how universalism and increased attention to difference are both possible, culminating in inclusive, cosmopolitan definitions of citizenship. Crucially, in relation to suggestions made that Habermas's or Linklater's kind of language games and 'ideal' citizen practices are male games inimicable to feminist practices (eg Carol Pateman (1991), *The Disorder of Women: Democracy, Feminism and Political Theory*, Cambridge: Polity Press). Such critiques are valuable in that they emphasise the importance of achieving substantive as well as formal realisations of citizen rights. However, an emphasis on essential sexual differences and entirely separate and incommensurable epistemologies neglects the openness to discourse provided in Millian terms, especially by the Feyerabendian conception of 'Two Chains', in the way I have interpreted this. This is endorsed by Anne Phillips (1993), *Democracy and Difference*, Cambridge: Polity Press, a critic of Pateman, who argues that the idea of citizenship ought to include, and in this sense, transcend differences. As sometimes proposed, this may involve special mechanisms of representation and involvement for disadvantaged groups, including women. On the other hand, we should not neglect the huge general influence already achieved by women's movements alongside other 'new social movements' of recent times, for example on global and environmental and peace issues, as well as issues of sexuality and gender. As argued by Habermas and also Anthony Giddens (*The Transformations of Intimacy*, Cambridge: Polity Press, 1994, and elsewhere), it is the universal implications of such movements that are perhaps most striking. An emphasis on common humanity—on 'humanity as the touchstone of citizenship' as Kimberley Hutchings ('Feminist theory and citizenship', Centre for the Study of Democracy, Bulletin, 1988, 6 (1)) has put it, need not undermine the challenge to exclusionary practices or be predicated on the abolition of difference.

19 As well as Habermas's own writing, I have drawn here on the sophisticated summary of Habermas's thinking provided by Peter Dews in his introduction to Habermas's *A&S*, also taking note of the terms of Linklater's deployment of Habermas's writing in his more specific focus on the evolution of political community.

20 The crucial point to note in fending off criticisms is that, as we shall see, Habermas is far from denying 'contingency' and the necessity for detailed soci-

ological analysis of both the generality and particularity of the passage of states to modernity. S. Sanderson (1995), *Social Transformation: a General Theory of Historical Development*, Oxford: Blackwell, provides a highly useful account of the general issues surrounding evolutionary thinking on the context of general history.

21 These consist of (i) civil rights, rights to freedom of expression and access to information, and the right to freedom of association and organization and equality before the law, including property rights; (ii) political rights, the right to vote and to seek political office in elections; (iii) social rights, rights to welfare and social security, and perhaps full employment, but stopping short of the right (especially collective labour rights) to share in the management of economic organisations, to break the prerogative of managers to manage and of capitalists to own and direct the use of their capital.

22 A. Giddens (1985), *The Nation-state and Violence*, Cambridge: Polity Press. For a critique of Giddens's objections to evolutionism see D. Jary and J. Jary, 'The transformations of Anthony Giddens', *Theory, Culture and Society*, 12 (2), 141–160.

23 As long as no assumption is made that 'evolutionary learning processes' are inevitably institutionalised and all associations with positivist-empiricism are expunged. As Habermas remarks in 'Citizenship and national identity—some reflections on the future of Europe' (paper presented to an invited European Union conference 'What Identity for Europe?' Brussels, May 1991): '[the] image of linear progress arises from a description that remains neutral towards increases or losses in autonomy; it says nothing about the actual use made of active citizenship by means of which the individual can himself bring influence to bear on democratic changes of his own status'. Thus significantly,

> Liberal or negative and social or positive rights can also be conferred by a paternalistic authority. In principle, . . . the rule of law and the welfare state can exist without the concomitant existence of democracy. Liberal and social rights remain ambiguous in Western countries where all three categories of rights are institutionalized. It is true that both individual freedom and social security can be considered as the legal basis for the social independence necessary for an effective exercise of political rights in the first place. Yet, this link is contingent. For rights of individual freedom and social security can just as well facilitate a privatised retreat from citizenship and a particular 'clientelization' of the citizen's role.

24 B. Moore (1971), *Reflections on the Causes of Human Misery*, London: Allen Lane.

25 Especially see U. Beck (1992), *Risk Society. Towards a New Modernity*, London: Sage; A. Giddens (1990), *The Consequences of Modernity*, Cambridge: Polity Press.

26 Especially see Habermas's 1991 paper, 'Citizenship and national identity', op. cit.; and also the interview with Jürgen Habermas, 'There are alternatives', *New Left Review*, 1998, No. 231.

27 As discussed in Held (1992), op. cit., R. Falk (1991), *Positive Prescriptions for the Near Future*, NJ: Princeton University Center for International Studies, Occasional Paper, No. 20, and also interestingly Anthony Giddens. Both have argued for an 'embedded' or 'utopian realism', a systematic extrapolation from existing tendencies, as a vital part of thinking about alternative futures.

28 D. Cesarani and M. Fulbrook (eds) (1996), *Citizenship, Nationality and Migration*

© The Editorial Board of The Sociological Review 1999

in Europe, London: Routledge. Especially see the 'Introduction' and 'Conclusion' to their edited volume and the individual chapters by Fulbrook, by Patrick Well and by Karen Schowalder. See also C. Bryant (1997), 'Citizenship, national identity and the accommodation of difference: reflections on German, French, Dutch and British cases', *New Community*, 23 (2), 157–172.

29 The difficulties involved are indicated by the fact that, in association with media campaigns, one poll shows more than 50 per cent of Germans think that Germany has too many 'foreigners' and only 7 per cent are at ease 'with more immigration'.

30 P. Anderson (1999), 'The German Question', *London Review of Books*, 7 Jan, 10–16. See also chapters by Anderson in P. Gowan and P. Anderson (eds), (1997), *The Question of Europe*, London: Verso.

31 P. Well (1996), 'Nationalities and citizenships: the lessons of the French experience for Germany and Europe', in M. Fulbrook and Cesarani, *Citizenship, Nationality and Migration in Europe*, London: Routledge.

32 Habermas, however, points to the growing significance of English as a universal second language.

33 P. Anderson (1988), 'The German Question', op. cit.

34 M. Mann (1994), 'The Sources of Social Power', vol. 2, *The Rise of Social Classes and Nation-States, 1760–1914*, Cambridge: Cambridge University Press.

35 See also J. Hall (1996), 'How homogenous need we be? Reflections on nationalism and liberty', *Sociology*, 30, 163–171.

36 Grimm's article 'Does Europe need a constitution?' and Habermas's 'Reply to Grimm' are contained in P. Anderson in P. Gowan and P. Anderson (eds), (1997), *The Question of Europe*, London: Verso.

37 S. O'Leary (1996), *The Evolving Concept of Community Citizenship, Kluwer Law International, and European Union Citizenship: the Options for Reform*, London: IPPR.

38 In Germany especially between 1987 and 1994, 7 million foreigners residing in Germany were joined by 1.6 million more, plus another 2 million or so ethnic Germans from Eastern Europe.

39 Following Anderson, the reasons for regarding Europe thus are two fold. First, Europe's contemporary form arose from the French-initiated decision to control Germany by 'cooptation' in a context in which the goal of national self-sufficient domination was thus removed. Second, within Europe 'devolved' accommodations have been effectively achieved, for example in post-Franco Spain (and hopefully soon in Ireland and in Scotland) in recognition of the advantages of both a larger and local context of operation in a globalising world. Post-national arrangements for 'dual citizenship' are likely to also flourish further in this context. Fears of the threat of a 'fifth column' from this source are exaggerated given that no obvious enemy of Europe now exists. Whether a continued European openness to immigration is a significant doubt about the new Europe and a lack of international pressure in this area may indicate likely limits on multinationalism in the medium term. Nevertheless more complex multi-national/multi-citizen identities remain the likely way forward in the longer-term with no epistemological, or ontological barriers to this. Anderson's analysis is especially pertinent given their grounding in his monumental 'evolutionary' historical studies of East-West and North-South variations in European social and political institutions.

40 A. Giddens (1994), *Beyond Left and Right: The Future of Radical Politics*, Cambridge: Polity Press.

41 J. Hall (1996), op. cit.

Processes

Making Europe—processes of Europe-formation since 1945

Dennis Smith

Abstract

Dennis Smith argues that the development of the European polity that has become the European Union has been shaped by social processes similar in many respects to those analysed by Norbert Elias in *The Court Society* and *The Civilizing Process*. However, these processes have occurred at the supra-state level whereas Elias described them as they occurred at the level of the developing national state, especially during the sixteenth and seventeenth centuries. During the 1940s and 1950s the United States played a key role in pacifying the European nations and imposing a framework of rules for the conduct of their economic and diplomatic affairs. States in western Europe were increasingly locked into tight bonds of interdependence. This movement towards integration was complemented by the disembedding of regions and large businesses from their close ties to the national state; they became 'Europeanised'. Brussels became Europe's Versailles, a place where the courtier's skills were employed by the lobbyist. It is suggested that just as France represented, in Elias's eyes, a vanguard society within Europe in respect of the civilising process at the level of the national society, the European Union may play such a role globally in respect of developments at the supra-state level.

Europe and America

The European Union is a bold political experiment. It is quite surprising that 'Europe' has survived for nearly half a century since its early manifestation as the European Coal and Steel Community, created in 1951. A similar expression of surprise could have been made about the continuing survival of the American Republic into the early decades of the nineteenth century. In fact, half a century after its foundation in 1776, the American Republic was running into problems that are rather similar to those troubling the European Union now: how to make a single currency work, how to increase the number of states within the Union without too much political disruption, how to manage internal conflicts between northern and southern interests, how to reconcile the decentralisers with the federalists, how to overcome distrust between the executive and the legislature, and so on.

Obviously, the two cases are different in important respects. For example, the Republic joined together colonies revolting against a common master, not national states that had recently been engaged in full-scale war against each other. Furthermore, the dominance of English as the language of public business in early nineteenth-century America gave that polity a degree of cultural cohesion among its élites not yet achieved in Europe.

However, the similarities are striking. The American experiment, like the later European experiment, was justified in terms of Enlightenment ideals. Both enterprises were undertaken by leaders who claimed they were creating a rational framework for human action so that citizens could pursue prosperity in conditions of relative freedom and security.

The two cases, America and Europe, are linked by more than historical similarities. Their histories are intertwined. In the late eighteenth century, the American Republic was brought into being in the course of a unilateral declaration of independence from a European sovereign. That is a well-known and celebrated fact. A less well-known and less celebrated fact is that in the mid-twentieth century, American power played a crucial role in driving forward the movement towards European unity. However, that is to anticipate the argument.

Tocqueville's *Democracy in America* (Tocqueville, 1968) has helped the Americans to understand themselves.[1] Tocqueville investigated American society approximately half a century after the Republic's inauguration. Roughly the same amount of time has passed since the end of World War II and the beginnings of the process of institution-building that led to the European Union. Half a century, give or take a few years, is a reasonable time after which to review the early progress of any Enlightenment experiment in political union. In other words, it is a good time to ask about the social processes that are shaping it and to identify the key tensions and dynamics at work within its social networks.

Now Europe needs to be subjected to an analysis of similar depth. It is true that the European Union has spawned a large literature, especially in the last decade. There is a mountain of polemic as well.[2] There are also careful scholarly studies of institution-building, political processes, social trends as well as essays in futurology.[3] However, what we do not yet have is a work that does for Europe at the turn of the millennium what Tocqueville did for early nineteenth-century America.[4]

Tocqueville showed links between the mentality and social habits of its population, its sense of self-identity, its patterns of community life and the dynamics of its class and political relations. This analysis related these characteristics of the society to the way its laws and customs were monitored and enforced, the development of relations between that society and its neighbours, and the location of these structures and processes within the flow of history.

Europe does not yet have its Tocqueville. Whoever eventually fills this role will benefit from studying the work of Norbert Elias. In some respects Elias and Tocqueville could not be more different. Tocqueville, born in 1805, was a French aristocrat whereas Elias, born in 1897, was a German bourgeois of Jewish origins. However, their central problem was shared. They were both preoccupied with the question of how a large, dynamic and complex society could survive the removal of its aristocratic ruling class without collapsing into violent anarchy or turning into a centralised dictatorship.[5] For Tocqueville as a French politician this was a vital issue in the 1830s and 1840s. For Elias as a potential victim of Nazism it was a vital issue in the 1930s and 1940s.

Both Tocqueville and Elias were interested in the roots of human discontent and social disorder. Like Tocqueville, Elias saw powerful connections between our sense of identity and broader socio-historical processes. Elias had a multi-layered identity—European, German and Jewish—and spent his whole life trying to make intellectual sense of the tensions between the different layers.[6] His technique was to use historical evidence to track down the social forces and networks that generate tensions within the personality and between social groups.

Elias's main achievement was to produce four books that examine these issues from different angles.[7] Two of these books are *The Court Society* (Elias, 1983), which looks at the French court at Versailles between the sixteenth and eighteenth centuries, and *The Civilizing Process* (Elias, 1994a) which is an extended study of the European case covering the thousand years from the eighth century to the eighteenth. The other two works are *The Germans* (Elias, 1996), and *The Society of Individuals* (Elias, 1991a). Norbert Elias's work can help us towards the kind of analysis we need. His approach to long-term social processes can increase our understanding of how Europe has taken shape, socially and politically, over the past half-century.[8]

Elias on the civilising process

Elias believes that increased economic and political integration within Europe is part of a long-term civilising process whose earlier phases can be traced as far back as the early Middle Ages. In his view this process is not inevitable; nor can its timing be predicted. It may slow down or be reversed. In fact, civilising and decivilising tendencies may coincide.

The civilising process is rooted in the incessant competition that goes on within and between human groups for survival. People compete for resources and opportunities, and struggle to get the upper hand in exchange relationships. In the early stages of the civilising process the key survival units are families or tribes, later the key units are states.[9] Four aspects of the civilising process are especially relevant.

Firstly, competition between survival units leads to monopoly. The new monopoly power imposes strict rules of behaviour upon its former competitors. It makes them co-operate with each other or, at least, compete in a more peaceful and orderly manner. For example, military competition between powerful medieval families eventually led to the triumph of a small number of royal houses (in France, England and so on) that were able to establish stable power monopolies, in other words, states with powers to tax and make enforceable laws. The states took control over the means of violence and disarmed the aristocracy, the old medieval warrior-dynasties.

Secondly, people who have been pacified by a dominant power centre learn to exercise self-control, to become increasingly self-aware, to pursue their goals carefully and rationally. In other words, they impose constraints upon their inner drives, develop strong ego and superego controls. This is what happened to the warlike medieval lords when they were forced to become royal courtiers. They became 'civilised' people, able to hide their feelings, make long-term calculations, and obey detailed rules of conduct that imposed delicacy and discretion. A steadily increasing range of types of behaviour was brought under surveillance and control. Everybody monitored themselves and each other very closely. Later in the civilising process, this civilised *habitus* or psychological make-up[10] spread to the bourgeoisie and, later still, to the whole population within modern societies.

A third aspect of the civilising process is that the self-images people have are shaped by the networks of social relationships in which they are embedded. These might include, for example, the family, the tribe, the social class or the national state. These networks provide their members with a sense of belonging to a group or groups who can refer to themselves collectively as 'we'. Individuals within them have a shared 'we-identity'. A person's sense of being a separate and distinct individual, an 'I', is always linked to a sense of being part of a 'we'.[11] In the course of the civilising process, the figurations to which people belong change in fundamental ways and so do the self-identities which people acquire.

Finally, courtiers, professional establishments, business élites and other social groups closely linked to stable power monopolies are able to exclude 'outsiders' and impose an inferior 'we-image' upon them. However, the boundaries between established groups and outsiders are constantly shifting in the course of the civilising process. Elias argues there is a long-term tendency within the civilising process for outsiders to become more like established groups, to adopt their habits, merge into their social circles, and become more equal with them.

All these tendencies are liable to go into reverse if decivilising processes occur. For example, power monopolies break up, behaviour becomes less controlled and more openly aggressive, 'we-identities' such as nationalism may become very pronounced and outsider groups (such as the Jews) are violently excluded.[12] However, argues Elias, insofar as the civilising process prevails, it has a long-term tendency to democratise societies.[13]

America in post-war Europe

These ideas may be found in *The Court Society* and *The Civilizing Process* which are mainly about the sociogenesis of the state and the civilised habitus. Elias did not write directly about the sociogenesis of the European movement. However, *The Court Society* provides us with some important clues to understanding that process.

In *The Court Society*, Elias argues that the structure and organisation of key political institutions are shaped by the struggles that bring them into existence. The victors use these institutions to try and stabilise their supremacy and keep the upper hand. As Elias puts it, 'Every form of rule is the precipitate of a social conflict—it consolidates the distribution of power corresponding to its outcome' (Elias, 1983: 146). He develops this argument in the case of France in the seventeenth and eighteenth centuries.

France had been internally divided during the long wars of religion during the sixteenth century. This was at a time when the family or dynasty was still regarded by many powerful people as the most important survival unit. You fought for your own family against other families. Finally, however, the French crown imposed its authority upon the competing noble families. It disarmed them and made the leading nobles come to the royal court where the king could keep a close eye on them. In other words, the king won and he imposed his rules on the losers. Rough feudal warriors became elegant courtiers.

This process did not happen overnight. Half a century after Henry IV of France promulgated the Edict of Nantes (1598)[14] at the end of the French religious wars, French nobles were still ready to engage in armed revolt against the crown during the Fronde rebellion. However, when Henry entered Paris as king of France in 1594 the social climate was strongly for peace and order:

> The rural population of France was weary of ceaseless war. Starvation and plague were threatening, and in a devastated Brittany great packs of wolves were on the prowl . . . It was to the idealized figure of a patriarchal king, the upholder of justice, the champion of order, that . . . [the peasantry] now instinctively turned . . . It was an extraordinary spontaneous movement, compounded of hatred of anarchy and social oppression, and a mass rallying of the people of France to their anointed king . . . It was as if the country were purging itself of the religious hatreds of half a century. 'We all promise and swear before God to love and cherish each other'. There would be 'no more war among them, nor reproach for diversity of religion, and each would be free to live as he desired'. (Elliott, 1968: 356)

Lurking behind this rather idealised and romantic picture of human tolerance are indications of a climate of receptivity to strong regulation from above, an almost Hobbesian willingness to be ruled. The locus of this rule shifted 'upwards' during the century following the end of the French religious wars.

By the mid-seventeenth century the most prominent survival units in Europe were no longer families but states. It is true that during the eighteenth century the resources of the state were often mobilised to serve the ambitions of royal dynasties in France, Austria, Russia and elsewhere. However, as royal heads rolled throughout Europe between the French and Russian revolutions, governments identified themselves increasingly with the population at large. By the early twentieth century, the violent struggles that shaped European politics were not between dynasties but between national armies.

A central argument of this paper is that the balance of power yet again shifted decisively 'upwards' during the mid-twentieth century. Two things happened. First, in the course of two world wars, the competition between states in Europe merged into an inter-state competition at the global level. Second, by 1945 a clear winner in this global competition had emerged in the form of the United States. America's leading position was eventually eroded to some degree but during the late 1940s and 1950s it was virtually unchallenged.

As a victorious 'super-state' the US government behaved like a monarch that had subdued an unruly nobility. The American government set about imposing rules and protocols that would encourage peaceful cooperation and impose limits on disruptive forms of competition and conflict. One example of this is the General Agreement on Tariff and Trade (1947), a watered-down version of the American plan for an international trade organisation that would coordinate different nations' counter-cyclical policies. Another example is the United Nations, founded in 1945 and symbolically sited in New York.

In 1946 the US Government committed itself to defending the principles of the UN Charter 'in the interest of world peace'. In practice, this entailed a strategy of 'containing' the Soviet Union.[15] American anxieties about Europe focused on its economic and military weakness in the face of potential Soviet aggression or the advance of left-wing organisations in Western Europe, for example in Italy and France. From the American point of view, the defence situation was improved by the establishment of North Atlantic Treaty Organization in 1949 based in Brussels.[16] In the following year an integrated force for the defence of Western Europe was established under a Supreme Headquarters Allied Powers Europe (SHAPE). Its first chief was the man who had commanded the Allied forces during the final victory over Germany a few years earlier: General Eisenhower.

The economic condition of Europe in the late 1940s was dire. Loss of agricultural stock, disruption of trade, declining population and rising prices were all widespread. Capital had been eaten up by the war and many European governments were heavily in debt and short of assets.[17] The American response was set out in a speech at Harvard University in 1947 by Secretary of State George C. Marshall. Discussing 'the rehabilitation of the economic structure of Europe', Marshall declared that 'Europe's requirements for the next three or four years . . . —principally from America—are so much greater than her present ability to pay that she must have substantial additional help or face economic, social and political deterioration of a very grave character'.[18]

Within a month of this speech the French and British governments, with strong American behind-the-scenes encouragement, invited over twenty European countries to a conference in Paris. The object was to draw up a plan that would set out what help the Europeans wanted from the Americans. Although the American government was not officially represented at the Paris conference, American officials made it quite clear unofficially that: 'Participating countries should take effective steps to create internal monetary and financial stability . . . Steps should be taken to diminish trade barriers, with the eventual goal of complete uniformity with the International Trade Organization . . . [and] . . . A permanent organization should be created'.[19]

Marshall Aid under the Economic Recovery Plan (ERP) was channelled through the Organisation for European Economic Cooperation (OEEC), a body that represented the sixteen European nations benefiting from Marshall Aid.[20] The money was not given without strings attached. The Americans insisted that OEEC should produce a pan-European plan aimed at encouraging free trade and reducing protectionism.[21] Furthermore, under the rules of the programme the Americans had to give their agreement before funds could be spent on specific projects. For example, approval was not given for contracts with firms recognising communist trade unions.[22]

The Americans offered Marshall Aid to ex-enemies and friends alike. In this respect, the Marshall Aid programme has some resemblance to the strategy adopted by Henry IV of France who, at the end of the French religious wars, said that he wanted to put a chicken in the pot of every French household. This offer applied to Protestants and Catholics alike.[23] The ERP injected nearly $12.5 billion into Europe between 1948 and 1952. During the decade after 1945 the total amount of American support for Europe added up to nearly $25 billion. The UK received $6.9 billion, France $5.5 billion, the Federal Republic of Germany $3.9 billion and Italy $2.9 billion.[24] This freed up domestic funds for capital formation.

The point is that although there were vocal enthusiasts for pan-European institutions in most European nations and had been for decades,[25] it was the Americans who, in the late 1940s, pushed the West European states into cooperating with each other. In 1947 George Kennan argued that the Europeans had no shared sense of direction and that the US State Department would have to 'decide unilaterally' what was in Europe's best interests.[26] For a few years in the late 1940s this is what they tried to do although with slightly more subtlety than Kennan's words imply.

There was a massive propaganda campaign in support of Marshall Aid, especially in countries such as Italy thought to be in danger of 'going communist'. As David Ellwood has shown, the Marshall Plan was presented to Italians (and other Europeans) as the gateway to American standards of material life. During the 1948 general election in Italy the State Department made it clear 'that Communist voters would be banned from emigration to the US, and Marshall himself declared that should the Left win, the country would be excluded from the benefits of the ERP' (Ellwood, 1998: 34).

Marshall Aid was administered on the American side by the Economic Cooperation Agency (ECA). Its chief administrator, Paul Hoffman, was a moderate Republican who had previously worked in the automobile business. In 1953 he described his approach to dealing with his European counterparts:

> I have learned from experience that if you want enthusiastic cooperation, you have to get those concerned to do the planning, or at least to participate in the development of the planning. If, for example, in Studebaker, I believed that our body department was not as efficient as, say, that of Oldsmobile, I wouldn't go to the Oldsmobile company, study what they are doing and then give an order to the head of our body department. Instead, I would talk to our man, saying that they seem to be doing some interesting things in connection with bodywork at Oldsmobile, and I would suggest that he go and take a look.
>
> He comes back, and if he is any good, he will have ideas. He will say that Studebaker has developed this or that which is desirable, but of course it needs modification and improvement— for which he takes the initiative in suggesting improvements, and he accepts the responsibility. In a larger way, we were successful in getting this done in Europe. There was development by each

country of its own plans and proposals. It was their initiative and enthusiasm, and they took responsibility for the plans.[27]

This vignette of a 'good' relationship between a company boss and a managerial subordinate nicely sums up the relationship with Europe that the Americans were looking for in the late 1940s and early 1950s. It is the equivalent, in a more commercialised and bureaucratic world, of the relationship between the absolute monarch who commands the key military and economic resources and the court noble available to serve and eager for preferment.

One of Hoffman's chief aides, Richard Bissell, later commented that 'Before the Marshall plan began, there was a clear intention to try in a four-year period to bring about some structural changes in Europe. It was recognised that the things that were wrong were deep-seated and that, therefore, deep-seated efforts would be needed to cope with them'. In Bissell's view, the 'structural change' of 'European unification' received 'a good deal of intelligent attention all through' but not enough was done to 'really come to grips with . . . the problem of the relatively decadent managerial class and weak labour especially in France and Italy (not in North Europe, Germany etc. generally)'. Bissell regretted that the Americans had not managed to do 'something important on that front'.[28]

By October 1949, American frustration at the slow pace of structural change in Europe led to a more forceful and direct approach. Paul Hoffman made a major speech at a conference of the OEEC insisting that the price for continued dollar aid was 'integration', a word he used repeatedly. By integration he meant 'the formation of a single large market in which quantitative restrictions on the movement of goods, monetary barriers to the flow of payments and, eventually, all tariffs are permanently swept away'.[29] As a step in this direction, the Americans supplied the Europeans with a plan for a European Payments Union (EPU), in other words a system for handling debts between European states so that national currencies could become fully convertible.[30] The EPU began operating in September 1950.

The Americans did not always get their way any more than Henry IV or Louis XIV did. However, they gave a powerful shove in the direction of pan-European institution-building. They wanted a regime of increasingly rational, increasingly rule-bound behaviour and they got it. Their capacity to control this regime gradually diminished. In part this is because after 1950 the outbreak of the Korean War shifted American attention to the Pacific. At the same time, the European economies began to revive rapidly.

The weakening capacity of the United States government to force its views about institution-building on their European allies was made clear in 1953 when the Americans gave their support to federalists such as Jean Monnet who were arguing for the creation of a European Defence Community. The EDC would control a new European Army including a German contingent. The American government made military aid under the Mutual Security Program of 1953–4 contingent on the EDC being created; if it was not created half the planned aid would be withdrawn. This strategy of winning policy victories by the carrot of aid had been reasonably successful in the days of Marshall Aid. However, by 1954 it no longer worked. French opinion was hostile. The French National Assembly refused to ratify the EDC and the plan collapsed.[31]

Nevertheless, during the 1950s it became clear that there would be no return to the 'old days' of direct military confrontation between West European states. This did not mean that national interests were forgotten, any more than court aristocrats stopped caring about the size of their hereditary estates during the seventeenth century. The point is that the way these interests were pursued changed. Just as French nobles learned to pursue their dynastic interests by intrigue at Versailles, worming their way into and up the networks of influence, so Europe's politicians tried to shape the institution-building process to serve their own national ambitions.

Take the case of the Schuman Plan which led to the setting up of the European Coal and Steel Community launched in 1951. In retrospect, this is sometimes presented as one of the building blocks for a new pan-European institutional order moving beyond petty national rivalries. However, one motive for establishing the ECSC was that it gave the French a means of exerting influence over German reindustrialisation, making sure their own interests were protected. The crucial difference from the 'old days' is that by the early 1950s peaceful and 'civilised' strategies were used to pursue national interests.

This approach was significantly different from the one adopted by the French government a quarter of a century earlier. In 1923, it sent in troops to occupy the German district of the Ruhr in order to neutralise the threat posed by its industrial capacity. This was equivalent, at a higher level of social integration, to the French aristocracy conducting its disputes by laying siege to each other's castles. By ceasing to behave in this way European governments were, in Elias's terms, giving evidence of a significant advance in the civilising process.

Just as the court nobility were permitted to keep their swords, as long as they did not use them, so the leading West European states have maintained their 'independent' nuclear arsenals. Instead of jousting, there are NATO exercises. Western Europe was not disarmed and pacified to the same extent as Eastern Europe under Soviet control but military expenditure certainly dropped as a share of national budgets.[32] Between 1953 and 1970 defence spending fell from eleven per cent of GNP in Britain to five per cent. In France the drop was from eleven per cent to four per cent, in Italy and West Germany from five per cent to three per cent. This reduction would not have been possible without an immense American military presence on European soil.

According to Michel Jobert, French foreign minister in 1973–4, West Europe in the immediate post-war decades was 'Lined up in one camp, under strict US control, taking orders and reporting for duty'. Jobert added: 'Europe was reassured but at a cost of irresponsibility'.[33] Jobert's comments may be exaggerated but they show how it felt to be subject to the constraints of a new power monopoly.

The disciplinary power of the Americans was certainly shown during the Suez adventure of 1956 when Britain and France were punished for acting like 'over-mighty subjects'. The secretly-organised attack by Britain, France and Israel on Egypt was an act straight out of the old closed book of imperialism. As Colin Cross put it, John Foster Dulles, the American secretary of state, 'did not equate the containment of Communism with the maintenance of British authority in the Middle East' (Cross, 1970: 327). Caught in the glare of American disapproval, the British and French faced utter condemnation at the United Nations where they secured only five votes of support in the General Assembly; sixty-four members voted against them. The British Prime Minister, Anthony Eden, did not lose his head as he might have done had he been similarly disobedient at Louis XIV's court. However, he lost his job, his health and his reputation.[34]

Processes of Europe-formation

My argument is that the sociogenesis of the European Union is a process that has a similar structure to the sociogenesis of the state, except that this process operates at a higher level of integration. In the period after 1945 in Europe, American economic, political and military power imposed higher standards of restraint in the use of violence. It also encouraged a regime of increasingly rule-bound interdependence between West European states, a regime that fostered strong links between their major economic enterprises such as coal, steel, nuclear energy and agriculture. The European Union after the Maastricht Treaty is the latest expression of this regime.

At the turn of the millennium, most of Western Europe has a major stake in this highly developed figuration. Laws made in Brussels affect the lives of citizens in all member states. In 1994 the British government calculated that a third of all British law was, in effect, written in Brussels. In 1988 Jacques Delors, President of the European Commission, suggested that at some time in the future 80 per cent of economic legislation affecting national states would be enacted in Brussels.[35] These laws range from employment legislation to the environment. A notable aspect of these laws is that they impose standards, for example in water purity, hours of work, and so on. They express new thresholds of decency.

The penetrative powers of the European Union have some resemblance to those previously exercised by the national state. One of the main attributes of the state, according to Elias, is its capacity to 'individualise', in other words, to disembed people from their family, tribe or other 'pre-state forms of integration' (Elias, 1991b: 181) and treat them according to the state's own rules and categories. This has the effect of weakening the hold on people of these older forms of integration. People become less constrained by their attachments to specific dynasties, clans or tribes and more attached to the national state.

The European Union is doing this, in turn, to its member states.[36] For example, it is giving special recognition to the regions (Emilio-Romagna, Rhône-Alps, Baden-Württemberg, Catalonia, Scotland and so on),[37] providing them with an alternative source of funding and legitimacy, an alternative, that is, to relying on the national state. The European regions are being disembedded from their national states.

The European Union is also contributing to the disembedding of large business corporations from the national state, a process that has clearly been considerably encouraged by the development of large-scale multinational and transnational corporations. EU regulations can have a direct impact on profit levels. It is highly advantageous for large companies to have lobbyists working for them in Brussels.

According to a recent study of the 'informal politics' of the European Union, the influence of firms 'ought not to be measured only by the number of experts implanted or lobbyists employed. The firm's long-term influence may be directed towards creating an attitude of mind among officials, a predisposition towards a particular technology, or fuel, or standard, or even a recognition of one firm's status *vis-à-vis* another' (Middlemas, 1995: 461). In this passage, the author, Keith Middlemas, is describing a strategy of psychological manipulation that Elias traces back to the royal court,[38] to La Bruyère and Saint-Simon.

Brussels, home of the European Union and NATO, has become a modern Versailles. Middlemas compares companies' lobbying strategies to trench warfare involving 'periods of low-key surveillance and monitoring followed by intensely fought battles, resulting in what are usually marginal gains' (456). This is reminiscent of La Bruyère's comment that 'Life at court is a serious, melancholy game, which requires us to arrange our pieces and our batteries, have a plan, follow it, foil that of the adversary, sometimes take risks and act on impulse. And after all our measures and meditations we are in check, sometimes checkmate' (Elias, 1994a: 475).[39]

This careful, realistic, calculating attitude of mind is highly developed among those lobbyists, diplomats and officials who spend long months and years at Brussels. They all play a long game. In the medium term, simply by joining in they strengthen Europe-wide exchange networks and develop a commitment to those very networks. As Middlemas puts it, 'Entry to the European game imposes a sense of interdependence. Where information exchange transactions with Commission officials (which comprise the largest single part of firms' activities) are concerned, even commercial firms have to accept an element of shared interest, which makes them much more acceptable in officials' eyes' (Middlemas, 1995: 458).

When the disembedding processes analysed previously combine with the integrative processes just described they work together to create a psychological and political 'space' for the development of a new European identity. Where should we expect to find the growth points for this European 'we-image'? I would suggest two. The first is in the newly liberated regions. Here the enthusiasm for 'Europe' may be less a matter of adopting the ideals of the federalist founders and more a matter of cheering on your master's master: in other words, giving support to a higher authority, the European Commission, who may be able to right the wrongs inflicted by the immediate oppressor, the national state.

A second growth point may be the professional classes within those national states that have been 'outsiders' within Europe.

Much of the German enthusiasm for Europe stems from the opportunity the European movement gives to escape from the stigmatising effects of history. For the Irish, Europe provides an affirmation of Ireland's emancipation from its old colonial subjection to British rule. For the Spanish, the Portuguese and the Greeks, membership of the European Union is a sign of acceptance within the European establishment.

However, ranged against this is what Elias describes as 'the drag effect' (Elias, 1991b: 211) coming from the *habitus* or social personality created by the national states. As far as survival is concerned, the crucial level of integration is now above the level of the national state. However, generations of experience within competing national states have caused the populations that make up Europe to think of themselves as primarily 'English', 'French', 'Swedish' and so on. If this sense of national identity is lost or diminished, this is experienced as a fundamental loss of meaning, a kind of 'death' for those generations that have to confront this challenge.

Exaggerating to make his point vividly, Elias suggests that the situation of the national state merging within a European super-state is comparable to that of a native American tribe having to give up its hunter-gatherer existence and find a future in the big city. In Elias's view, 'it usually takes at least three generations for these profess-conflicts to die down' (214). If Elias is right, Europe is about half to two-thirds of the way through its period of adjustment.

Conclusion

To recall the words used at the beginning of this chapter, Elias's model of the civilising process makes a very useful contribution to the Tocquevillean task of tracing links between the mentality and social habits of Europe's population, its sense of self-identity, its patterns of community life and the dynamics of its class and political relations. Elias helps us to understand some aspects of how these characteristics of European society are related to the way its laws and customs are monitored and enforced, the development of relations between that society and its neighbours (especially the United States), and the location of these structures and processes within the flow of history.

At the centre of Europe-formation is a shift from national states that mainly *impose* discipline on those subject to their domination to national states which are themselves to a very considerable extent *subject* to continuing discipline from 'above'. Closely related to this process is another: just as, at an earlier stage of the civilizing process, individuals were disembedded from kinship-based institutions, so, within the European Union, regional and business interests are being disembedded from the national state.

The layers of identity entrenched within the social personalities of European men and women are being slowly and sometimes painfully 'loosened up' and reshuffled. At the same time, as European interest groups have become more tightly bound together across national boundaries, the European Commission and the European Court of Justice have spun an increasingly dense web of rules and regulations, setting standards and defining rights. Meanwhile, the boundaries of the Union have gradually extended outwards, turning outsiders into committed members of the European professional establishment.

In a recent issue, *The Economist* commented that while most of the world, including the United States, Japan, China, and most of Asia, Latin America and Africa hold on to 'traditional ideas about the husbanding of state power', in Europe the situation was very different. In their words, 'In no other part of the world is the idea of a diminution of national sovereignty anywhere near so readily accepted'. Compare, for example, the Association of South-East Asian Nations (ASEAN) whose 'cardinal principle . . . is a mutual pledge of non-interference in internal affairs'.[40]

The extent to which the EU has penetrated the boundaries of its member states and influenced their internal workings is astonishing. This is now so much taken for granted by most people within the EU that it is surprising to discover how unusual it is. In the late 1930s Norbert Elias judged that France had played a vanguard role in the civilising process within Europe. There are signs that the European Union may be playing a similar part in a global context.

Notes

1 First published in 1835. The second volume appeared in 1840. See also Smith, 1990: 17–36.
2 See, for example, Connolly, 1995; Johnson, 1996; Hama, 1996. For a carefully argued essay which makes the case that ' "Europe" is more than a geographical notion but less than an answer' see Judt, 1996. The quotation is from page 141.
3 See, for example, Middlemas, 1995; Therborn, 1995; Ash, 1994; Smith, 1997.
4 Tocqueville did not believe that the American republic was the best political system possible. He much preferred an enlightened aristocratic system and wanted

to know how a democracy could exist without collapsing into violence and disorder. This work was an instant success, not least in America. (See Mayer, 1968: xxxi–xxxiii.) People influenced by Tocqueville included Francis Lieber, the 'father of American political science', who met Tocqueville during his visit to the United States and corresponded with him afterwards (xxxi). The reception of Tocqueville's work benefited from, and contributed to, a climate of critical reflexivity within the United States. This capacity for critical reflexivity, however, flawed, must have helped American society weather the storms of civil war, immigration and urban-industrial change still to come in the rest of the nineteenth century. The idea of critical reflexivity overlaps with the notion of 'social control' as developed by the Chicago School (for example) and expounded by Morris Janowitz. See Smith, 1988; Janowitz, 1978: 27–52. The Soviet Union, yet a third experiment in implementing Enlightenment ideals, might have had a better chance of weathering its own storms if it had cultivated a similar capacity. Take the case of Aleksandr Solzhenitsyn. For a while his work was encouraged by Khrushchev who authorised the publication of *One Day in the Life of Ivan Denisovich* (Solzhenitsyn, 1963) in the early 1960s. However, in 1968, just over half a century after the Russian Revolution, Solzhenitsyn was expelled from the Union of Soviet Writers for publishing *The First Circle* (Solzhenitsyn, 1988) and *Cancer Ward* (Solzhenitsyn, 1970). Solzhenitsyn's *The Gulag Archipelago* (Solzhenitsyn, 1986), first published in the 1970s, was a strong critique of the Soviet system. Like Tocqueville, Solzhenitsyn was formed by a set of values (Christian in his case, aristocratic in Tocqueville's) that were rejected by the system he was critically analysing. Compare the Soviet enthusiasm for Mikhail Sholokhov who was fundamentally loyal to the values of the system (Sholokhov, 1970; Sholokhov, 1978; Sholokhov, 1988; Sholokhov, 1992). For Elias's comments on the importance of self-reflection see his essay entitled 'Thoughts on the Federal Republic', in *The Germans* (Elias, 1996), especially 407–12, 418–19.

5 For both Elias and Tocqueville, the question was not just intellectual, it was deeply personal. Members of Tocqueville's family lost their lives during the French Revolution; Elias's mother was killed in Auschwitz. For further discussion see my forthcoming critical study of Elias to be published by Sage.

6 In a very obvious way the Jews did not 'fit in' to German society; they were threatened outsiders. However, Elias also felt that Germany's history, not just in the twentieth century but since the Middle Ages, made his native country a threatened outsider within Europe as a whole.

7 For other work by Elias developing related themes, see bibliography.

8 Europe-making processes were of interest to Elias. He comments in *The Society of Individuals* that 'It would make rational sense and possibly bring benefits if the European national states combined into the United States of Europe' although he adds immediately: 'the difficulty lies in the fact that intellectual awareness of the logic of integration meets the tenacious resistance of emotive ideas which give the integration the character of ruin, a loss that one cannot cease mourning' (Elias, 1991a: 225). Elias is referring to the feeling that Europe-making processes entail a loss of national identity. Elias had a strong sense of his own German-ness but at the same time he was able to identify strongly with the wider entity of Europe. When in his late eighties he was asked what nationality he identified with. He replied: 'Basically, I am a European' (Elias, 1994b: 74). Elsewhere he described himself as 'a person who feels deeply bound to the European tradition' (Elias, 1996: 428). Elias was born in 1897 in Breslau, then part of the German

Empire, now part of Poland. As a young man he worked in the universities at Heidelberg and Frankfurt but in 1933 he joined the exodus of Jewish intellectuals from Germany. He spent time in Switzerland and Paris before arriving in England in 1935. He spent the next three and a half decades in Britain. However, by the late 1960s Elias was frequently travelling to Germany and the Netherlands. After 1975 he spent most of his time in those two countries. By the time he was in his early nineties he had received the Adorno prize from the city of Frankfurt, an award from the West German president, an honorary doctorate from the University of Strasbourg, and the insignia of the Order of Orange-Nassau from Queen Beatrix in the Netherlands. See Mennell, 1989: 25.

9 Elias acknowledged but paid relatively little attention to the part played by economic enterprises or businesses as survival units in spite of the fact that the monopoly mechanism had first been explored in the sphere of the economic market by earlier writers.

10 The *habitus* of a social group is its code of feeling and behaviour or learned behavioural and emotional disposition. Some aspects of habitus may be peculiar to specific individuals, others are shared by the group. Each person's habitus is multi-layered, expressing (for example) the codes and dispositions specific to themselves as individuals, the social groups to which they belong, the nations of which those groups are a part, and so on.

11 Although Elias argues that in later phases of the civilising process the I-identity may become very pronounced and its links to the we-identity may be ignored, forgotten or not acknowledged. See *Changes in the we-I balance* (Elias, 1991b).

12 See Elias, 1996.

13 On 'functional democratisation' see Elias, 1994a: 503.

14 As is well known, the Edict of Nantes gave Protestants equal political rights with Catholics and also allowed Protestants a certain amount of religious freedom. Henry IV also worked with his minister Sully on a 'grand design' to establish a universal Christian polity in Europe comprising six hereditary monarchies (France, England, Spain, Denmark, Sweden, Lombardy), five elective monarchies (the empire, the papacy, Hungary, Poland and Bohemia) and four republics (Switzerland, Italy, Venice and Belgium). In practice, for all its pan-European rhetoric, this scheme was in effect a proposed alliance against the Hapsburgs.

15 Secretary of State Byrne announced this intention at the Overseas Press Club in New York on 28 February 1946 (van der Beugel, 1996: 20). This approach was enshrined as the Truman Doctrine. The thinking behind it was set out in George F. Kennan's article in *Foreign Affairs* setting out the American administration's intention to engage in 'firm and vigilant containment of Russian expansive tendencies' (Kennan, 1947: 581).

16 The original treaty powers were Belgium, Canada, Denmark, France, Iceland, Italy, Luxembourg, the Netherlands, Norway, Portugal, the UK and the USA. Greece and Turkey joined in 1951, the Federal Republic of Germany in 1955.

17 Europe's need for imports and consequent chronic trade deficit left the continent short of dollars at a time when the dollar was on the way to becoming the global currency. As *The Economist* put it on 31 May 1947, 'the whole of European life is being overshadowed by the Great Dollar shortage' (833).

18 Quoted in van der Beugel, 1966: 50–1.

19 Quoted in van der Beugel, 1966: 80.

20 In 1961 the OEEC became the Organization for Economic Cooperation and

Development (OECD), expanding its membership to include advanced industrial countries (such as USA and Canada) outside of Europe.

21 See Griffiths, 1995: 8–15.

22 Griffiths, 1995: 8–9.

23 Henry IV was a Protestant and, of course, most of his French subjects were Catholic.

24 Judt, 1997: 37. Between 1945 and 1971 US aid to Europe (military and civilian) amounted to $53 billion gross and $43 billion net, of which $39 billion was in the form of grants (Maddison, 1976: 475). It is worth mentioning that Elias wrote about the position of the French Protestants in an essay published in 1935 (Elias, 1935).

25 A United States of Europe was advocated by *Le Moniteur*, a French newspaper, in 1848. An International Steel Cartel had linked Germany, France and several other European producers between 1926 and 1929. Aristide Briande and Gustav Stresemann had worked for greater Franco-German cooperation leading to a united Europe with its own single European currency, during the 1920s. During the 1930s organisations such as Jeune Europe provided a forum for enthusiasts such as the Belgian Socialist Paul-Henry Spaak. See Judt, 1997: 6–9, 14. Other enthusiasts for a united Europe have included Alterio Spinelli, Luigi Einaudi, Giovanni Agnelli, Andrea Cabiati, Maurice Renoult, Bertrand de Jouvenel, Roger Manuel, Herman Kranold, Sobei Mgoi, Edo Fimmen, to name but a few.

26 Quoted in Judt, 1997: 17.

27 Taken from an interview with Paul Hoffman conducted by 'HBP' on 28 January 1953. Located in the Truman Presidential Library Digital Archives. This may be located through the Internet at the following address: www.whistlestop.org/study_ collections/marshall/large/folder 7

28 Taken from an interview with Richard M. Bissell Jr conducted by Sam Van Hyning, Harvey Mansfield, Guy Horsley and 'HBP' on 19 September 1952. For location see previous note.

29 Quoted in Griffiths, 1995: 10

30 This plan was drawn up by Richard Bissell. Griffiths, 1995: 10.

31 Judt, 1996: 17–18. Congressional Record, 83rd congress, 1st session, p. 8683; van der Beugel, 1996: 287.

32 It would be interesting to compare the West European and East European versions of the civilising process after World War II at greater length than is possible here. Just one question: from an Eliasian perspective, does the breakup of the Soviet Union after 1989 represent a decivilising process of equivalent dimensions to the collapse of the German Empire in 1918? The USSR was in existence just two decades longer than the *Kaiserreich*.

33 *Le Monde*, 10 August 1991; Judt, 1997: 29, n 7; Elias, 1994a: 512–13.

34 President Eisenhower made it clear he thought that the strategy of using force in settling disputes such as that over the Suez Canal was 'out of date' (quoted in Moseley, 1978: 409). See also the chapters in Louis and Owen, 1989.

35 *The Economist*, 3 January 1998: 28.

36 These comments apply also to the EU's previous incarnation, the European Community.

37 See Middlemas, 1994: 383–434.

38 Although it was, no doubt, also to be found in the monastery and the cathedral chapter house.

39 The quotation is from La Bruyère, 1922: 237.

40 *The Economist*, 3 January 1998: 28.

Bibliography

Ash, T. G. (1993), *In Europe's Name. Germany and the divided continent*, London: Cape.

Connolly, B. (1995), *The Rotten Heart of Europe*, London: Faber and Faber.

Cipolla, C. M. (ed), *The Fontana Economic History of Europe. The Twentieth Century*, London: Collins/Fontana.

Cross, C. (1970), *The Fall of the British Empire*, London: Paladin.

Drost, H. (1995), *What's What and Who's Who in Europe*, London: Cassell.

Elias, N. (1935), 'Der Vertreibung der Hugenotten aus Frankreich', *Der Ausweg*, 1 (12), 369–76.

Elias, N. (1950), 'Studies in the genesis of the naval profession', *British Journal of Sociology*, 1 (4), 291–310.

Elias, N. (1971), 'The sociology of knowledge: new perspectives', *Sociology*, 5 (2), 149–68, 355–70.

Elias, N. (1978), *What is Sociology?* translated by Stephen Mennell and Grace Morrissey, with a foreword by Reinhard Bendix, Hutchinson: London; originally published in 1970.

Elias, N. (1982), 'Scientific establishments', in Elias, Martins and Whitley, 1982, 3–69.

Elias, N. (1983), *The Court Society*, translated by Edmund Jephcott, Oxford: Basil Blackwell.

Elias, N. (1985), *The Loneliness of the Dying*, translated by Edmund Jephcott, Oxford: Basil Blackwell.

Elias, N. (1986), 'Soziale Prozesse', in Schäfers, 1986.

Elias, N. (1987a), 'On human beings and their emotions: a process-sociological essay', *Theory, Culture and Society*, 4, 339–61.

Elias, N. (1987b), *Involvement and Detachment*, edited by Michael Schröter, translated by Edmund Jephcott, Oxford: Basil Blackwell.

Elias, N. (1991a), *The Society of Individuals*, edited by Michael Schröter, translated by Edmund Jephcott, Oxford: Basil Blackwell.

Elias, N. (1991b), 'Changes in the we-I balance', in Elias, 1991a, 155–237.

Elias, N. (1991c), *The Symbol Theory*, London: Sage.

Elias, N. (1992), *Time: An Essay*, translated in part by Edmund Jephcott, Oxford: Basil Blackwell.

Elias, N. (1993), *Mozart: Portrait of Genius*, edited by Michael Schröter, translated by Edmund Jephcott, Cambridge: Polity Press.

Elias, N. (1994a), *The Civilizing Process*, two volumes (vol. 1: *The History of Manners*, vol. 2: *State Formation and Civilization*), translated by Edmund Jephcott, Oxford: Basil Blackwell; originally published in 1939.

Elias, N. (1994b), *Reflections on a Life*, translated by Edmund Jephcott, Cambridge: Polity Press.

Elias, N. (1996), *The Germans. Power struggles and the development of habitus in the nineteenth and twentieth centuries*, edited by Michael Schröter, translated and with a preface by Eric Dunning and Stephen Mennell, Cambridge: Polity Press.

Elias, N. and E. Dunning (1986), *Quest for Excitement. Sport and leisure in the civilizing process*, Oxford: Basil Blackwell.

Elias, N. and J. L. Scotson (1994), *The Established and the Outsiders*, London: Sage.

Elias, N., H. Martins, and R. Whitley (1982), *Scientific Establishments and Hierarchies. Sociology of the Sciences, vol. iv*, Dordrecht, Netherlands: D. Reidel.

Elliott, J. H. (1968), *Europe Divided 1559–1598*, London: Fontana.

Ellwood, D. W. (1992), *Rebuilding Europe. America and West European Reconstruction*, London: Longmans.

Ellwood, D. W. (1998), ' "You too can be like us": Selling the Marshall Plan', *History Today*, 48 (10), 33–39.

Gastelaars, M. and A. de Ruitjer (eds) (1988), *A United Europe. The quest for a multi-faceted identity*, Maastricht: Shaker Publishing.

Griffiths, N. (1996), *Disintegrating Europe. The Twilight of the European construction*, London: Adamantine Press.

Johnson, C. (1996), *In With the Euro, Out With the Pound*, Harmondsworth: Penguin.

Judt, T. (1997), *A Grand Illusion. An essay on Europe*, Harmondsworth: Penguin.

Kennan, G. E. (writing under the pseudonym of 'X') (1947), 'The sources of Soviet conduct', *Foreign Affairs*, 25, July.

La Bruyère, J. de (1922), *Caractères*, Paris: Hachette; originally published in 1688.

Maddison, A. (1976), 'Economic policy and performance in Europe 1913–1970', in Cipolla, 1976, 442–508.

Louis, W. R. and R. Owen (eds) (1989), *Suez 1956: The Crisis and the Consequences*, Oxford: Clarendon Press.

Mayer, J.-P. (1968), 'Tocqueville's *Democracy in America*: reception and reputation', in Tocqueville, 1968, xvii–xxxvi.

Mennell, S. (1989), *Norbert Elias. Civilization and the human self-image*, Oxford: Blackwell.

Middlemas, K. (1995), *Orchestrating Europe. The informal politics of European union 1973–95*, London: Fontana.

Milward, A. S. (1992), *The European Rescue of the Nation State*, London.

Moseley, L. (1978), *Dulles*, New York: Dial Press.

Sholokhov, M. (1992), *And Quiet Flows the Don*, Harmondsworth: Penguin.

Sholokhov, M. (1970), *The Don flows to the Sea*, Harmondsworth: Penguin.

Sholokhov, M. (1988), *The Virgin Soil Upturned*, London: Pan Books.

Sholokhov, M. (1978), *Harvest on the Don*, Harmondsworth: Penguin.

Smith, D. (1997), 'Eurofutures', *Five scenarios for the next millennium*, London: Capstone.

Smith, D. (1983), *Barrington Moore. Violence, morality and political change*, London: Macmillan.

Smith, D. (1988), *The Chicago School. A liberal critique of capitalism*, London: Macmillan.

Smith, D. (1990), *Capitalist Democracy on Trial. The transatlantic debate from Tocqueville to the present*, London: Routledge.

Smith, D. (1991), *The Rise of Historical Sociology*, Cambridge: Polity.

Smith, D. (1999), *Zygmunt Bauman. Prophet of postmodernity*, Cambridge: Polity.

Smith, D. (forthcoming), *Norbert Elias*, London: Sage.

Solzhenitsyn, A. (1963), *One Day in the Life of Ivan Denisovich*, Harmondsworth: Penguin.

Solzhenitsyn, A. (1970), *Cancer Ward*, Harmondsworth: Penguin.

Solzhenitsyn, A. (1988), *The First Circle*, London: Harvill Press.

Solzhenitsyn, A. (1974–8), *The Gulag Archipelago*, London: Harvill Press.

Solzhenitsyn, A. (1980), *The Oak and the Calf*, London: HarperCollins.

Therborn, G. (1995), *European Modernity and Beyond. The trajectory of European societies 1945–2000*, London: Sage.

Dennis Smith

Tocqueville, A. de (1968), *Democracy in America*, 2 vols, translated by George Lawrence, edited by J.-P. Mayer and A. P. Kerr with an introduction by J.-P. Mayer, New York: Collins; originally published 1835–40.

National pride and the meaning of 'Europe': a comparative study of Britain and Spain

Pablo Jáuregui

Abstract

In this chapter, Pablo Jáuregui questions the idea that the development of the European Union means Europe is entering a 'post-nationalist' era. He suggests that nationalism and Europeanism are not necessarily opposed to each other or mutually incompatible. Taking the two cases of Spain and Britain, Jáuregui argues that their specific national self-images and feelings of collective pride have influenced the particular discourses on Europe in those two countries. Drawing in part on the ideas of Norbert Elias, this chapter examines the political rhetoric employed to legitimate or contest the idea of 'going into Europe' in Spain and Britain, paying particular attention to the different ways this decision impacted upon perceptions of national status and sentiments of collective self-esteem. In Britain, the idea of going into Europe was associated with a decline in national status and the 'loss of world power'. In contrast, for Spain entering Europe meant a considerable enhancement of national prestige following the collapse of a 'backwards dictatorship'.

Introduction

Nations are not something eternal. They began, so they will come to an end. A European confederation will probably replace them.

More than a century has passed since Ernest Renan (1996: 59) made this prophetic statement in his celebrated lecture 'What is a nation?', delivered at the Sorbonne in 1882. To what extent can one say that his vision has come true? How far would it be accurate to claim that over the course of time, a supranational confederation has begun to replace the nations of Europe, and their respective nationalisms? It seems undeniable that since Renan's day, great progress has been made towards the goal of European unification. A new territorial unit has gradually emerged which today encompasses fifteen nation-states and is represented by a common name-symbol, the 'European Union', a number of 'European' political and legal institutions, a 'European' flag, a 'European' anthem, the 'Euro' currency, ritualised commemorations such as 'Europe Day', and so on.[1] In many ways, Renan seems to have hit the nail on the head, and Europe does appear to be moving towards an increasingly 'post-nationalist' era.

Nevertheless, one has only to consider the euphoric passions ignited by the latest World Cup football contest in order to realise that the ideals and sentiments of nationhood have hardly disappeared within the context of the European Union. Indeed, a quick look at any newspaper can reveal what Michael Billig (1995) has called the 'banal nationalism' of the contemporary world: the taken-for-granted, routine ways in which every nation's achievements are constantly 'flagged' in the daily language of politicians and the mass media, highlighting national triumphs not just in athletic arenas, but in military, economic, cultural, and many other spheres of international competition. Within the EU's member states, policies concerning 'Europe' are in fact typically legitimated in political discourse through the invocation of 'national interests' (Ruane, 1994). Hence, as soon as one takes into account the resilient habits of 'banal nationalism', it becomes very clear that Renan's vision of Europe does not fit the facts at this stage, and that the conclusion reached by Raymond Aron more than thirty years ago still sounds like a much more accurate description of reality: 'I believe that consciousness of the nation remains infinitely stronger than a sense of Europe . . . The old nations still live in the hearts of men, and love of the European nation is not yet born, assuming that it ever will be' (1964: 60–61).

However, is it always right to assume that people's emotional attachments to 'the old nations' are necessarily incompatible with 'a love for the European nation'? Should nationalism and Europeanism be seen as irreconcilable enemies or polar opposites that cannot co-exist with one another? This certainly seems to be a widespread belief. Alain Touraine, for instance, has suggested that 'the reason for our uneasiness when we speak about Europe is that it is an indirect way of speaking about something else, or more precisely, about the opposite of European integration, namely our national states' (1994: 13). Indeed, the project of European unity is often depicted as a struggle *against* nationalism. Like in Renan's prophecy, many supporters of 'Europeanism' hope that loyalty to a new supranational confederation will ultimately transcend, erode, and *replace* the traditional sentiments attached to nation-states, which are seen as selfish and dangerous emotions.

Some authors, for instance, have suggested that European integration was fundamentally constructed 'in opposition to the nationalist, atavistic instincts' (Gladwyn, 1967: 58) or 'the welter of ultra-nationalistic attitudes' (Davies, 1996: 42) which were held to be responsible for the outbreak of the Second World War. In the years that followed this devastating conflict, 'the reaction against nationalism went naturally together with the notion of European solidarity' (Seton-Watson, 1985: 12), and hence 'committed "Europeans" saw European union as *replacing* the failed nation-states out of which it would be built' (Wallace, 1990: 63–4). From a 'pro-European' perspective, one writer has therefore lamented the fact that as the twentieth century draws to a close, there is still 'no European feeling or identity', due to 'the predominant emotional fixation on our nation-states' (Papcke, 1992: 66). Another author has suggested that the 'nationalism of the peoples' should indeed be seen as one of the 'major problems besetting the idea of a European supernation-state' (Llobera, 1994: 207). Nationalism and Europeanism are thus often seen as contrary tendencies or conflicting movements.

The aim of this chapter is to look closer at the relationship between national sentiments and the process of European unification. My objective is to show that it can be highly misleading to make a rigid distinction between national and European affiliations, as if the two were necessarily opposed to each other or mutually incompatible. I shall firstly outline a theoretical approach to national identity as a symbolic, an emotional, and a political phenomenon. From this perspective, I shall then compare the way in which national self-images and feelings of collective pride have influenced the development of different discourses on 'Europe' in two member states of the EU, Britain and Spain. By focusing primarily on the political rhetoric which was employed to either legitimate or contest the concept of 'going into Europe' in these two countries, I shall contrast the diverse impacts this decision had on perceptions of national status and sentiments of collective self-esteem. It will be argued that while in Britain the idea of 'entering Europe' inevitably became associated with a decline in national status after the loss of 'world power', in Spain, on the contrary, this event represented a great enhancement of national prestige follow-

ing the collapse of a 'backwards dictatorship'. Hence, EC membership became a potent source of national pride for Spaniards, in a
way which could hardly have been possible in Britain. On the basis
of this comparison, I shall propose that instead of making a sharp
distinction between 'nationalism' and 'Europeanism', one should
rather consider the way in which national sentiments have provoked
different degrees of enthusiasm or hostility towards the concept of
'becoming European' in each member state of the EU.

We-images, we-feelings, and power struggles: the symbolic, emotional, and political components of national identity

In the contemporary world, most human beings think of themselves
as members of collectivities they refer to as 'nations'. Hence, an
individual may routinely state, in relation to himself, 'I am Spanish'
or 'I am British'. National identity can thus be defined in the first
place as one aspect of people's self-understanding in the modern
world: their symbolic concept of themselves. At the same time, as
the example of the World Cup football championship vividly illustrates, these same human beings often display an acute emotional
sensitivity towards the shifting fortunes of their particular nation.
National identity must therefore also be seen as an aspect of
people's self-esteem in the modern world: the positive or negative
emotions they experience in relation to themselves and their sense
of worth.

These symbolic and emotional components of national identity
can be conceptualised, following Norbert Elias (1991a), as 'we-
images' and 'we-feelings': the ideals and sentiments which people
acquire not in relation to who they are as unique individuals, but in
relation to the societies of which they are members. Human beings
are uniquely equipped with the biological capacity to orientate
themselves through the acquisition of symbols (Elias, 1991b). From
the beginning of their lives, all newborn individuals undergo a social
process of symbol-learning within a particular linguistic community, and this includes the internalisation of symbols about themselves, or self-symbols. The human self, however, should be seen as
both an I-self and a we-self. In other words, people's self-images are
composed not only of concepts of themselves as distinct individuals,
but also as members of groups to which they belong: 'A person's we-
image and we-ideal form as much part of a person's self-image and

self-ideal as the image and ideal of him or herself as the unique person to which he or she refers as "I"' (Elias, 1994a: xlii). People's emotional sensitivities can therefore be triggered off at both individual and collective levels, because part of their self-love or self-esteem may be attached to the societies of which they are members (Elias, 1987a: xi–xii). They can feel admired or humiliated, respected or insulted, not only in relation to their 'I'-identity, but also with regard to the communities in which they classify themselves and of which they say 'we'. As Elias illustrated in his study of the relationships between established and outsider groups, in collaboration with John Scotson (Elias and Scotson, 1994), an individual's sense of self-worth can be intensely affected by the 'group charisma' or 'group disgrace' of a community to which he or she belongs, depending on its varying power and status *vis-à-vis* other groups. Hence, human associations typically develop a 'self-praising vocabulary' through which their members often derive 'an immense narcissistic gratification' (Elias, 1987a: xi–xii).

This affective or emotional component of collective identification has been further explored in a very illuminating manner by the American sociologist Thomas Scheff (1990, 1994a, 1994b). Following the insights of earlier authors such as Charles Cooley (1922) and Erving Goffman (1967), Scheff has illustrated how people's social behaviour cannot be properly understood without considering the role of emotions, particularly pride and shame. Essentially, his argument is that individuals constantly monitor the amount of respect or disrespect they are receiving from others, and this self-awareness triggers off varying degrees of pride or shame. As a result of what Scheff calls the deference-emotion system, 'conformity to exterior norms is rewarded by deference and the feeling of pride, and nonconformity is punished by lack of deference and feelings of shame' (1990: 95). This phenomenon, however, may be observed not only in the Goffmanian 'interaction ritual' between particular individuals, but also in the relations between large-scale societies such as modern nation-states. On both personal 'I' and collective 'we' levels, according to Scheff, self-esteem can be defined as 'a sort of pride-shame balance', a 'moment-by-moment social status' which individuals and groups constantly seek to increase in their relationships with each other (1994a: 285).

In the case of national identity, one could say that part of the face or the self-esteem of individuals becomes attached to the power and status of their respective nations. Hence, national triumphs and defeats can conceivably affect their pride-shame balances, their feelings of superiority and inferiority, in the same way as their own personal successes and failures. On the basis of numerous criteria, such as military strength, economic might, moral respectability, cultural and scientific achievement, technological advancement, athletic skill, and so on, the world's nation-states are all tacitly ranked on a competitive ladder of power and status. Nationalised individuals therefore typically view their own country's classification on this hierarchic pyramid of international prestige as an aspect of their own self-importance in the world.

Much of the literature on nationalism has concentrated exclusively on the modernity of this phenomenon: for instance, the functional economic role it fulfils in industrial societies which require a standardised mass culture (Gellner, 1983), or the way in which national communities were 'imagined' by millions of people who did not personally know each other, through the spread of printed books and other modern forms of mass communication (Anderson, 1983). It is undeniable that in certain respects, nationalism is relatively new or modern, as these and other authors have shown. However, the we-images of nations, as well as the we-feelings of national pride and shame, can also be seen as cultural variations of a common human theme, or as long-term, socio-historical developments of certain anthropological universals. As Durkheim (1976 [1915]) originally argued, all human societies construct 'collective ideals' and 'collective sentiments' which they typically reaffirm through the celebration of assemblies and rituals. Variants of this phenomenon, in his view, could be observed in modern states as much as in ancient tribes.

From Elias's 'process-sociological' perspective, one could argue that the human population has always been divided into 'survival units': relatively self-sufficient groups of people who have constructed we-images of themselves, in opposition to they-images of rival others, and who have organised themselves to provide security for their members from all external threats (Elias, 1987b; Mennell, 1994). Over the course of history, however, it is clear that there has been a long-term trend towards the development of larger survival units, and the expansion of emotional identification throughout wider territorial spaces: 'From small bands of twenty-five to fifty members, perhaps living in caves, humans coalesced into tribes of several hundred or several thousand, and nowadays more and more into states of millions of people' (Elias, 1987b: 225). Nation-states can therefore be seen as modern versions of earlier human survival units. They are inwardly pacified and outwardly defensive associations, which have developed their own particular brand of collective we-images and we-feelings.

In the contemporary world, there are many other layers of we-images and we-feelings: less inclusive groupings such as the family, the city, the region, and so on, or more inclusive ones, such as supranational associations, religious communities, and even the concept of humanity as a whole (Elias, 1991a: 202). To some extent, it is clear that as webs of contact and interdependence have spread across the globe, identification with all peoples has increased over the course of time (De Swaan, 1995). Indeed, in many contemporary nation-states a contradictory code of moral norms exists in which nationalist and humanist values uneasily co-exist with each other: the use of violence against all human beings is generally forbidden, but in the context of a war this taboo may be broken for the good of 'the nation' (Elias, 1996: 160). Hence, although it is undeniable that the concept of 'human rights' has gradually expanded, the national we-layer of emotional identification has simultaneously remained an important component of people's habitus, ie the psychological make-up or affective structure they have acquired through a social learning process.[2]

The symbolic and emotional components of national identity, however, must necessarily be linked with the distinctive political aspects of this phenomenon: the role which national we-images and we-feelings can perform in the maintenance of power and authority. As many authors have stressed, the birth of nationalism was historically intertwined with the rise of modern states and of democracy as a novel form of political legitimation (Elias, 1970; Anderson, 1983; Calhoun, 1994). The psychogenesis of national ideals and sentiments must therefore be linked to the sociogenesis of modern states, which have legitimated their authority more or less successfully by claiming to represent a particular 'nation' within a particular territory.[3] For this reason, those who are involved in the struggles to acquire or maintain positions of power within each state often invoke the well-being and pride of their respective national communities in order to gain popular support.[4] In other words, the defence of 'the nation' and the 'national interest' is clearly one of the fundamental symbolic strategies of political legitimation in the contemporary world. One could say that there is an ongoing political contest to flatter the national ego of each country's population: aspiring or established leaders, through the platforms of the mass media, typically present themselves and their programmes as the most effective guardians of national prosperity and self-respect.

The concept of 'the nation' can therefore be seen as an emotionally charged, political symbol which is routinely invoked and manipulated by aspiring or established leaders, in their daily struggles to acquire power and prestige within particular territories. Following the terminology of Abner Cohen (1979), 'the nation' can be defined as a 'bivocal symbol' of modernity, in the sense that it may simultaneously fulfil both personal, existentialist functions of self-meaning, as well as political functions of power-legitimation. As Elias put it, 'people in power can usually count on a warm response of approval and often of affection or love from their compatriots whenever they praise or add to the glory of the social unit they all form with each other' (1987a: xii). Hence, within the public sphere of each state, the leaders of different political organisations constantly offer to populations what one could call *conflicting paradigms of national greatness.*[5]

In spite of the remarkable progress which the project of European integration has made this century, every member state of the EU has clearly maintained its own nationally bounded arena of political conflict, its own distinctive battlefield of discursive struggles. National we-images and we-feelings have therefore functioned and continue to function as highly contested objects of political dispute within the public sphere of each state. In fact, what one can observe is that the idea of 'going into Europe' has been primarily embraced or rejected in every country on the basis of what it has been claimed to represent for 'the nation' in question by leading political figures. This is what I shall now attempt to illustrate through a comparison of Britain and Spain.

Britain: 'Europe' as a symbol of diminished status and a weak source of national pride

When the project of European integration began to take shape in the aftermath of the Second World War, the dominant paradigm of British national greatness depicted the United Kingdom as a 'world power' with global aspirations and responsibilities (Wallace, 1991; Butt Philip, 1992; Radice, 1992; Haseler, 1996). Britain, it was proclaimed, had 'stood alone' against the Nazis, she had heroically avoided the foreign occupation of her territory, she remained at the head of a 'great Empire', and hence she was still symbolically classified as one of the so-called 'Big Three', with a secure place at the 'Top Table' of international diplomacy. Hence, from such a standpoint, the very idea of British submersion into a European federation was simply inconceivable amongst its leaders, for Britain was considered to be much more than *just* another European country.

In fact, this proud we-image of Britain was displayed quite clearly by Winston Churchill during his influential Zurich speech of 1946, in which he famously called for the creation of 'a sort of United States of Europe'.[6] This address was one of the events which got the ball of European integration rolling after the war, and it earned Churchill a rightful place among the 'founding fathers' of European unity. Nevertheless, the discourse he employed made it plain that in his mind, Britain could not be a part of this continental association. Rather, along with the other 'world powers', the British nation would simply encourage the construction of 'Europe' from the sidelines:

> Great Britain, the British Commonwealth of Nations, mighty
> America, and, I trust, Soviet Russia—for then, indeed, all would
> be well—must be the friends and sponsors of the new Europe and
> must champion its right to live.

Churchill's grand vision, therefore, did not include Britain within the future 'United States of Europe', since this would be completely at odds with its distinctive status as one of the world's giants. At the most, Britain would warmly support this project from its powerful position of global strength and influence. In other words, from this perspective, while 'they, the Europeans' needed to unite in order to survive, 'we, the British' were not seen as part of this continental grouping, because this was a 'we' which could allow itself greater, more prestigious aspirations.

It is worth considering Churchillian discourse in some detail, given the historic influence of this leader and his symbolic role as one of the most popular icons of modern British nationhood. The paradigm of British national greatness which Churchill clearly believed in and publicly promoted was one of Anglo-American world leadership. In the preface of his popular *History of the English-Speaking Peoples*, he wrote:

> For the second time in the present century the British Empire and
> the United States have stood together facing the perils of war on
> the largest scale known among men, and since the cannons
> ceased to fire and the bombs to burst we have become more
> conscious of our common duty to the human race . . . Vast

numbers of people on both sides of the Atlantic and throughout the British Commonwealth of Nations have felt a sense of brotherhood. (1956: vii)

The national we-image which Churchill defended therefore sought the maintenance of British status and pride through an Atlantic union with the USA, rather than by merging with 'the Europeans'. Indeed, his highly influential theory of Britain's place in the world placed the United Kingdom at the intersection of three great circles: the Empire, America, and Europe. Britain's links with 'the Continent' were thus perceived as merely one aspect of the nation's global importance, a relatively minor component of its self-image as an established world power. From this perspective, which was widely shared, both Britain's imperial links and responsibilities, as well as the 'special relationship' with America, were viewed as much greater sources of national pride than the highly unattractive idea of losing sovereignty by joining a European federation.

Although the war had seriously weakened Britain economically, the discourse of its leaders continued to display the resilience of this proud, self-confident we-image. In spite of the relative inferiority of its military might and its material strength in comparison to the new American and Soviet 'superpowers', Britain was nevertheless portrayed as a nation with an unparalleled moral prestige which still had a unique influence in the world (Blackwell, 1993: 98–100). Even as independence was increasingly granted to its colonies, and as the Empire was transformed into the Commonwealth, the dominant paradigm of national greatness continued to place Britain on a much higher plane of status and prestige, in comparison to the lower ranking which was ascribed to the continental European countries. Although the days of imperial glory may have been over, it was widely believed that Britain still had to play a unique global role, for it maintained a special responsibility towards the progressive development of its old dependencies and could act independently as a 'go-between' between America and the Soviet Union in the cause of world peace.

This historical and socio-psychological background is crucial in order to understand that when British leaders ultimately decided to put forward the idea of 'joining Europe', such a policy was a rather difficult one to sell to the public, for it inevitably appeared to symbolise a lowering of rank in the hierarchic ladder of international status. As one author has put it, when Britain turned to Europe, this occurred 'more by a process of elimination than one of choice'

(Allen, 1988: 169), only when the loss of its strength had seriously eroded the possibility of maintaining a distinctive 'world power' status. The concept of 'going into Europe' could not easily be portrayed as a source of national pride in Britain, for in many ways it seemed to imply the recognition of a humiliating defeat, the collapse of loftier aspirations, the end of 'greatness' as this concept had been understood until that time.

For many years, British leaders had maintained a stance of relative indifference and aloofness towards the major steps which were initially taken in the process of supranational European unification, the European Coal and Steel Community in 1952 and the Treaty of Rome in 1957. Indeed, to some extent they attempted to frustrate such projects by promoting the alternative of a wider, looser trading unit: the European Free Trade Association. It had been widely assumed that the British Commonwealth, as well as the 'special relationship' with the United States, would be sufficient to maintain British prosperity and prestige, without having to resort to a submersion in the pooling of national sovereignties which the EEC represented. However, events such as the 1956 Suez crisis slowly began to reveal the gradual process one British historian has defined as the fall 'from primacy back to mere ordinariness' (Hill, 1988: 34). By the early 1960s, Britain no longer possessed the great military weight of its past, it had become entirely dependent on the United States for its defensive nuclear capacity, it had lost its previous world-wide dominance, and in fact it was now even beginning to slip in the economic league tables in comparison to the members of the European Common Market (Sanders, 1990: 143–44). Hence, the old we-image of global preeminence increasingly began to lose its plausibility, and the decision to 'join Europe' was in fact a key aspect of Britain's painful adaptation to the new reality of reduced power. When other, more ambitious and prestigious alternatives had failed, British leaders ultimately turned to the EEC as the only option which remained to avoid the possibility of further decline. In the British case, 'Europe' was thus a sort of last straw rather than a widely desired aspiration.

Given this particular context of national we-images and we-feelings, it is not very surprising that when Prime Minister Harold Macmillan timidly announced the decision of his government to open negotiations with the European Common Market on 31 July 1961, he was immediately interrupted by an emotive cry which was yelled from both sides of the Parliament floor: 'Shame!'[7] A member of his own party, Mr Anthony Fell, stood up and called him a 'national disaster' for 'his decision to gamble with British sovereignty'. At the same time, however, Macmillan's announcement was greeted with loud cheers which warmly supported the move towards 'Europe' as a new hope for Britain. In fact, what was essentially inaugurated on that day was a symbolic and emotional battle concerning the fate of 'the nation' and its relationship to 'Europe'. It was a passionate conflict between two rival paradigms of national greatness which to some extent is still going on today: the older we-image which saw British pride as fundamentally linked to the leadership of its Commonwealth and its distinctive global preeminence through the 'special relationship' with the United States, in opposition to a new we-image which aimed to find a new source of power and status through collaboration in the project of European unity.

In the discourse with which Macmillan attempted to legitimate the decision to begin negotiations with the EEC, he emphasised that the best hope for security and prosperity, both for Britain as well as for its Commonwealth, could now only be found through the opportunities offered by the Common Market. During a televised speech to 'the nation' which the Prime Minister delivered as Britain's negotiations with the EEC proceeded, he essentially asked the public to give up the grand ideals of the past and wake up to the new reality of a more humble status:

> Now it's no good pretending. Some people naturally feel like this, that we can go back to the old world, before the war. A lot of people do look backward, but the real test you must bring to this question is are you going to look forward?[8]

At this point in national history, Macmillan assured his countrymen that the best way to maintain British influence was through the European solution: he claimed that the 'great historic reason' why his government had applied to enter the EEC was 'to preserve the power and strength of Britain in the world'. It was thus a direct appeal to the British pride-shame balance: 'Europe' was the right way forward, the most realistic alternative to retain as much national strength as possible, given that the old grandeur of the past had been lost. The Prime Minister was essentially arguing that 'Europe' was now the best Britain could do, even if admittedly it was not everything 'the nation' might have wished.

However, the traditional British we-image could hardly have died down so easily, and in fact was kept fully alive by the harsh, discursive counter-attack pronounced by the Leader of the Opposition,

Hugh Gaitskell. On the day after Macmillan's address, the leader of the Labour Party seized his own opportunity to speak to 'the nation' through a television broadcast, and proclaimed that the Common Market was certainly not the only way for Britain to be 'strong and prosperous'. Indeed, he warned that membership in a European federation would be a devastating blow to everything that Britain had represented since its foundation:

> Let us be clear what it means. We become no more than Texas and California in the United States of Europe. It means the end of a thousand years of history. It means the end of the Commonwealth, for the Commonwealth cannot be just a province of Europe.[9]

Gaitskell declared that the British people felt much stronger ties to countries like Australia, New Zealand, and Canada, with 'our institutions and language', than with the countries of Europe. Furthermore, the British Commonwealth represented the best hope for human welfare as a whole, given its world-wide character, and so it was presented as the most appropriate and honourable source of national pride:

> The Commonwealth is a tremendous force for peace because it embraces so many races and so many continents. Do not think the British people, given the chance to decide as they should be, will in a moment of folly throw away a tremendous heritage of history.

The two main British leaders therefore put forward two radically opposed views: 'Europe' as the best, most realistic hope for the maintenance of Britain's strength, and 'Europe' as an unacceptable, humiliating reduction of Britain's historic role. Nevertheless, it should be noted that they both proclaimed 'the good of the nation' as their fundamental concern, even if this 'good' was defined in very different terms: either 'in Europe' or 'outside Europe'.

This first attempt to enter the Common Market, however, was blocked by Charles de Gaulle, who feared that British entry would reduce France's preeminent position within the EEC and subordinate it to the dictates of the 'Anglo-Saxon' partnership formed by London and Washington. It was not until 1967 that Britain, this time under Prime Minister Harold Wilson, once again knocked on the European door to find a solution to its declining economic situation, as well as a new source of political influence. At the time of the first attempt, Wilson had voiced his opposition to the idea of EEC entry, due to Britain's 'position in the world'.[10] Indeed, after his election victory in 1964, he was still proudly maintaining the traditional we-image with proclamations such as 'we are a world power and a world influence or we are nothing'.[11] Nevertheless, only a few years later his own government also came to the conclusion that Britain had become too weak to 'go it alone', and on 2 May 1967 Wilson announced the decision to re-open negotiations with the EEC in the House of Commons. His discourse during the parliamentary debates which followed this event clearly revealed a conversion to the idea that given Britain's undeniably diminished position, entry into the Common Market now represented the best opportunity for economic advancement, political influence, and moral service.[12] Like Macmillan before him, in his own televised address to 'the nation', Wilson also appealed directly to national we-feelings and made it clear that 'Europe' represented a novel source of British power and status: 'It is the beginning of a new greatness for Britain. I believe this is a great historical turning point'.[13] Nevertheless, such discursive efforts to transform the British we-image into that of a more humble 'European' country once again proved to be futile for the time being, since this second attempt to join the EEC was also blocked by the recalcitrant de Gaulle.

It was ultimately under the leadership of the Conservative Prime Minister Edward Heath that Britain 'entered Europe' in January 1973. Heath firmly believed in the European paradigm of national greatness, the idea that a declining Britain could only be resurrected and strengthened through membership of the EEC. One has only to consider some excerpts from his own ritualised television broadcast to 'the nation' in July 1972, when his government's negotiations with Brussels had been completed. Again, it was a speech full of patriotic invocations and emotive appeals to national pride:

> Why should we go in? As Prime Minister, my answer is that we must go in if we want to remain Great Britain, and have the chance of becoming a Greater Britain . . . Let's look at the facts. Today we don't occupy the place in the world we once did . . . The European Community provides us with our chance. It opens up one of the biggest markets in the world to us. It gives us the opportunity to grow again, to become a greater Britain in a Greater Europe . . . We have the chance of new greatness. Now we must take it.[14]

Once again, the message was that the imperial glory days of the past were over ('we don't occupy the place in the world we once did'), and hence that the best 'the nation' could now do to remain 'great', and perhaps to become even 'greater', was to fuse with other European countries in the pooling of economic power represented by the Common Market.

This use of national symbolism and sentiment to legitimate entry into the EEC was also very evident in the propaganda of organisations such as the British European Movement, which distributed pamphlets across the country featuring the Union Jack with the headline: 'It's time we carried our flag into Europe! It's time Britain woke up, stopped being a looker-on, and grabbed a share of the European gravy!'[15] Meanwhile, however, 'anti-Marketeers' contested such claims and battled back with their own patriotic appeals. For one thing Harold Wilson, now as leader of the opposition, claimed that Heath had not protected the 'national interest' in his negotiations. Although he could hardly reject the principle of 'going into Europe', given that his own government had previously attempted to do so, the Labour Party remained bitterly divided on the whole question of EEC membership and was unwilling to allow Heath an easy triumph on this matter. Wilson, therefore, opposed the terms of entry that the Conservative Government had achieved, for selling 'the nation' short.[16] Meanwhile, organisations such as Keep Britain Out and the Anti Common-Market League staged mock funerals outside Parliament when the EEC entry was being approved, announcing 'the Death of British Democracy' and proclaiming that:

> It is therefore now the duty of every patriotic citizen—everyone who wants to save this country from the national decline inevitable if we are driven into the EEC—to resist the Government's proposed legislation by all means in our power.[17]

One can see, therefore, the way in which national we-images and we-feelings were the fundamental weapons that were employed in the British political arena to either legitimate or de-legitimate the idea of 'going into Europe'. It was a discursive conflict between 'Europe as national salvation' versus 'Europe as national disaster', which flared up at the time of the adhesion and to some extent has never fully died down. According to the historian Kenneth O. Morgan, in spite of Edward Heath's patriotic invocations, Britain's entry into the EEC was 'coloured by fateful resignation rather than passionate enthusiasm' (1990: 317). In fact, a spokesman of Heath's government recognised that, as the evidence of opinion polls repeatedly demonstrated, the EEC remained an unpopular policy, in spite of all the propagandistic efforts to link the concept of 'national greatness' to membership of Europe: 'It is like going to the dentist: the country knows we've got to join, but it doesn't want to go'.[18]

On 6 June 1975, under the renewed leadership of Harold Wilson, the issue of EEC membership was put forward to the British public in the first referendum of the country's history, after the government had re-negotiated new terms which were now claimed fully to protect the 'national interest' (Butler and Kitzinger, 1976). The conflict of paradigms continued, with leaders on each side of the debate appealing to the national pride-shame balance, either in favour or against membership of the Common Market, as the following examples can illustrate:

> One of the sadder aspects of the campaign is the way that the anti-Marketeers are talking Britain down. They tell us that the British people are too weak to hold their own in the European Community . . . I reject totally that kind of defeatist talk. (Edward Heath, 12 May 1975)

> What the advocates of membership are saying, insistently and insidiously, is that we are finished as a country, that the long and famous story of the British nation and people has ended. (Peter Shore, 27 May 1975)[19]

In the end, the cross-party alliance on the 'European' side of respected figures such as Heath, Roy Jenkins and Jeremy Thorpe, as well as the Prime Minister, the Conservative leader of the opposition, Margaret Thatcher, and most of the media, ensured a 2–1 'Yes-vote' in favour of remaining 'in Europe'. Membership of the Common Market was thus successfully sold to the public as the most sensible option for the protection of British interests at that stage. When the results were announced, Prime Minister Wilson proclaimed that 'fourteen years of national argument' were finally over.[20]

Nevertheless, as is well known, Britain's relations with the European enterprise have continued to reflect tension, hesitancy, reluctance, and even outright hostility. Britain has been labelled 'the awkward partner' (George, 1990) or the 'semi-detached member' (Bulmer, 1992) of the EC/EU, and European issues have remained highly contested both between as well as within parties. Particularly during the Thatcher era, any further moves towards the loss of sovereignty to 'Brussels bureaucracy' were strongly resisted, and the 'special relationship' with America was promoted as a greater source of national pride. It seems as if in Britain, membership of 'Europe' has continued to be more a source of status-anxiety than of status-security, especially as the supranationalism of the project has gathered strength. Popular newspapers such as *The Sun* famously campaigned in 1991 against the federalist vision of the President of the European Commission, Jacques Delors, with their 'Up Yours, Delors' headlines.[21] Others, like the *Daily Express* asked their readers in 1996 to fly 'an alternative flag' on Europe Day, as 'your chance to make a patriotic protest against Euro-rot'.[22] This 'alternative flag' depicted Saint George on horseback, ripping through the twelve-starred European flag and uncovering a Union Jack in the background.

I am not suggesting that such extreme representations of British 'Euro-phobia' reflect the views of the majority. In fact, the popularity of Tony Blair, who has shown a more sympathetic attitude towards the EU than his Conservative predecessors, suggests that 'Europe' is becoming more attractive. My point is simply that in Britain it has been relatively difficult for leaders to promote the European cause and to transform it into a source of national pride. The symbolic association of 'Europe' with the dwindling of British power and prestige, or from world-wide responsibilities to what one author has termed 'a falling back into European parochialism' (Hill, 1988: 29), have always made this an extremely complicated task. In short, it has been very difficult to overcome the idea that for Britain, 'going into Europe' represented a shift downwards from the world's first division to a rather inferior league, and hence that limiting national aspirations through submersion in a European superstate would be an intolerable reduction of British potential.

Spain: 'Europe' as a symbol of enhanced prestige and a potent source of national pride

The case of Spain presents a fascinating contrast to that of Britain, since in this country 'Europe' became the symbol of a great collective aspiration, a widespread hope for national resurgence and improvement. By the time the Spanish state became a member of the EEC in 1986, the idea of 'entering Europe' was widely viewed as a necessary achievement for the full recovery of national self-esteem, after the downfall of an authoritarian regime and the successful transition to a 'modern' and 'democratic' status. Hence, in comparison to Britain, this decision was much more easily transformed by political leaders into an unquestioned potent source of national pride.

When the project of European integration began to take shape after the Allied victory in the Second World War, the Spanish state remained in the hands of a man who had risen to power with the support of Hitler and Mussolini.[23] The incompatibility between the ideals of European unity and the principles defended by Francisco Franco's regime are evident when one considers that *el Generalísimo* himself originally defined his military uprising in 1936 as a 'national crusade' to protect the 'essential' Catholic values of *la patria* from what he called the 'bastardized, Frenchified, Europeanizing' doctrines of modern liberalism (Franco, 1975: 116). The paradigm of national greatness which Franco defended was essentially that of *la España imperial*, the imperial Spain of the Catholic Kings, of Charles V and of Philip II, the Spain of global prestige whose mission was 'to defend and extend all over the world a universal and Catholic idea, a Christian Empire' (Franco, 1975: 116). Throughout his dictatorship, any mention of democratic pluralism was derided in official discourse as a dangerous conspiracy of 'reds' and 'freemasons'. In opposition to what he labelled the 'inorganic democracy' of other European countries, Franco promoted 'organic democracy', a 'natural order' based on traditional 'Spanish institutions' such as the Church and the family.

Hence, in spite of the Franco regime's numerous efforts to gain acceptance in the EEC, Spain could hardly be allowed to 'enter Europe' as long as *el Generalísimo* held the reins of power. For this very reason, however, as the legitimacy of his dictatorship eroded over the years, 'Europeanization' increasingly became a fundamental component of the national we-image defended and promoted by all those Spaniards who opposed the regime and demanded political change. From their perspective, Spain desperately needed to overcome its shameful *atraso*, or 'backwardness', and to recover respectability in the world through a process of modernisation and democratisation. The idea of 'going into Europe' was thus seen as the ultimate culmination of this national ambition.

In Spain, the symbolic identification of 'Europe' with modernity can be traced back to the intellectual and political debates which were stirred up after the so-called 'disaster' of 1898.[24] This was the year in which Spain lost Cuba, the Philippines, and Puerto Rico, the last remnants of its once-great Empire, after a short war with the United States. Such a humiliating loss of imperial status, at a time 'when the possession of colonies was seen as the hallmark of a vigorous nation' (Balfour, 1996: 107), provoked an outpouring of books on the nation's shameful downfall, the loss of its historic greatness, and hence the disappearance of its prestige in the world. Numerous writers attempted to explore the roots of Spanish decadence, and many of them claimed that the nation's problems could only be remedied through a gradual process of 'Europeanisation'. Indeed, already at this time, the idea of 'becoming European' had become synonymous in Spanish reformist circles with all the policies which were deemed to be vital for national salvation: industrialisation, secularisation, educational improvement, and scientific advance.

The most famous and influential exponent of this idea was undoubtedly José Ortega y Gasset, for whom it was clear that 'European regeneration' was the only possible solution for the Spanish predicament. As he put it in a public lecture delivered in Bilbao in 1910:

> To feel the ills of Spain is to desire to be European . . .
> Regeneration is inseparable from Europeanization; for this
> reason, from the moment in which the reconstructive emotion
> was felt—the anguish, the shame and the desire—the idea of
> Europeanization was conceived. Regeneration is the desire;
> Europeanization is the means to satisfy it. It was clearly seen
> from the beginning that Spain was the problem and Europe the
> solution. (1989: 18–19)

Ortega was convinced that his country was in danger of dissolution and chaos, that it has become an 'invertebrate' nation, and that only a new enlightened élite with a fully modern or 'European' mentality could save it from self-destruction.

However, in the rival discourse promoted by Spanish conservatives during the same period, such 'Europeanisers' were frequently stigmatised as enemies of *la patria*. For the defenders of Spanish tradition, national greatness was essentially founded on the maintenance of conventional social hierarchies and Catholic values. Hence, from this perspective, the project of 'European' modernisation was defined as fundamentally 'alien' or 'anti-Spanish':

> The 'real' Spain was defended by reactionaries as an immutable
> social hierarchy dominated by the traditional triumvirate of

crown, church, and aristocracy. Any attempt to challenge the socio-economic status quo could be condemned as the sinister manoeuverings of national apostates and foreign agents: 'Europeanizers'. (Preston and Smyth, 1984: 26)

During the constant polarised conflicts between conservatives and liberal reformists which characterised Spanish political life right up to Franco's 1936 revolt against the Second Republic, the contest of national paradigms defended by political leaders was thus largely one between the maintenance of traditional 'Hispanic' values versus the project of 'European' modernisation (Pollack and Hunter, 1987: 129).

It would be inaccurate, however, to define Francoist discourse as 'anti-European'. In fact, what one can observe is that a particular symbolic representation of the 'true Europe' was developed in order to coincide with Franco's conception of the 'true Spain'. Essentially, the crusade of 'national Catholicism' represented by his forces was placed within the larger context of a continental struggle for the preservation of 'Europe's Christian civilisation', threatened by the 'evil forces' of liberalism and communism. As in earlier centuries, when Spain had been entrusted with the salvation of Europe from Moorish invaders, it would now proudly continue this role against new infidels. Franco explained his position as follows, in a speech delivered during the Civil War in Burgos:

> This is a conflict for the defense of Europe, and, once again, Spaniards have been entrusted with the glory of carrying at the point of their bayonets the defense of civilization, the mainte-nance of a Christian culture, the maintenance of a Catholic faith. (Franco, 1975: 49)

When the forces of *el Generalísimo* emerged victorious in 1939, Francoist discourse divided Spanish society into two camps: the *vencedores* (victors), who represented the 'true' Spain, and the *venci-dos* (vanquished), who represented 'anti-Spain'. The very survival of 'the nation' was thus symbolically identified with the maintenance of the regime, while all of its opponents, including those classified as liberal 'Europeanisers', atheists, and Communists, as well as periph-eral Basque and Catalan nationalists, were classified as 'traitors'. Until the final years of his dictatorship, during which all media institutions of symbolic power were controlled by the Francoist state, only this vision of the 'Spanish nation' and its foreign-inspired 'enemies' could be officially promoted in the public sphere.

Although Spain remained formally neutral throughout the Second World War, Franco did not conceal his moral identification with the kind of 'European order' envisioned by Hitler and Mussolini, and provided logistical support to their cause. There were many occasions during the course of this conflict in which 'Europe' was invoked as a way of identifying the Francoist national project with the ambitions of the Axis powers. For instance, on 17 July 1941, the fifth anniversary of the outbreak of the Spanish Civil War, Franco delivered a public address in which he presented the World War as an interrupted sequence of Axis triumphs, and spoke of:

> these moments when the German armies lead the battle for which Europe and Christianity have for so many years longed, and in which the blood of our youth is to mingle with that of our comrades of the Axis as a living expression of our solidarity. (Cited in Preston, 1993: 441)

In fact, it seems clear that until the victory of the Allies became increasingly obvious in 1944, Franco attempted to flatter the we-image of Spaniards by presenting himself as the leader who would wipe out the shame of 1898 and guide them to a new age of imperial splendour in which 'the nation' would finally recuperate its lost prestige in the world, through a powerful partnership with Hitler's Germany and Mussolini's Italy.

The Allied victory, however, radically altered Franco's plans of renewed glory for the Spanish *patria*. Instead, his regime's collaboration with the defeated totalitarian powers led to a harsh period of international ostracism and economic penury. Spain was excluded from the United Nations, as well as from the Marshall Plan for post-war recovery. Nevertheless, after this difficult period, the Franco regime ultimately found a renewed source of wealth, prestige, and moral legitimacy through a Cold War alliance with the United States in 1953. In return for allowing the establishment of US military bases on its territory, Spain would receive over one billion dollars of aid over a period of eight years. Two years later, Spain was admitted into the United Nations, diplomatic relations were re-established with most Western countries, and hence the days of total international isolation were over. The regime's propaganda now constructed a we-image of Spain as 'the sentinel of Occident', an honourable partner in the Western family's struggle against Soviet Communism. Furthermore, its disastrous traditional policies of economic autarky were abandoned, and a successful, full-scale programme of capitalist development was implemented. Until the end of his life-long rule in 1975, Francoist propaganda therefore claimed that *el Generalísimo* had saved 'the nation' from economic ruin and transformed it into an advanced, prosperous society.

The regime, however, was much less fortunate with regard to the project of European integration. While Uncle Sam warmly embraced Franco, 'Europe' always gave him the cold shoulder. Hence, in this sphere of the international stage, Spain remained a humiliated outsider throughout his dictatorship. Although in 1962, the Francoist state officially requested entry into the EEC, 'entry into Europe' could hardly be allowed to an old ally of Hitler and Mussolini, for in many ways his regime stood for everything the 'new Europe' had been constructed against. The official Francoist propaganda claimed that Spain had a 'European vocation', that it wanted to participate in the great collective project of the Common Market, but nevertheless it continued to classify the liberal politics of other European countries as 'dangerous' and 'inferior'.[25] Nevertheless, in opposition to this official 'European vocation' which the regime tried to promote, all those Spaniards who rejected Francoism began to unify under the symbolic banner of a very different 'Europeanism' which stood for the political modernisation and democratisation of their country. In fact, one of the most notable gestures of anti-regime protest which occurred during the Franco dictatorship took place in Munich during the IV Congress of the European Movement in 1962, when Spaniards of many political tendencies demanded that the EEC should reject the Francoist request to enter the Common Market, unless a full-scale programme of democratic reform was implemented in their country (Tusell, 1977). Not surprisingly, the official regime media branded all those Spaniards who had participated in the Munich reunion as 'filthy conspirators' who had stabbed *la patria* in the back.[26] Egged on by the official propaganda, thousands of people gathered to demonstrate in many Spanish cities to denounce these 'traitors', and Franco delivered several addresses to publicly condemn their 'betrayal of the nation'. At that time, it seems undeniable that the Francoist manipulation of national we-images and we-feelings was still very effective.

Over the course of time, however, the legitimacy of Francoist 'patriotism' began to dwindle, while the rival paradigm of a modern, democratic, and hence 'European' Spain slowly gained the upper hand. By the 1970s, Spain had been transformed into an industrialised, mobile, better educated society by Franco's own regime. At this point, students, intellectuals, workers, Basque and Catalan nationalists, and even many representatives of the Catholic Church were publicly rejecting the official discourse of the regime. A new we-image was increasingly spreading, which sought the recovery of collective pride through the achievement of the kind of 'freedom' and 'liberty' enjoyed by 'the rest of Europe'. Although the regime had repeatedly made the promise that it would satisfy the country's 'European vocation', the most it ever accomplished was a commercial trade agreement with the EEC in 1970. Full membership, however, always remained out of the question. Hence, by the time Franco died in 1975, it had become obvious, even amongst many élites within the authoritarian power structure, that if Spain truly wanted to become 'European', political democratisation would be a necessary condition for this ideal to become a reality. Francoism was increasingly seen by broader and broader sectors of the population as something which was still keeping Spain at the shameful levels of so-called 'Africanism'. From this perspective, it was thus only through a complete 'Europeanisation' of the country that national self-esteem could be regained.

In the Spanish case, therefore, a very different historical and socio-psychological background to that of Britain ultimately identified 'going into Europe' with a major promotion of national prestige, a shift upwards in the international hierarchy of power and status. In the aftermath of Franco's death, a new élite of political leaders promoted the vision of a Spain which aspired to 'freedom', 'modernity', and 'democracy', ideals which were all identified with the desire to achieve a 'civilised' and 'European' status. King Juan Carlos I, initially stigmatised amongst all the forces of the opposition for being Franco's appointed successor, clearly positioned himself on the side of 'European' democratisation, and therefore managed to legitimate his rule amongst a population that was now overwhelmingly demanding political change. There is no space here to analyse the delicate process through which the Spanish political system was transformed relatively quickly from Franco's authoritarian 'national-Catholic' regime to a liberal pluralist democracy, but the important point one should make is that leading figures of the transition such as the first democratically elected prime minister, the centrist Adolfo Suárez, continuously identified modernisation and democratisation with the idealised concept of 'becoming European'.[27] Indeed, the aspiration to become a full member of the EEC was one of the fundamental issues on which there was a broad consensus in Spain amongst the political forces which made the negotiated transition to democracy possible. As Morán has put it:

> At the time of the transition from dictatorship to democracy, [Spain's Europeanism] attained almost a metapolitical worth and constituted one of the facts on which the unanimity which permitted change was established. (1980: 289)

'Europe', in the collective consciousness of Spaniards, was thus never only a question of economic benefit, but furthermore a necessary condition for the recovery of moral self-respect after many years of international opprobrium.

One of the best ways to illustrate the proud. 'Europeanised' we-image which was constructed in post-Franco Spain is by briefly considering the spectacular signature ritual which was organised in Madrid to formalise the country's accession to the EEC. The official entry of Spain into the Common Market did not take place until 1 January 1986, after a prolonged period of complex negotiations, but the signing of the treaty of adhesion on 12 June 1985 was transformed into a major 'national event' by the socialist government of Felipe González.[28] The ceremony, which took place at the Royal Palace of Madrid, was attended by King Juan Carlos and his entire cabinet, the President of the European Commission, Jacques Delors and other EEC authorities, the leaders of all political parties, the heads of Spain's regional governments, bankers, businessmen, trade union leaders, artists, writers, sportsmen, and many other national personalities. The mayor of Madrid, Tierno Galván, published a special proclamation on that day in which he called Europe 'the Reason of the universe that guides the rest of the world's peoples with the light of intelligence and the health of its sentiments'.[29] After declaring that on this day 'we are more European than we have ever been', he asked his fellow citizens to show the world their exuberant happiness on such a joyous occasion. The enormous importance which Spanish authorities gave to the event was further illustrated by the fact that the main public television channel broadcast the entire ritual live from the grand hall of the Royal Palace. In this way, the entire country was invited to participate in this civil liturgy of national self-veneration.

The main highlights of the ritual were speeches delivered by the King and Prime Minister González, in which 'Europe' was depicted as the culmination of Spain's triumphant passage to modernity and democracy. Juan Carlos I, for instance, welcomed Europe's dignitaries as follows:

Spain is proud to receive the most illustrious dignitaries of the
European Communities and the nations which integrate them.
You represent what the Spanish people understand by Europe:
the principles of liberty, equality, pluralism, and justice, which
also preside over the Spanish Constitution. The Spanish people
welcome you with satisfaction, and conscious of the great
significance which this event implies.[30]

González, similarly, called the event an 'historic occasion' for Spain,
a country which identified entry into the EEC 'with participation in
the ideals of liberty, progress, and democracy' and with 'the challenge of modernity'.[31] The symbolism of Spanish political discourse
on 'Europe' therefore reached its ultimate climax: 'the nation' had
finally become 'European' through a democratic transformation
and a passionate desire to be 'modern'. In this way, the project of
European unification was equated with all the ideals that represented major sources of pride for a country that until very recently
had suffered the painful stigma of 'backwardness'.

I do not wish to suggest that there has been an absolute unanimity in Spain with this sort of discourse. For one thing, the whole
concept of 'the Spanish nation' remains a highly contested one, and
the leaders of nationalist parties in the Basque Country, Catalonia,
and Galicia promote we-images and we-feelings for their own
regional communities as separate 'nations in Europe'. Nevertheless,
my fundamental point is that on the whole, the dominant paradigm
of *Spanish* national greatness has incorporated the concept of
'belonging to Europe' with much greater ease than in Britain, since
it has essentially symbolised the quasi-mythical success of *la transi-
ción* to democracy. It has therefore been seen as a major improvement in the nation's global ranking not only in terms of political
power and economic advance, but also in terms of ethical
respectability. The European flag is indeed much more conspicuous
in Spain than in Britain, since for the most part it remains an
uncontested prestige-symbol, and it is even used by advertisers to
promote their products.[32] Hence, in the case of the Spanish collective psyche, one could say that on the whole, adopting a European
supranationality and showing enthusiasm for the project of
European integration has hardly clashed with national sentiments.
On the contrary, 'entering Europe' was exactly what the national
self had been thirsting for.

Conclusion: 'Europe' as a disputed, emotionally charged symbol in the political arena of each member state

I began this chapter by citing Ernest Renan's prophetic claims about a future Europe in which nations would ultimately be replaced by a continental confederation, a hope shared by many contemporary 'Europeanists'. The cases of Britain and Spain, however, clearly illustrate that the undeniable progress which has been made towards the goal of European unification has in no way transcended, eroded, or replaced the ideals and sentiments of nationhood. On the contrary, national we-images and we-feelings can in fact be seen as the fundamental factors which have conditioned the development of different discourses and collective representations of 'Europe' in these states. In each country, the idea of 'going into Europe' has been legitimated more or less successfully by the appeals of political élites to national interests, memories, aspirations, and pride-shame balances. One could therefore say that the fundamental issue in the discursive battles which have taken place within the context of each nationally-bounded, media-transmitted political arena has always been: What does 'Europe' mean for 'us' (the national 'we')? What does 'becoming European' represent for 'our' interests, 'our' reputation, 'our' honour, 'our' self-respect?

The contrast between Britain and Spain makes this particular clear, because it illustrates how national sentiments can produce two very different outcomes: a largely lukewarm, reluctant, insecure attitude to 'Europe' in Britain, and a generally enthusiastic, eager, self-confident 'Europeanism' in the Spanish case. In both countries, the invocation of national interests and the appeal to national feelings was similarly performed in order to sell the European idea, but while in the British case this process turned out to be a highly contested, difficult, unresolved struggle which met much resistance, in Spain the whole idea was accepted with greater east. As I have argued, this can be linked to the fact that while for Britain the European road represented a loss of rank in the world's hierarchic pyramid of power and status, for Spain it was exactly the opposite. Hence, 'Europe' was quickly transformed into a potent source of pride or 'group charisma' amongst Spaniards, in a way which one could hardly have expected in Britain.

What this means, however, is that although national sentiments are often seen as barriers which can only stand in the way of European unification, this is not necessarily the case. In many ways it may be true that the ideals and sentiments of nationhood act like a 'drag effect' which blocks the development of European integration (Elias, 1991a: 213). For instance, in all countries, the cognitive and affective dispositions of national habitus can still make it very difficult for people to accept the authority of power-holders or decision-makers who are not of their own country. Nevertheless, national sentiments should not be classified *a priori* as obstacles in the process of European integration, for to a considerable extent they have also played a key role in the acceptance of EC/EU membership among populations. Instead, sociologists should investigate the more or less harmonious interplay between national sentiments and the concept of 'belonging to Europe' which has developed (and is developing) in each country.

In conclusion, although it may be true that 'the old nations still live in the hearts of men', as Raymond Aron asserted in the quotation cited earlier, this does not necessarily mean that 'a love for the European nation' is inconceivable or impossible. 'Nationalism' is clearly incompatible with European unity, if this concept refers solely to the channelling of national sentiments towards the cause of aggression and domination over others. The collective self-esteem of nations, however, can also be identified with the successful achievement of other, less destructive objectives. It may be possible to make national sentiments compatible both with European unity, as well as with what Durkheim called 'world patriotism' (1992: 75), if peaceful co-existence, solidarity, and respect for other peoples is successfully transformed into a fundamental source of national pride, while the violation of these principles becomes a potent source of national shame.

Acknowledgements

This chapter is based on my work as a doctoral researcher at the European University Institute in Florence. I would thus like to thank both the EUI and the Spanish Ministry of Foreign Affairs for their financial support, as well as my supervisors, Christian Joppke, Gianfranco Poggi, and Arpad Szakolczai.

Notes

1 The symbolic construction of a European identity is explored in Shore and Black (1994).
2 On the concept of habitus, see, for instance, Elias (1991a: 182–3).

3 On the concepts of psychogenesis, and sociogenesis, see Elias (1994b [1939]) Nationalist movements generally grew out of dominant ethnic communities, as Llobera (1994) has illustrated, and so inevitably many minority languages and cultures were repressed or obliterated during the processes of state-building. Of course, the effectiveness of a state's identity-construction as the legitimate representative of a particular 'nation' has been more successful in some territories than in others, as the contemporary struggles in areas such as Scotland, Wales, the Basque Country, or Catalonia illustrate.

4 This point has been explored by Bloom (1990). Bourdieu (1991: 105) has also referred to 'nations' as one example of the symbolic 'struggle over classifications' which characterise the discursive power contests of the modern world.

5 The concept of competing paradigms in political arenas was proposed by Turner (1974).

6 *The Times*, 20 September 1946.

7 On this event, see *The Times* and *The Guardian*, 1 August 1961.

8 *The Times*, 21 September 1962.

9 *The Times*, 22 September 1962.

10 Cited in Kitzinger (1968: 11).

11 Cited in Robbins (1994: 272).

12 *The Times*, 9 May 1967.

13 *Daily Mirror*, 9 May 1967.

14 *The Times*, 9 July 1971.

15 Cited in Kitzinger (1973: 222).

16 See, for instance, Wilson's televised address, published in *The Times* on 10 July 1971.

17 Cited in Kitzinger (1973: 239, 247).

18 Cited in Spanier (1972: 175).

19 Both excerpts are cited in Butler and Kitzinger (1976: 183).

20 *The Times*, 7 June 1975.

21 *The Sun*, 1 November 1990.

22 *Daily Express*, 3 May 1996.

23 On Franco and Francoism, see Carr and Fusi (1981), Payne (1987), Preston (1993).

24 This has been explored by Torregrosa (1996).

25 See, for instance, the address on 27 May 1962 cited in La Porte (1992: 396).

26 See, for instance, *ABC* and *Arriba*, 9 June 1962.

27 On the transition, see Carr and Fusi (1981) and Preston (1986). On the EEC as an aspiration during this period, see Preston and Smyth (1984).

28 See, for instance, the widespread media coverage of this event in *El País*, *ABC*, *Diario-16*, 13 June 1985.

29 Cited in *Diario-16*, 13 June 1985.

30 Cited in *El País*, 13 June 1985.

31 Cited in *El País*, 13 June 1985.

32 For instance, the Spanish savings bank Caja de Madrid published a two-page newspaper advertisement displaying the European flag, alongside its own company logo, with the slogan: 'The project of a unified Europe compels us to work harder every day for our customers' (*El Mundo*, 26/12/96).

Bibliography

Allen, D. (1988), 'Britain and Western Europe', in M. Smith, S. Smith, and B. White (eds), *British Foreign Policy: Tradition, Change, and Transformation*, London: Unwin Hyman.

Anderson, B. (1983), *Imagined Communities*, London: Verso.

Aron, R. (1964), 'Old Nations, New Europe', in S. R. Graubard (ed.), *A New Europe?* Boston: Houghton Mifflin.

Balfour, S. (1996), '"The Lion and the Pig": Nationalism and National Identity in Fin-de-Siècle Spain', in C. Mar-Molinero and A. Smith (eds), *Nationalism and the Nation in the Iberian Peninsula: Competing and Conflicting Identities*, Oxford: Berg.

Billig, M. (1995), *Banal Nationalism*, London: Sage.

Blackwell, M. (1993), *Clinging to Grandeur. British Attitudes and Foreign Policy in the Aftermath of the Second World War*, London: Greenwood Press.

Bloom, W. (1990), *Personal Identity, National Identity, and International Relations*, Cambridge: Cambridge University Press.

Bourdieu, P. (1991), *Language and Symbolic Power*, Cambridge: Polity Press.

Bulmer, S. (1992), 'Britain and European Integration: Of Sovereignty, Slow Adaptation, and Semi-Detachment', in S. George (ed.), *Britain and the European Community: The Politics of Semi-Detachment*, Oxford: Oxford University Press.

Butler, D. and U. Kitzinger (1976), *The 1975 Referendum*, London: Macmillan.

Butt Philip, A. (1992), 'Westminster versus Brussels—the Last Crusade?' in M. Maclean and J. Hoyworth (eds), *Europeans on Europe*, New York: St Martin's Press.

Calhoun, C. (1994), 'Nationalism and Civil Society: Democracy, Diversity, and Self-determination', in C. Calhoun (ed.), *Social Theory and the Politics of Identity*, Oxford: Blackwell.

Carr, R. and J. P. Fusi. (1981), *Spain: Dictatorship to Democracy*, 2nd edn, London: George Allen & Unwin.

Churchill, W. (1956), *A History of the English-Speaking Peoples. Vol. I: The Birth of Britain*, London: Cassel & Company.

Cohen, A. (1979), 'Political Symbolism', *Annual Review of Anthropology*, 8, 87–113.

Cooley, C. (1922), *Human Nature and the Social Order*, New York: Scribner's.

Davies, N. (1996), *Europe: A History*, Oxford University Press.

De Swaan, A. (1995), 'Widening Circles of Identification: Emotional Concerns in Sociogenetic Perspective', *Theory, Culture and Society*, 12, 25–39.

Durkheim, E. (1976 [1915]), *The Elementary Forms of the Religious Life*, London: George Allen & Unwin.

Durkheim, E. (1992), *Professional Ethics and Civil Morals*, London: Routledge.

Elias, N. (1970), 'Processes of State-formation and Nation-building', *Transactions of the World Congress of Sociology*, 3 (3), 274–284.

Elias, N. (1987a), *Involvement and Detachment*, Oxford: Basil Blackwell.

Elias, N. (1987b), 'The Retreat of Sociologists into the Present', *Theory, Culture and Society*, 4, 339–61.

Elias, N. (1991a), *The Society of Individuals*, Oxford: Basil Blackwell.

Elias, N. (1991b), *The Symbol Theory*, London: Sage.

Elias, N. (1994a), 'Introduction: A Theoretical Essay on Established and Outsider Relations', in N. Elias and J. Scotson, *The Established and the Outsiders*, London: Sage.

Elias, N. (1994b [1939]), *The Civilizing Process*, Oxford: Blackwell.

Elias, N. (1996), *The Germans*, Cambridge: Polity Press.

Elias, N. and J. Scotson (1994), *The Established and the Outsiders*, London: Sage.

Franco, F. (1975), *El Pensamento Político de Franco*, Madrid: Ediciones del Movimiento.

Gellner, E. (1983), *Nations and Nationalism*, Oxford: Blackwell.

George, S. (1990), *An Awkward Partner: Britain in the European Community*, Oxford: Oxford University Press.

Gladwyn, L. (1967), *The European Idea*, London: New English Library Mentor.

Goffman, E. (1967), *Interaction Ritual*, New York: Anchor.

Haseler, S. (1996), *The English Tribe: Identity, Nation, and Europe*, London: Macmillan.

Hill, C. (1988), 'The Historical Background: Past and Present in British Foreign Policy', in M. Smith, S. Smith, and B. White (eds), *British Foreign Policy: Tradition, Change, and Transformation*, London: Unwin Hyman.

Kitzinger, U. (1968), *The Second Try: Labour and the EEC*, Oxford: Pergamon Press.

Kitzinger, U. (1973), *Diplomacy and Persuasion: How Britain Joined the Common Market*, London: Thames & Hudson.

La Porte, M. T. (1992), *La Política Europea del Régimen de Franco, 1957–62*, Pamplona: Ediciones Universidad de Navarra.

Llobera, J. R. (1994), *The God of Modernity. The Development of Nationalism in Western Europe*, Oxford: Berg.

Mennell, S. (1994), 'The Formation of We-Images: A Process Theory', in C. Calhoun (ed.), *Social Theory and the Politics of Identity*, Oxford: Blackwell, 175–97.

Morán, F. (1980), *Una Política Exterior Para España*, Barcelona: Planeta.

Morgan, K. O. (1990), *The People's Peace: British History, 1945–89*, Oxford: Oxford University Press.

Ortega y Gasset, J. (1989), *Ensayos Sobre la Generación del 98*, Madrid: Revista de Occidente en Alianza Editorial.

Papcke, S. (1992), 'Who needs European identity and what could it be?' in B. Nelson, D. Roberts, and W. Veit (eds), *The Idea of Europe: Problems of National and Transnational Identity*, Oxford: Berg.

Payne, S. (1987), *The Franco Regime: 1936–75*, Madison: The University of Wisconsin Press.

Pollack, B. and G. Hunter. (1987), *The Paradox of Spanish Foreign Policy: Spain's International Relations from Franco to Democracy*, London: Pinter Publishers.

Preston, P. (1986), *The Triumph of Democracy in Spain*, London: Methuen.

Preston, P. (1993), *Franco: A Biography*, London: HarperCollins.

Preston, P. and D. Smyth (1984), *Spain, the EEC, and NATO*, London: Routledge and Kegan Paul.

Radice, G. (1992), *Offshore: Britain and the European Idea*, London: I. B. Tauris & Co.

Renan, E. (1996), 'What is a Nation?' in S. Woolf (ed.), *Nationalism in Europe, 1815 to the Present*, London: Routledge, 48–60.

Robbins, K. (1994), *The Eclipse of a Great Power. Modern Britain 1870–1992*, London: Longman.

Ruane, J. (1994), 'Nationalism and European Community Integration: The Republic of Ireland', in V. Goddard, J. Llobera, and C. Shore (eds), *The Anthropology of Europe*, Oxford: Berg, 125–41.

Sanders, D. (1990), *Losing an Empire, Finding a Role: British Foreign Policy Since 1945*, London: Macmillan.

Seton-Watson, H. (1985), 'What is Europe, Where is Europe? From Mystique to Politique', *Encounter*, July–August 1985, LXV (2), 9–17.

Scheff, T. (1990), *Microsociology. Discourse, Emotion, and Social Structure*, Chicago: University of Chicago Press.

Scheff, T. (1994a), 'Emotions and Identity: A Theory of Ethnic Nationalism', in C. Calhoun (ed.), *Social Theory and the Politics of Identity*, Oxford: Blackwell, 277–303.

Scheff, T. (1994b), *Bloody Revenge: Emotions, Nationalism, and War*, Boulder: Westview.

Shore, C. and A. Black (1994), 'Citizens' Europe and the Construction of European Identity', in V. Goddard, J. Llobera, and C. Shore (eds), *The Anthropology of Europe*, Oxford: Berg, 275–98.

Spanier, D. (1972), *Europe, Our Europe*, London: Secker & Warburg.

Torregrosa, J. R. (1996), 'Spanish International Orientations: Between Europe and Iberoamerica', in G. Breakwell and E. Lyons (eds), *Changing European Identities: Social Psychological Analyses of Social Change*, Oxford: Butterworth Heinemann.

Touraine, A. (1994), 'European countries in a post-national era', in C. Rootes and H. Davis (eds), *A New Europe? Social Change and Political Transformation*, London: UCL Press.

Turner, V. (1974), *Dramas, Fields, and Metaphors. Symbolic Action in Human Society*, Ithaca and London: Cornell University Press.

Tusell, X. (1977), *La Oposición Democrática al Franquismo*, Barcelona: Planeta.

Wallace, W. (1990), *The Transformation of Western Europe*, London: Royal Institute of International Affairs.

Wallace, W. (1991), 'Foreign Policy and National Identity in the United Kingdom', *International Affairs*, 67 (1), 65–80.

Democracy in Eastern Europe as a civilising process

Harald Wydra

Abstract

In this chapter, Harald Wydra argues that the rise of democracy in Eastern Europe has been a long-term social process interwoven with the collapse of communism whose origins are long before 1989. He challenges the vision of East and West as two isolated blocs that prevailed in the 1950s and the assumption of gradual convergence that became widespread in the 1970s and 1980s. His main focus is upon the East where, he believes, dissident movements created a 'second reality', undermining the myths propounded by the official communist establishment. He argues that there was an increase in self-restraint on the part of the communist state accompanied by the growth of civil society and non-violent political opposition. The East experienced a feeling of 'unrequited love' in its relationship to the West. Dissidents took their standards and aspirations from Western experience but found themselves largely ignored by the West. Since 1989, democratisation has increased the influence of western models and standards but it has also led to a breakdown of self-restraint and an upsurge of violence.

Introduction

The recent rise of democracy in Eastern Europe[1] is arguably the most important process of political and social change in Europe since World War II. In an astonishingly short time-span, most of the old Eastern bloc countries have introduced democratic governments with political pluralism, division of powers, the rule of law, and free mass media. Politicians, scholars and public wisdom very rapidly concluded that the regime changes in Eastern Europe added up, in a straightforward way, to a peaceful transition to democracy. Unlike other revolutions or regime changes, vindictive violence was virtually absent from the collapse of Communism. In a few years democracy in Eastern Europe was transformed from a cherished illusion to an apparent fact, guaranteeing peace not only within the region but also *vis-à-vis* the West.

An optimistic view of the future has been produced by the surprisingly peaceful character of the end of Communism and by the supposed benefits of democracy. In those cases where investigators look to the past, taking historical differences or path-dependence effects[2] into account, these factors are only examined with reference to how a country's type of non-democratic regime have affected its current prospects for democratic consolidation (Linz and Stepan, 1996). In the meantime, scholars have moved on from their previous concern with the weakness of the trend away from autocracy in the East. They are adjusting to a new situation, one apparently characterised by 'consolidated democracy', a condition that now seems prosaic, routine and over-determined.[3] Democracy is being treated as the expected end-point of a normal historical sequence. This goes along with a *tabula rasa* conception of democracy, which is treated as if it was created from scratch after the demise of Communism. Following the Cold War with its ideological and political standoff, democracy's advent has been seen as an élite-based, actor-driven and largely spontaneous process of institutional change occurring entirely post-1989.

The literature mainly deals with the institutional design of democracies.[4] The conceptual focus is on changes in the state apparatus following the transition to a democratic government (Schmitter and Karl, 1994; Linz and Stepan, 1996: 15; Elster *et al.*, 1998). Democratisation is seen as a regime change involving transformation of the institutional and constitutional pillars in these countries. Part of the literature also examines the vacuum of state authority arising in the new democracies and tries to find remedies for this (Holmes, 1997b). Neither way of approaching the rise of democracy in Eastern Europe investigates pre-1989 structures and processes.[5] As a result, the modalities of the non-violent breakdown of Communism and the enthusiastic 'return to Europe' have received too little attention so far.[6]

This chapter challenges any assumption that the process of democracy began with a decisive rupture in 1989. It offers an alternative view: the demise of Communism and the advent of democracy were intertwined long before the actual breakdown of Communism in 1989. By treating the rise of democracy in Eastern Europe as a long-term process, it is intended to fill the conceptual gap that exists in the literature between that process and the end of Communism. Democracy, in these terms, is not strictly understood as the shaping of a political system by institution-building or political competition. The focus is on the development of the meaning, expectations, and content of democracy before 1989 as a result of interdependencies and reciprocity between Eastern Communism and Western democracies.

The civilising process and the east–west divide

In this context, I examine the historically rooted causes for the gradual, non-violent convergence between non-democratic Eastern Europe and the democratic West. The end of the systemic confrontation between Communism and the West is closely related to the taming of political, social and military violence in Communist societies. This pacification, itself a precondition for democracy, can be treated as a civilising process, an idea developed in the work of Norbert Elias.

In his early works (Elias, 1939, 1969), Elias examined the reasons for the pacification of human relations in politics and society. During the Middle Ages, social competition in courts and increasing interdependence among territorial states and societies led to increasing monopolisation of institutional and physical violence. Pacification at the collective level was intertwined with individual civilising processes. These latter processes involved the internationalisation of a social habitus favouring increased calculation, affect-control and individual self-restraint. Conflicts that were previously dealt with by force and aggression increasingly became subject to peaceful negotiation or the decision of whoever held a monopoly of violence; for example, the king.

Elias repeatedly stressed the importance of understanding the part played by networks of interdependence and reciprocity as aspects of civilising processes (Elias, 1978, 1994). He argued that growing competition and increasing long-term interdependence with others were favourable to greater control of affects and emotions. The first place where this happened was the European court (Elias, 1969). The development of self-control and competition for influence among courtly ruling groups at the outset of modernity was a paradigmatic instance of the civilising process.

The concept of figuration conveys the notion of a dynamic network of interdependencies between human actors or collectivities. It undermines any assumption of division or polarisation between isolated individuals within society (Elias, 1978: 132f.; 1978a). According to Elias, individuals are not *'homo clausus'* but *'homines aperti'*. There is no 'I' without a 'you', no 'he' or 'she' without a 'we', or 'you' (Elias, 1978: 125).[7] Seen in this context, the rationalisation of violence is both individual and collective, a psychological and social reality at the same time (Elias, 1939 (2): 386). In modern democracies, rationalisation of the emotions is extended and generalised. So is the rational exercise of the monopoly of violence. Monopolies of violence, formerly held by kings, princes or territorial rulers, become the province of constitutional governments and legal bureaucracies. Participatory democracy is based on mutually shared attitudes such as trust, self-restraint, and mutual respect.

At first, it seems curious to base an analysis of democracy on the characteristics of the figuration linking the Eastern bloc and Western democracies. After all, East and West appeared quite alien to each other for decades. The Communist path leading to the monopolisation of violence differed greatly from Western European patterns.[8] From the outside, Eastern European societies appeared to consist of inchoate masses. Almost the only identifiable individuals were the old, staid party leaders. Due to the military stalemate imposed by the Cold War and the incompatibility of the Eastern and Western systems, it was taken for granted that their life-worlds were hermetically closed to each other. This assumption of isolation was reflected in the tradition of Western historiography that treated 'civilisation' and European history as being synonymous with what happened in the West.

Various incorrect assumptions recurred in this Western historiography. One was that West and East, however defined, have little or nothing in common. Another was that the division of Europe is justified by natural, unbridgeable differences. A third was that the West is superior. A fourth was that the West alone deserves the name of Europe (Davies, 1996: 16–25).

In a similar vein, the social sciences were dominated by a vision of isolated blocs. On the whole, western analysts since the 1950s focused on the violent character of Soviet-type regimes and the techniques of totalitarian government that pervaded society.[9] It was argued that Soviet Communism was ruled by suspicion and indoctrination accompanied by ruthless spying, purges, and acts of aggression against its own population. It was seen, in short, as a dehumanising regime[10] and evil empire, whose development towards civilisation was retarded. In the wake of Khrushchev's reforms and rising inner-party dissidence in Eastern Europe, the essence of totalitarianism shifted towards the supremacy of its ideology. This was epitomised by the institutionalised totalitarian lie and the systematic destruction of memory (Rupnik, 1988: 269). In whatever form, Communism continued to be seen as a form of deviance, either openly repressive or exercising subtle 'civilised violence'.[11]

The opposite tendency was represented by the modernisation and convergence approaches which became popular during the 1960s and 1970s. Essentially, they assumed that economic and technological rationalisation would lead to intensified cooperation. Communist governments and economies would gradually converge with Western-type democracies. Although convergence approaches minimised the incompatibility of East and West, the former was still seen as inferior to the democratic West on account of its political system, its economic backwardness and its cultural marginality.

However, East and West were part of one social configuration, mutually dependent. Dependence is an ambiguous term. 'Paradoxically, although Eastern Europe finds itself in the situation of dependent countries that are late entrants to capitalism and the international division of labour, it sees itself and its own problems in terms of European categories'.[12] This apparent paradox disappears if we move beyond a mere economic understanding of periphery and centre. Dependence applies also to cultural equity and identification. Adopting Elias's work as a general methodological approach to social and political reality (Kuzmics, 1988), we may shift from the objective-institutional to the subjective level of perceiving the other.

Eastern Europe's dependence on Western democracy operates at both individual and collective levels. 'On the left as on the right, the West is not just a place on the map where democracy and industrial capitalism emerged, it is also an empire of the mind, imposing belief in an essential form of human society emerging from a progressive pattern of history, including the modern tradition of revolutionary democracy'.[13] In this context, a figurational approach takes account of complex emotional involvements or double-binds within collective mentalities and individual psychologies. I will now explore these aspects in more detail.

Eastern Communism and western democracy as a figuration

As Elias suggests (1939, 1992), a figurational approach to Eastern Communism and Western democracy should take account of the moulding of social habitus (or psychological make-up) and identity-formation. In his studies on the Germans, Elias (1992) argues that the decivilising turn through Nazism had its origins in the socio-genetic peculiarities of German history. In his view, large-scale disruptions such as the Thirty Years War had permanent effects upon the national *habitus* of the Germans, their typical ways of thinking and feeling. More recent history also made a profound impact. Catching up with the other major European powers required violent military action by Germany through internal and external wars. The defeat of 1918 came as a traumatic event.

Compared to France and England, which enjoyed solid continuity in their political and social evolution, Germany's history has many more political breakdowns and disruptions of social order. If we transpose this picture to Eastern Europe, we see that social and political discontinuity made an even greater impact than in Germany. Boundaries, governments, nation-states, bureaucracy, and élites were all precarious throughout modern Eastern European history (Bibó, 1992; Okey, 1992; Schöpflin, 1993). In these circumstances, social and national *habitus* became stamped with a political psychology of collective fear (Bibó, 1992). Communist Eastern Europe was, likewise, in a permanent state of transition (Szakolczai, 1998). It is no accident that in the post-1945 period East Central Europe was the most fragile part in the Soviet bloc (Arnason, 1993; Holmes, 1997). There is good reason to assume that East Central Europe formed a fraught community of fate, one ruled by a feeling of grievance, a sense of European destiny denied, of merit unperceived (Okey, 1992: 130).

Interrupted development and late modernisation brought isolation and backwardness (Janos, 1982; Szücs, 1988; Schöpflin, 1993). Eastern Europe was cut off from Western democracies at many levels: for example, in terms of its ideological premises, political structure and economic system.[14] During the Cold War, ideological and political stalemates deepened. The East's isolation was most conspicuous in political, military, and economic terms but also extended to constraints on occupational mobility, information flows and freedom of travel. This worsening of the empirical divide intensified the East's psychological dependence on the Western model. The underlying reciprocity and interdependencies were much stronger than is commonly acknowledged.[15] Behind the East's many disruptions and its relative backwardness lay a strong desire to normalise, to achieve Western standards.

The powerful demonstration effect of democracy, capitalism, and industrialisation stimulated and diffused the image of the West in

Eastern Europe (Bauman, 1992; Feher, 1995). The more sclerotic Communism became, the more Easterners identified with the West. This assessment is confirmed when the value and belief systems in some Eastern European countries are compared to those of Western democracies. Recent research has shown that in those countries where socialism was established at the beginning of a world war (Baltic countries) rather than in its aftermath and in those countries where national culture, especially the dominant religion, remained strong (as in Poland), beliefs and value systems diverged from the communist norm, showing a strong resemblance to Western countries (Szakolczai and Füstos, 1996).

An essential feature of the civilising process is the reduction of hierarchical contrasts within society. This happens as a result of differentiation processes, including a growth in the complexity of the division of labour as societies become increasingly commercialised, industrialised and urbanised (Elias, 1939 (2): 342 ff.). Long-term competition in Western societies diminished the distinctions between high and low strata. One aspect of this process was an increase in democratic rights and social claims.

Modernisation also led to a reduction of hierarchical contrasts in Eastern Europe. However, unlike in Western Europe, this reduction was a conscious project launched long before the Communists came to power. This project originated in 19th-century Russia where intellectuals formed a distinctive class, the intelligentsia (Seton-Watson, 1964: 53). Aware of the backwardness of their region and inspired by Western examples, élites throughout Eastern Europe have pursued great projects of modernisation such as nationalism but also democracy (Schöpflin, 1993: 29 f.). Contrary to the Western tradition, weak differentiation between state and society in the East gave scope for the intelligentsia to play leading roles inside state bureaucracies.

Elites in the East were caught within two, closely-related, double-binds. As a group, they were at the same cultural level as the democracies they admired. However, at the same time, they were representatives of backward people and societies.[16] As a consequence, the emotionally fraught double-bind relationship of Eastern élites with Western democracy was intertwined with a second double-bind between these aspiring intelligentsias and the half-despised masses within their own societies.[17] In both cases, strong positive and negative feelings were present. These conditions sustained a collective psychology which combined fear for the integrity of state and nation with an intense desire to catch up with the Western democracies.

Civilising processes towards democracy

Without claiming to provide a complete picture, a sociogenetic analysis of the demise of Communism identifies at least four civilising processes[18] tending towards democracy. The first relates to the developing monopolisation of power and violence. As Elias notes, within societies political and economic competition reduces the number of competitors and gradually makes them dependent (directly or indirectly) on a steadily decreasing number of powerful players (Elias, 1939 (2): 144). Soviet Communism was a competitive arrangement that emerged as a rival version of its democratic counterpart and aimed to catch up or overcome it.[19] During its attempted consolidation, the Soviet model of civilisation took a particularly violent path that resulted in systematic terror and millions of deaths.[20] Although Communist regimes remained repressive, the peak of Stalinism of the late 1940s and early 1950s was followed by growing pluralism inside Communist parties and a limited political liberalisation.[21]

Competition between East and West embraced political, economic, social, and technological issues such as the model of democracy, the rate of economic growth, and the pattern of industrialisation (Brus and Laski, 1989; Dembinski, 1991). Shortly after World War II, the Soviet bloc rejected the option of being 'Eastern' and, instead, adopted a self-image as 'the most developed . . . Western stage of our civilization'.[22] Effective educational policies were one of the major achievements in Soviet-type countries, including literacy and technical skills.[23]

Soviet-type regimes declared themselves to be socialist only during a period of transition leading towards Communism, the true revolutionary democracy.[24] Democratic achievements such as constitutionality were always a fiction (Aron, 1965: 240 ff.). However, while 'third way solutions' such as market socialism or the political normalisation of Communist societies largely failed as political strategies, they indirectly opened up democratic niches in social and political life.

Political, economic, and technological competition are tightly linked to a second civilising process, one that resulted in growing criticism of the ideological premises and everyday practices of Communism. This process, which gradually led to the emergence of dissident communities which distanced themselves from Communist regimes, can be characterised as a bifurcation of realities. During the 1960s and 1970s the number of non-conformist associations and dissident groups increased. A growing independence from state authorities came about in different areas of social and cultural life. The dynamic growth of dissident movements materialised in counter-publics, 'second' economies or 'second' societies (Skilling, 1989). While the political and ideological stalemate between East and West persisted at the level of official politics, the penetration of Western modes of life and values and their acceptance in Eastern Europe increased.

Within these second societies, 'civilised' standards of civic freedom, humanitarian values, and social rights—all denied by Soviet Communism—were partly re-established. The *Samizdat*[25] provided spaces for uncensored information. Meanwhile, a quasi-market type of economy parallel to the planned economy provided Western-style commodities. The growing scope of this second reality made some parts of Eastern everyday life the mirror image of the West. Because of the restrictions imposed by collective social and political control, democratic ideals were easier to experience at the personal level in the course of the individual's everyday life. In other words, democracy was embodied at the level of the 'I-image', in personal lifestyle, rather than in formal political practices expressing the Communist state's official 'we-image'.

The I-image of democracy was perhaps best developed in Hungary, Poland, and former Yugoslavia, where citizens could travel freely to the West, enjoying the highest degree of freedom of expression and standard of living. Hungary's market socialism, for instance, allowed 'bourgeoisified life styles' to develop (Szelényi and Szelényi, 1994: 229). Poland's miracle on credit created a 'second Poland' in the 1970s and made Western goods and travel available. Given the repressive political environment and the lack of non-communist mass movements, western-style democratic we-images were more difficult to enact. At face value, only large-scale dissidence movements such as the Solidarity movement in Poland fulfilled these requirements. Despite martial law and the imprisonment of its leadership, after 1981 Solidarity survived through the continuity of individual lives which maintained its values within a multitude of I-images.[26]

These tendencies towards the development of an independent society or second reality gradually strengthened a third civilising process. In the wake of de-stalinisation, physical violence was gradually replaced by growing self-restraint on the part of the Communist state. Relations between Communist countries and

Western democracies improved as shown by the process of détente and the Conference for Security and Cooperation in Europe. This process of pacification developed the roots of civil society and became known as the 'politics of anti-politics' (Konrad, 1985; Ost, 1990).

The most sweeping version of an anti-political second polity was embodied in the Polish Solidarity trade union in 1980. Before the development of this mass social movement, extensive writings and oppositional activity had created a climate of consensus among dissident forces in society.[27] The creation of a second polity in Poland and a moral opposition in Czechoslovakia were both based on explicitly non-violent action. Solidarity pursued self-imposed self-restraint in explicit opposition to the uncivil methods of Communist power. Systematic non-violence was a spiritual force that aspired to power without politics. Notions such as the power of the powerless (Havel, 1985) or of the self-limiting revolution (Staniszkis, 1984) express this voluntary self-restraint. Solzhenitsyn's entire work argues that resistance to totalitarian violence is possible. Acquisition of a certain amount of Western goods and a limited degree of freedom to travel went along with some democratisation of the regime. In an environment ruled by foreign control and authoritarian constraint, beliefs in the 'solidarity of the shaken' (Patocka), 'living in dignity' (Michnik), or 'living in truth' (Havel) expressed the reality behind the image of democracy.

The effects of competition, the emergence of second realities, and non-violent political opposition were closely related to a fourth process: the development of an emotional bond between Eastern Europe and Western democracy. According to Elias, increasing economic and military interdependence has fostered a higher degree of co-operation among European nations. The European Union is, perhaps, the best example of this. The tendency to favour the 'national interest' is balanced by a rational inducement to accept the functional advantages of supra-nationalism. An entity such as the European Union hardly arouses any affection but it has practical advantages for its members (Elias, 1939 (1): 303). These advantages include material prosperity, welfare, political stability and the military shield against Russia.

This rationality at work in the European Union contrasts in an interesting way with the hazy concept of Western European democracy[28] that has pervaded Eastern Europe. This Eastern concept of the West was deeply conflictual and fraught with rejection. According to the Lithuanian born Polish Nobel Prize winner Czeslaw Milosz:

East European intellectuals knew everything about France, about Germany, England or Italy. Western European culture was European culture, Western European political history was the core of the continent's past, while the cultural and political monuments of the second part of Europe were out of sight ... There was never reciprocity. The secondary and marginal status of the culture and peoples of Eastern Europe was a pity but an acknowledged truth.[29]

It was resented as Hungarian Prime Minister Józef Antall made clear:

We are not the back-yard of Europe [...] I hope [...] that they will at last pay more attention to our region and that they will be sensitive to the fact that the nations of this area, from the Poles to the Hungarians and others, have viewed the Western world with unrequited love for centuries. This unrequited love must end because we stuck to our posts, we fought our own fights without firing one shot and we won the third world war for them.[30]

The bonds of sympathy and affection are coloured by a sense of rejection and disappointment.[31]

This emotional reciprocity is one aspect of the interdependence between Communism and Western democracies, the interdependence of two dominant 'paradigms' (Hankiss, 1994: 116–118). When the Communist regimes took power they dismantled established institutions, social networks, identities, dignity and self-esteem. The created the 'paradigm of the prisoner' which was especially strong in the Visegrad countries. For the Easterners, 'Western freedom and prosperity was not only a goal to emulate but also invincible proof that life was worth living, that it was not devoid of value and meaning, that oppression, humiliating compromises, and an existence without dignity were only a transitory episode in their lives'.[32] At the same time, the existence of Eastern Communism helped people living in the West to develop the 'paradigm of the missionary'. The fate of the prisoners behind the Iron Curtain was an indispensable source of meaning for Western identity, reinforcing its missionary zeal towards the East.

Civilising processes are not historical laws expressing an evolutionary gradualism or an optimistic teleology. The ideological and political journey towards democracy was neither evolutionary nor inevitable (Szelényi and Szelényi, 1994). The peaceful end of the

Cold War was all the more surprising, since peace in international relations is the least certain of things. Elias repeatedly stressed that the levels of pacification inside territorial units were much higher than they were in inter-state relations.[33] While the monopolisation of physical violence and increased self-restraint between individuals in national societies renders life more secure, at the international level the control and use of physical violence remains subject to the factual force and will of hegemonic states. It is thus all the more striking that, despite the war in Afghanistan, the Soviet Union dropped its monopoly of externally imposed violence in Eastern Europe.

While at the end of the Nazi regime the masses still showed an amazingly high degree of identification with the regime (Elias, 1992: 498 ff.), the ideological and psychological cracks in the Soviet bloc were huge. Although they initially complied with the Soviet regime, the people of Eastern European societies became gradually drawn to Western lifestyles. The prospect of a democratic future offered Eastern Europeans a way out of their despair. It was a dream that gave hope. Eastern European societies were caught up on the unreality of the real (Engler, 1992: 80). The onset of Soviet decay in the 1970s (Schöpflin, 1993) deepened the political crises, the economic hardship, and the experience of shattered identities. All these factors reduced expectations for the future of the Communist system. At the same time as many Easterners were becoming increasingly influenced by images of Western democracy, their own living standards and economic performance were rapidly declining, especially during the second half of the 1970s.[34] When hope for improvement is low, and expectations are gone, the social and political order lacks a long-term perspective (*Langsicht*).[35]

The simultaneity of civilising and decivilising processes

Without doubt the transformations in East Central Europe since 1989 have strengthened the legitimacy of political rule, increased personal freedom, and enhanced the chances for peaceful changes of government.[36] Furthermore, there is the prospect of integration into the community of democratic countries through international organisations such as NATO and the European Union. It is a difficult process of transition since the greatest challenge for democracy lies in the *simultaneous* occurrence of political, economic, and social reforms (Schmitter and Karl, 1994; Offe, 1996). Furthermore, evidence from post-1989 Eastern Europe strongly suggests that democratisation has had a double-edged effect. On the one hand, the political stalemate and ideological competition of the Cold War was 'undermined' by the manifold tendencies in Eastern European countries which reduced the civilisational gap. The rise of democracy in East Central Europe depended on the struggle to achieve specific political, economic, cultural models and was anchored in the future-oriented belief in ethical and universal values such as personal freedom, dignity, and human rights.

On the other hand, however, a fierce nationalism has become the most important feature of post-1989 Eastern Europe (Ignatieff, 1993; Hassner, 1995; Brubaker, 1996). Paradoxically, while the end of the Cold War has rendered peace more likely, war has become less improbable (Hassner, 1995: 381 f.). Uncivil wars (Keane, 1996) have deconstructed monopolies of power and force and blurred the distinction between war and crime.[37] The destructiveness of this pervasive conflict undermines the ecology of the human personality.[38]

The young Eastern European democracies are characterised by simultaneous civilising and decivilising processes involving an increase in violence, a reduction in self-restraint, and the breakdown of power monopolies. Decivilising processes were occurring before 1989 but they were not perceived as such by social scientists inspired by Marxism or optimistic views on modernisation (Lipset and Bence, 1994). These processes were more fully recognised only after 1989.[39] Taking a broader view, it should be recognised that the sudden and unexpected breakdown of Communism was not the result of a sudden or spontaneous attraction to democracy. Only the transitory nature of the Communist regimes and the long-term dissolution of Communist values can account for the apparently instantaneous forming of mass movements asserting new we-identities, such as those expressed in the demonstrations in favour of democracy in 1989. The rise of the image of democracy was a response to two aspects of decivilising processes: on the one hand, the deliberate intervention in intimate aspects of social life through totalitarian methods of discipline and surveillance; and, on the other hand, the feeling that most self-imposed constraints were historically obsolete (Engler, 1992: 45–46).

The simultaneous civilising and decivilising processes in Eastern Europe present striking parallels with the situation of the German middle-class in the 18th and 19th centuries, as analysed by Elias. A shift from ethical, humanistic, or moral ideals towards national (and even nationalistic) sentiments, values and historical traditions was the general tendency of the middle-classes in most European countries between the 18th and 20th century (Elias, 1992: 174 ff.). The emancipation of the middle class was linked to their adoption of a notion of 'culture' that was a-political or even anti-political. Humiliated, deprived of rights, and excluded from political power, the German middle class found the universe of culture was the only realm where their emancipatory endeavours could be successful (Elias, 1992: 164 ff.). Essentially, a similar process occurred in an accelerated manner in Eastern Europe between World War II and the early 1990s.

For the Eastern intellectual middle class after 1989, 'emancipation' through culture after 1989 came in the form of a painful redis-covery or reappropriation of the past, epitomised by two divergent tendencies. On the one hand, the Communist past was jettisoned in the euphoric moments of 1989. Most obviously, this happened through the changing of names: of streets, institutions, historical periods, and countries. Some countries substantially revised their history, others attempted to draw a veil over the past. On the other hand, other pasts were rediscovered. Obfuscation of the past had been a central feature of official Communist politics.[40] The Soviet-driven mythologisation of the liberation from Nazi Germany by the Soviets in the name of equality, fraternity, and liberty froze the past. After 1989, it unfroze, uncovering many different pasts.[41]

Suspicion, envy, and pure hostility between East and West were deepened after 1989 by their reciprocal ignorance combined with the sudden need on both sides to reassess the myth-laden past; all these feelings were more dominant among Eastern than Western countries (Hassner, 1995: 314). Virtually overnight the emotional focus shifted from the future (evoking universal values and progress-oriented) to the past and present (coming back to national particularities and traditions) (Elias, 1992: 176). The victory of democracy is thoroughly intertwined with the politics of memory and a retrospective drawing up of accounts in respect of Communist violence. The bright future of democracy suddenly became bur-dened with a dark past. Strategies to cope with or overcome the past have not been very successful so far.[42] Rediscovering the past has evoked images that incite emotions, hatred, and may lead to a drastic relapse into barbarism, as epitomised by the open war in ex-Yugoslavia and Chechnya.

The impact of new images of the past was accompanied by a widely perceived and tangible breakdown of individual self-restraint, a shown by increasing crime and homicide rates.[44] These tendencies have been strengthened by a general inclination towards discrimination and the marginalisation of ethnic and social minorities.[45] Loss of social and individual self-restraint is also shown by the demographic collapse throughout the entire region,[46] expressed in a sharp increase in crude death rates, accelerated emigration, and high mortality rates among adolescents due to accidents, poisoning and violence.[47] On the whole,

> social cohesion and protection indicators reflect increasingly divided and tense societies bending under the strain of rising individualism, uncertain social values and precarious security, including personal safety, where even the bough of parental commitment is becoming more fragile.[48]

This complex interweaving of civilising and decivilising processes evokes Elias's (Elias, 1987b) sociological interpretation of Edgar Allan Poe's Fishermen in the Maelstrom.[49] In this tale, a fishing boat sailed by two brothers is sucked into the abyss of an enormous whirlpool. The older brother, immobilised by fear, cannot escape his fate and is drawn into the maelstrom. The younger brother, exercising more self-control over his emotions, observes the objects being drawn into the depths and notices certain regularities in this process. Certain smaller objects were rising to the surface and escaping the maelstrom. By using this information (tying himself to a small barrel) he behaves in a rational way and so avoids his brother's fate. Uncritical and fearful involvement is contrasted with critical and detached reflection on one's own situation.

Heated emotions threaten to draw parts of Eastern Europe deeper into the maelstrom of post-communist violence. Despite the intimations of civil society and democratic political systems that occurred within Communist societies, they did not develop fully-fledged élites. After 1989, these élite-less Eastern European societies (Szakolczai, 1998) have clung to their memories and their myth-laden national pasts. In many respects, Eastern Europe suffers from a vicious circle of socio-psychological double-binds. In other words, high exposure to dangers heightens the emotionality of human responses. The deep emotions engendered by fear and insecurity weaken rationality and realism. This provokes even greater emotionality, and so on (Elias, 1987b: 48).

As Elias convincingly showed, the decivilising turn in Nazi Germany was closely linked to the historical genesis of a distinctive social *habitus* and national identity. In Eastern Europe, the civilising process leading towards democracy made some headway as social *habitus* and identification came to focus on universal democratic values and a conscious orientation towards the more successful Western mode of living. This aspect of the Eastern social *habitus* encouraged convergence with the Eastern image of Western democracy and, as a result, favoured the process of extrication from the maelstrom of Soviet Communism. However, the East European social *habitus* has also been deeply affected by the return of suspicion and hatred, political instability, individual violence, ethnic conflicts, and war. After 1989, many areas of political, social, and private life fell prey to the dynamics of a political psychology of collective fear. If democratic stabilisation is to succeed, Western democracies must continue to guide their Eastern neighbours. In the Yugoslav war, Slavic brothers were drawn into the abyss because the European democracies failed. Similarly, the different speeds at which the Eastern enlargement of NATO and the European Union are occurring threatens to incite symptoms of unrequited love, reciprocal envy, and fear among Eastern European countries. Democracy remains the possible outcome of a civilising process that is constantly threatened by decivilising turns. Western democracies must continue to perform their missionary work in order to liberate the prisoner from its mental chains, even though the price for this may be much higher than it was during the Cold War.

Notes

1 This paper refers primarily to Eastern Europe but includes references to the former Soviet Union as the cradle of the systemic alternative to democratic regimes.

2 This concept was first introduced by Stark (1992).

3 See Schmitter and Karl, 1994: 183.

4 A concise overview is found in Holmes (1997b).

5 Typically, the historical background is synthesised or by-passed as in the programmatic introduction to a recent study: 'What we want to understand in this comparative study is not so much the breakdown of the old order but the problematic emergence of the new' (Elster *et al.*, 1998).

6 Exceptions are Bauman (1992), Szakolczai (1997, 1998), Horvath (1998).

7 Elias, 1939 (2): 372.

8 The concept of monopoly of violence in the context of Soviet Communism requires careful use. While both democratic and Soviet-type governments factually hold a monopoly of power and violence there are substantial differences. According to Aron (1965) democratic (constitutional-pluralist) regimes are distinguished from monopolistic regimes by four antitheses: 1) competition versus monopoly; 2) constitution versus revolution; 3) pluralism of victimisation and multiple double-binds between self and social groups versus bureaucratic

absolutism; 4) party state versus partisan state. Unlike Germany (Elias, 1992), Communism could not rely upon strong legitimacy for the state and thus had to create such a faith from scratch. 'While under Nazism the giving up of civilized self-control went through a self-abandonment to the Nazified state, under Communism it implied a self-abandonment to the Communist Party through feelings of self-pity and self-victimisation . . . multiple double-binds between self and other' (Szakolczai, 1997: 10). For an Eliasian approach to Soviet civilisation see also Arnason, 1993.

9 See summary discussion of totalitarianism in Aron (1965), Rupnik (1988) and Hassner (1995).

10 The emblematic reform attempts linked to the Prague Spring proclaimed the slogan 'socialism with a human face' which was an attempt to reverse the dehumanising aspect of Soviet Communism.

11 Here one can think of the concept of 'civilised violence' or the concept of 'totalitarianism from below' or non-violent social control, all of which stress the overall psychological manipulation that makes resistance by *homo sovieticus* meaningless (Rupnik, 1988).

12 Staniszkis, 1984: 284.

13 Joravsky, 1994: 844.

14 This statement applies strictly to the institutional pillars of constitutional government. Several authors have shown that Eastern Europe's social and political traditions took separate ways from the outset of modernity, that is in the 15th and 16th century, see: Szücs (1988), Bibó (1992), Schöpflin (1993).

15 See the 'Eastern European syllogism' whose major premise in 1989 was 'if it were not for communism, we would have been like the west', and the minor premise is 'now communism is gone'. The conclusion points to the adoption of democracy and capitalism and their success in Eastern Europe (Przeworski, 1993: 141).

16 'The people were the inert clay to the intelligentsia's active zeal, the slothful against the energetic, the superstitious against the educated, the benighted against the enlightened, the ignorant against the knowledgeable; in short the backward against the progressive' (Bauman, 1992: 85).

17 A third double-bind situation refers to emancipation from Soviet Russia, although the detailed circumstances varied between cases. The historical motives for the resentment of Polish élites against Russian interference in internal affairs, for instance, differed substantially from those underlying Tito's rupture with Stalin in the late 1940s. Some authors convincingly argue that East Central Europe's own path and its affinity with the West are essentially distinct from Russia's authoritarian political traditions (Kundera, 1983; Szücs, 1988).

18 Conceptually, a civilising process differs substantially from a traditional path dependence approach (Stark, 1992). In the latter approach, historical habits, routines, and legacies are unilateral or linear. By contrast, civilising processes presuppose interdependencies, reciprocity, and figurational double-bind situations.

19 ' . . . the Soviet Union was not an island unto itself. Far from it. On the contrary, it was locked in an ideological competition with the capitalist world, involved in a race for both economic and military preponderance . . . ' (Gellner, 1994: 157).

20 The recent attempt to quantify Communist crimes all over the world estimates the victims of Communism at some 20 million dead in the USSR and some 1 million dead in Eastern Europe (Courtois *et al.*, 1997: 14). Although the absolute numbers and the validity of a comparison with fascists' crimes were contested among the authors themselves, their evidence on the scope of violence in Soviet

Communism is impressive. The record starts with the Russian Civil War, the process of industrialisation and rural collectivisation, political realignment and control of the party through the Great Terror in Stalin's Russia 1936 and 1938, forced mass deportations of ethnic groups and a vast network of concentration camps (Archipelago Gulag), and continues up to the purges in Soviet Russia and Eastern Europe in the early 1950s. Several popular uprisings such as in Hungary, 1956, in Czechoslovakia in 1968, or in Poland 1970 (and in 1981) were also heralded by violence (Courtois *et al.*, 1997: 49–496).

21 See the Polish road to Socialism, economic liberalisation in Hungary, or self-management models and decentralisation in Yugoslavia.

22 Feher, 1995: 64.

23 Levels of illiteracy in Eastern Europe were still very high on the eve of World War II, with 32 per cent in Bulgaria, 40 per cent in Yugoslavia, 50 per cent in Romania, and 85 per cent in Albania (Jelavich, 1983: 242).

24 See the appeals of Hungarian party leader Mátyás Rákosi for the strengthening of democracy. His never-ending repetition of the pathological condition of experiencing betrayal and suffering is a good illustration of reciprocity and interdependence with an imagined democracy. This torment went together with a desire for future happiness and a readiness to serve this purpose (Horváth, 1998: 338).

25 The term *samizdat* was derived by analogy from the acronyms used for official publishing houses. It refers to unofficial publications of all kinds and to the entire process of unofficial publication. It can best be translated by the awkward 'self-publication' (Skilling, 1989: 4–5).

26 Elias claimed that 'the individual bears in himself or herself the habitus of the group, and . . . it is this habitus that he or she individualises to a greater or lesser extent' (Elias, 1991: 182 f.). The we-image of Solidarity as a collective subject survived the period of martial law because it was preserved through the individual I-images of the leaders of Solidarity and Polish people. The link between individual destiny and collective identity was expressed by the dissident Adam Michnik whose letter to General Kiszczak—responsible for the proclamation of martial law—said: 'For me General, prison is not such a painful punishment. On that December night it was not I who was condemned but freedom: it is not I who is being held prisoner but Poland' (Wydra, 1997: 30–32). Turning to another case, in spite of the absence of large-scale opposition in Czechoslovakia, the I-image that crystallised in the Charter 77 created the possibility of a we-image that relied on universalistic ethical and moral claims such as freedom of expression and human rights.

27 Polish opposition to Communism rested on three broad social groups: the Catholic Church, the workers, and the intellectuals. It took nearly two decades and the experience of bloody and failed uprisings to achieve the convergence of intellectuals with workers, and the left with the Catholic Church tradition.

28 'People yearned for Western political institutions, a Western standard of living, Western freedom, etc. but not for capitalism . . . ' (Szacki, 1995: 120).

29 Milosz, 1997: 164.

30 Excerpts of this speech are printed in *East European Reporter* V (II), March–April 1992, 67.

31 Yugoslavs, being able to travel freely since the late 1950s, could perhaps best grasp the invisible walls between Easterners and Westerners. After the demise of Communism ' . . . citizens from Eastern Europe are going to be second-class citizens still for a long time to come' (Drakulić, 1996: 21).

32 Hankiss, 1994: 118.

33 While in 1939, Elias seemed to be quite optimistic about a global pacification of the world, in 1985 he assessed the likelihood of a war between the superpowers as being relatively high (Elias, 1985: 68–69).

34 Several countries such as the GDR, Czechoslovakia, Bulgaria, and Hungary were catching up in terms of economic growth and industrial production until the mid 1970s. Between 1975 and 1989 their growth slowed and the gap between capitalist and socialist countries widened again (Szelényi and Szelényi, 1994: 216 ff.). A comparison in time between Poland's GNP with other formerly peripheral economies in Europe reveals the extent to which Communist progress actually aggravated backwardness. While Finland, Spain, and Italy had nearly been at the Polish level in 1938, in 1989 GNP in Finland was 12 times higher, in Italy 9 times, in Spain 5 times, in Greece 3 times, and in Portugal 2.5 times higher than in Poland (Landau and Roszkowski, 1995: 287–289). Similarly, good results of industrial production went along with worsening demographic structure (Eberstadt, 1990; Lipset and Bence, 1994).

35 Many strategic and programmatic publications in the 1970s expressed hope for improvement. Popular mobilisation that peaked in Poland in 1981/81, and in other Eastern European countries in 1989 was followed by a high degree of political and social apathy, even a demobilisation of élites. The demise of civic forums or citizens' committees and the low voter turnouts (sometimes below 50 per cent in national elections) all over Eastern Europe is symptomatic.

36 Take the electoral defeat of the authoritarian Vladimir Meciar in Slovakia in the parliamentary elections of october 1998.

37 The war in former Yugoslavia left an estimated 200,000 dead, 4.2 million refugees and displaced persons. The war in Chechnya caused at least 40,000 dead, while other armed conflicts in the former Soviet Union such as between Armenia and Azerbaijan, Georgia, or Tajikistan caused some 2.5 million refugees (UNICEF, 1997: 29–30).

38 Land mines scattered over Bosnia are only the most extreme example for the destructiveness of uncivil wars (Keane, 1996: 15 ff.). Estimates say that during the war some 750,000 land mines were put in around 30,000 minefields. So far, only 50,000 mines have been cleared away while 17,000 minefields were located, see: *Frankfurter Allgemeine Zeitung*, 26 July 1997.

39 See especially the pertinent essays by Engler, 1992.

40 All Communist regimes imposed strict silence over the founding moments of violence. In this vein, Tito's Yugoslavia never ever problematised the civil war and the reciprocal violence between Ustasha and Chetnika. The fundamental consensus of Hungary's Kadarism lay in silence about its violent genesis (Varga, 1991: 173). This also applies to Soviet war crimes against Poles (Katyn) and to the Soviet intervention after the Prague spring.

41 The division into three parts such as the pre-Communist period, the Communist period and the very recent period of extrication from the Communist regimes remains too sketchy (Elster *et al.*, 1998: 35 f.). It seems much more adequate to point to the many disruptions in the past such as those occurring in 1918–21, 1938, 1939, 1941, 1944, 1945, 1948, 1956, 1968, 1989 (Judt, 1992).

42 There is no single English word for the German *Vergangenheitsbewältigung*. Garton Ash (1998) suggests 'treating' the past, 'working over' the past, 'confronting it', 'coping, dealing or coming to terms with', even 'overcoming' the past. Numerous examples show this process has only begun in Eastern Europe.

43 The re-emergence of past images played a crucial role in warmongering in ex-Yugoslavia. In this vein, as of 1989, Croatia was systematically identified by the Serbian press with the fascist Croatian Ustasha of World War II (Banac, 1991).

44 Crime rates increased drastically between 1989 and 1995. A sub-regional summary shows for Central Europe an increase of 108.9 per cent, for South Eastern Europe 269.3 per cent, for the Baltic states 84.0 per cent and for the former Soviet Union (without Caucasus) 59.2 per cent. Homicide rates went up in Central Europe by 78.0 per cent, in the Baltic states by 174.4 per cent, and in the former Soviet Union (without Caucasus) by 92.3 per cent (UNICEF, 1997: 10).

45 The more than 5 million Romany population in Eastern European states have become a leading scapegoat exposed to physical violence, not only in Romania but also in the Czech Republic (Barany, 1994). Anti-Semitism has become a political issue in Poland since the early 1990s and has become a paradigmatic political weapon in Russia: 'Overt anti-Semitism is mostly at the fringes of society, and it has been flourishing ever since the mid-1980s . . . ', see: *International Herald Tribune*, 16 April 1997. Ethnic discrimination is high in the Baltic countries, Slovakia, Romania, and Bulgaria. The most extreme case of ethnic hatred is the Yugoslav war.

46 With the exception of Poland, Czech Republic and Slovakia, there was a net natural decrease of the population, which has been further compounded by out-migration (UNICEF, 1993: 15 f.).

47 Crude birth rates fell steadily between 1980 and 1996, in some countries (Czech Republic, Poland, Slovenia, Romania) by almost 50 per cent (UNICEF, 1998: 94), 'There is almost no current demographic fact about Russia that would fail to shock: *Per capita* alcohol consumption is the highest in the world . . . a wider gap has developed in life expectancy between men (59) and women (73) than in any other country; the mortality rate of 15.1 deaths per 1,000 people puts Russia ahead of only Afghanistan and Cambodia among the countries of Europe, Asia and America; the death rate among working-age Russians today is higher than a century ago', *International Herald Tribune*, 9 June 1997.

48 UNICEF, 1997: 13.

49 I owe this idea to Arpád Szakolczai (1998).

Bibliography

Ash, T. G. (1998), 'The Truth about Dictatorship', *The New York Review of Books*, 19 February 1998.

Arnason, J. P. (1993), *The Future that Failed*, London and New York: Routledge.

Aron, R. (1965), *Démocratie et totalitarisme*, Paris: Gallimard.

Barany, Z. D. (1994), 'Living on the Edge: The East European Roma in Postcommunist Politics and Societies', *Slavic Review*, 2, 321–344.

Banac, I. (1992), 'The Fearful Asymmetry of War: The Causes and Consequences of Yugoslavia's Demise', *Daedalus*, 2/121, 141–174.

Bauman, Z. (1992), 'Love in Adversity: On the State and the Intellectuals, and the State of Intellectuals', *Thesis Eleven*, 31, 81–104.

Bibó, I. (1992), *Die Misere der osteuropäischen Kleinstaaterei*, Frankfurt/Main: Verlag Neue Kritik.

Brubaker, R. (1996), *Nationalism Reframed*, Cambridge: Cambridge University Press.

Brus, W. and K. Laski (1989), *From Marx to the Market*, Oxford: Oxford University Press.

Courtois, S. *et al.* (1997), *Le livre noir du communisme*, Paris: Robert Laffont.

Davies, N. (1996), *Europe. A History*, Oxford: Oxford University Press.

Dembinski, P. (1991), *The Logic of the Planned Economy*, Oxford: Oxford University Press.

Drakulić, S. (1996), *Cafe Europe. Life after Communism*, London: Abacus.

Eberstadt, N. (1990), 'Health and Mortality in Eastern Europe 1965–1985', *Communist Economies*, 2(3), 347–71.

Elias, N. (1939), *Über den Prozess der Zivilisation*, 2 vols. (1994), ed., Frankfurt/Main: Suhrkamp.

Elias, N. (1969), *Die höfische Gesellschaft*, Neuwide: Luchterhand.

Elias, N. (1978), *Was ist Soziologie?* 3, ed., München: Juventa.

Elias, N. (1985), *Humana conditio. Beobachtungen zur Entwicklung der Menscheit am 40. Jahrestag eines Kriegsendes (8. Mai 1985)*, Frankfurt/Main: Suhrkamp.

Elias, N. (1987a), *Die Gesellschaft der Individuen*, Frankfurt: Suhrkamp.

Elias, N. (1987b), *Involvement and Detachment*, Oxford: Basil Blackwell.

Elias, N. (1988), 'Violence and Civilization: The State Monopoly of Physical Violence and its Infringement', in John Keane (ed.), *Civil Society and the State*, 177–198.

Elias, N. (1992), *Studien über die Deutschen*, Frankfurt/Main: Suhrkamp.

Elster, J., C. Offe and U. K. Preuss (1988), *Institutional Design in Post-Communist Societies*, Cambridge: Cambridge University Press.

Engler, W. (1992), *Die zivilisatorische Lücke. Versuche über den Staatssozialismus*, Frankfurt/Main: Suhrkamp.

Feher, F. (1995), 'Imagining the West', *Thesis Eleven*, 42, 52–68.

Gellner, E. (1994), *Conditions of Liberty. Civil Society and its Rivals*, London.

Hankiss, E. (11994), 'European Paradigms: East and West, 1945–1994, *Daedalus*, 123 (3), 115–126.

Hassner, P. (1995), *La violence et la paix*, Paris: Seuil.

Havel, V. (1985), 'The Power of the Powerless', in John Keane (ed.), *The Power of the Powerless: Citizens against the State in Central-Eastern Europe*, London: Hutchinson, 23–96.

Havel, V. (1991), *Open Letters. Selected Prose 1965–1990*, selected and edited by Paul Wilson, London/Boston: faber and faber.

Holmes, L. (1997a), *Post-Communism*, Cambridge: Polity Press.

Holmes, L. (1997b), 'The Democratic State or State Democracy? Problems of Post-Communist Transition', Jean Monnet Chair Paper RSC No. 97/48.

Horváth, A. (1998), 'Tricking into the Position of the Outcast: A Case Study in the Emergence and Effects of Communist Power', *Political Psychology*, 19 (2), 331–347.

Ignatieff, M. (1993), *Blood and Belonging. Journeys into the New Nationalism*, London: Chatto & Windus.

Janes, A. C. (1982), *The Politics of Backwardness in Hungary 1825–1945*, Princeton: Princeton University Press.

Jelavich, B. (1983), *History of the Balkans: Twentieth Century*, Cambridge: Cambridge University Press.

Joravsky, D. (1994), 'Communism in Historical Perspective', *American Historical Review*, June 1994, 837–857.

Judt, T. (1992), 'The Past is Another Country: Myth and Memory in Postwar Europe', *Daedalus*, 121 (4), 83–118.

Keane, J. (ed.) (1988), *Civil Society and the State. New European Perspectives*, London: Verso.

Keane, J. (1996), *Reflections on Violence*, London: Verso.

Konrad, G. (1985), *Antipolitik*, Frankfurt/Main: Suhrkamp.

Kuzmics, H. (1988), 'The Civilizing Process', in John Keane (ed.), *Civil Society and the State*, London/New York: Verso, 149–176.

Kundera, M. (1983), 'Un occident kidnappé', *Le Débat*, November 1983, 3–22.

Landau, Z. and W. Roszkowski (1995), *Polityka Gospodarcza II RP i PRL (Economic Policy of the Second Republic and of the Polish People's Republic)*, Warszawa: Wydawnictwo Naukowe PWN.

Linz, J. and A. Stepan (1996), *Problems of Democratic Transition and Consolidation. Southern Europe, South America and Post-Communist Europe*, Baltimore and London: The Johns Hopkins University Press.

Lipset, S. M. and G. Bence (1994), 'Anticipations of the Failure of Communism', *Theory and Society*, 23, 169–210.

Milosz, C. (1997), *Zycie na wyspach* (Life on Islands), Kraków: Znak.

Moore, B. (1966), *Zur Geschichte der politischen Gewalt. Drei Studien*, Frankfurt/Main: Suhrkamp.

Offe, C. (1996), *Varieties of Transition. The East European and East German Experience*, Cambridge: Polity Press.

Okey, R. (1992), 'Central Europe/Eastern Europe: Behind the Definitions', *Past and Present*, 137, 102–133.

Ost, D. (1990), *Solidarity and the Politics of Anti-Politics*, Philadelphia: Temple University Press.

Przeworski, A. (1993), 'Economic Reforms, Public Opinion, and Political Institutions. Poland in the Eastern European Perspective', in Bresser Pereira *et al.*, *Economic Reforms in New Democracies*, Cambridge: Cambridge University Press.

Rupnik, J. (1988), 'Totalitarianism Revisited', in John Keane (ed.), *Civil Society and the State*, 263–289.

Seton-Watson, H. (1964), *Nationalism and Communism*, London: Methuen and Co. Ltd.

Schmitter, P. and Karl (1994), 'The Conceptual Travel of Transitologists and Consolidologists: How Far to the East Should They Attempt to Go?' *Slavic Review*, 53 (1), 173–185.

Schöpflin, G. (1993), *Politics in Eastern Europe 1945–1992*, Oxford/Cambridge: Blackwell Publishers.

Staniszkis, J. (1984), *Poland's Self-Limiting Revolution*, Princeton: Princeton University Press.

Skilling, G. (1989), *Samizdat and an Independent Society in Central and Eastern Europe*, Columbus: Ohio State University Press.

Stark, D. (1992), 'Path Dependence and Privatization Strategies in East Central Europe', *East European Politics and Societies*, 6 (1), 17–54.

Szacki, J. (1995), *Liberalism after Communism*, Budapest: Central European University Press.

Szakolczai, A. (1997), *Decivilizing Processes and Dissolution of Order with Reference to the Case of East Europe*, paper presented at the Norbert Elias Centenary Conference, 20–22 June, Bielefeld.

Szakolczai, A. (1998), *In a Permanent State of Transition. Theorizing the East European Condition*, paper presented at the conference 'Die Osterweiterung der Europäischen Union', 6–7 May 1998, Bonn.

Szakolczai, A. and L. Füstös (1996), *Value Systems in Axial Moments: A Comparative Analysis of 24 European Countries*, EUI Working Paper SPS, No. 96/8, Florence.

Szelényi, I. and B. Szelényi (1994), 'Why Socialism Failed: Towards a Theory of System Breakdown—Causes of Disintegration of East European State Socialism', *Theory and Society*, 23, 211–231.

Szücs, J. (1988), 'Three Historical Regions of Europe', in John Keane (ed.), *Civil Society and the State*, 291–332.

UNICEF (1993), *Public Policy and Social Conditions*, Regional Monitoring Report, No. 5, Florence.

UNICEF (1997), *Children at Risk in Central and Eastern Europe: Perils and Promises*, Regional Monitoring Report, No. 4, Florence.

UNICEF (1998), *Education for All?* The MONEE Project Regional Monitoring Report, No. 5, Florence.

Varga, L. (1991), 'Geschichte in der Gegenwart—Das Ende der kollektiven Verdrängung und der demokratische Umbruch in Ungarn', in Rainer Deppe *et al.* (eds), *Demokratischer Umbruch in Osteuropa*, Frankfurt/Main: Suhrkamp, 167–181.

Wydra, H. (1997), *Imitating Capitalism and Democracy at a Distance*, EUI Working Paper SPS 97/2, Florence.

Notes on Contributors

Barrie Axford is Principal Lecturer in Politics at Oxford Brookes University. He has held posts at the universities of Stanford and Southampton, and been a Visiting Professor at the University of Genoa. Books include: *The Global System: Economics, Politics and Culture* (1995); *Politics: An Introduction* (1997) joint author; *Unity and Diversity in the New Europe* (1999) joint Ed; and *Democratization and the Nature of Democracy* (2000) (joint author).

Andeas Føllesdal is a Senior Researcher at ARENA, a research programme on the Europeanisation of the Nation State, under the auspices of the Research Council of Norway. He is also Professor of Philosophy at the University of Oslo, Norway. He publishes on European political theory and on topics of applied and social ethics. Recent publications include, 'Democracy, Legitimacy and Majority Rule in the EU', 'Subsidiarity', 'Sustainable Development, State Sovereignty and International Justice', 'Minority Rights: a Liberal Contractualist Case', *Restructuring the Welfare State*, Springer-Verlag, (1997), and *Democracy and the European Union*, Springer-Verlag, (1997).

Reiner Grundmann is a Lecturer at Aston Business School. He has just published a book on the protection of the ozone layer. The study analyses the science controversy, the political controversy, the public discourse and how they influenced each other. Publications include *Marxism and Ecology*, Oxford University Press, (1991), *Transnational Environment Policy*, Routledge, *Werner Sombart: Economic Life in the Modern Age*, Transaction Books (with Nico Stehr), (forthcoming). His current research interests are the transformation of the European public sphere, innovation networks, cross national comparisons of risk regulation in Europe with regard to environmental and health aspects and issues in social and political theory.

Charlotte Hoffmann is currently Senior Lecturer at the University of Salford where she teaches German language and lectures on Sociolinguistics and Bilingualism. She is also Associate Director of the European Studies Research Institute. She is interested in a variety of aspects of individual and social multilingualism. Her publications are in the fields of child bilingualism, trilingualism and trilingual competence, and on language contact, maintenance and planning in Europe, particularly with regard to German and Spanish speaking areas.

Richard Huggins is Senior Lecturer in Politics at Oxford Brookes University. Recent and forthcoming publications include *Politics: an Introduction* (1997) and *Democratization and the Nature of Democracy* (forthcoming 2000) and he has published a number of articles on the information society and politics.

David Jary is Professor of Sociology and Dean of the Graduate School at Staffordshire University. Previously he lectured at Salford University. He has written extensively on social theory, most recently on Anthony Giddens and on 'McDonaldization'. He has a long standing interest in the relations between epistemology and politics, which is reflected in his chapter in this volume. He is also Director of the Institute for Access Studies at Staffordshire University and edits the journal *Widening Participation and Lifelong Learning*.

Pablo Jáuregui is currently completing his PhD thesis entitled 'National Identity and the European Union: a Comparative Study of Britain and Spain' at the Department of Political and Social Sciences of the European University Institute in Florence. His current empirical interest is in the field of national identity and its influence on the process of European integration. He is also interested in collective identification, political symbolism and ritual, the sociology of emotions, historical sociology and social anthropology.

John Markoff is Professor of Sociology, History and Political Science at the University of Pittsburgh. His books include *Waves of Democracy*, Pine Forge Press, (1996), *The Abolition of Feudalism*, Pennsylvania State University Press, (1997), and (with Gilbert Shapiro), *Revolutionary Demands,* Stanford University Press, (1998), the latter two of which received prizes from the Society for French Historical Studies. He is currently writing on the history of democratisation.

Stephen May is a Lecturer in the Sociology Department at the University of Bristol. He has written widely on issues to do with language, education and minority rights. His major publications include, *Making Multicultural Education Work*, Multicultural

Matters, (1994), *Critical Multiculturalism,* Falmer Press, (1999), and *Language, Education and Minority Rights*, Longman, (forthcoming).

John Rex is Professor Emeritus at the University of Warwick. Previously he was Associate Director, Centre for Research on Ethnic Relations and has been a Visiting Professor in numerous European and American universities. Recent publications include, *The Ghetto and the Underclass*, (1990), *Ethnic Identity and Ethnic Mobilisation in Britain*, (1991), editor with Beatrice Drury, *Ethnic Mobilisation in a Multi-Cultural Europe*, (1995), and, *Ethnic Minorities and the Modern Nation State*, (1996).

Dennis Smith is Professor of Sociology at Loughborough University. He previously held positions at Leicester University and Aston University. He is researching on globalization and modernity. He has written several books including *The Rise of Historical Sociology*, and *Capitalist Democracy on Trial*. His most recent publication is *Zygmunt Bauman. Prophet of Postmodernity*. His current research projects include a critical study of Norbert Elias and a study of the implications of the Balkan War for the development of the European public sphere (with Sue Wright and Reiner Grundmann).

Sue Wright has been a member of the School of Languages and European Studies at Aston University since 1991 and the editor of *Current Issues in Language and Society* since 1994. She has written extensively on language planning and the non-planned changes in language use in response to societal change. Her book *Community and Communication,* on the difficulties of democracy in plurilingual polities, is about to appear.

Harald Wydra is Assistant Professor of Political Science at the University of Regensburg (Germany). He holds a PhD in the Social and Political Sciences from the European University Institute in Florence. He is the author of *Continuities in Poland's Permanent Transition*, Macmillan, (forthcoming). His research interests focus on comparative analyses of East European transitions and their relevance for contemporary political social theory.

Index

Index

Index